The Hidden Holmes

THE
HIDDEN
HOLMES

His Theory of Torts in History

David Rosenberg

Harvard University Press
Cambridge, Massachusetts
London, England
1995

Library of Congress Cataloging-in-Publication Data

Rosenberg, David.
The hidden Holmes : his theory of torts in history / David
Rosenberg.
p.   cm.
Includes bibliographical references and index.
ISBN 0-674-39002-4 (alk. paper)
1. Holmes, Oliver Wendell, 1841–1935—Contributions in torts.
2. Torts—United States—History.   3. Strict liability—United
States—History.   I. Title.
KF1250.R67   1995
346-7303—dc20
[347.3063]
95-24264

For Catherine, Jason, and Samantha

Preface

Modern thinking about the law of torts begins with Oliver Wendell Holmes. Yet his scholarly contributions to its theory and practice are little understood today. In this book I show that the current portrayal of Holmes as a legal formalist in torts, who replaced strict liability with a universal negligence rule chiefly to subsidize industrial development, is a case of mistaken identity.

Indeed, Holmes's theory of torts established the intellectual foundation for expansive use of strict liability to augment the negligence rule in preventing and redressing injuries from industrial enterprise. It played a crucial intellectual role in the development of his revolutionary jurisprudence of judicial policy-making that launched the American legal realist movement. My recovery of Holmes's theory of torts also contradicts standard interpretations of the history of tort law. I show that his contemporaries recognized and shared his support for strict liability, joined him in reconciling both strict liability and negligence on policy as well as doctrinal grounds, and invoked his ideas in promoting far-reaching reforms of tort law to protect society from the hazards of industrial enterprise.

What happened to Holmes—what often happens to such seminal thinkers—is that others who built an edifice from his foundation have in the course of time distorted his original thinking, intent, and the historical context of his work. This process of errant revision is particularly tenacious and destructive in law, where historical pedigree counts far too much in judging the worth of ideas that determine not merely the pecking order in academia, but the incidence of state power exercised by courts. The importance of the stakes involved seems only to have increased the influence of political preferences in the interpretation of historical evidence. Indeed, the rise in the early 1950s of the current misconception of Holmes's views on strict liability corresponds with the mysterious disappearance from scholarly literature of discussion of a major portion of *The Common Law*—conspicuously titled "The Theory of Torts." Thus, while my ultimate aim is to reopen and reorient the agenda of research on Holmes and his times, showing the rudimentary neglect of plain evidence in the primary sources also raises questions about the present state of legal scholarship.

I too accepted the prevailing orthodoxy on Holmes in my own work, principally regarding mass torts. By sheer accident, while skimming through "The Theory of Torts" in search of a pithy passage to quote for his purported opposition to strict liability, to my surprise I found in it clear statements of support for strict liability, particularly for the rules that addressed industrial and other business risks. I read the entire book, reread it, and then read his other scholarly writings, expecting with the turn of every page to find evidence of the orthodox view. I found the opposite everywhere I looked. In fact, my reading revealed previously unnoticed connections between his thinking in torts and jurisprudence, and a new perspective on the historical relationship between negligence and strict liability. My curiosity about what path commentators took to arrive at the mistaken current consensus on Holmes led to the discovery of its departure from the general understanding of his contemporaries.

The main theses of the book were contained in the first draft circulated generally in 1988, but its final form has greatly benefited from the substantive and editorial criticism by many persons. In particular, I wish to thank several students for their research and editorial assistance: Heather Cornell, Robert Fisher, Susan Granoff, Sally Hadden, Crystal Nix, Melanie Oxhorn, Barbara Schneider, and Richard Wareing. My thanks go to Donna Andon for help in gathering and organizing the primary source materials and in proofreading. I also thank Harry Martin and his talented and resourceful staff at the Harvard Law School Library. I am grateful for the attentive and expert editorial assistance from Michael Aronson and Anita Safran of Harvard University Press. I also thank my colleagues at Harvard and elsewhere for their thoughtful advice on various portions of the book: Harold Berman, Scott Brewer, Edward Dangel, Richard Epstein, Bruce Hay, William Fisher, Charles Fried, Stephen Gilles, Mary Ann Glendon, Robert Gordon, Thomas Jackson, Andrew Kaufman, Patrick Kelley, John Mansfield, Diana Moses, Charles Nesson, Richard Posner, Jeffrey O'Connell, Gary Schwartz, Arthur von Mehren, and Paul Weiler. For their valuable comments and enormously generous expenditure of time in reviewing drafts of the book, I am especially indebted to Phillip Areeda, Charles Donahue, Frank Michelman, Thomas Reed, Catherine Rosenberg, David Shapiro, Steven Shavell, and Hiller Zobel.

Contents

The Hidden Holmes

Introduction

The law of torts exerts the most extensive power of social control known to the common law, vesting judges with a virtual roving commission over all aspects of life, however intimate to the parties or vital to the public welfare. Yet the political legitimacy of that authority remains no less a matter of vigorous debate today than it was during the formative stage of modern tort law in the late nineteenth century. The question at the heart of this debate focuses on the fundamental concept of individual responsibility that courts invoke to justify the imposition of tort liability. Should the power to coerce a defendant to bear a plaintiff's loss depend on the reasonableness of the defendant's conduct? In other words, is the threshold basis for recovery in tort negligence, or is it liability without negligence (strict liability)? From the beginning, this debate has been shaped by the ideas of Oliver Wendell Holmes, the most illustrious jurist in American law.

Surprisingly, Holmes's theory of torts—a descriptive, not a normative theory—and its response to the choice between negligence and strict liability are generally misunderstood today. Despite the enormous literature on this preeminent legal thinker, his theory of torts is believed to be essentially the opposite of what it was in fact. The view prevails today that Holmes opposed strict liability, and that he dogmatically insisted upon a universal negligence threshold for recovery in tort. Many scholars also contend that his main purpose in establishing the hegemony of negligence was to subsidize the industrialization of America.

This perception of Holmes as an enemy of strict liability is relatively recent and entirely mistaken. Holmes's theory of torts consistently and forthrightly supported strict liability. Indeed, his theory provided the intellectual foundation of philosophical and policy arguments that convinced leading commentators and courts in this century to favor strict liability for industrial activities. It is fair to say that the modern understanding of strict liability as a general and independent branch of tort law was his invention. Moreover, Holmes was recognized by his contemporaries and most of their successors up to 1950 as a strong proponent of strict liability for many types of cases, especially those concerned with industrial injury.

My purpose in writing this book is to explain Holmes's theory of torts and clarify the intellectual legacy it left to twentieth-century legal thought and practice. In addition to correcting the erroneous orthodoxy that depicts Holmes as an opponent of strict liability, I also suggest how it came about that his views have been misconstrued by legal scholars today. In the process, I offer new perspectives on his jurisprudence as well as on the backdrop of nineteenth-century law and commentary in torts. My findings also raise questions about the practices and quality of current legal scholarship.

This inquiry canvasses the familiar body of Holmes's scholarly work spanning the period from 1870 to 1900. The centerpiece consists of two celebrated lectures on torts delivered at Boston's Lowell Institute in 1880 and published the following year in *The Common Law*.[1] I draw interpretive guidance from Holmes's judicial opinions, correspondence, and informal speeches and essays, and from the writings of contemporaries over the six decades of his life in the law. I also review the literature on Holmes to verify my interpretation of his views on torts and to determine how they have been perceived through history. Additionally, a complete understanding of Holmes's theory of torts requires consideration of his jurisprudential writings on the nature of law and the process of its development. Holmes never wrote a free-standing work on torts; all of his major essays, including the torts lectures, were integral parts of his larger enterprise to construct a "new jurisprudence."[2]

Torts and the New Jurisprudence

Like many leading intellectuals of his time, Holmes was greatly influenced by the momentous practical and theoretical developments in science. When he began writing on torts and jurisprudence in the early 1870s, an industrial society was emerging that promised a phenomenal bounty of goods and the triumph of reason over superstition, brute power, and unruly fate. But the science that was building that society also revealed and demanded recognition of the new and more devastating risks of industrialization. Industrial production, as Holmes observed, generated systematic risks to person and property of such unprecedented volume and technological sophistication as to overwhelm the law of torts crafted from more prosaic and "ungeneralized" cases of assault, carriage collision, and slander.[3]

Science was also transforming the understanding of law. The "official theory" of jurisprudence, according to Holmes, was formalism, a preoccupation with the "formal connection of things, or logic."[4] Formalism professed scientific aspirations but amounted to little more than a closed "syllogistic[]" system like Euclidean geometry.[5] Presuming its postulates fixed and true, *a priori* formalist legal science maintained that the decision of any particular case was mathematically certain, "merely [a] logical consequence of [those] simple postulates."[6] Formulated in the image of the syllogistic ideal, law thus would become not only entirely consistent and determinate but, more importantly, untroubled by choices among competing policies and social interests. Gapless and timeless, the formalist system precluded the need and opportunity for judicial legislation, especially for making policy that might alter existing distributions of economic and political power. But irreparable cracks were appearing in the intellectual edifice of formalism as scientific empiricism and relativism, stunningly exhibited by Charles Darwin's theory of evolution, challenged the syllogistic structure of all classical sciences, of law as well as of nature.

Holmes re-envisioned torts and jurisprudence in the light of the new predicaments and understandings of modern empirical science. He formulated the torts theory on the realization that rather than merely extrapolating an autonomous and immutable set of concepts and rules, courts were making policies that necessarily balanced the conflicting interests of different classes and ideologies vying for ascendance in the harsh and crowded conditions of industrial society. Studying tort law scientifically meant focusing on the legal reality of judges exercising a discretionary power to make policies motivated not by dictates of logic but by "experience" of the "relative worth and importance of competing legislative grounds" of social needs and values.[7] From this vantage, Holmes effectively rescued torts from dissolution. One of the most important and enduring contributions of his theory of torts was to overturn the traditional system of classification based on the antiquated and artificially limited structure of procedural forms of action. Holmes developed a thoroughly pragmatic and empirical organization of the various liability rules through comprehensive examination of their actual substantive requirements and effects, as well as their consequences for the primary functions of tort law: compensation and deterrence.[8] The resulting arrangement created the division of torts into intentional wrongs, negligence, and strict liability[9]—the three principal independent branches that organize study of torts to this day.[10] Ultimately, in clarifying and rationalizing the three branches according to their actual operations and functions, Holmes provided torts, and strict liability in particular, with the theoretical coherence and policy justifications necessary to deal with the mass risks of the industrial age and beyond.

Holmes's reconstruction of torts informed as well as reflected his thinking in jurisprudence. Torts provided the chief ammunition for his relentless war against formalist legal science. Indeed, the principal defect of the leading formalist theories of torts was their inability to reconcile the rules of strict liability and negligence with a coherent conception of responsibility. In contrast, the success of his theory in accounting for both strict liability and negligence was a singular triumph for his new jurisprudence.

The empirical scientific approach necessarily rejected the syllogistic ideal that divorced law from the political, economic, and moral life of society. Holmes's work in torts demonstrated the need for commitment to the working hypothesis (empirical science never claims ultimate truths) that the process of legal development was an integrated part of evolving social history. Judges should be regarded as "law-makers," continuously engaged in making and revising "policies" to provide "expedient" solutions for new social problems.[11] But, as Holmes's work in torts also showed, courts generally concealed their policy choices behind the form of logical arguments from precedents, customs, and doctrines—covertly adapting old rules to new uses. Therefore, historical analysis of the rules was necessary to unravel this "paradox of form and substance" to determine what, if any, policies the rules were actually serving.[12] History should be studied, he emphasized, simply for a better understanding of how and why the law developed as it did, not for the formalist purpose of finding in the past or in the process of evolution grounds to sanctify the present. Indeed, the perspective of history, the time dimension of law in science, revealed the contingent and chance character of judicial policy choices; they were entirely dependent on the changing conditions in particular places and periods. Law thus was best seen as the prophecy of what courts will do in the future, and Holmes concluded that only empirical science could usefully provide the method and basis for such understanding. Knowledge of the underlying political, economic, and moral motives for judicial policy choices would enhance prediction of the trends in legal development—thereby reducing uncertainty's burden on freedom while also promoting deliberate and effective law reform. Holmes founded his new jurisprudence on this radical reconceptualization—stimulated and tested by his work in torts—of the "legislative function of the courts."[13]

Torts and Strict Liability

Holmes's theory of torts explained the threshold norm of moral "responsibility" "at the bottom of all liability in tort."[14] "[T]he true starting-point" of state coercive power was, in his view, a broad free-will notion of responsibility.[15] This norm authorized the imposition of *prima facie* liability for causing harm that the defendant could be "expected to contemplate as possible," and therefore could exercise a "choice" to avoid.[16] Applying the conceptual structure of responsibility and excuse in classic moral philosophy, Holmes stated that on his theory of responsibility in tort "[a] harmful act is only excused on the ground that the party neither did foresee, nor could with proper care have foreseen harm."[17]

Holmes concluded that foresight-informed choice had become the norm of responsibility by judicial legislation at the most fundamental level of law, enacting a social ethic

> "that it is felt to be impolitic and unjust to make a man answerable for harm, unless he might have chosen otherwise . . . [and that] the choice must be made with a chance of contemplating the consequence complained of, or else it has no bearing on responsibility for that consequence."[18]

This finding confirmed the central hypothesis of the new jurisprudence, as stated in the famous opening paragraph of *The Common Law*:

> "The felt necessities of the time, the prevalent moral and political theories, intuitions of public policy, avowed or unconscious, even the prejudices which judges share with their fellow-men, have had a good deal more to do than the syllogism in determining the rules by which men should be governed."[19]

Holmes's theory unified the branch of strict liability with the branches of negligence and intentional wrongs by putting them "all on the footing of the reasonably-to-be-contemplated."[20] The theory held that rules of strict liability qualified by a foresight condition (hereafter *foresight-based strict liability*) were just and rational according to the prevailing norm of responsibility.[21] Foresight-based strict liability satisfied the ends of justice by protecting individuals from being held responsible for unforeseeable harms that they had no power of choice to avoid. These rules also rationally served the functions of compensation and deterrence. Strict liability provides appropriate incentives for reasonable conduct and a sensible means of compensation only if, as Holmes explained, it takes account of the ability of prospective defendants to predict risk.

The sole form of strict liability excluded by the theory was what Holmes called the "rule of absolute responsibility" (also referred to here as *cause-based strict liability*).[22] That rule would impose liability on the mere fact of causing harm, regardless of its foreseeability. The classic case is that of a defendant who, without knowing or having any reason to know about the existence of a nearby mink ranch, conducted non-negligent blasting operations that frightened the mink into killing their young.[23] Holmes found little or no precedent for cause-based strict liability, as was to be expected of a doctrine that contravened the prevailing norm of responsibility. Indeed, cause-based strict liability was morally incoherent. The causation element has no rational purpose if not to make the choice to avoid harm a prerequisite for liability. Yet by itself—without the further requirement of foreseeability—the causation requirement was wholly insufficient to guarantee choice in any meaningful sense. As Holmes concluded: "A choice which entails a concealed consequence is as to that consequence no choice."[24]

The relationship of the two versions of strict liability to each other and to intentional wrongs and negligence is illustrated by the following diagram of their respective necessary and sufficient elements ("X"), over and above the universal requirement of cognizable, accrued injury.

Holmes applied the foresight theory to rationalize all of the major rules of strict liability then in force, and which remain at the core of strict liability today: trespass to land; conversion of personal property; injury to person and property from domestic and wild animals, nuisance, and necessity; defamation; and what in effect were judicial "takings" of property to promote the general welfare. By far the most important application of the foresight theory concerned the strict liability rule for "dangerous escaping things" established in the famous English case of Rylands v. Fletcher.[25] In holding a mill owner strictly liable for the damage done when his reservoir collapsed and flooded a neighboring mine, *Rylands* became the flagship

	Necessary and sufficient elements			
Liability rules	Causation	Foreseeable harm	Unreasonable conduct	Malice
Intentional wrongs	X	X	X	X
Negligence	X	X	X	
Foresight-based strict liability	X	X		
Cause-based strict liability	X			

and most controversial symbol of the expansive use of strict liability for industrial activities.

Holmes's support for *Rylands* best exemplifies his intellectual contributions and commitment to strict liability. He voiced unwavering support for *Rylands* long before he gained scholarly and judicial status, and despite the intense opposition to it of leading American courts and commentators. In fact, this support provoked an immediate public rebuke in 1873 from Charles Doe, the highly respected Chief Judge of the New Hampshire Supreme Court, at the opening of his renowned opinion in Brown v. Collins rejecting *Rylands*.[26] Nevertheless, Holmes steadfastly resisted efforts by contemporaries to deny both the precedential support for and the very strict liability character of the *Rylands* rule. Indeed, he boldly founded his conception of the strict liability branch on the test of inherently dangerous things drawn from *Rylands*.

Most significantly for the development of strict liability in this century, particularly in industrial cases, Holmes used *Rylands* to demonstrate the far-reaching scope of strict liability when harnessed to generalized and statistical foresight of risk. Thus, while theoretically important, the difference between the scope of strict liability based on causation alone and that based on generalized statistical foresight was potentially negligible in practice, distinguished by nothing more than the wildly freakish case. On this understanding of *Rylands*, Holmes created the classification of "extra-hazardous sources" to explain the imposition of strict liability predicated simply on the choice to engage in an activity recognized as systematically posing residual risks, such as the characteristic dangers of flooding from reservoirs, crop damage from straying cattle, and injury from the debris of blasting.[27] The extra-hazardous classification, though rarely associated with Holmes today, provided the broadest warrant for strict liability ever adopted in this country.[28] As Morris Cohen noted, had the courts heeded Holmes's teachings, the movement toward strict liability for industrial injury would have been far less tortuous and protracted.[29]

Holmes Revised

Holmes's contemporaries and their immediate successors generally recognized his support for strict liability. An article by Fleming James in 1950 marks the start of sustained advocacy of the view that Holmes was a diehard opponent of all forms of strict liability and dogmatic advocate of making negligence the universal rule in tort.[30] In 1963, Mark DeWolfe Howe was the first to include this erroneous view in a full-scale consideration of Holmes's theory of torts as developed in *The Common Law*.[31] Still, it was not until the 1970s and early 1980s that the negligence-dogma interpretation gained its present dominance. In that period most of the leading scholars of legal history and torts adhered to the view held by G. Edward White, that torts for Holmes "was virtually synonymous with negligence."[32] For example, according to Lawrence Friedman, Holmes considered strict liability generally "primitive" and "indefensible," while Richard Posner asserted that Holmes rejected its "compensation rationale as alien to the system."[33] Similarly, Guido Calabresi stated that Holmes denied deterrence objectives for strict liability on "invalid premises," and Morton Horwitz concluded that Holmes found strict liability an anathema on various grounds of "policy and/or morality."[34]

Many proponents of the negligence-dogma interpretation connect it to a long-standing and widely accepted thesis that nineteenth-century tort law established a "lax negligence standard" as the universal rule, to provide nascent industry with a covert "subsidy."[35] Developed independently of the negligence-dogma interpretation, this industrial-subsidy thesis offers alternative explanations of the negligence hegemony, theorizing that the leading courts and commentators either "transformed" the existing system, dominated for centuries by cause-based strict liability or, regardless of what rule if any dominated the existing system, simply throttled the rise of strict liability, particularly as exemplified by *Rylands*.[36] Holmes is charged with playing a pivotal intellectual role in fostering the subsidy goal of formalizing the negligence hegemony and the economic redistribution that accompanied it. He is accused of establishing, through guileful analysis and mesmerizing rhetoric, the historical inevitability, functional superiority, and moral necessity of the negligence threshold for liability. The torts lectures were essentially, in Robert Gordon's view, "a polemic from political economy against strict liability."[37] *Rylands* was the chief nemesis of the subsidy goal, and according to Horwitz, Holmes "devoted [himself] to marginalizing this feared authority for redistribution in torts."[38] Grant Gilmore went further than most when he claimed that in securing the triumph of negligence, Holmes was laying the groundwork for his ultimate goal of insulating industry from liability "to anyone for anything."[39]

A number of those advocating the negligence-dogma interpretation also suggest that it undermines Holmes's standing as the progenitor of modern legal realism and its "progressive" tradition.[40] The apparent contradiction between Holmes's antiformalist jurisprudence, based on a legislative conception of tort law, and the moralistic as well as dogmatic nature of his supposed arguments for a negligence hegemony has spurred these advocates to reassess his thinking (but not their own). They see a deep philosophic confusion, a mind "at war with itself."[41] Many consider Holmes's purported negligence-dogmatism as sufficient cause to brand him a closet formalist. Even if Holmes never accepted the teleology of natural law, they argue, he arrived at the same formalist result through the evolutionary creed of normative social Darwinism, deeming negligence the fittest rule for the needs of an industrial society built by free-wheeling entrepreneurs engaging in economic competition. Some claim that formalism characterized Holmes's early writings only through *The Common Law*, while others think it persisted for his entire scholarly career.

The negligence-dogma interpretation remains the unchallenged orthodoxy today. Its proponents never confront, let alone discuss, the evidence of Holmes's support for strict liability in his scholarly writings. Even those who note that Holmes recognized certain strict liability rules dismiss this as a minor inconsistency, an aberration, or sheer whimsy. His support for *Rylands* is trivialized when not ignored altogether.[42] On the few occasions that his arguments for strict liability in industrial cases are acknowledged, commentators nonetheless claim that as a general proposition—without explaining their criteria—Holmes was a negligence-dogmatist.[43] Many proponents of the negligence-dogma interpretation admit to being perplexed by Holmes's advocacy of the "external or objective standard" of negligence—a standard that ignores personal deficiencies—which he clearly favored precisely for its affinity to strict liability in demanding "a certain average of conduct, a sacrifice of individual peculiarities . . . necessary to the general welfare."[44] Yet, again, they find that the inconsistency lies not with their interpretation but with contradictions in Holmes's theory.

Perhaps the most flagrant example of scholarly neglect by these commentators is the failure to discuss a crucial portion of Holmes's torts lectures. In the nearly fifty years of advocacy of the negligence-dogma interpretation, its proponents have ignored the second half of Lecture IV entitled "The Theory of Torts."[45] This section contains Holmes's culminating arguments in the torts lectures, which were intended to "review the principal branches of the law of torts," as he said, "and state the theory to be discovered."[46] To this end, Holmes applied the foresight theory to justify the various strict liability rules in force, and, most importantly, marshaled *Rylands* in support of the conclusion that strict liability was a just and functionally rational means for redressing and preventing foreseeable injury.

My investigation of Holmes's theory of torts proceeds in three phases: Holmes's jurisprudence, his thinking on torts, and the history of scholarly views about his theory of torts and strict liability.

First, the book explains Holmes's central ideas on jurisprudence and illuminates the role played by his thinking on torts (particularly regarding strict liability) in providing the motive and proving ground for his new jurisprudence. Chapter 1 focuses primarily on the first decade of Holmes's writings, before publication of *The Common Law*. Its aim is to explore the fruits of that labor for his work on torts, and also to disprove the currently prevailing formalist portrayals of his jurisprudential thought during that period. It will be seen that all of the major components of his antiformalist conception of legal reality, including the well-known perspectives of the "bad man," law-as-prophecy, and legislative function of courts, were in place from the beginning. Chapter 2 explains the model of empirical science embodied in Holmes's new jurisprudence and delineates the framework which its test of experience provided for working out a general theory of torts. The chapter also discusses Holmes's vision of the practical benefits of such general theories in improving the realism and utility of legal knowledge and reform. Both the formalist characterizations of Holmes's classificatory objectives and the equation of his evolutionary historicism with normative Social Darwinism are shown to be profoundly mistaken.

Second, the book elaborates the development, nature, and implications of Holmes's theory of torts. He worked out his theory in the process of rebutting the two leading formalist theories for unifying torts. The first, advanced by the English jurist John Austin, held that the threshold of responsibility in tort was personal culpability akin to *mens rea* in criminal law. Even before writing the torts lectures, Holmes considered that he had effectively refuted Austin's theory by showing its empirical failure to account for the pervasive use in tort of external standards of negligence and strict liability, under which the existence of personal culpability is irrelevant. The main focus of Chapter 3 is on Holmes's refutation of the other formalist theory, which posited responsibility in tort on the mere causing of harm, however unforeseeable, and justified cause-based strict liability. The chapter presents Holmes's attack on this causation theory, an attack that denied not only the theory's descriptive validity, but also its moral coherence. This discussion of Holmes's arguments against the causation theory provides a new understanding of his view of the relationship of negligence and strict liability in the history of tort law, a view that was prevalent among his contemporaries but which has been lost from sight today. The recovered view offers unexplored perspectives on this history by challenging the "transformation" and other standard interpretations as well as the related industrial-subsidy thesis.

In accord with the structure of classic moral philosophy, Holmes divided his torts theory in two parts, distinguishing "responsibility" and "excuse" from "justification."[47] Chapter 4 discusses the first part of his theory, which located the threshold of moral responsibility in tort on foresight-informed choice. In large part, the chapter is devoted to demonstrating that Holmes's theory of responsibility supported all liability rules that required foreseeable harm as a minimal condition for recovery, including *Rylands* and the other major rules of strict liability. Chapter 5 looks at the second part of Holmes's theory, which was concerned with justification. In contrast to the first part, which focused on the abstract, enduring conception of moral responsibility changing only gradually over centuries, the second part accounted for the more short-term policies courts make (consistent with the general conception of responsibility) to deal with concrete cases and the immediate needs of society. Specifically, it explained how courts exercise discretionary power to justify on public policy grounds "escapes" for a given class of cases from *prima facie* responsibility for inflicting foreseeable harm.[48] Depending on their views of policy, courts may select any of the foresight-based rules of liability or, indeed, may deny liability altogether. Chapter 5 elaborates Holmes's view of the policy choices courts make in determining whether negligence or strict liability should govern a particular class of cases. This discussion provides a comprehensive outline of his innovative policy arguments for using rules of strict liability and negligence to achieve the compensation and deterrence functions of tort law in cases arising from industrial and other business activities. Although many of these arguments have become commonplace today (albeit without recognition of their source in Holmes), examination of his thinking still offers fresh insights on tort policy even on the eve of the twenty-first century.

Third, the book traces the history of scholarly interpretations of Holmes's theory of torts. Chapter 6 shows that the consensus among Holmes's contemporaries recognized his support for strict liability. It further substantiates this support by demonstrating a correspondence between his ideas and terminology and those of his contemporaries. This evidence undermines both the negligence-dogma interpretation and industrial-subsidy thesis. The chapter next identifies the sources of the negligence-dogma interpretation and the factors that have perpetuated its dominance, including scholarly neglect and ideological presuppositions. Beyond removing obstacles to understanding the ideas of Holmes and his contemporaries, this book thus serves an additional purpose—to provide a case study of the current state of legal scholarship.

1

Formalist Legal Science

Holmes's views on torts were part and parcel of his thinking on jurisprudence. He developed and presented his analyses of negligence and strict liability to serve the purpose of generating, testing, and illustrating his jurisprudential arguments. "I am not trying to justify particular doctrines," he cautioned, "but to analyze the general method by which the law reaches its decisions."[1] Thus, to understand his theory of torts, we need to begin with an examination of his jurisprudence.

In this chapter I examine Holmes's jurisprudential thinking as it developed during the 1870s. In particular, I focus on his conception and criticism of formalist legal science, leaving for later a review of the basic components of the "new jurisprudence," his scientific methodology for deriving general theories of law. My aim is to explore previously unrecognized connections between Holmes's jurisprudence and his theory of torts.

The Genesis of Holmes's Antiformalism

The prevailing understanding of Holmes's jurisprudence is that he began as a committed formalist, progressing in relatively discrete stages through the 1870s to a position of antiformalism.[2] As one might expect from writings that reflect a decade of formative, intense thought and research, his interests and focus varied, and his ideas changed. But the antiformalist foundation for the new jurisprudence was in place from the start.

Legal Scholarship in the 1870s

Beginning with his earliest commentaries, Holmes denounced contemporary legal scholarship for lacking philosophical and scientific value.[3] It offered nothing but "unreal explanations . . . unreal formulas and inadequate generalizations," leaving the common law an incoherent "ragbag of details."[4] Most legal treatises continued to classify cases and rules under the old forms of actions and other archaic headings. Even those commentaries that departed from tradition proceeded simply by "enumeration," grouping cases and rules on the basis of partial and usually superficial characteristics.[5] "Most men think dramatically, not quantitatively," he complained.[6] To his mind, mere compilation of particulars, however accurate and complete, fell far short of theoretical explanation: "A fact taken by itself is gossip; seen in its connections and relations it is part of science and philosophy."[7]

No common law subject needed coherent theory more than torts. Holmes dismissed torts scholarship as "pretty poor stuff."[8] Indeed, its lack of doctrinal "cohesion and legal relationship" prompted him initially to doubt the possibility of salvaging torts as a "proper subject for a law book."[9] Most astonishing was that philosophical default in the field muddled even the basic distinction between the two principal liability standards: negligence and strict liability. Instead of illuminating the necessary elements of these standards, torts literature was still "darkened by arguments on the limits between [the ancient writs of] trespass and case."[10] Holmes considered this inexcusable, because the leading American jurisdictions had formally discarded the writ system several decades before.[11] Moreover, the logical and empirical speciousness of the causal test demarcating Trespass from Case—"[t]he distinction between a direct application of force, and causing damage indirectly, or as a more remote consequence of one's act"—had been obvious for centuries.[12]

When not founded on the obsolete writ system, the method of classification favored by tort scholars arbitrarily distributed cases and rules among trade categories—"Railroads or Telegraphs"—or traditional legal titles—"assault and battery, libel and slander, nuisance, trespass, conversion, etc."[13] Holmes was not surprised that these scholars had no inkling of the extent to which the negligence and strict liability standards actually governed—and therefore could be generalized to organize—the seemingly infinite variety of unrelated cases and rules. The degree of philosophical bankruptcy afflicting torts was such that, according to Holmes, "no one dreamed . . . that the different cases of liability were, or ought to be, governed by the same principles throughout."[14]

In Search of a True Science of Law

To overcome the jurisprudential chaos, Holmes proposed applying the philosophy and methodologies of modern empirical science to the study of law. Clearly, science was triumphing in every field of inquiry about the natural world, providing empirically testable descriptions and explanations of causal relationships in place of the unverifiable dogmas of metaphysics and religion. He was most profoundly affected by Darwin's theories of evolution, which extended the power of scientific theory to all living nature. Holmes recognized that empirical science could provide only provisional hypotheses—"never proved, but always to be proved"[15]— rather than an absolute, fixed order and justifications of a metaphysical postulate or a theological final cause. Yet he was convinced that only empirical science could lead to a coherent and socially useful understanding of legal reality.

Although "science was at the bottom" of all thinking, Holmes derived most of his learning on this subject, as with law, through informal self-instruction.[16] His 1859 undergraduate botany class at Harvard, taught by Asa Gray, was a noteworthy exception. Gray was both a proficient empirical scientist and an innovator of modern pragmatic philosophy and methods of scientific classification.[17] As a primary mover in establishing the "natural system" of classification—an arrangement of inclusive, flexible, and purely empirical categories chosen solely for their convenience in communicating ideas and information—Gray was instrumental in replacing the Linnaean "artificial system" of metaphysical *a priori* postulates, narrow and immutable categories, and syllogistic logic.[18] Gray vehemently opposed "natural theologians" like his Harvard colleague Louis Agassiz and the philosopher Herbert Spencer, who subordinated the findings of empirical science to the concept of final cause and other *a priori* doctrines.[19] Upon the publication of *On the Origin of Species* in 1859, Gray became the leading American advocate of Darwin's evolutionary theories and empiricist science.[20]

Holmes's "scientific way of looking at the world" was also nurtured in the home—by his mother's "skeptical temperament," and by his father, who was "brought up scientifically" and sided with Gray in combating Agassiz and promoting Darwin's theories.[21] The young man's reading in

science during the late 1860s was current if eclectic, and included the
works of John Stuart Mill on empiricism, as well as the studies of Henry
Buckle on evolution as applied to sociology, and the foundational work of
Edward Tylor in anthropology.[22] But the primary influence shaping the
pragmatic understanding of science that Holmes brought to law came
from his discussions in the early 1870s with Charles S. Peirce, William
James, Nicholas St. John Green, Chauncey Wright, and other members of
the Metaphysical Club in Cambridge.[23]

Wright appears to have been Holmes's principal source on modern scientific philosophy and methodology, and the importance of Darwin's theories.[24] A protégé of Gray's, Wright was a talented physicist and
mathematician and a profound philosopher whom Peirce acknowledged
as a cofounder of American pragmatism. Wright armed Holmes and his
fellow club members for combat against metaphysical and other *a priori*
theorists by elaborating for them the empiricist maxim that a scientific
theory should posit only those causal relationships susceptible to falsifi-
cation by the test of experience. He explained the ideas of chance and
relativism in scientific philosophy as illustrated by Darwin's probabilistic
theories of variation and natural selection. On this basis, Wright demonstrated the error of those like Spencer who presumed that historical evolution necessarily brought about social progress.[25] Wright also strongly
reinforced Holmes's commitment to intellectual skepticism by stressing
the "neutrality" of science—that science provides causal, not justificatory
explanations and therefore should not become involved with final causes,
metaphysical postulates, and other *a priori* systems.

Wright's teachings echo throughout Holmes's writings. Wright's theory
of scientific neutrality may be seen, for example, in the distinction Holmes
drew between the prior orthodoxy of "explain[ing] any part of the universe by showing its fitness for certain ends . . . demonstrating what they
conceived to be its final cause according to a providential scheme," and
the present "less theological and more scientific day [in which] we explain
an object by tracing the order and process of its growth and development
from a starting point assumed as given."[26] Explanations based on supernatural forces beyond the physical relationship between a "phenomenon
and its antecedents and consequents" were not science but "miracle."[27]
"It is outside the [postulated] law of cause and effect, and as such tran-
scends our power of thought, or at least is something to or from which we
cannot reason."[28] More than a half-century after their discussions,
Holmes recollected the significance of Wright's lessons: "Chauncey

Wright, a nearly forgotten philosopher of real merit, taught me when young that I must not say *necessary* about the universe, that we don't know whether anything is necessary or not. So I describe myself as a *bet*-tabilitarian. I believe that we can *bet* on the behavior of the universe in its contact with us."[29]

Unscientific Legal Science

According to Holmes, law was in a state of disarray not for want of a scientific direction, but rather because of misdirection by bogus science. Formalist legal science was then dominant, having achieved ascendance in America by the appointment in 1870 of its strong if untutored promoter, Christopher Columbus Langdell, as Dean of the Harvard Law School.[30] The salient "foreign" schools of formalist legal science in Holmes's view were the analytic and historical approaches, the former founded in England on the work of Jeremy Bentham's disciple John Austin, and the latter advocated in Germany by the Pandectist followers of Friedrich Carl von Savigny.[31] Throughout the 1870s and the ensuing decades of his scholarly career, Holmes pressed his fundamental objections to "all theories which consider the law only from its formal side, whether they attempt to deduce the *corpus* from *a priori* postulates, or fall into the humbler error of supposing the science of law to reside in the *elegantia juris,* or logical cohesion of part with part."[32] He concentrated most of his fire against analytic and historical legal science, dismissing Langdell's "humbler" version as shallow, and apparently discounting other American contributions as merely derivative.[33] It was clear to him that their overthrow and replacement by a new jurisprudence fully committed to the philosophy of modern empirical science was a prerequisite to developing a sound theory of torts and the other common law subjects.

Emulating Euclidean geometry, formalist legal science presented law as a syllogistic scheme operating from fixed postulates and deductively derived rights to produce mathematically determinate decisions.[34] "[T]he notion," Holmes noted, "[is] that a given system, ours, for instance, can be worked out like mathematics from some general axioms of conduct."[35] Even though formalist legal science rejected the supernatural postulates of metaphysics and theology, it purported to find timeless truths by induction (or conclusive presumption) from the phenomena under study. The analytic school focused on legal language; the historical school drew its truths from evolving national customs and mores.

Formalism "pursue[s] an inspirational combined with a logical method, that is, the postulates are taken for granted upon authority without inquiry into their worth, and then logic is used as the only tool to develop the results."[36] Analytic legal science, for example, called on jurisprudence to "imitate the method so successfully pursued by geometers."[37] According to Holmes, Austin presupposed the major premise "that all law emanates from the sovereign, even when the first human beings to enunciate it are the judges," and deduced that tort liability, being a direct sovereign command like criminal liability, required personal culpability on the defendant's part and therefore excluded strict liability.[38] Advocates of historical legal science, which also excluded strict liability, presumed "that law is the voice of the Zeitgeist," but "cunningly adjusted" it to an idealized conception of Roman law.[39] Modeling a syllogistic structure from this understanding of Roman law would enable jurists to "calculate with their notions," as Savigny said, "[achieving] a certainty which is found nowhere else, except in mathematics."[40]

In formulating syllogistic systems from language and custom respectively, the aim of both analytic and historical legal science was to establish—preferably by codification—an apolitical, comprehensive, and self-sufficient set of norms for logically extrapolating solutions to virtually all new problems. In a perverse twist of scientific neutrality, formalist legal science claimed that it could stop the "struggle for life" from affecting the formulation and application of legal rules by courts, and that its mechanical gapless systems precluded the need, let alone the opportunity, for judicial policy-making, particularly that which would effect a redistribution of wealth and political power.[41] A central purpose of legal science was, Roscoe Pound observed, "complete separation between jurisprudence and the theory of legislation . . . to exclude all ideas of policy from the domain of legal thought."[42]

Holmes did not reject analytic and historical legal science wholesale. Indeed, his new jurisprudence amalgamated central tenets from both approaches as well as from other schools of jurisprudential thought in pursuing the common philosophical goals of classificatory clarity, conceptual generalization, and unifying theory. Thus he concurred in Austin's positivist premise that the law was the empirical product of human will rather than of an absolutist order of *a priori* metaphysical postulates to be discovered.[43] Moreover, Holmes relied upon the apparent recognition by both analytic and historical legal science that law implemented and signified public policy (in its broadest political and moral sense) and, according to the historical school at least, was an evolving and thus culturally and temporally relative process.[44]

Despite this shared orientation, Holmes concluded that formalism disqualified legal science from being a "true science of law."[45] The scientific study of law should seek explanatory theories based from start to finish on the actual experience of legal systems. Formalism blinded legal science to the real world. Contrary to formalist presumptions, the common law was a historically evolving process driven by judicial choices of expedient policy to satisfy socially contingent needs; therefore, it could never be reduced to a "syllogism" of "seemingly self-sufficient propositions."[46] As Holmes declared: "[C]ertainty is only an illusion . . . Views of policy are taught by experience of the interests of life. Those interests are fields of battle."[47]

Indeed, to Holmes, such a political experience of clashing ideologies and competing classes was "the secret root from which the law draws all the juices of life."[48] The law grows and changes as it continuously adjusts these conflicts in basic values and needs. The process of adaptation takes the guise of logical form, but the propelling substantive force is "legislative"—judicial "inventions" of "public policy."[49] Legal evolution was probabilistic; it followed no final or other necessary course but rather was an indeterminate process of dynamic interplay between "history" and "theories of legislation."[50]

Fallacies of Formalism: A Capsule Overview

The bulk of Holmes's writing in the 1870s was aimed at demonstrating two basic fallacies of formalistic legal science: disregard of experience (the law in operation), and the politics of law (legislative function of courts). First, Holmes showed that legal science validated theories without regard to the law in operation, violating the "first call of a theory of law . . . that it should fit the facts . . . [and] explain the observed course of legislation."[51] Holmes surmised that both the analytic and historical schools often mistook idealized notions of law for existing legal systems. Second, and most significantly for the development of twentieth-century legal realism, Holmes exposed the neglect or concealment in legal science of the politics of law: "[e]very important principle which is developed by litigation is in fact and at bottom the result of more or less definitely understood views of public policy."[52] The crucial operative facts ignored by legal science, he argued, were precisely those that revealed the determinative role of judicial policy preferences in the development of common law rules as well as in the decisions of particular cases.

The chief failing of both analytic and historical schools of legal science was that neither could account credibly for the operational and political reality of strict liability. Both schools developed elaborate unifying theories of tort law, which were founded on negligence and which Holmes refused to accept. Indeed, his main attacks on the analytic and historical approaches culminated respectively in two articles focusing on the failure to explain prevalent rules of strict liability: "The Theory of Torts" (1873), and the largely overlooked "Common Carriers and the Common Law" (1879).[53] The next two sections of this chapter take a closer look at the interplay between Holmes's development of his theory of torts and his evaluation of the two major schools of formalist legal science.

Analytic Legal Science

Basic Concepts

For the "analytical jurist," the language of law provided the key to the logical structure of legal reality.[54] Austin's supposition was that embedded in language was a universal system of semantic logic. Logical parsing of basic concepts would reveal this system in the form of a permanent syllogistic hierarchy of major premises and derivative rights, which could dictate the decision of particular cases with near mathematical certainty. Because the conventional grammar and usage of legal concepts involve them in "thicker obscurity," analytical legal science endeavored to clarify popular as well as technical legal terminology.[55]

The foundation of Austin's system was the postulate that the sovereign's command was the ultimate source and authority of law.[56] This equation was essential to the idea of legal order, and it defined the character of all systems, regardless of specific social and historical context. Austin reasoned that the idea of positive law limiting sovereign power was "a flat contradiction in terms," and that judicial anarchy would reign without the existence of a supreme political will, such as the Crown and Parliament in England and the several states in America.[57]

Consequently, all legal relationships and status were determined by a set of absolute rights decreed by the sovereign. Austin regarded the notion of "rights" as logically prior to the notion of "duties" and other concepts that specified the entailed prerogatives of right-holders and obligations of those in subordinate positions. "[U]nfold[ing] the notions which are signified by the term 'Right' " would, he argued, "indicate the import of the terms with which it is inseparably connected."[58]

From the major premise of sovereign command, Austin deduced a comprehensive scheme of common law rights and correlative duties that could be applied to particular cases with mechanical precision. Political choices and influences were thus removed from the judicial process, and in that sense adjudication was politically neutral. Any changes in policies were the province of the science of legislation, as distinguished from the science of law, and for the sovereign and not the courts to make.[59]

Critique of Absolute Rights

Holmes's first line of attack was to turn this use of analytic logic on itself. Austin committed the same elementary error as the metaphysicist in supposing that deductive logic, whatever the first principle, could specify absolute, generally applicable rights of sufficient definiteness to render their scope and application impervious to judicial policy discretion. What Austin failed to recognize was that the statement of any right necessarily implies a limiting case where a counterright takes precedence. No amount of parsing by analytical legal science of the phrase "property right," for example, could define away or reconcile competing rights, or logically determine the degree to which those excluded from the property would be obliged to respect its boundary lines and bear its risks. Absolute conceptions always foundered on this basic dilemma: their logical extension eventually conflicted with equally powerful opposing conceptions, a collision of interests that always necessitated political compromise. Courts resolved this inevitable conflict through political compromises usually expressed in the doctrinal terms of variable duties that determine the scope of a right by "limit[ing] freedom of action or choice on the part of a greater or less number of persons in certain specified ways."[60]

The scope of a right—the policy allocation of benefits and burdens— was determined by judicial discretion to specify the relative scope of related duties—"acts or forbearances, imposed on other persons, the claim to which constitutes the rights."[61] By limiting duties, directly or through the specification of more or less qualified privileges, judicial policy-making reconciled competing social interests. One of Holmes's recurrent examples was the use of malice in defamation to limit a privilege that absolved

derogatory statements in employment references, thereby balancing the
need both for candid advice and for protecting personal and business reputations.[62]

Indeed, as Holmes explained in "Theory of Torts" (1873), legal evolution was pervasively characterized by this struggle between competing
claims of moral, political, and economic interest. Initially, "[t]wo widely
different cases suggest a general distinction, which is a clear one when
stated broadly," but as "new cases . . . begin to approach each other," the
distinction becomes a battle ground of competing values and uses.[63] To
resolve these disputes, courts must draw fine lines of policy (especially in
specifying the scope of duties)—even "arbitrary" bureaucratic ones when
it was "better to have a line drawn somewhere . . . than to remain in
uncertainty."[64] Torts provided the best examples of the inevitability of
judicial policy discretion, particularly in determining the relative functional benefits of using strict liability or negligence in a given class of cases.
And, again in torts, courts frequently calibrated external negligence standards in varying degrees of "arbitrariness" to balance competing policies
of compensation, deterrence, and administrative economy.[65]

Even in criminal law, which Austin ("a criminalist"[66]) believed most
susceptible of logical determinancy, there was inevitable need for judicial
legislation, drawing policy lines between conflicting claims of right. As
Holmes explained:

> The law does not punish every act which is done with the intent to
> bring about a crime.
>   Eminent judges have been puzzled where to draw the line, or even
> to state the principle on which it should be drawn, between the two
> sets of cases. But the principle is believed to be similar to that on
> which all other lines are drawn by the law. Public policy, that is to
> say, legislative considerations, are at the bottom of the matter; the
> considerations being, in this case, the nearness of the danger, the
> greatness of the harm, and the degree of apprehension felt.[67]

Austin's presumptive logical priority for rights over duties masked the
inevitable drawing of policy lines by the courts. Even if Austin followed
Bentham in recognizing rights and duties as merely "fictitious entities,"
Holmes would not be satisfied.[68] Concepts are almost as dangerous when
they are treated as fictions as when they are mistaken for reality, especially
when they are "invented to conceal the fact."[69] "[A] legal fiction [such as
implied contract] does not change the nature of things," he declared; to

avoid thinking otherwise, even admitted fictions must be tested against the reality of the actual effects and consequences of the rules as applied.[70] Indeed, giving primacy to duties rather than rights would more clearly represent the real relationship and the political conflicts between classes of individuals, and between sovereign and subjects.[71] Focus on duties highlighted the differences in facts and interests presented by particular cases that preoccupation with absolute, general rights tended to disregard.[72] Here Holmes aligned himself with Comte: "To take rights and not the corresponding duties as the ultimate phenomena of law, is to stop short of a complete analysis, and to make 'entities of abstractions.' "[73] This was one of Holmes's main objections against Austin's aim to found a syllogistic code on a system of purified rights; that code simply could not decide the conflicting claims of real cases.[74] "We are not studying etymology, but law," Holmes declared, and "[l]aw, being a practical thing, must found itself on actual forces."[75]

Holmes broadened this view into a basic antiformalist tenet. Studying the law from the perspective of fixed *a priori* concepts without testing their scope against the reality of what courts were actually doing leads to "dangerous reliance on . . . glittering generalities, and a distaste for the exhaustive analysis of a particular case, with which the common law begins and ends."[76] Later, he captured this antiformalist precept in the famous aphorism, "[g]eneral propositions do not decide concrete cases."[77]

Critique of Sovereign Command Postulate

From an empirical perspective, Holmes concluded that Austin's major premise of equating law with sovereign command suffered from its disregard of the operation and the politics of law.[78] The forced equivalence ignored the way in which law actually operated by focusing obsessively on identifying a sovereign ruler whose actions were beyond the control of positive law. Even if such a sovereign could be identified in reality—a difficult logical conundrum in itself—the important feature of a command's compulsory effect is not "by whom a duty is imposed," but rather "the definiteness of its expression and the certainty of its being enforced."[79] On this test, as Holmes pointed out, even purely social and customary obligations often entail social and commercial penalties of a sufficiently stern nature to qualify as sources of law.[80] But Austin could never accept this dose of reality, because it would make impossible the logical containment of what counts as authoritative, legitimate law. More

important, Austin's semantics diverted him from the real locus of sover-
eignty—the judiciary. "A sovereign or political superior secures obedience
to his commands by his courts," Holmes noted, and hence a sovereign's
will is what the courts "*say* is his will."[81] Judges are not mere puppets of
logic. They frequently contravene the plain commands of their sovereign.
Indeed, in reality, they have virtually complete policy-making discretion.[82]
The most emphatic statutory prohibition "may be emptied of its contents
by construction."[83]

A more fundamental fallacy of Austin's approach was its disregard of
the politics of law. Austin's syllogistic conception of law presented judicial
decisions as logically determined and unaffected by any outside considerations such as custom, public policy, moral precepts, or political ideology.
Although he was aware of this problem, he attempted to make reality
conform to theory by rationalizing judicial enforcement of custom as a
mere implementation of "the tacit consent of the sovereign" that the custom should be law.[84] Holmes rejected this rationalization of imputed sovereign consent; when courts enforced a custom, statute, or precedent, they
were exercising virtually unfettered "discretion."[85] Moreover, the reality
of law for lawyers anticipating what judges would do consisted of predictions concerning the ideas, interests, and other factors in experience which
would motivate judicial discretion. This reliance on prediction exploded
the notion of an autonomous, self-contained, and mathematically determinate system. Logical consistency with a sovereign command was barely
a factor.

Thus even the most formal inside source of law, be it constitution or
statute, merely provides motives for judicial discretion. By calling attention to the forces outside the law that influence judicial discretion, Holmes
further clarified the continuous interrelationship of the law and social life.
His examples of these outside motives are inclusive and provocative, suggesting an infinite array of policy and personal considerations. In addition
to custom, all but "[s]ingular motives" are "ground[s] of prediction" and
might include "a doctrine of political economy, or the political aspirations
of the judge, or his gout."[86]

Fallacies of Austin's Theory of Torts

Analytical legal science led Austin to adopt what Holmes dubbed "a criminalist theory" of torts, following the semantic logic (reinforced by notions
of Roman law) that tort liability was "a penalty for disobedience [to the

sovereign's commands]."[87] Because both criminal and tort sanctions flowed directly from the sovereign will, unconditioned by contract, status, or other relationships, Austin reasoned that tort imposed general absolute duties of obedience equivalent to those of the penal law. It followed that, like its criminal counterpart, liability for breach of tort duties required "culpability as a state of the defendant's consciousness."[88] This requirement and its punitive policy explained and ordered all tort rules and decisions. By providing not only explanation but logical structure, Austin's personal culpability theory confined the scope of tort liability accordingly. Logic outlawed any discretion to diminish the culpability requirement and expand the scope of liability. For courts to disregard their logical constraints would constitute judicial legislation tantamount to a *coup d'état*.

Austin's theory simply did not square with the facts as Holmes saw them. Given Austin's definition of tort duties as connoting an "absolute command" and a corresponding obligation of obedience, one would expect to find with few exceptions that the cases implemented a sovereign intention to prohibit the conduct in question rather than make it "an option at a certain price."[89] While noting that courts occasionally attached "collateral consequences" to achieve a prohibitory result, such as requiring forfeiture in trover, Holmes insisted that the punitive explanation failed to account for the great majority of cases.[90] In operation, tort liability neither comported with nor implied the notion of punishment. By imposing damages for "ordinary liability," he pointed out, tort exacts no "penalty or sanction," but merely a "tax on a certain course of conduct."[91]

Equally untenable was Austin's suggestion that tort liability itself "impl[ied] culpability, or a breach of duty."[92] The deduction failed on grounds of semantic logic alone; as Holmes reasoned, "the possibility that I may have to pay the reasonable worth or market value of my neighbor's property cannot be said to amount to a penalty on conversion, much less to make it my duty not to convert it."[93] But his principal objection, again, was Austin's disregard of experience, which indicated clearly that courts applied external standards in most tort cases. This was true in the "great mass" of negligence cases.[94]

Thus, while initially accepting Austin's claim that a breach of a civil duty usually resulted in a penalty akin to criminal punishment for personal culpability, Holmes did so strictly on empirical grounds, finding some conflict in the evidence but concluding that Austin's characterization was an "accurate enough" description of actual practice.[95] Within two years, however, Holmes's research led to a changed estimate: the rules predominating in torts and civil liability generally applied external standards, which did not "imply culpability, or a breach of duty, as Austin thought, who looked at the law too much as a criminal lawyer."[96] Significantly, the critical edge of Holmes's empiricist attack on Austin's conceptualism was honed on the reality of "lawyers' law"[97]—previewing the new jurisprudence perspectives that stripped law down to the raw probabilistic phenomena of lawyer "prophecies" and "bad-man" concerns of what courts will do in fact.[98]

The most telling point against Austin, however, was the external standard of strict liability, in which "negligence is not an element."[99] Holmes placed particular reliance on the modern expansive doctrine of strict liability established by *Rylands,* which holds defendants "liable for damage resulting from extra-hazardous sources, without any allegation of negligence."[100] "Extra-hazardous" was a term Holmes coined and often applied to industrial and other commercial activities which generate substantial residual (non-negligent) risks, ranging from the danger of flooding posed by the reservoir in *Rylands* to crop damage caused by trespassing cattle.[101]

The emphasis on the absence of negligence in the operational requirements of *Rylands* and the other principal doctrines of strict liability had special relevance in refuting Austin's theory. Writing some time before the decision in *Rylands,* Austin nonetheless recognized that strict liability posed the greatest problem for his theory. Negligence decisions were susceptible of a personal culpability characterization; strict liability holdings were not. To buttress his theory, Austin attempted to eliminate strict liability as a doctrinal category by recasting the major traditional rules of such liability (for example, injuries from animals) as presumptive negligence standards—arguing that there was either misfeasance by the guilty party in conducting the activity or per se unreasonableness—"remote inadvertence"—in the choice or place of the activity.[102]

Contrary to what one might expect from a supposed negligence-dogmatist, Holmes flatly rejected this maneuver as thoroughly belied by the facts. Although he agreed that under the negligence doctrine the reasonableness of the defendant's conduct would be scrutinized both in the choice of activity and in its management, neither the doctrines nor cases of strict liability entailed any such negligence as a matter of fact or law. Holmes concluded that nothing "savoring of culpability" could be found in any of the major traditional rules of strict liability, such as those governing trespass to land, conversion of personal property, defamation, and personal and property damage from domestic and wild animals.[103] Even in the cases concerning wild animals, where presumptive negligence interpretations were most plausible, analysis disproved the formalist position. "[T]here is usually no question of negligence in guarding the beast," Holmes concluded, so the "risk is thrown upon the owner for other reasons than the ordinary one of imprudent conduct."[104] Nor could these cases be treated as instances of "remote inadvertence"—unreasonableness in choosing to engage in the activity at all (however carefully) or of doing so at an unsuitable location—as the "law does not forbid a man to keep a menagerie, or deem it in any way blameworthy."[105] Yet liability was imposed nonetheless.

In rebutting Austin, Holmes emphasized that contemporary courts already applied traditional rules of strict liability, both in their own right and under the encompassing *Rylands* principle, to deal with the modern problems presented by "sources regarded as extra-hazardous."[106] These rules applied to activities that were plainly "prudent and beneficial to the community."[107] If such strict liability doctrines represented the future direction of tort in an increasingly industrialized society, then external standards were not only in the majority but on the leading edge of legal development.

By indicating that courts exercise discretion in shaping and choosing among various liability rules, Holmes also pointed to the inevitable politics of torts. Policy—not semantic logic—explained decisions to make external negligence or strict liability, rather than personal culpability, the basis of liability for any given class of cases. The choice was functional: courts selected the rule which they believed would "best accomplish" the compensation and deterrence ends of tort law.[108] For support, Holmes stressed the multiple compensation and deterrence rationales for strict liability under *Rylands*.

The decision in *Rylands* to apply strict liability instead of negligence was based solely on a pragmatic determination that making defendants bear the entire risk in a given class of cases would better achieve the deterrence and compensation objectives than would allocating the non-negligent portion of the risk to plaintiffs. Generalizing this insight, Holmes argued that resort to strict liability or negligence always depended on the balance of social advantage in the circumstances. A notable example was the contemporary abandonment of strict liability in favor of negligence for cattle trespass in some western states, on the social calculus that "the enclosure of their vast prairies is necessarily for a long time out of the question."[109] Thus Austin's notion of reducing tort law to a consistent and settled code was fantasy, especially given the contingent and widely varying conditions of American life. Logic could neither anticipate nor balance the conflicting and changing social interests at stake in tort cases. "Public policy must determine where the line is to be drawn."[110]

The Prototype Theory of Torts

A crowning triumph over Austin for Holmes would be to synthesize a unifying theory of torts on antiformalist grounds. This was the aim of his 1873 essay, "The Theory of Torts." While the essay was a great intellectual achievement, it fell short of its goal.

This unified-theory objective sharply contrasted with Austin's aspirations for a classification system based on the *a priori* postulate of sovereign command and built in the shape of a hierarchical structure of logically purified, compartmentalized, and fixed concepts. In contrast, Holmes's approach to classification was antiformalist. Consonant with modern scientific theories of classificatory empiricism developed and exemplified by the work of Darwin and Gray in the natural sciences, Holmes's was a thoroughly empirical and pragmatic arrangement.[111] His theory of torts would contain no structure of immutable categories. Rather, the results of legal evolution would be depicted in fluid, connected relationships that accorded with his view of the real substantive mechanism of development—judicial policy responses to evolving social and political conflicts. Cases and rules would be organized according to their operational scope (measured by their actual requirements, effects, and consequences) as ultimately delimited by corresponding policy motives. Furthermore, all classification would remain provisional and subject to the test of experience. Holmes hypothesized that the resulting policy-based arrangement would be more comprehensive and reveal a far more continuous relationship between legal phenomena than was provided by Austin's *a priori* system of syllogistically derived, fixed concepts.

To a large extent "The Theory of Torts" succeeded in satisfying Holmes's antiformalist aims. Within three years of expressing doubts that torts was a coherent subject, Holmes provided a realistic, pathbreaking arrangement of it. This classification system did not stop at demonstrating the dominance of external standards. More fundamentally, it innovated the division of tort law into three independent branches and inventively consolidated the diverse strict liability rules into a distinct branch, coequal with those for negligence and intentional wrongs.

The core of the strict liability branch comprised rules governing the expansive class of extra-hazardous activities. Holmes explicitly and repeatedly presented *Rylands* as epitomizing the rules of strict liability that should govern the future of extra-hazardous risk. Far from presenting *Rylands* as anomalous, Holmes made it central to the strict liability branch and its distinction from the negligence branch. To him, *Rylands* revealed the empirical unity of the apparently disparate rules of strict liability. Despite their factually varying contexts, the operationally significant fact common to all of those rules was their application to inherently dangerous activities—"things having an active tendency to do damage; *e.g.* Reservoirs."[112] Admittedly, the "particular things" deemed inherently dangerous would vary from jurisdiction to jurisdiction, and thus would "have to be considered separately."[113] Yet when the facts of the "particular instances" were examined, the "general principle" of recognizable inherent danger would emerge "as the tacitly assumed ground of decision."[114]

On the empirical finding of this common element, Holmes conjectured that the modern development of all of the strict liability rules stemmed from the same motivating policy: "that it is politic to make those who go into extra-hazardous employments take the risk on their own shoulders."[115] His proposed strict liability classification encompassed not only such traditional rules as vicarious liability, cattle trespass, and the rules governing personal and property damage from domestic and wild animals, but also the two strict liability rules that would become the dominant means of regulating industrial activity in the twentieth century: *Rylands* and liability for latent product defects.

Despite the intellectual achievement of formulating a broad-based strict liability classification and of dividing torts into the three "principal branches"[116]—intentional wrongs, negligence, and strict liability—"The Theory of Torts" failed to state a unifying general theory based on empirical, not *a priori* grounds. Holmes based his unifying theory on the general duty concept. Stripped of Austin's moral culpability connotations, the general duty concept represented the usual policy in tort law to impose obligations on defendants without regard to contractual, status, or other special relationships between the parties. The generalized nature of these duties reflected the increasing tendency of courts to employ "arbitrary" (bureaucratic or "concrete") rules that constrained individual freedom by a collective "criterion of social welfare."[117]

In accord with his understanding of the policy basis of judicial duty-setting decisions, Holmes recognized that an undifferentiated general duty category would obscure the different policy considerations underlying the three branches of liability rules. In particular, a realistic classification had to account for the irreducible differences arising from the economic and political effects of negligence and strict liability. To sharpen the focus, he assigned each of the three branches of liability rules to a separate subcategory of general duty: "Duties of All to All" (negligence); "Duties of All to Persons in Particular Situations" (intentional wrongs); and "Duties of Persons in Particular Situations to All" (strict liability).[118]

This subcategorizing of the duty concept, however, undermined the unifying theory objective, especially in highlighting the distinction between strict liability and negligence. Holmes was compelled to admit that the duties of the former "cannot satisfactorily be resolved into duties" of the latter.[119] In a vain effort to patch together the three subcategories, he simply invented an ether-like medium. The "element in common" was that all three liability standards establish generalized duties "irrespective of the special relation between the parties."[120] Following this reasoning, Holmes reconciled the strict liability and negligence branches in Darwinian fashion, as comprising a continuous spectrum of kindred species that "shade away from . . . [each other] by insensible degrees."[121] By this device Holmes salvaged enough unifying elements to claim that, despite their ineradicable distinctions, strict liability and negligence duties were nevertheless general in nature and therefore "discerned to tend in the same direction."[122]

It was obvious, however, that the label "general duty" added nothing of substance. Filament-thin nearly to the point of transparency, the general-duty arrangement had neither source nor shape independent of the liability rules it contained. Rather than unifying the three branches, the scheme merely reproduced the fractured and internally contradictory tort system under a different set of names, albeit now winnowed down to the three main rule classes. Holmes conceded as much, in acknowledging that the "enumeration of the actions which have been successful, and of those which have failed, defines the extent of the primary duties imposed by the law."[123]

This failure to develop a unified theory of tort liability apparently taught

Holmes the final lesson about the "trap which legal language lays for us."[124] Conceptualization of experience was necessary, of course, but forgetting that the meaning of a concept is grounded in the facts it symbolizes posed a constant danger of making "entities of abstractions." Even after all Austinian meaning had been distilled away, the duty concept could induce the mistake of confusing a conclusion with an explanation. After completing "The Theory of Torts," Holmes virtually banished the terms "right" and "duty" from his lexicon. "[O]pen to objection" and, in future, to be "avoid[ed]," these concepts received negligible mention in the torts lectures and only derisive reference thereafter.[125] Instead, he intensified his commitment to empirical inquiry. The search for a unifying theory with power to explain the law in operation must seek the practical and policy motives underlying the duty and right conclusions. This would entail determining the actual requirements of liability rules as they arose and operated in an ever-changing social and historical context. "What I am seeking to discover," he stated, "is the theory [of tort liability]—or the ground of fact, by or out of which the law creates those rights or duties . . . to find out why it does create them when it does."[126]

Historical Legal Science
Basic Concepts

Historical legal science rejected the analytic approach as abstract and static, yet zealously pursued the syllogistic ideal. The formalist historians' *a priori* major premise equated law with "customary law": the steadily unfolding "consciousness of the people"—"as a natural unity . . . the bearer of positive law"—that jurists were perfecting in the image of Roman law.[127] Historical legal science attracted strong followings in England and America both because of its perceived methodological advantages, and because the conceptual structure of German custom worked out by Savigny and the Pandectists seemed ready-made for the English common law, given its Teutonic origins.

According to Savigny, German law developed initially through customary practice, which supplied the "political element" and "true grammar of law." As it matured, the process took a scientific direction in the hands of juristic scholars.[128] Influenced by Kantian metaphysics, their own professional interests, and aspirations for a centralized legal system, the German jurists added the "technical element," which entailed methodically elaborating and restating the essential meaning of custom into a syllogistic structure.[129] "Law based on the external authority of an immediate conviction of the people and legislative power is traced to its principles by scientific activity and grasped as a system, a whole composed of reciprocal principles which presuppose and condition each other."[130]

What gave this structure closure as well as comprehensiveness and deterministic conclusiveness was an idealized conception of Roman law, with which the jurists suffused the system through the guise of interpreting and adapting indigenous mores. The result of these juristic ministrations was a network of legal principles—the custom of the jurist class—that was more "Roman" than German or even than the original Roman law. Once this idealized Roman structure had been fully elaborated, it would be codified to preclude judicial policy-making. While Savigny opposed the early German codification movement, arguing that more development of the structure of custom was required, by the 1840s his Pandectist followers claimed to have substantially satisfied this condition, and by the 1870s they were drafting a comprehensive code of German law. This code based tort liability generally on negligence.

Critique of Historical Legal Science

Holmes and proponents of historical legal science shared common ground in conceiving of law as reflecting as well as shaping social evolution. They also agreed that the analytic approach was woefully inadequate for its neglect of this historical perspective. Holmes asserted that a "rule of law that has been gradually developed can only be understood by knowing the course of its development."[131] He repeatedly deployed history to support his analytic as well as empirical criticisms of Austin's conclusions.[132] Most notably, he marshaled history in "The Theory of Torts" to support his previously published arguments that both logic and experience contradicted Austin's personal culpability theory of tort liability. According to Holmes, the tort system evolved from conceptions of blame and responsibility that were poles apart from Austin's hypothesis. Tort liability found its source not in the sense of punishment for personal wrongdoing but rather in primitive animism—expressing a personal but wholly vengeful form of blame, "vengeance on the offending thing"—which later gave way to damages as an expedient to avert clan feuds and violence.[133] Holmes developed this insight into the grand historical theme of *The Common Law*. The law began with personalized blame and the desire for revenge suitable to the isolated existence of individuals in primitive times, but, he hypothesized, the notion of responsibility in torts changed in response to the needs of organized society and was "continually transmuting those moral [subjective] standards into external or objective ones."[134]

From the beginning, however, Holmes clearly distinguished his evolutionary historicism from that of historical legal science. He rejected the culturally deterministic arguments of historical legal science that equated law with custom or Roman law or any other legal authority over and above what "judges *say*." Rather than deny with Savigny that the law developed "by the arbitrary will of the law-giver,"[135] Holmes affirmed that the law did and would continue to develop precisely through judges exercising discretion, including decrees of "arbitrary" external standards to cut "through the region of uncertainty."[136] To the extent that it equated law with the autonomous and paramount authority of custom (molded to the idealized model of Roman law), historical legal science was simply a metaphysical project to convert the contingent product of history into *a priori* doctrine. Holmes denied that a system of law evolving as part of social history could ever conform or reduce to a syllogistic structure of fixed ultimate postulates dictating what always must and ought to be. "The truth is," he said, "that the law is always approaching, and never reaching, consistency . . . It will become entirely consistent only when it ceases to grow . . . However much we may codify the law into a series of seemingly self-sufficient propositions, those propositions will be but a phase in a continuous growth."[137] Scholars who professed to see the syllogistic ideal in legal evolution—particularly, the necessary progress of history—were entirely misguided and, Holmes strongly suspected, less interested in studying historical change scientifically than in freezing it at a point that favored their class and political preferences.[138]

In Holmes's view of the historical perspective, law was an integral but not a mechanical part of the process of evolving social life. Law shaped as well as reflected that development. Social forces—whether expressed as a "doctrine of political economy," "positive morality," "custom," or otherwise—provided the motives for judicial policy choices; they generated substantive policy options and imposed cultural and intellectual constraints on thought and action.[139] But nothing in the nature or substance of historical growth automatically foreclosed freedom of judicial discretion, requiring courts to "sacrifice good sense to a syllogism."[140] "[C]ontinuity with the past," Holmes repeatedly affirmed, was "only a necessity and not a duty . . . That continuity simply limits the possibilities of our imagination, and settles the terms in which we shall be compelled to think."[141] Law was thus not a mechanical unfolding of pure reason, semantics, or custom, but rather largely the result of "expedient" judicial public policy responses to social contingency and conflict. Conversely, history as a critical tool was useful for more than demonstrating the political, asyllogistic character of law. To combine history with the tools and perspectives of other disciplines—including anthropology, sociology, economics, political theory, ethics, and logic—would greatly facilitate understanding of the actual policies shaping and driving the law in operation. The purpose of gaining this knowledge was entirely instrumental: to improve predictions of what courts will do, and—contrary to the admonitions of historical legal science against interfering with the natural growth of custom—to stimulate and enhance law reform efforts.

During the 1870s Holmes relentlessly applied the tool of historical criticism along several fronts to demonstrate the formalistic fallacies of historical legal science. Its reliance on Roman law for structural backbone supplied a principal example of the fallacy of ignoring the law in operation. It was absurd to think that wholesale importation of Roman law would well serve the political needs of Germany or any other modern society. Moreover, in the passage of time, whatever logical structure Roman law might have possessed had been obscured from view; more important, its "principles of classification . . . have lost their significance, and . . . [its] philosophy . . . is no longer vital."[142] Indeed, to Romanize German law contravened the idea of cultural autonomy advocated by historical legal science.

Most current commentators miss the basic thrust of Holmes's intricate anti-Romanist arguments, dismissing them as intellectual filigree and antiquarianism. What he was attempting to show was central to the new jurisprudence hypothesis of legal evolution driven by judicial policy choices. By disproving the Romanists' conception of how English common law developed, Holmes removed a major obstacle to understanding that law is not a permanent logical structure but rather the historical product of sociopolitical contingency. More important to new jurisprudence methodology, by denying the presumed universal application of Roman law he embraced the ideas of historical and cultural relativism. Law must be studied as an evolutionary process, but always with a view to particular contexts of time and place—whether it be the experience of England or America, or that which emerges more locally from New England's "granite rocks and barberry bushes."[143] In fact, according to Holmes, German custom bore little resemblance either to the idealized versions of Roman law or to its actual content, which was far more pragmatic and contextual than the jurist scholars claimed. The alleged correspondence had been a concoction of the "German professors."[144] To foreclose application of German theories of historical legal science to the English common law, Holmes used highly charged rhetoric in repeatedly denying comparisons between Roman law and the "modern law" in England and America.[145] He expended much energy in proving that Roman law, in either the original or the Germanized version, was not the source of many basic and long-standing common law rules, including, as discussed below, those governing the crucial area of bailment—"[t]he test of the theory of possession which prevails in any system of law."[146] Whatever the contentions about a connection to German law, he concluded, the notion that Roman law permeated English common law was "perniciously false."[147]

Holmes's objections to reliance on Roman law also pointed more broadly to the basic error of historical legal science in denying the politics of law. That error lay in the supposition that custom represented the shared, natural, and politically neutral expression of a nation's developing moral sense, and, as such, precluded courts and even legislatures from "legislating" public policies that swerved the evolving law from its inevitable path. Holmes insisted that English and American common law never regarded custom as the exclusive, let alone apolitical, fountainhead of law. Whatever the case might be in Germany, the common law treated custom—whether of a particular business interest, economic class, or more widespread social practice—as merely one among numerous motives for judicial choice in making law.[148] Holmes ridiculed Savigny's "latitudinary theorizing," which gave political primacy to custom such that it could even "repeal a statute."[149] "A custom, as such, is a fact," albeit often difficult to determine, and its existence is sought only "to suggest a rule of law to the court."[150] Whether a court chooses the standard of conduct suggested by its own view of public policy, or by custom, or by some other relevant fact, such as a statute, precedent, or a jury determination, "depends on the discretion of the court."[151]

Moreover, Holmes thought it ludicrous after Darwin for anyone to maintain the quasi-metaphysical conception that legal customs evolve according to a set of innate and shared mores. Custom was shaped not by a stable social consensus but by pressures from irreconcilable competing interests and, at any given time, from the most powerful contenders. Political conflict was endemic to the process of defining the scope of rights. Declaring his opposition to all absolutist conceptions of law, historical as well as analytic, Holmes emphasized his point that a right-holder's claim to freedom reduces merely to predictions of the duties courts will create to curtail the freedom of others. In defining duties, courts necessarily took sides on the basic political issue of the individual versus social welfare, as well as on the particular interests of vying factions. The net result was that judicial policy preferences tended to favor powerful and usually majority ideologies and interests, but this by no means represented a social consensus. The losers never relented and often, in league with other factions, succeeded in swaying judicial policy views in the direction of their thinking. Holmes considered it a "singular anomaly" that any proponent of an evolutionary understanding of law could presume "the solidarity of interests of society."[152]

Common Carrier Strict Liability

Holmes's attack on historical legal science culminated in "Common Carriers and the Common Law" (1879).[153] The purpose of the article was to refute the effort of historical legal science to explain the law of bailment in terms of Romanized English custom. The focus was on the particular class of bailees denominated "common carriers," and the evolution of the contemporary rule of strict liability governing their responsibility for damaged and stolen goods. "[T]he true history" of this liability showed that it derived from neither Roman law nor English custom.[154] More broadly, Holmes wanted to demonstrate that the evolution of law does not represent the unfolding of any syllogistic ideal, but rather follows an indeterminate course marked out by contingent judicial choices among competing public policies.

Contrary to the supposition of Roman law origins, which implied that common carrier liability started from the Roman predicate of negligence, Holmes vigorously asserted that the governing standard was always strict liability.[155] The rule derived from Teutonic folk custom, but the common law incorporated and thereafter enforced the rule for centuries on expedient and changing judgments of public policy, independent of and without reference to early Teutonic or subsequent English custom. Here again was proof of the lack of descriptive and explanatory power in general propositions, whether derived by semantic logic or from the teachings of

Roman jurists; consistency could not be found in a body of law shaped by experience.

Far from suggesting any deep and logical connection to customary mores, the history of common carrier liability revealed that often, and sometimes at crucial junctures, the rule developed simply from a "confusion of ideas."[156] The most significant instance was when outmoded procedural policies prompted courts to "extend[]" the strict liability rule for stolen goods to cover damaged goods.[157] This extension of coverage occurred even though the reasons for applying strict liability for stolen goods "had lost their meaning centuries before," following certain procedural changes and the advent of contracts to provide insurance for loss. In any event, the strict liability rule for stolen goods lacked relevance to damaged goods because there was no risk of bailee collusion or slack in safeguarding and retrieving goods from wrongdoers.[158] Like the clavicle in the cat that belied final cause assumptions of progress in biological evolution, this demonstration of the existence of "dry precedent," which is "likely to be followed according to the letter, because the spirit had departed," undermined similar progressivist assumptions supporting the syllogistic ideal in historical legal science.[159]

While courts sometimes enforced dry precedents by mistake or out of uncritical habit, Holmes argued that courts very often used such outmoded "survivals" as a means of sensibly adapting the law to deal with changing social conditions. But instead of acknowledging that they are really "legislating" by "invent[ing]" new policies for old rules, the courts usually conceal this law-making behind a pretense of logical analogy.[160] Holmes illustrated the point with the pivotal bailments case of Coggs v. Bernard, which on his analysis perpetuated the strict liability rule for common carriers by relating them to certain public callings (such as innkeepers) on the fictive analogy that both types of activities offered services to the general public.[161] This analogy created a singular exemption for the two classes of bailees from the negligence and contract rules applicable to bailment generally. But the analogy was superficial; while strict liability served to hold proprietors of public callings "up to the mark," at least in early times, when travelers were at the mercy of innkeepers and blacksmiths, no similar need existed to deter exploitative practices in the commercial and competitive market of shippers and carriers.[162] Conceptualistic explanations were equally unavailing, in Holmes's view. The meaning and logic attributed to the merged concept of callings-carriers was not intrinsic but fictitious. "We do not get a new and single principle by simply giving a single name to all the cases to be accounted for."[163]

In reality, the fictive amalgamation of public callings and common carriers disguised a policy innovation principally designed to provide insurance. Previously, in "The Theory of Torts," Holmes suggested that *Rylands* illustrated this policy-making mechanism of legal evolution by effecting a similar amalgamation of various extant rules of strict liability—including archaic remnants of early animistic notions later incorporated into newly invented policies, such as the rule governing cattle trespass. This showed that there was nothing historically anomalous about *Rylands,* deriving as it does from "very sensible and intelligible rules of modern law."[164] In finding it "politic" to retrofit traditional legal forms to solve the modern social problems presented by extra-hazardous industrial and other business activities, the courts that authored and enforced *Rylands* represented the mainstream of the common law process of growth.[165] Holmes's affirmation that *Rylands* constituted a "sound" extension of traditional strict liability rules stands in direct conflict with his current portrayal as a negligence dogmatist.[166] In fact, he provided the controversial doctrine with vital and timely support. Opposition to *Rylands* was mounting on both sides of the Atlantic in the 1870s. The chief complaint was that by generally classifying this category of risks (escaping dangerous things) within the scope of strict liability, the court created a novel rule of untested economic and social consequence. In his 1873 "Theory of Torts" Holmes validated this classification by demonstrating that the element of inherent danger was common to all of the major traditional doctrines of strict liability—on which the court in *Rylands* had relied for precedent—and, indeed, that *Rylands* supplied the core rationale for the growth of strict liability in the future.[167]

Yet as Holmes underscored in "Common Carriers and the Common Law," when courts deal in fictions they tend to lose sight of the underlying policies and over- or underenforce the doctrine.[168] Even more inexplicable than *Coggs*'s limitation of strict liability solely to two classes of bailees were the subsequent decisions that confined strict liability to common carriers alone. Moreover, this remaining exception to the general rules of bailment arbitrarily excluded similar activities (such as grain-elevators or deposit-vaults), while indiscriminately including many others (such as a privately owned "public cab") regardless of their relation to the insurance rationale.[169]

"Common Carriers and the Common Law" offers a comprehensive summary of the antiformalist critique of historical legal science that Holmes had been developing for nearly a decade. In "[t]he little piece of history" on common carriers, he intended to explain why historical legal science could never grasp the reality of law.[170] By adhering to the "official theory . . . that each new decision follows syllogistically from existing precedents," legal science would always be misled by "the paradox of form and substance in the development of law."[171] From the formalist perspective, courts will often be seen to perpetuate outmoded doctrines. But it would be erroneous to treat such survivals as meaningless and simply impediments to consistency. "[W]hen ancient rules maintain themselves in this way, new reasons more fitted to the time have been found for them."[172] It should be noted that this explanation of the process of legal evolution—whereby judicial policy inventions adapt old rules to contemporary uses—amplified views Holmes expressed earlier in the decade.[173]

Holmes concluded that all efforts to make the law logically consistent were futile. They could not succeed because logic could not explain a process driven by discretionary judgments of public policy responding to sociopolitical contingencies. For a real explanation of how and why the law developed as it did, it was necessary to recognize that "in substance the growth of the law is legislative."[174] This was not simply the conventional positivist denial of a "brooding omnipresence"—a law that is found rather than made.[175] Holmes meant "legislative" in the "deeper sense": that courts make law by making public policy choices among competing "considerations of what is expedient for the community concerned."[176]

Policy explanations revealed by historical analysis were, however, neither justifications for accepting the status quo nor suggestions for regarding legal development as an inevitable process beyond the power of courts and legislatures to reform. "The importance of tracing the process" was precisely to gain a clear understanding of the operation and politics of the law, so that "we are at liberty to consider the question of policy with a freedom that was not possible before."[177] Indeed, Holmes concluded his historical analysis of the strict liability rule for common carriers by suggesting that most cases should be governed by the negligence and contract rules applicable to bailment generally. This was not a recommendation for conceptual uniformity or historical continuity, but rather for functional, discriminating use of rules to achieve specific public policy objectives. Holmes was thinking of the usual common carrier situations involving commercial parties and competitive markets, where contract or trade custom would distribute the insurance burden efficiently and fairly. He noted, however, that public policy might well call for strict liability even in the commercial context to deal with market failures, systematic bias in bargaining relationships, and the potential for political domination. He had in mind industrial cases like those involving "railroads, who may have a private individual at their mercy, or exercise a power too vast for the common welfare."[178]

The Powers of Darkness

In a brief book review of Langdell's casebook on contracts, published shortly after "Common Carriers and the Common Law," Holmes reiterated and amplified his denunciation of formalist legal science. Lumping together all syllogistic theories of law, whatever the source and articulateness of the *a priori* postulate, he declared "the failure of all theories which consider law only from its formal side," and pronounced the whole enterprise "unscientific."[179] Privately, Holmes used harsher terms: legal science represented the "powers of darkness."[180]

This book review was Holmes's first direct attack on Langdell.[181] Although Langdell's program for legal science eschewed interest in Roman law and was close to deeming cases the authoritative source of law, his methods and objectives were inveterately formalistic. "Mr. Langdell's ideal in the law, the end of all his striving," Holmes asserted, "is the *elegantia juris*, or *logical* integrity of the system as a system."[182] Langdell not only confirmed his presumed principles by preselected cases but, against the teachings of Hume, claimed to determine the absolute truth and permanency of these principles by induction. He then deduced particulars from given ultimates, "less concerned with his postulates than to show that the conclusions from them hang together."[183] In his fixation on the "formal connection of things, or logic," Langdell fell prey to the paradox of form and substance.[184] "[T]he law finds its philosophy not in self-consistency," Holmes declared, but rather in the political conflicts of "experience."[185] Holmes reprised the insight with which he closed "Common Carriers and the Common Law":

> The form of continuity has been kept up by reasoning purporting to reduce every thing to a logical sequence; but that form is nothing but the evening dress which the new-comer puts on to make itself presentable according to conventional requirements. The important phe-

nomenon is the man underneath it, not the coat; the justice and reasonableness of a decision, not its consistency with previously held views.[186]

Holmes closed the book review with a general warning to all schools of legal science. Their syllogistic ideal of "reduc[ing] the concrete details of an existing system to the merely logical consequences of simple postulates" misapprehended "the nature of the problem and the data."[187] The law will never be consistent "so long as it continues to grow."[188] More fundamentally, the law is a social institution, and thus "[n]o one will ever have a truly philosophic mastery over the law who does not habitually consider the forces outside of it which have made it what it is . . . history and the nature of human needs."[189] In short, as a product of policy choices, the making of law by courts is appropriately an "object of science" just as "the theory of legislation is a scientific study."[190]

By the end of the 1870s, Holmes's accumulated writings had not only swept legal science from the center stage of American legal thought, but they had also laid a comprehensive and enduring intellectual foundation for a realistic and functionally directed law of torts. He was now prepared to unveil his new jurisprudence and its fruition—a general theory of torts—in *The Common Law*.

2

The New Jurisprudence

The paramount goal of *The Common Law* and the writings that followed was to move beyond criticism of formalist legal science and to present an affirmative program, a new jurisprudence for deriving general theories of the common law. The new jurisprudence posited that legal developments resulted from an evolutionary process of courts adapting old rules to a contingent environment of new and competing social needs and values. Accordingly, a scientific explanation of substantive law and its probable course of future growth would be found not by searching for an innate meaning in language or custom, but rather by examining the rules in light of their historical context. The famous opening paragraph of *The Common Law* brilliantly captures the essence of Holmes's prescription: "The life of the law has not been logic: it has been experience."[1]

The notion of experience is pivotal to Holmes for achieving his jurisprudential objective of formulating general theories of law. This is also true of his approach to developing a unified theory of tort liability. After exploring that subject, the chapter concludes with a discussion of the role Holmes envisioned for general theories in the practice and reform of the common law. The evidence amassed in this chapter continues to refute the conventional view current today that Holmes's thought with respect to legal reality and theory contradicted itself, particularly by lapsing into formalism. His new jurisprudence was antiformalist throughout; and its skepticism, evolutionary historicism, law-as-prediction equation, "bad man" perspective, classification aims, and other component ideas were all internally coherent emulations of modern scientific philosophy and methodology.

Experience and Legal Evolution

The idea of experience at the core of the new jurisprudence expressed both a substantive concept of legal reality and a methodology for studying it. In substance, experience connoted the political nature of law-making—of law as the product of judicial legislation. The methodological meaning imported the tenets of empirical science that were designed to avoid the pitfalls of conceptualism—"mak[ing] entities of abstractions"—by subjecting all theories, classifications, and other statements to the test of experience, which is the law in operation.

Legislative Function of Courts

The new jurisprudence located courts at the center of the "process of law-making."[2] In contrast to formalist legal science, which assigned normative and interpretative policy questions to nonjudicial authorities—the sovereign ruler or social custom—the new jurisprudence asserted that courts exercised "the sovereign prerogative of choice."[3] Indeed, Holmes said, the courts perform a "legislative function."[4] Judicial decisions, in common with legislative decisions, necessarily take sides in "a concealed, half conscious battle on the question of legislative policy."[5] Courts decide "[q]uestions of policy" by choosing among competing "considerations of what is expedient for the community concerned."[6]

By denying that logical consistency was the predominant motive for judicial decisions, Holmes focused inquiry on the social factors that were likely to influence judicial policy choices in given cases—the "important phenomena," the judicial views of "justice and reasonableness" that shape a decision.[7] As expressed in his classic summary at the beginning of *The Common Law*, they included "The felt necessities of the time, the prevalent moral and political theories, intuitions of public policy, avowed or unconscious, even the prejudices which judges share with their fellowmen."[8]

The legislative growth of the law was neither determinate nor the unfolding or presentist embodiment of any final cause. Rather, the law evolved through a process of pragmatic judicial policy choices, adapting "old implements . . . to new uses" to address the exigencies of changing social conditions.[9]

Holmes hypothesized an atomistic process of gradual legal evolution similar to Darwin's "population" theory of evolution—a style of theory that propelled advances in many domains of contemporary thought, including economics, politics, physics, chemistry, and geology.[10] At the macro level, the law developed without deliberation or purposeful direction, taking on the aggregate shape at each moment in time of the judicial decisions of individual cases. At the micro level, judicial law-making proceeded opportunistically, with courts fashioning and enforcing their views of expedient policy for the particular situation at hand. The contingency of social conditions as well as the limits of human knowledge and ingenuity denied judges the means to make policy "determinations that shall be good for all time."[11] Holmes warned against presuming any necessary result. He advised approaching the law as simply a fact of discretionary power, and regarding a court's decision as "no more than embody[ing] the preference of a given body in a given time and place."[12]

Many obstacles impeded discovery of the substantive legislative grounds underlying judicial policy choices. Crucial policy choices were deliberately and deeply "hidden" behind the logical form of reasoning by analogy and distinction from traditions of precedent, doctrine, and custom.[13] Most judges, preferring to appear the servant of unbending logic, were extremely hesitant "to discuss questions of policy, or to put a decision in terms upon their views as law-makers."[14] The myth of the syllogistic ideal shielded judges from criticism and responsibility, and they did not want to give it up, for "the moment you leave the path of merely logical deduction you lose the illusion of certainty which makes legal reasoning seem like mathematics."[15] Perpetuation of the formalist illusion greatly distorted the adjudicative process. Because the most self-reflective and well-informed judges were silent or evasive, many others remained insufficiently aware of the policy influences affecting their decisions, and thus "failed adequately to recognize their duty of weighing considerations of social advantage."[16] According to Holmes, a candid look at the influences would reveal, for example, that much of the judicial opposition to strict liability arose from visceral fear of socialism.[17]

A central mission of the new jurisprudence therefore was to penetrate the "logical form" that cloaked the animating "judgment as to the relative worth and importance of competing legislative grounds."[18] Just as modern empirical science sought to explain the inner workings of opaque natural phenomena, so Holmes proposed to infer the nature of judicial policy motives that lay beneath the surface. "In order to know what it [the law] is, we must know what it has been, and what it tends to become."[19] This inquiry obviously required the tools of historical and logical criticism.

More than that, the task of determining the policy motives underlying legal decisions demanded analysis from the widest range of perspectives, from "anthropology, the science of man, to political economy, the theory of legislation, ethics."[20] Once the legislative grounds of decisions were revealed and understood, it would be possible to formulate a unifying general theory that could both explain how and why the law in a particular area such as torts developed as it did and predict what might be its likely course. For the future, to save the costs of unraveling the paradox of form and substance, Holmes urged courts to execute their judicial policy-making role deliberately and forthrightly. He called for reform of law school curricula, to better "train . . . lawyers . . . habitually to consider more definitely and explicitly the social advantage on which the rule they lay down must be justified."[21]

Despite current assumptions that the late nineteenth century was wedded to formalism and to the idea that law was discovered rather than made, it is unclear whether Holmes's politics-of-law message was really a revelation to his contemporaries. Reviewers of *The Common Law* seemed to take it in stride, apparently less impressed with the novelty of the author's antiformalism than with the style and boldness of its expression. The reviewer selected by the *American Law Review* (of which Holmes was the former editor), praised the book for "bring[ing] into unaccustomed clearness the legislative office of the courts," which "has hitherto been much disguised."[22] "[P]rofessing only to discover and apply" pre-existing law, and keeping up a "fictitious and unsubstantial deference to precedents," compelled courts to make policy covertly and ineffectively— "through the ingenious shifts which patch the new, in gradually increasing pieces, on to the old"—leaving "the law . . . some way behind the demands of society."[23] While confident that "such unconsciousness and such pretense are sure to weaken under the matter-of-fact scrutiny of modern thought" promoted by Holmes, the reviewer—anticipating the New Deal deadlock on the Supreme Court—forecast the political pressures and conflicts that would arise as more judges follow Holmes in making "avowed use of their legislative power."[24]

For many readers, Holmes's basic criticism of formalist legal science for relying on *a priori* moral postulates undoubtedly called to mind well-known antecedents in jurisprudence, and analogs in science, philosophy, history, and other disciplines. By the time *The Common Law* was published, Darwin's theories of evolution and their guiding scientific philosophy and methodology, on which Holmes modeled the new jurisprudence, had won general acceptance in the scientific community. Positivist empiricism and rejection of metaphysics held sway in science as well as in law. The demise of Spencer's teleological evolution and other final cause theories was imminent. Moreover, even though Holmes eschewed *a priori* laws of necessary purposes and stages of development, his conception of legal evolution driven by conflicting political interests resonated with the materialist interpretations of Marx and Maine. Certainly Holmes's views comported with those of his intellectual peers in Cambridge, especially Chauncey Wright, Nicholas St. John Green, and the other members of the Metaphysical Club who were publishing similar hypotheses.[25]

Indeed, Holmes may well have overestimated the extent to which judges were shy to acknowledge their policy-making role. A number of prominent American judges seemed quite prepared, particularly in deciding tort cases, to exercise this role deliberately and explicitly. In various leading opinions on strict liability, for example, judges expressly repudiated the syllogistic ideal of absolute *a priori* concepts (notably property rights), and instead openly balanced competing interests in light of the particular circumstances of the case and its consequences for community welfare.[26]

Law in Operation

Holmes crafted the new jurisprudence with the methodological errors of legal science squarely in mind. Legal science was doomed not only for its misbegotten pursuit of the syllogistic ideal, but also because it ignored the empiricist prescription to ground theory on legal reality. He likened the ethereal theories of legal science to "a swarm of little bodiless cherubs."[27] Whenever called to account for legal reality, legal science resorted to fitting the evidence to its postulates. "Philosophy confirms dogma, and dogma philosophy," he declared.[28]

Holmes attributed the "inflated and unreal explanations" of formalist legal science to the vague, moralistic phraseology of legal concepts.[29] If one as astute as Austin could become mesmerized by the rhetoric of duty, then think of the far greater danger that the unwary would "drop into fallacy."[30] But formalist scholars manipulated language as much as they were misled by it. They tended to infuse language as well as history with *a priori* moral assumptions.[31] And to assert the moralistically laden concepts of right and duty as conclusive causal explanations was simply "a pontifical or imperial way of forbidding discussion."[32]

Although Langdell anchored legal science more realistically in case law,

Holmes nonetheless considered the improvement inadequate. To begin with, Langdell's focus on appellate cases constricted and distorted the scope of inquiry. Appellate decisions comprise a small fraction and provide an unsystematic sample of the law-making universe. Juries and trial judges render most of the formal decisions (reported and unreported). With respect to these other law-makers, appellate opinions were no better than secondary sources, characteristically flawed by misperception and post hoc rationalization. Moreover, as Holmes recognized, most of "lawyers' law" was fashioned not in court but rather in the law office. Nor did Langdell's own application of his method engender confidence. The method was easily perverted by selective samples and readings of leading cases to validate preferred principles and systems, and to construct *a priori* postulates for syllogisms that make everything seem to hang together.

A master of the arts of reasoning and rhetoric, Holmes was hardly unconcerned with what judges say in their opinions. He fully appreciated that the styles of argument and language judges employ in justifying their actions to the profession and public at large might throw light on their policy motives. But judicial opinions were very unreliable sources. Aside from the prevalence of moralistic verbiage and ambiguous terminology, judges by design or effect promoted the blurring of form and substance. Desiring certainty or being deceived by the "illusion of certainty," they tended to "dodge difficulty and responsibility with a rhetorical phrase" and camouflage their policy preferences in the guise of "hollow deductions from empty generalizations."[33] As Holmes concluded in regard to the oft-repeated example of defamatory employment references: "generalities are worse than useless, and the only way to solve the problem presented is to weigh the reasons for the particular right claimed and those for the competing right . . . Any solution in general terms seems to me to mark a want of analytic power."[34]

But the unreliability of judicial opinions appeared to be an ingrained part of the process of legal evolution, at least as it had worked in the past. Judges rarely looked beyond the case before them, and, given their myopia, they could not even be "trusted to state the *ratio decidendi*,"[35] let alone provide enlightenment on the trends and ideas reflected in the aggregate of individual decisions. While the judges "see well enough how they ought to decide on a given state of facts," they "did not begin with a theory . . . [and had] never worked one out."[36] Compounding all of these problems was the historical and social relativism of concepts. Holmes insisted on being as "accurate as we can," but he had no illusions about the precision and objectivity of knowledge.[37] "We live by symbols, and what shall be symbolized by any image of the sight depends upon the mind of him who sees it."[38] Theory itself depends on the theorist's empirically unverifiable "insight which tells him what details are significant [and] . . . investigations count."[39] Being conscious and in control of distorting influences, being committed ultimately to the test of experience, was the best way for one to keep thinking "cosmopolitan and detached . . . [and] able to criticize what he reveres and loves."[40]

The new jurisprudence's antidote to cognitive and linguistic distortions in formulating general legal theories was to "substitut[e] a scientific foundation for empty words."[41] The prescription was to focus on the rudimentary sensate conditions, the facts which are likely to trigger judicial action and the resulting coercive effects, whether imposed directly by the court judgment or indirectly by social stigma. "[T]o keep to the real and the true," Holmes enjoined, "think things not words."[42] By "[t]hings" Holmes meant how the actual requirements and effects of rules work in "influencing conduct by motives, and applying consequences."[43] Every intellectual construct, idea, classification, concept, and word must therefore be "thought out in things and results."[44] For example, the policy question posed by the application of strict liability to industrial activity—"how far it is desirable that the public should insure the safety of those whose work it uses"—becomes clearer with the realization that tort liability normally levies a "tax" on productive activity, and, however "disguised," like all taxes it "must be borne by the consumer, that is, mainly by the working-men and fighting-men of the community."[45]

Accordingly, any statement worthy of study must be capable of yielding empirical predictions of what the courts will do in fact (or explanations of what the courts have done). Those predictions must then be compared to the law in operation—the actual requirements, effects, and consequences of decisions and rules. Even the major generalizations, such as the "legal compounds, possession, property, and contract," must constantly be tested against the experience of what courts actually demand as necessary factual conditions for a cause of action, and what effects and consequences they actually impose on the interests at stake.[46] In Holmes's concise directive: "There are always two things to be asked: first, what are the facts which make up the group in question [that courts actually require for a cause of action]; and then, what are the consequences attached by the law to that group."[47]

To facilitate testing legal concepts and theories in the "dry light" of experience, Holmes advocated the "bad man" heuristic—examining the requirements and effects of the law as one who cares only about avoiding its sanctions.[48] "[W]ash it with cynical acid," Holmes instructed, and the "vague circumference" of "moral phraseology" and legal concepts, even the absolute duty premise of Austin's tort theory, "shrinks and at the same time grows more precise."[49] In his torts writings Holmes used the powerful "bad man" to strip away the veneer of negligence interpretations that contemporary commentators, following Austin, created to conceal the actual contours of strict liability in *Rylands* and other major doctrines. "[E]xpel everything except the object of our study, the operations of the law"; what remains is the basic material for constructing a unified theory of tort liability.[50]

Lon Fuller and Henry Hart are the principal sources of the present-day conventional view that the "bad man" device represented a positivist exclusion of morality from law-making.[51] This view suggests a simplistic understanding of positivism, which was critically concerned with questions of morality in law, only rejecting attempts to confine law to a theological, metaphysical, or other *a priori* system of morality.[52] Similarly, the view that Holmes walled off morality from law completely misconstrues his meaning. In saying that law was the prophecy of state (or social) sanctions, "right or wrong," Holmes was merely rejecting any preconditions on the analysis of judicial rules and practices based on a necessary correspondence between what courts do and some *a priori* "system of morals."[53] If law were studied otherwise than as "a part of the lives of men," Holmes declared, "it would become a matter for pedagogues, wholly devoid of reality."[54] But Holmes consistently affirmed that judges made policy choices by drawing upon "prevalent moral and political theories."[55] The moral ideas motivating judicial choices are reflected in the aggregate of individual decisions, and by this evolutionary process the law becomes "witness and external deposit of our moral life."[56]

Indeed, the "bad man" heuristic was premised not on the separation of law and morals but on their inseparability; its function was to unearth the moral and policy choices judges make but disguise in logical form or overblown, moralistic rhetoric. "We must alternately consult history and existing theories of legislation [the prevalent moral and political theories]," Holmes instructed, "to understand the combination of the two into new products at every stage."[57] Thus to understand what "duty," "tort liability," and the other words and rules of law mean "in the empirical sense in which lawyers use" them, the theorist must eschew normative connotations attached to them by "philosophers or moralists" from "outside" *a priori* systems, and study the law from inside its actual workings, focusing—without presupposed limits or purposes—on what the courts are doing in fact and why they are doing it.[58] Once this work was done—once this descriptive, explanatory theory of the actual moral and political motives for judicial policy choices had been formulated—Holmes fully endorsed normative "scrutiny and revision" of the law from moral and other policy perspectives, "weigh[ing] the ends of legislation, the means of attaining them, and the cost."[59]

Fuller, Hart, and their successors dismiss Holmes's repeated recognition of and concern for questions on the morality of law. Rather than seek or confront the coherence in Holmes's writings, these commentators denigrate any evidence contradicting their theses as the product of his intellectual confusion, or, in the latest fashion, his emotional conflicts.[60] In relying upon such makeweight and pseudo-psychological explanations rather than recognizing the intellectual consistency of Holmes's notion of empirical science and its application to law, these commentators not only misconstrue the new jurisprudence in general, but also obstruct understanding of the primary aim of the new jurisprudence in torts, which was precisely to discover the "moral starting point of liability."[61] By applying the "bad man" heuristic (or its equivalent, "lawyers' law") to remove the "influence" of "[m]oral predilections . . . in settling legal distinctions," Holmes determined that Austin's culpability theory of responsibility in tort could not account for the fact that liability usually operated as merely a tax.[62] This opened the way for his fundamental inquiry into the threshold basis of moral responsibility that tort law actually embraced.

A Unifying Theory of Tort Liability
Moral Basis of Responsibility

In tort law, the search was for some underlying "theory of responsibility" embedded in the aggregate of tort decisions that would provide a unifying explanation of the various liability rules.[63] While the particular requirements and uses of these rules were governed by a variety of policies, Holmes hypothesized that undergirding the entire tort system was a core policy of responsibility that, "still with a view to prediction," provides the rules with "some order, some rational explanation, and some principle of growth."[64] This search for the theory of responsibility in tort led Holmes

back millennia to look for its origins in the personalized blame characteristic of primitive animism, and vengeance that provoked individual retri-
bution and tribal feuds. Holmes found that nineteenth-century ideas of
responsibility stemmed from the time when primitive notions were dis-
placed by the emergence of organized society, with its need to monopolize
force and preclude individual violence and self-help.[65]

In response to the demands of increasingly organized life, courts rejected
two competing, polar theories of responsibility. On the one hand, they
refused to accept the anarchy of subjective moral theories that make liability depend upon an individual's "capacity for choosing rightly."[66] On
the other hand, courts opposed the complete determinism of pure causal
theories that equate responsibility with mere infliction of harm, regardless
of whether the defendant had any "fair chance to avoid doing the harm
before he is held responsible for it."[67] Instead, Holmes concluded, courts
generally founded tort liability on the conception of responsibility that
incorporated the external or social "moral element" of reasonably foreseeable harm and the corresponding choice to avoid harm.[68]

Some commentators today claim that Holmes's search for the moral
basis of tort liability contradicts his antiformalism; going even further,
they suggest that it evidences a commitment to metaphysics.[69] But I intend
to show that his theory of torts is formulated in complete accord with the
antiformalist, modern scientific precepts of the new jurisprudence. The
unifying theory he sought was a descriptive and explanatory hypothesis of
the "theory of responsibility"—the positive social morality—that the
courts themselves adopted and invoked, albeit implicitly and in the aggregate, to justify their exercise of coercive state power. Holmes's analysis
was directed neither to nor away from an *a priori* moral system or any
syllogistic ideal; quite the contrary, as he made clear at the outset of the
torts lectures, his object was to infer and test his theory of the unifying
moral basis of responsibility from experience of the law in operation—the
"common ground at the bottom of all liability."[70]

Application of Two-Part Test

In using the phrase "rational generalization" to describe the common
ground of foresight in tort, Holmes imported the two elements of the test
of experience as requirements for formulating a unifying general theory of
tort liability.[71] The first requirement was to probe for the law in operation: to distill the minimum factual conditions that courts actually estab-

lish as the threshold for liability under any rule in force. This involved application of the "bad man" heuristic, the prophecy conception of law, historical analysis, and other empirical methods, as well as the critical use of logic to reduce doctrines and case holdings to their essential factual elements and real effects and consequences—"ultimate or undecomposable phenomena."[72] Through "true induction" the analyst would hypothesize a generalization of the cases and rules grouped according to similar operational characteristics.[73] This categorization would lead to the more fundamental requirement of examining the operational generalization in light of history, political theory, economics, and other interpretative disciplines. This examination would reveal the nature of the underlying policy motives and the extent to which they relate to the operational categories. The resulting classifications would provide policy explanations of the operational relationship connecting the cases and rules, as well as empirically verifiable predictions of corresponding patterns and trends of judicial action. In turn, the stage would then be set for informed law reform. As Holmes summarized:

> The way to gain a liberal [realistic] view of your subject is not to read something else [e.g. Roman law or Kant] but to get to the bottom of the subject itself. The means of doing that are, in the first place, to follow the existing body of dogma into its highest generalizations by the help of jurisprudence; next, to discover from history how it has come to be what it is; and, finally, so far as you can, to consider the ends which the several rules seek to accomplish, the reasons why those ends are desired, what is given up to gain them, and whether they are worth the price.[74]

Functional Classification of Torts

In Holmes's view, tort law required a completely new system of classification, both in method and content. For him the existing artificial systems had no philosophic value. He vehemently objected to the aspirations of formalist legal science to devise a syllogistic structure of fixed hierarchical categories formed from the traditional named torts, such as nuisance, defamation, and trespass. He was equally opposed to the worthless "gossip" of treatises that merely enumerated cases by "dramatic" but operationally irrelevant facts, such as the defendant's trade. When various kinds of businesses were governed by the same liability rules and policies, they should be grouped accordingly. Some business categories, such as maritime insurance, reflected distinct operational and policy features and should be separately classified under the liability rule or under an independent heading. Holmes was not denying the importance of context in constructing classifications; he was rejecting only generalizations and distinctions based on functionally irrelevant criteria and facts. Thus businesses ought to be differentiated according to their relative market and political power even though they are governed by the same rules, as in the areas of strict common carrier liability or employer vicarious liability.

Holmes accomplished much of this classificatory work in "The Theory of Torts" (1873). In particular, as we have seen in the last chapter, he rebutted claims that tort liability was generally based on personal culpability, demonstrating instead that the vast majority of cases applied external standards of strict liability or negligence. These external standards could be grouped together because they served similar deterrence and compensation policies of organized society—aims that would be thwarted by the radical individualism of subjective standards. Notably, Holmes also confirmed the distinctive operational existence and policy grounds of *Rylands* and the major strict liability rules, saving them from becoming submerged in negligence. In doing so, he created the independent classification for strict liability and established the enduring three-branch arrangement of intentional wrongs, negligence, and strict liability.

The Common Ground of Tort Liability

What remained after completing this work of classification in "The Theory of Torts" was to determine whether the courts had adopted a conception of responsibility that established a common unifying threshold for liability in all three branches. Holmes hypothesized that the existence of such a unifying theory of responsibility would entail, and therefore would be inferable from, the core operational requirements of tort law, "a common ground for all liability in tort."[75] The common ground was essentially a minimum "common denominator" of necessary factual elements for recovery in tort—conditions that were universally required by all three branches and the "sufficient explanation" for liability under at least one.[76]

To qualify as a valid common ground for a general theory, however, the minimum set of factual conditions must also satisfy a second requirement: it must imply or signify an intelligible conception of moral responsibility.

Recognition of the legislative function of courts meant that the search for a general theory should not rest on a mere operational explanation. If certain operational conditions could not by themselves provide an intelligible conception of moral responsibility, then any cases holding them sufficient reflected not a principle of growth but evolutionary dross, "mere survivals" or, as Holmes labeled them in torts, "dry precedent."[77] Thus the common ground of a general theory was the most nearly universal set of minimum factual conditions for liability which could coherently legitimate the rule system as just and functionally rational.

The Torts Lectures

These lectures completed Holmes's quest for the common ground of tort liability and the embedded unifying theory of responsibility. He thought that the resulting general theory of torts best demonstrated the explanatory powers of the new jurisprudence methodology. A brief sketch of the course of his argument should serve both to illustrate that methodology and to introduce the general theory.

Holmes derived the general foresight theory through rebuttals of its chief competitors—in effect, reconstructing the evolutionary paradigm of the "struggle for life among competing ideas."[78] The first challenge was to Austin's personal culpability theory of responsibility. The second was to the causation theory which predicated liability on the mere fact of a causal connection between the defendant's act and the plaintiff's injury, maintaining that "under the common law a man *acts* at his peril," "however little intended and however unforeseen" the harm.[79] Holmes believed his foresight explanation triumphed because it alone satisfied the two general theory requirements, operational comprehensiveness and moral coherence.

Of the two competitors, Austin's personal culpability theory was the easiest for Holmes to dispatch. Having shown its inadequacy in several articles published during the 1870s, he understandably felt that the view did not deserve extended consideration. Incorporating his previous arguments against Austin's theory, the torts lectures simply reiterated prior demonstrations of its empirical deficiencies. In particular, Holmes emphasized that Austin's personal culpability theory disregarded most of legal reality in tort, which consisted of the external rules of negligence and strict liability. When judged by their actual effects, these rules amounted to no more than a regulatory tax on specified behavior.

Nevertheless, despite its narrow scope of explanation compared to the causation and foresight theories, Austin's personal culpability theory might still claim a common ground coverage if it expressed a morally exclusive conception of responsibility. Specifically, it would have to be shown that the external rules of negligence and strict liability—the reality of practice unaccounted for by Austin's theory—were demonstrably unjust and irrational, and nothing but "dry precedent." While recognizing the undoubted justice and rationality in holding individuals responsible for their personally culpable conduct, Holmes denied that such a radically individualistic norm set the moral bounds of liability for an increasingly organized society. Rather, he presented an abundant catalogue of ethical and functional arguments—anticipating virtually the entire modern repertoire of compensation, deterrence, and administrative efficiency rationales—in support of the far wider scope of social responsibility entailed by the external rules of negligence and strict liability.

Holmes's response to the causation theory consumed most of the torts lectures.[80] Essentially, while he denied the existence of any precedent in England or the United States of courts imposing strict liability for unforeseeable harm on the mere fact that the defendant's act caused it—that is, applying the rule of cause-based strict liability—his overriding objection to the causation theory was its moral incoherence. Predicating liability on mere causation was inexplicable by any intelligible conception of responsibility; moreover, it was not a rational (nonarbitrary) means of furthering the compensation and deterrence functions of tort law. Any case authority for the causation theory of responsibility was thus no more than dry precedent. Reasoning in a manner consistent with antiformalist tenets, Holmes reached this conclusion by deriving the testing norm of moral responsibility from the operational fact of the causation condition itself. The only morally intelligible reason for making the causal act a necessary condition of liability, he argued, was to have the power of informed, free-willed choice to avoid harm be the moral measure of individual responsibility. While causation is always necessary to assure the law's compliance with that norm, it was never a sufficient explanation without the addition of a foresight requirement. Cause-based strict liability was morally incoherent; it could not pass the threshold of justice and functional rationality which Holmes found implicit in the very requirement of a causal act. For "[t]here is no . . . power [of choice to avoid harm] where the evil cannot be foreseen."[81]

Purposes of a General Theory of Law

Holmes envisioned two seemingly opposed purposes for a general theory of law. It was "necessary both for the knowledge and for the revision of the law."[82] He reconciled these two aims through his understanding of legal reality as a continuing process of change driven primarily by judicial policy-making. By explaining the fundamental and unifying conception of moral responsibility in an area of law like torts, for example, a general theory would provide an understanding of its present order and a basis for predicting its future growth. At the same time, clarifying the basic policy of that area would facilitate informed and effective law reform.

Additionally, insofar as it enhanced the ability of lawyers to make more accurate predictions of judicial behavior, the new jurisprudence would benefit clients by reducing their exposure to uncertain and arbitrary sanctions, and by broadly promoting the ends of individual freedom and equality.[83] It should be noted that, contrary to a prevalent misconception today, Holmes did not confine this understanding of law as prediction and policy choice to practitioners while reserving the search for absolute, eternal truths to theorists.[84] He emphasized that the law could only be known through predictions grounded on the policy motives for judicial discretion, and that this route to understanding was necessary "both to speculation and to practice."[85]

Holmes's conception of a general theory complied with the philosophy and methods of modern science. The theory begins with a working empirical hypothesis of the public policy mechanism that generated the cases and rules in force. Based on this hypothesis, predictions of the substantive nature and trend of legal developments are deduced and stated in the form of classificatory distinctions and other specifications, and then they are put to the test of experience. The hypothesis remains provisional; the test of experience—of the law in operation—may falsify or require modification of the theory, but it can neither prove absolute truth nor affirm any *a priori* final cause or other assumption. This understanding contradicts currently prevailing formalist interpretations of Holmes's general theory objectives, which erroneously claim that his general theory envisioned making the law knowable as an *a priori* syllogistic system of classification and (at least in *The Common Law*) as effecting legal change solely by judicial incorporation of evolving and apolitical social custom.

Making the Law Knowable

Holmes argued that a scientific approach to law, like that applied to nature, should strive for explanations of perceived regularities to give some intelligible order to "what seemed a chaos of conflicting atoms."[86] "The mark of a master" was to give such a coherent explanation "that facts which before lay scattered in an inorganic mass, when he shoots through them the magnetic current of his thought, leap into an organic order and live and bear fruit."[87] In sum, a chief objective of a general theory was to "make the law *knowable*" by "discern[ing] the true basis for prophecy" in the policies motivating judicial discretion.[88]

In tort law, the search for the basis of prophecy focused on the concept of moral responsibility embedded in the common ground of liability. Discovery of a dynamic policy governing that area would explain the evolving patterns of decisions and rules, and make it possible to classify the universe of atomistic tort rulings in a logical "order, from its *summum genus* to its *infima species,* so far as practical."[89] Initially, Holmes arranged the rules of tort liability according to the differing policy choices indicated by the varying duties created by the courts. He distributed the three main branches of negligence, strict liability, and intentional wrongs along a spectrum calibrated by the scope and degree of responsibility which their respective duty constraints imposed on the freedom of defendants, and on the corresponding freedom of other, more or less protected classes. Beginning with *The Common Law,* and putting in practice his determination that the conception of moral responsibility underlying all tort duties was foresight-informed choice, Holmes revised this arrangement. He now explained the relationship between the rule branches as "a philosophically continuous series" of requirements of "manifest danger."[90] This new arrangement also conveyed the history of the legislative growth of tort law. It highlighted the increasing reliance on external standards to enforce policies defined by the "criterion of social welfare" to serve the complex needs of corporate life.[91]

Current commentators misconstrue Holmes's classificatory objective of his general theory, presumptively branding it formalist, if not metaphysical. They tag Holmes with the misguided assumption that nineteenth-century scientific classification necessarily meant systematization by formalist, *a priori* syllogism. This is a major theme in G. Edward White's recent biography of Holmes.[92] Specifically, White claims that although

Holmes's evolutionary historicism cohered with modern scientific empiricism, his classification objective followed the prevailing *a priorist* methodology in science and was inveterately formalist. Holmes "took 'science' as Darwin intended it to be taken," White contends, "as a concept encompassing two discrete methodological aims."[93] In his evolutionary historicism, Holmes's aim (like Darwin's) "more approximated the empiricist orientation that later generations would assume to be the central feature of 'scientific' inquiry."[94] But, in White's view, both Holmes and Darwin also pursued "the conventional [aim] of systematic classification": "an organization of subject matter based on assumed principles."[95] This is a misperception.

Holmes and Darwin, in their respective fields, pioneered and worked within the tradition of "experimental philosophy," the name given to empirical science since the time of Hume and Newton.[96] This tradition embraces the British empiricism of Mill, Bentham, Hume, and Bacon; the positivism of Mach and Comte; and Kant's secularization of science; and finds its source ultimately in ancient Greece and the thought of Aristotle and Thales.[97] Before the nineteenth century, experimental philosophy had blossomed with the brilliant and enduring theories of Copernicus, Galileo, Kepler, Harvey, Hooke, and Newton.

As received in the nineteenth century, this tradition stood resolutely for the proposition that " '*transcendental hypotheses*' . . . have no place in experimental philosophy"—in the words of Chauncey Wright, the philosophic "whetstone" on which Holmes and the other Metaphysical Club members sharpened their understanding of modern science.[98] Following Hume's teaching, Wright's philosophy of classification flatly denied the possibility of truth by induction: "a limited experience cannot prove an unlimited proposition."[99] Accordingly, scientific classification merely communicated empirical distinctions and predictions of the phenomenological relationships entailed by the general theory that governed their causal (empirical) mechanism. Based on the traditions of empirical philosophy, Wright observed, "one of the leading traits of modern scientific research is this reduction of ideas to the tests of experience."[100] These tests of empirical predictions against phenomena never cease; the distinctions and groupings hypothesized by classifications are provisional, always falsifiable, and never capable of being proven absolutely true. Passing the tests of experience has only the pragmatic significance of strengthening an individual's belief in a theory's explanation, as measured by his willingness to act.[101] Thus, as Wright concluded: "No system of classification, however natural or real, could be final. Classification would, indeed, be wholly inadequate as a representation of the organic world on the whole, or as a sketch of the 'plan of creation,' and would be falsely conceived as revealing the categories and thoughts of creative intelligence."[102]

With Darwin's evolutionary explanation of living nature, experimental philosophy became triumphant in all quarters of scientific inquiry. While Asa Gray and others were already replacing the *a priorist* Linnaean scheme with a thoroughly empirical natural system of classification, it was Darwin's theory of the probabilistic mechanism of descent by natural selection that provided the first testable causal explanation for the perceived relationships. To suggest that Darwin based his theory of evolution on empirical evidence, but predicated his classification system on a final cause or other *a priori* postulate, is clearly erroneous. The chief thrust of his theory was to oust *a priorism* from classification systems by destroying the idea of determinate and fixed categories of species. It was precisely Darwin's classificatory predictions of mutable species, formed under contingent circumstances by chance, that provided the key tests of experience for his natural selection theory of evolution and won over virtually all informed opinion. Indeed, Darwin took pains to deny room for *a priorism* in the resulting *"arrangement,"* insisting that classifying each group "in due subordination and relation to the other groups . . . [in] strictly genealogical . . . order" would reveal "the hidden bond which naturalists have been unconsciously seeking, and not some unknown plan of creation, or the enunciation of general propositions, and the mere putting together and separating objects more or less alike."[103]

Holmes applied experimental philosophy to law in full measure. "Law is not a science [like Euclidean geometry]," he declared, "but is essentially empirical," and therefore an "object of science."[104] Echoing Wright, Holmes denied the possibility of attaining "cosmic truth," explaining that as "the part cannot swallow the whole . . . our categories are not, or may not be, adequate for formulating what we cannot know."[105] It followed that as "I am in the universe, not it in me," the measure of a classification's validity is my willingness (and that of others) to act on its distinctions, and ultimately, its truth is simply that "I cannot help believing it."[106] And, as he concluded, "I therefore define the truth as the system of my limitations, and leave absolute truth for those who are better equipped. With absolute truth I leave absolute ideals of conduct equally on one side."[107]

The provisional character of classifications was imperative not only because of the impossibility of ultimate truth, but also because the understanding of experience, derived from sensations of that experience, is always relative. Social and historical contexts affect the content and bounds of ideas—in Holmes's words, "property, friendship, and truth have a common root in time."[108] The subjective and objective cannot be separated. Thus "one's experience . . . makes certain preferences dogmatic for oneself."[109] Clearly, Holmes well understood that theories and classifications could never express an absolute truth, but must forever remain working beliefs—taken in the pragmatic sense of motives for action—that proffer predictions for the test of experience. Accordingly, "Science has taught the world skepticism and has made it legitimate to put everything to the test of proof. Many beautiful and noble reverences are impaired, but in these days no one can complain if any institution, system, or belief is called on to justify its continuance in life."[110] Because no pre-determined way to organize phenomena exists, many classifications, like all ideas, will constantly vie with one another for acceptance. Some will be judged better and more fruitful than others, Holmes said, not by their logical consistency with assumed first principles or final causes, but rather, pragmatically, by the realism and utility of their explanations—by their "practical convenience."[111]

Holmes's method of classifying the evolving law as the results of the mechanism of judicial policy choices closely resembled Darwin's method for classifying the product of descent by natural selection.[112] Like Darwin, Holmes used the test of experience to overthrow *a priorist* systems. He rejected the idea that the gradual, political, and chance-like process of legal evolution would in reality take the form of an *a priorist* hierarchy of fixed, bright-line categories. In accord with his evolutionary theory of "legislative growth," he proposed classifications of "continuous, logical, philosophical exposition, setting forth the whole corpus with its roots in history and its justifications of expedience real or supposed."[113] Holmes explicitly predicted the existence of mutable, fluid, and connected relationships between the various legal "species," such as the "philosophically continuous series" of rules in torts.[114] While he used analytic logic to demolish Austin's system, Holmes relied solely on experience for confirmation of his own classificatory scheme, presenting a thickly textured and sophisticated array of data. This included evidence showing a linkage between tort and criminal liability based on similar external foresight conceptions of moral responsibility; the transmutation of personal culpability rules into external standards; and the shading of negligence into strict liability by virtue of the strict effect from external and concrete ("arbitrary") negligence rules.

In pursuing a general unifying theory, Holmes acknowledged its tension with the epistemic relativism of the new jurisprudence. Science can never prove itself or anything else true by induction. The scientific search for the causal mechanisms of perceived empirical relationships necessarily proceeds by skepticism founded, as Wright stated, "on the induction or *a priori* presumption, that physical causation is universal."[115] Holmes fully recognized the logical limitations of science as applied to law, and he made explicit the necessary assumption of causal intelligibility: "The condition of our thinking about the universe is that it is capable of being thought about rationally, or, in other words, that every part of it is effect and cause in the same sense in which those parts are with which we are most familiar."[116] He emphasized skepticism toward even this assumption by calling himself a "bet-tabilitarian" to symbolize the intellectual gamble he was taking.

Although Holmes's commitment to the test of experience justified his claiming the mantle of experimental philosophy for his general theory of tort law regardless of what might have inspired the idea, he highlighted the empirical grounds for his conjecture. Apparently, this was to give plausibility to a venture many among his contemporaries regarded as quixotic, considering the seeming chaos of the field as epitomized by the clashing titans of strict liability and negligence. In particular, Holmes stressed the conservative forces of social self-preservation and other natural instincts, and of demands by powerful (albeit changing) classes that exerted a constraining influence upon judicial policy choices. Moreover, the psychological need of judges for conformity, certainty, and repose, which makes formalism so appealing to them, would encourage imitation, stability, and predictability. The unreflective and slothful habits of mind exhibited by many judges would also induce reliance on tradition and custom. The established conventions were too firmly anchored by history and culture to be rearranged wholesale. This tendency towards consistency was not necessarily undercut by the continuous adaptations of the law to changing social conditions. In Holmes's view, social history was also a process of gradual evolution. Also, to the extent that the law did not hesitate to make expedient, if implicit, adjustments of policy, it avoided the need for precipitous change.

Scrutiny and Revision

Equal in importance to making the law better understood was the role of a general theory in spurring effective law reform. The reason for providing the best order and explanation for the existing system was to expose its workings and requirements to informed "scrutiny and revision."[117] Basing a general theory on the actual political forces shaping the law would encourage this process of criticism by making the legislative function of courts more conspicuous and the policy analysis more candid and deliberate. Holmes hoped that more conscious recognition of their legislative function would lead courts to found judgments on deliberate and candid appraisals of the competing policies, rather than on unreflective enactments of the passions and prejudices of class interest.[118]

For Holmes, then, a general theory was the necessary "first step toward an enlightened scepticism, that is, towards a deliberate reconsideration of the worth of those rules."[119] This was a mandate for top-to-bottom policy review to evaluate the rational fit of rules as means to given policy ends, referring "every rule ... articulately and definitely to an end which it subserves."[120] It also authorized going further to "consider the ends which the several rules seek to accomplish, the reasons why those ends are desired, what is given up to gain them, and whether they are worth the price."[121] A general theory, in Holmes's vivid summary, "get[s] the dragon out of his cave on to the plain and in the daylight, [so] you can count his teeth and claws, and see just what is his strength. But to get him out is only the first step. The next is either to kill him, or to tame him and make him a useful animal."[122]

Holmes imposed no conceptual or nonfunctional limitation on the scope and degree of law reform that courts might undertake.[123] In recommending judicial legislation "from molar to molecular motions," Holmes's license was exceedingly broad.[124] Indeed, the "doubtful case"—the *raison d'être* of most litigation—always required common law judges "to exercise the sovereign prerogative of choice" between competing policies.[125] Holmes understood that his advocacy of judicial deference in ruling on the constitutionality of economic and social welfare legislation entailed a major revision of established precedent and doctrine as well as a substantial restructuring of the social order.[126]

This law reform mission of the general theory, as well as the theory's source in experience, refute those commentators who have characterized Holmes's jurisprudence as "Social Darwinist." Never bothering to define social Darwinism, these commentators essentially adopt its popular association with the notion of progressivity, that law evolves as an inevitable, determinate, and socially beneficial and virtuous expression of some final cause or other *a priori* design. Holmes flatly rejected all such normative accounts of history. Chastising Spencer and other normative Darwinists, Holmes admonished that "[the true] evolutionist will hesitate to affirm universal validity for his social ideals, or for the principles which he thinks should be embodied in legislation."[127]

In rejecting all "necessities" of history, Holmes was reflecting the lessons taught by Wright. Wright demolished the scientific pretensions of what he called "German Darwinism."[128] Speaking directly to Spencer's notions of inevitable progress and development in evolving social customs, Wright responded that "progress and development, when they mean more than a continuous proceeding, have a meaning suspiciously like what the moral and mythic instincts are inclined to," and he called for science to be "purified of this idea."[129] Accordingly, Holmes regarded the changing policy choices made by courts as nothing "but a phase in a continuous growth."[130] Hence despite his evident belief in the utility of external standards, Holmes underscored that no normative inference should be drawn from the finding that the law, referring to criminal law specifically, generally employs such standards. While one might readily doubt that "criminal law does more good than harm" by using external standards, the question simply was whether the law is "enacted or administered on that theory."[131] A general theory sets the stage for scrutiny and revision by giving "a true account of the law as it stands."[132]

Holmes emphasized the same descriptive purpose for the study of history generally; that it was not pursued for any intrinsic normative meaning, but solely as a critical tool for determining how and why the law has come to be what it is. Resort to history was pragmatic, and indeed more contingent than the use of economics, ethics, logic, political theory, sociology, or any other tool of analysis. History is studied simply because law is still made by "judges trained in the past," and it is for this reason alone that knowledge of "what the law has been is necessary to the knowledge of what the law is."[133] Much of the established doctrine "might as well be different," and a good deal of it is of no use whatsoever.[134] Far from seeing any unfolding virtue in judicial attempts to give law historical continuity, Holmes considered this effort not only a sham of logical form but, to the extent it succeeded, "the government of the living by the dead."[135]

Within the new jurisprudence, history had only one practical purpose for lawyers, and that one was "negative and skeptical"—to cut all moral imperialisms down to size.[136] "[I]nflated and unreal explanations," Holmes boasted, "collapse at the touch of history."[137] Yet "the present has a right to govern itself."[138] To achieve social progress, the law must liberate itself from its dependence on history and the need to study it, and should concentrate instead on making policy for the "here and now."[139]

He looked to "a time when the part played by history in the explanation of dogma shall be very small, and instead of ingenious research we shall spend our energy on a study of the ends sought to be attained and the reasons for desiring them."[140] Policy would then be scientifically based on deliberate and open choices that reflect and admit to the test of experience. "An ideal system of law should draw its postulates and its legislative justification from science."[141]

Yet despite this evidence of Holmes's antiformalist perception of history, a view is currently taking hold that even if Holmes was not a social Darwinist in his later years, the formalist characterization fits at least through *The Common Law* and well into the 1890s. In a recent book, Morton Horwitz elaborates such a thesis, aligning Holmes with historical legal science insofar as he equated law with naturally evolving apolitical custom.[142] According to Horwitz, Holmes postulated *a priori* an apolitical, "autonomous realm of custom" and, in particular, advocated the external negligence standard precisely for its supposed automatic incorporation of customary due care and therefore its capacity to "reconcile individual and social morality" without resort "directly [to] considerations of policy."[143] In a single stroke, Holmes purportedly achieved his chief objectives: finding an apolitical, collectivist alternative to the anarchic individualism of Austin's personal culpability standard; avoiding functional arguments that might favor use of strict liability in industrial cases; and reinforcing the formalistic precept that courts discover rather than make the law. It was not until "The Path of the Law," Horwitz claims, that Holmes completely abandoned the "customary law perspective" and accepted the inevitability of political controversy, the unavoidability of judicial policy discretion, and the choice between negligence and strict liability as simply a question of public policy.[144]

This formalist characterization lacks foundation. Even before *The Common Law*, Holmes completely repudiated historical as well as analytic legal science for committing the fallacy of disregarding the legislative function of courts. He denied precisely the equation of custom, law, and political consensus attributed to him by Horwitz, pointing out the error of thinking that judges really decide cases by logically extrapolating norms and analogies from custom. That is the *form* of their argument, not the *substance* of their decision—and "form is nothing."[145] In substance, the growth of the law results from judicial policy judgments based on discretionary choices—not logical deductions—from among various policy suggestions offered by a spectrum of formal and informal sources of experience, custom being only one.[146] Holmes maintained, moreover, that the law evolves through conflict, not consensus (or synthesis). At the poles are clear cases, but most "nice cases" worth litigating are close and present conflicts of value and interest that defy consensus resolution.[147] Far from achieving political harmony, the inevitable policy choices establish a temporarily "favored class" whose law-enforced advantage is "certain [to be] ... inconsistent with [the interests of] others ... [who] have competed unsuccessfully."[148] Indeed, Holmes suspected it was more by method than by mistake that historical legal science professed the social progress and solidarity of evolving custom. This claim not only overlooked the universal "struggle for life," but reflected a thinly disguised "theory of government intended to establish its limits once for all by a logical deduction from axioms."[149]

Horwitz fails to address any evidence from Holmes's early writings. Instead, for proof of the "customary law perspective," he relies on a single phrase in Lecture I of the *The Common Law*, quoted as follows: "[Holmes] saw the evolution of law as *'the unconscious result of instinctive preferences and inarticulate convictions.'* "[150] From this the writer concludes that Holmes labored under a social Darwinist conception of legal evolution, which "did not yet presuppose social engineering by a coercive state" or view law as "the product of social struggle," but which saw courts automatically absorbing customary mores so that "[n]othing stands between the state and the individual."[151] This characterization is not obvious from the quoted words, which evoke the opening references in Lecture I to "[t]he felt necessities of the time, the prevalent moral and political theories, intuitions of public policy, avowed or unconscious."[152]

Horwitz's interpretation is selective reading in the extreme. He omits the balance of the sentence following the quoted phrase, where Holmes states that while judges rarely examine or make definite the political assumptions they legislate into law, those assumptions, far from representing absolute truth, class solidarity, or political consensus, are in fact "none the less traceable to views of public policy in the last analysis."[153] In the next sentence, Holmes makes clear that many judges make policy deliberately and intelligently, and notes that the "law is administered by able and experienced men, who know too much to sacrifice good sense to a syllogism."[154] They have adapted old rules to new uses on policy "inventions."[155]

Holmes fully appreciated that these policy inventions represented the coercive power of the state over the individuals taking sides in their ongoing social struggle. This was indeed a principal theme both before and throughout *The Common Law*. Almost a decade before publication of his book, Holmes declared "false" any "theory of evolution" that proceeded on the "assumption of the solidarity of the interests of society," disregarding the "sacrifice" of one group for the benefit of another in the relentless "struggle for life."[156] Much of this sacrifice was the result of adopting external bureaucratic rules that deliberately subordinated individual rights to the needs of social control and welfare:

> No society has ever admitted that it could not sacrifice individual welfare to its own existence. If conscripts are necessary for its army, it seizes them, and marches them, with bayonets in their rear, to death. It runs highways and railroads through old family places in spite of the owner's protest, paying in this instance the market value, to be sure, because no civilized government sacrifices the citizen more than it can help, but still sacrificing his will and his welfare to that of the rest.[157]

Moreover, in the phrase Horwitz last quotes ("the unconscious result of instinctive preferences and inarticulate convictions"), Holmes was denouncing judges who "rarely mention, and always with apology"—or, worse, never evaluate—their policy views, leaving the process secretive, uncoordinated, and unselfcritical.[158] Indeed, Holmes regarded this result as a cost, not a benefit, of using myth-making form to conceal substantive policy inventions. Far from calling for obeisance to custom to preclude deliberate and explicit policy-making, he "insist[ed] on a more conscious recognition of the legislative function of the courts."[159] This would not only enhance understanding and prediction of what courts will do. More significantly, it would free courts both to evaluate "the various grounds of policy" that have been invented *sub rosa* to justify "large and important branches of the law," and to "decide anew whether those reasons are satisfactory."[160] This was not to prejudge their worth, but because deliberate "scrutiny and revision are justified."[161]

The torts lectures also contradict Horwitz's interpretation. They contain no suggestion (and Horwitz cites none) that torts was or should be a process of automatic cultural osmosis; rather, the lectures leave no doubt of Holmes's politics-of-law approach. This is made clear from the start, where Holmes observes, with obvious approval and prescriptive import, that in contemporary tort law it is "natural and unavoidable that judges as well as others should openly discuss the legislative principles upon which their decisions must always rest in the end, and should base their judgments upon broad considerations of policy."[162] The stakes in many cases were nothing short of large-scale choices between policies favoring the "absolute protection of property" and those serving "the requirements of modern business."[163]

The torts lectures repeat "The Theory of Torts" in making clear that custom, whether emanating from the practices of a particular class or the general public, was merely one of a number of advisory sources, including statutes and precedents, which "suggest" rules, standards, and policies. They were "only motives for decision upon the law—grounds for legislation, so to speak"—which may be consulted and used "depending on the discretion of the court."[164] Indeed, the primary advisory source was the court's own independent policy judgment, which preempted other sources unless the judge felt unclear, indifferent, or inexpert on the matter. Self-recognition of its lack of competence would usually prompt a court in ordinary negligence cases to consult jury opinion for assistance in devising standards of conduct to govern daily experience. But this was a purely instrumental choice, and it by no means equated law with the jury's opinion. Jury opinion merely "aids its [the court's] conscience" in deciding the best policy; the court retained the power to determine whether jury advice would be helpful in the particular type of case, and ultimately to define the standard of care that ought to be taken, giving pragmatic consideration to the type of activity involved and the capacities for precautions of the persons likely to engage in such an activity.[165] Consensus was hardly to be expected even in ordinary, common sort of cases, in which a court frequently finds "the jury oscillating to and fro, and will see the necessity of making up its mind for itself."[166] Certainly Holmes did not regard the jury opinion in industrial cases as particularly useful, let alone politically neutral.[167]

Finally, contrary to Horwitz's claims that Holmes supported the external negligence standard as a means of suppressing resort to strict liability, throughout the torts lectures Holmes consistently affirmed the existence and promoted the "politic" uses of *Rylands* and other major strict liability rules. He made it clear that courts decide to make personal culpability, negligence, or strict liability the basis of recovery in a given class of cases not by deduction from custom or idealized concepts, but always and necessarily by judgment of "public policy."[168] Horwitz also fails to mention Holmes's advocacy of external standards based on "concrete," regulatory presumptions to implement the policies of strict liability as well as negligence. Indeed, "The Path of the Law" affirmed not only the general fore-sight theory of liability as developed in the torts lectures, but also its support for the functional rationality and justice of using strict liability in industrial cases.[169]

Tort law was the proving ground of the new jurisprudence. The torts lectures worked out the general foresight theory not to "outline" or "jus-tify particular doctrines, but to analyze the general method by which the law reaches its decisions."[170] The theory supported Holmes's basic hypotheses of the adaptive evolution of subjective standards to objective ones; of a process of judicial legislation by which courts compromise the interests tied to "tradition and precedent on the one side and the free conception of the desirable on the other"; and that experience not logic exerts the greatest influence over the law's development.[171] Yet the gen-eral foresight theory was applied both broadly and specifically enough for Holmes to conclude "there really is a Law of Torts," and *Rylands* was a central part of it.[172]

3

The Common Ground
of Liability

In *The Common Law* Holmes examined and ultimately rejected the causation theory of the unifying common ground in tort. On that theory of responsibility, strict liability could fasten on mere causation of harm, however unforeseen. The torts lectures begin with the precise question posed by the causation theory: whether anything more than "dry precedent" supported the "rule of absolute responsibility" (that is, cause-based strict liability) that holds a defendant "answerable for all the consequences of his acts, or, in other words, that he acts at his peril always, and wholly irrespective of the state of his consciousness upon the matter."[1]

Lecture III carried most of the burden of analysis demonstrating the formalistic fallacies of the causation theory. In it Holmes showed that neither precedent from the law in operation nor intelligible moral arguments supported liability for "accidental" harm—"accident" being a term-of-art in the torts lectures meaning "a [harmful] consequence which could not have been foreseen."[2] The crux of Holmes's criticism of the causation theory was that it presumed the specious postulate of causal essentialism or singularity. As such, the theory could never explain the practice or morality of tort liability in the real world, where harm results from multiple contributing causes, necessitating judicial policy choices of whether and to what extent the defendant's act would be held responsible.

Holmes's foresight theory emerged most fully from this lengthy critique of the causation theory.[3] At every juncture, as will be seen, his arguments debunking the causation theory concurrently buttressed his foresight theory; what he found wanting in the former were precisely the virtues inhering in the latter. Moreover, in focusing on the causation theory's claim of precedent as well as morality for cause-based strict liability, Holmes consistently affirmed the prevalence and moral coherence of all rules predicated on more than mere causation, including *Rylands* and the other major rules of foresight-based strict liability.

In the course of reconstructing Holmes's analysis, this chapter presents evidence of a previously unnoticed interpretation of the role of negligence in the traditional writ system developed by Holmes and his contemporaries.[4] This "some-negligence interpretation" offers scholars today a new perspective on the history of tort liability that not only contradicts prevailing views of Holmes as a dogmatic proponent of negligence but also challenges two opposing monolithic portraits: on the one hand, the orthodox claim of a nineteenth-century shift to negligence from cause-based strict liability, and, on the other, the conventional view that negligence continuously reigned in tort.

Absolute Responsibility in Trespass

If precedent existed for cause-based strict liability, Holmes surmised it would most likely be found in the unintentional torts classified under the writ of trespass ("Trespass"). Cause theorists maintained that Trespass traditionally authorized recovery on mere causation. It was only the writ of trespass on the case ("Case") that required more than causation—foresight at a minimum. Whether a claim was processed under Trespass or Case—and hence on mere causation or more—was decided, cause theorists asserted, according to the distinction between direct and indirect causation.

Lecture III methodically attacked the claimed Trespass "stronghold" for cause-based strict liability.[5] Holmes began by challenging the possibility of logically consistent precedent for the causation theory of responsibility, arguing that the distinction between direct and more remote causation alone could never on its own terms explain divergent decisions. The law in operation confirmed his logical analysis. In fact, no significant authority existed for cause-based strict liability, and thus none existed for the notion that mere causation constituted the common threshold of moral responsibility in tort.

The need for elaborating these arguments arises because they are central to Holmes's thinking in torts, and particularly to his notion of strict liability. Yet current commentators have only superficially examined the pertinent portions of Lecture III. Many, like Howe, Horwitz, and White, simply ignore these arguments, apparently deeming them esoteric. Others, like Gilmore, obfuscate their significance by dismissing them as merely "nine pages of closely reasoned discussion."[6] The resulting gap in the understanding of Holmes's insights on causal multiplicity and relativity leaves current commentators to reinvent the wheel in present day debates over neocausation theories of responsibility in torts.[7] More important for present purposes, this scholarly neglect explains why so many leading commentators have grossly misconceived Holmes's tort theory and its accommodation of strict liability.

Logically Consistent Precedent

Cause theorists claimed that by applying the direct causation requirements for Trespass, courts established consistent precedent for cause-based strict liability. Holmes, of course, rejected such appeals to the "official theory ... that each new decision follows syllogistically from existing precedents," arguing instead that decisions reflected the legislative function of policy-making.[8] But, just as he had done in attacking the logic of Austin's theories of torts and jurisprudence generally, Holmes refused to grant the causation theory even formalistic coherence. To count as precedent for cause-based strict liability, a holding that causation alone was sufficient for liability must consistently resolve "every case" where the defendant's "act was a factor in the result complained of."[9] But "in principle" no such precedent could exist, precisely because the defendant's act is never the sole contributing cause of the plaintiff's harm.[10] In determining whether the legally responsible cause of the plaintiff's harm was the defendant's act rather than any one or combination of numerous other contributing causes—environmental, animal, or human—courts must resort to some criterion outside the causal paradigm. For Holmes, this criterion was foreseeability.

A main thrust of Holmes's arguments was refutation of attempts by cause theorists to surmount the problem of multiple causation by limiting their claims of precedent for cause-based strict liability to cases where the defendant's act was a "direct" as opposed to a "more remote" contributing cause of the plaintiff's harm.[11] That distinction "does not touch the theory of responsibility, if that theory be that a man acts at his peril."[12] This was so because, he reasoned, "if principle requires us to charge a man in trespass when his act has brought force to bear on another through a comparatively short train of intervening causes, in spite of his having used all possible care, it requires the same liability, however numerous and unexpected the events between the act and the result."[13]

Moreover, the notion of "directness" itself lacked objective meaning as a procedural test for issuing writs of Trespass. Courts invariably exercised discretion in choosing among the numerous more or less "direct" contributing causes of injury. Even in cases seeming to involve the most direct cause-and-effect relationship, as where the defendant shoots the plaintiff at point-blank range, a "vast series of physical changes" always combines with the defendant's act to produce the plaintiff's injury.[14] Causal indeterminacy requires courts to make judgments of policy. This was apparent from the many Trespass decisions that redressed consequences, as Holmes observed, "more remote from the defendant's act than in other instances where the remedy would be case."[15]

In remonstrating that there was an "awful lot of rot talked about causes," Holmes particularly had in mind Francis Wharton's "ordinary natural sequence" test for causal directness.[16] This test determined whether an abnormal intervening cause superseded the defendant's act, rendering it "remote," by comparing the facts of the given case against a presumed normal chain of events. To Holmes, such purportedly determinate tests of direct causal relationships were nothing but sophistical fronts for judicial policy decisions regulating the scope of liability.[17] Because every case arises from a unique mix of circumstances, no objective measure could be derived from the causal paradigm to detect when the "intervening" presence of some causal factor represented the type of variation or departure from the presumed normal course of events (assuming this notion had some objective meaning) that would cut off a defendant's responsibility for harm. Moreover, although extraordinary intervening causes usually involve statistically unlikely events, they remain, physically and philosophically, natural and contributing causes. It also was arbitrary to focus on likelihood alone, since this neglects the element of severity, which can raise the level (and palpable nature) of even the most remote risk above far more likely but less severe hazards. Thus courts relying on such a fallacious "efficient cause" formula to determine responsibility for the harmful consequences of a defendant's act obscure the real reasons, which are outside the causal paradigm: "the intervening events are of such a kind that no foresight could have been expected to look out for them, [and therefore] the defendant is not to blame for having failed to do so."[18]

Cause theorists might further limit their directness conception to cases where the defendant's act was the last sufficient human cause, and where "only physical or irresponsible agencies, however unforeseen, co-operated with the act complained of to produce the result."[19] But, Holmes argued, the position of these theorists remained indefensible. There was no principled basis in the causal paradigm for deeming all nonhuman factors to be noncauses, or for making the last human contribution, however minor, the responsible agent. Nor could the causal paradigm explain the preference for a synchronous, after-the-fact conception of sufficiency that varies the defendant's responsibility according to the fortuitous sequence of events, or, equally arbitrary, if "by good fortune no harm comes of his conduct in the particular event."[20] As exemplified by the law of criminal attempts, society often holds individuals responsible for the disruptive effects they caused by merely contributing to the creation of a risk.[21] Moreover, limiting cause-based responsibility to the last human actor would resolve few if any cases. In every case, the presence of the plaintiff's person or property—the result of a choice by the plaintiff to use or continue using a certain area or thing in conflict with the defendant's attempted use—was always a necessary *sine qua non*. As courts were fully aware, causal reasoning could not solve the dilemma posed by the joint contributions to risk from both parties in modern tort cases arising from conflicting claims of priority, such as over land usage, access to information for business purposes, or rights-of-way on highways, sea lanes, and rail crossings.[22]

The famous hypothetical instance offered by counsel in the ancient *Thorns* case supplied Holmes with an apt illustration of the multiple cause conundrum as well as an opportunity to emphasize the paucity of the supposed support for cause-based strict liability.[23] The *Thorns* hypothetical assumed that a court would impose cause-based strict liability on a defendant for "accidentally [meaning 'could not have been foreseen'] striking the plaintiff," who was standing behind him, "when lifting a stick in necessary self-defense" against a third party.[24] To demonstrate its inadequacy as a source of precedent, Holmes varied the hypothetical slightly, so that the plaintiff happened to be there because a horse suddenly pushed him "just as it [the stick] was lifted."[25] This variation put cause theorists in a bind; they were unlikely to concede such a bizarre application of cause-based strict liability, given that the defendant's act was certainly not the exclusive or most proximate cause, let alone the responsible one by any ordinary standards. Nor could they attribute the injury to the plaintiff, whom cause theorists would regard as merely the "passive instrument of an external force."[26] Yet if cause theorists would not apply strict liability on mere causation to the hypothetical involving the horse, logic precluded its application to the original *Thorns* hypothetical. "[T]here is no difference between [the two cases]," Holmes concluded, "provided that it was not possible, under the circumstances, in the one case to have known [of 'a person standing in one's rear,' and], in the other [involving the horse] to have anticipated, the proximity."[27] If responsibility is denied in one case, it must be denied in the other, not for lack of direct causation, but rather because when the risk is unforeseen, "there is wanting the only element which distinguishes voluntary acts from spasmodic muscular contractions as a ground of liability."[28]

Cause theorists could not elude the vise of Holmes's reasoning by arguing that in cases like his variation of the *Thorns* hypothetical, courts treated the defendant's act, one that "directly" contributed to the plaintiff's harm, as merely a "passive instrument" of uncontrollable circumstance and hence a noncause. Of course, "passive" was surplusage if it signified simply that the defendant's physical will power had been overcome by some irresistible force, or that such a force would have inflicted the plaintiff's harm regardless of the defendant's conduct. While suggesting that the causal paradigm might allow a simpler conception of the causal connection, Holmes generally granted cause theorists their assumed premises that the defendant's act must be self-willed—more than mere "spasmodic muscular contractions"—and that it must be a but-for cause of the plaintiff's harm, "a factor in the result complained of."[29] If both of these conditions were satisfied, however, nothing in the causal paradigm could logically warrant calling the defendant's act a "passive" noncause.

Referring to the classic runaway horse case of Gibbons v. Pepper, Holmes demonstrated that the passive characterization generally turned on more than causation, and that it implicitly invoked the foresight condition for liability.[30] In *Gibbons,* the defendant's horse, a quietly ridden and otherwise docile animal, bolted and ran down the plaintiff-pedestrian upon being "frightened by accident" by a sudden and unexpected gun shot.[31] Cause theorists claimed that *Gibbons* stood for cause-based strict liability, reading the decision to suggest that the ruling against the defendant might have been different had the pleadings shown that the harm resulted from a third person's act.[32] It was sheer nonsense, in Holmes's view, for cause theorists to rely on *Gibbons.* Under no plausible account of the case could the defendant deny the causal contribution of his riding the horse just when it heard the gunshot and reacted in panic. Moreover, whatever might be said of the defendant's conduct at that precise moment, the demand for an active causal relationship could always and easily be supplied, Holmes asserted, by referring the plaintiff's harm "more remotely" to the defendant's act, for example, "of mounting and taking the horse out."[33] All of these acts were willed. At all relevant times, the defendant could have—if adequately forewarned—physically prevented the horse from bolting by reining it in, tying it up, or not taking it out in the first place.

Therefore, Holmes concluded, the only cogent explanation of cases like *Gibbons* was in foresight terms. If, then, the court was prepared to treat the defendant's act as simply another background condition in the environment, it was not because that act had not causally contributed to plaintiff's harm. Rather, it was because the harmful consequences were rendered unavoidable by intervening causes "of such a kind that no foresight could have been expected to look out for them."[34]

Case Authority

Examination of the law in operation confirmed that no evidence of authority existed in Trespass to sustain cause-based strict liability. Holmes acknowledged that nonetheless the doctrine of absolute responsibility had an impressive following among contemporary commentators, practitioners, and some leading judges. He pointedly referred to supportive arguments in *Rylands* (by counsel for plaintiff) and to Lord Cranworth, in his opinion for the House of Lords.[35] But Holmes regarded Justice Blackburn's opinion as the authoritative statement of the *Rylands* rule, and took it as a call to abjure absolute responsibility in favor of foresight-based strict liability.[36] Indeed, Holmes determined that the law in operation "has never known such a rule [absolute responsibility], unless in that period of dry precedent which is so often to be found midway between a creative epoch and a period of solvent philosophical reaction."[37]

Vainly culling centuries of English and American reports for authority applying cause-based strict liability in Trespass, Holmes concluded that there, as in Case, the courts always coupled causation with foresight when setting the threshold of responsibility. This was true whether the Trespass claim involved harm to person or property. Moreover, in accord with his theory, Trespass traditionally enforced a number of major rules of foresight-based strict liability. Under Trespass liability was sometimes imposed for unforeseeable harm, but (as discussed later) Holmes rationalized this precedent under the some-negligence interpretation: that Trespass granted recovery for unforeseen harm only if it resulted from the defendant's negligence toward some other, foreseeable risk. In the absence of such negligence, the defendant's act would be treated as one of many "irresponsible agencies."

Holmes began by reviewing the classic English Trespass cases involving personal injury. This analysis showed that mere causation never sufficed for liability, despite language suggesting the contrary. In every case, the foresight condition was satisfied in fact or as a matter of law—often by actual malice—"full [subjective] foresight"—or negligence.[38] When recovery was granted for the harmful consequences of non-negligent conduct, he found that foresight-based strict liability had been applied. Moreover, the early cases, which supposedly founded the rule of absolute responsibility, generally required pleading direct force and violence ("vi et armis"), and predominantly arose from criminal attacks and related intentional and unlawful acts of assault and battery.[39] Holmes thus denied that cause theorists could rely on suggestions in some ancient reports indicating the sufficiency of pleading a direct causal relationship. The additional requirement of foresight was readily inferable in these cases from the allegations (and facts) of force and violence as well as, in any event, from the assertion of direct causation itself.[40] Also, many Trespass cases predicated liability on undeniable evidence of negligence. In some of the most prominent eighteenth- and nineteenth-century Trespass cases, "there was . . . no question of absolute responsibility for one's acts before the court, as negligence was admitted."[41]

The most telling cases Holmes marshaled against the causation theory, however, were those which refused to attach responsibility to a harmful act despite a sufficiently close causal relationship between act and injury to qualify the claim for Trespass. The causation theory predicted that no such cases existed; thus the contrary experience falsified the theory. For Holmes, only the foresight theory could explain these different outcomes in Trespass.

A principal example was Scott v. Shepherd—"the famous squib case"—involving a Trespass claim "against one who had thrown a squib [firecracker] into a crowd, where it was tossed from hand to hand in self-defense until it burst and injured the plaintiff."[42] On the causation theory, the more proximate acts of the intervening actors should have been treated by the court as superseding causes, terminating the responsibility of the defendant although he had initiated the chain of events. But, against the predictions of the causation theory, the court sustained the claim of Trespass, denying that the intervening actors were responsible. Only the foresight theory could explain this result. According to Holmes, the court excused the intervening actors because the sudden and unexpected danger provoked an "instantaneous" and "more or less nearly automatic" reaction—tantamount to an "unconscious spasm."[43] It is apparent that he took the decision to exonerate the intervening actors and impose liability on the defendant as clear proof that the law never deems it a "sufficient foundation for liability . . . that the proximate cause of loss was an act."[44]

To similar effect, Holmes dealt with the court's suggestion in *Gibbons* that liability might be imposed if the horse were being spurred rather than ridden quietly when it ran away. He asserted that causal considerations were entirely irrelevant to the decision. Surely, whatever difference the court perceived to exist between hard spurring and quiet riding could have nothing to do with the notion of remoteness, let alone with the distinction between "results which are and those which are not the consequences of the defendant's acts."[45] Rather, the difference taken by the court between modes of riding corresponded to the crucial distinction between the act's foreseeable and unforeseeable consequences. "Hard spurring is just so much more likely to lead to harm than merely riding a horse in the street, that the court thought that the defendant would be bound to look out for the consequences of the one, while it would not hold him liable for those resulting merely from the other."[46] Although the "possibility of being run away with when riding quietly" was "familiar," it was "comparatively slight," and consequently not an event the defendant was "bound as a reasonable man to contemplate ."[47]

Contrary to current supposition, Holmes's treatment of *Gibbons* nowhere equates slight risks with reasonable conduct (non-negligence), or high risks with unreasonable conduct (negligence). His analysis is explicitly and solely grounded on the foreseeability of risk.[48] He equated the unexpected runaway in *Gibbons* with "coming to a place where one is seized with a fit and strikes the plaintiff in an unconscious spasm."[49] Indeed, in cases where the defendant had any reason to believe that the horse was prone to being spooked by sudden, loud noises, Holmes would apply the prevailing rule of strict liability based on foresight *(scienter)*.[50] Given that it was an "exceptional phenomenon" for domestic animals to become wild, vicious, or a danger to the person of others, the policy of courts was that the keeper of an apparently tame animal does not act "at his peril as to the personal damages which they may inflict, unless he knows or has notice that the particular animal kept by him has the abnormal tendency which they do sometimes show."[51]

After demonstrating the explanatory power of the foresight theory in Trespass cases involving personal injury, Holmes proceeded to attack the last and best fortified bastion of supposed precedent in tort for cause-based strict liability: cases involving "innocent trespasses upon land, and conversions" of personal property.[52] In those cases, while the courts did apply strict liability, they provided no decisional authority for liability based solely on causation. In every case, the facts and holdings fully satisfied the foresight requirement. Not incidentally, many of these cases also confirmed Holmes's multiple cause critique of the causation theory. Indeed, foresight explained even the *Thorns* case, which purportedly provided the foundational precedent for cause-based strict liability. The court in *Thorns* sustained the Trespass claim against the defendant for allowing cuttings from his hedge pruning to fall onto the plaintiff's adjacent land and, also without permission, for entering the property to retrieve the cuttings. But the ruling exemplified the foresight rather than the causation theory. "When he [defendant] cut the thorns," Holmes pointed out, "he did an act which obviously and necessarily would have that consequence [of their falling on the plaintiff's property], and he must be taken to have foreseen and not to have prevented it."[53]

Experience had shown, Holmes observed, that trespass to neighboring property was an inherent danger of such activities as walking or keeping animals, and that these dangers were clearly foreseeable by the respective classes of pedestrians and animal keepers. Indeed, mere knowledge of the rudimentary nature of the activity involved was usually enough to engender foresight of this risk and subject the defendant to strict liability. Recognition that one is walking not on a "treadmill" but "over the surface of the earth" provided the individual with knowledge that "he is surrounded by private estates which he has no right to enter, and . . . that his motion, unless properly guided, will carry him into those estates."[54] Having thus been "warned" of these harmful consequences of walking, the defendant's decision to engage in the activity constituted a choice to undertake the risks of trespass, which, in Holmes's view, was why the law deemed it appropriate that the "burden of [defendant's] conduct is thrown upon himself."[55]

Holmes's foresight explanation of the land trespass cases provided firm underpinnings for his foresight rationalization of strict liability in industrial and other cases of business-related risk. In discussing land trespass cases, he made clear that foresight-based strict liability was not limited to situations such as the hard spurring of a horse in *Gibbons,* where consciousness of danger coincides with the act that was proximate to the plaintiff's injury. Rather, the foresight basis for strict liability could be extended to the outer limit of reasonable risk cognition, where the defendant makes the choice to engage in the activity itself. At this remote point, the foreseeable risks are highly generalized, being extrapolated from the nature of the activity rather than from any aspect of the defendant's particular circumstances. Indeed, the boundaries of this generalized risk cognition are marked and are constantly being enlarged by statistical, actuarial, expert, and other methods and factors which enhance the capacity to understand and communicate empirical experience.

Holmes used the cattle trespass cases to illustrate the breadth of strict liability based on such generalized foresight. Strict liability applied whenever crop damage occurred, because the empirical correlation between that risk and the activity of keeping cattle in general was sufficiently high to satisfy the foresight requirement from the start. But, while the cattle owner was always "bound at his peril to keep them off his neighbor's premises," there was no similar injunction "in all cases to keep them from his neighbor's person."[56] This was because the risk of personal injury from otherwise docile horses, cattle, and other domestic animals was too slight to enter the consciousness of the reasonable owner at any level of meaningful generality to furnish notice in time to avoid the harm. In accord with the foresight requirement, however, courts applied strict liability for personal injuries from cattle and other domestic animals in *scienter* actions, where the owner had reason to know of an "abnormal tendency" in the particular animal involved.[57] Holmes's insight regarding foresight-based strict liability for animals, which he generalized to support *Rylands,* anticipated the use of activity or industry-wide foresight classifications in formulating the broad modern rules of strict enterprise liability.[58]

Accident and Unforeseeable Harm

The history of English Trespass showed that courts generally refused to impose liability on mere causation. Instead, they defined the threshold boundary of responsibility and excuse in terms of foresight-informed choice. This conception of moral responsibility required that the law afford the defendant "an opportunity of choice with reference to the consequence complained of—a chance to guard against the result which has come to pass."[59] But choice was meaningless in any moral sense without foresight. As Holmes declared: "A choice which entails a concealed consequence is as to that consequence no choice."[60] Directly following this finding, Holmes capsulized it in his well-known formulation: "[t]he general principle of our law is that loss from accident must lie where it falls."[61] In the next sentence he emphasized the unforeseeable harm meaning of "accident": "[R]elatively to a given human being anything is accident which he could not fairly have been expected to contemplate as possible, and therefore to avoid."[62]

Holmes's formulation of the "general principle" denying liability for "accident" corresponded to what George P. Fletcher called, in his exposition of the principal Trespass cases, the "Aristotelian excusing categories of compulsion and unavoidable ignorance," traditionally asserted through defenses of irresistible force and unforeseeable harm under the rubrics "act of God" and "inevitable accident."[63] While Holmes noted the possibility that an external force by itself might overpower a defendant,[64] he appears to have concluded that without the added elements of suddenness and unexpectedness few if any such cases were likely to arise. In most cases, a "natural cause or physical factor" would not be irresistible unless it "intervenes, unknown at the time," to affect the defendant's act, "in some way not to be foreseen, and turns what seemed innocent to harm."[65] Also, the malleability of the notion of irresistible force implied an excuse (as opposed to possible justification) in cases of "necessity," where, in contrast to cases of automatism like *Scott,* the defendant inflicts harm under duress, but nonetheless with the physical and conscious power to choose otherwise (albeit at great personal or social cost). But, Holmes noted, a classic line of cases with modern significance recognized no excuse for harm inflicted by such necessity, and, consistent with his theory of foresight-informed choice, such cases imposed strict liability as a means of just compensation.[66] For these reasons he avoided using the term "irresistible force" and, instead, defined a voluntary act by the inclusive notion of an act that was "willed," as opposed to mere "spasmodic muscular contractions."[67] When, as in virtually all cases, the harmful act was willed, the defendant could "only [be] excused on the ground that the party neither did foresee, nor could with proper care have foreseen harm."[68]

Holmes's definition of "accident" as unforeseeable and hence unavoidable harm comported with conventional usage.[69] For example, in discussing the scope of strict liability for nuisance, Thomas Cooley noted that "[o]nly sudden and unavoidable accident, which could not have been foreseen by due care, could be an excuse."[70] Austin defined "*casus or accident*" similarly as the "broad principle ... [that] the party could not foresee the mischievous event."[71] The scientific meaning of "accident" was to the same effect. According to Wright, Darwin used "accident" to characterize events "which are quite beyond the power of finite minds to anticipate or to account for in detail."[72] In fact, prior to Holmes, Joseph Story had elaborated the defense of "pure accident" that excused harms "which human prudence could not foresee or prevent," dictating "that the loss must be borne by the sufferer, according the maxim, that it falls where it lights."[73]

Holmes's preference for just plain "accident" may be explained by the ambiguities and limitations of the other standard phraseology, in particular "inevitable accident" and "act of God." By the late nineteenth century, the classic role of "inevitable accident" in excusing unforeseeable harm was beginning to blur into its present-day usage as a justification of non-negligence applicable to cases of foreseeable as well as unforeseeable injury.[74] Moreover, although Holmes illustrated the unforeseeable harm meaning of accident with traditional examples of unforeseeable "acts of God"—tempests, disease, wild animal attacks, and lightning—he never mentioned that phrase in the torts lectures.[75] This was not however, owing to any confusion on Holmes's part regarding its "unforeseeable harm" meaning or its accommodation of strict liability.[76] His contemporaries well understood that this defense applied only to harms, as Pollock stated, "such as human foresight could not be reasonably expected to anticipate."[77] Moreover, as Pollock hastened to make clear, a strict liability reading of *Rylands* was reconcilable with the defense given that "it is not because due diligence has been used that an accident which nevertheless happens is attributable to the act of God."[78] Holmes probably jettisoned the "act of God" metaphor because of its traditional application to unforeseeable harms resulting solely from natural forces without any human contribution.[79] In stating the general principle of no liability for accident, he thus emphasized that its scope was inclusive and "not affected by the fact that a human being is the instrument of misfortune."[80]

The "Some-Negligence" Interpretation

Although a number of Trespass decisions awarded damages for unforeseeable harm, Holmes denied that they supported the causation theory. Rather, he argued, these cases conformed to his foresight theory. In every one the courts treated the principal harm sued upon as unforeseeable, and conditioned recovery for such harm on proof or presumption of "some negligence" on the defendant's part in regard to some other (causally related) foreseeable risk.[81]

Current commentators mistake Holmes's reference to this some-negligence doctrine in Trespass as an effort to transform a purported universal rule of cause-based strict liability into a general rule of negligence. In fact, his showing that Trespass was grounded on the some-negligence doctrine was designed to refute the doctrine of absolute responsibility and related solely to cases where the harm sued upon was unforeseeable—"accidental trespasses."[82] He never suggested that the some-negligence interpretation precluded strict liability in Trespass or Case where the harm involved was foreseeable; indeed, his theory of responsibility fully accommodated all of the traditional and most modern rules of foresight-based strict liability. While my reconstruction of Holmes's some-negligence interpretation of "accidental trespass" is new to present-day literature, his contemporaries widely recognized and shared that view.[83]

Although the exchange between court and counsel in *Thorns* contained intimations of the some-negligence doctrine, Holmes determined that the doctrine was generally established in Weaver v. Ward, the pivotal seventeenth-century case which cause theorists claimed as one of their "principal authorities."[84] In his view, they patently disregarded the court's decision to reject the defendant's plea of inevitable accident for failing to show that the harm involved (defendant shot plaintiff during a military drill) occurred "utterly without his fault." To be "excused of a trespass,"[85] the defendant should have shown not only that the injury resulted from an unforeseen turn of events, such as the court suggested: " 'if here the defendant had said, that the plaintiff ran cross his piece when it was discharging.' "[86] But the court also required allegations, as Holmes underscored, " 'that the defendant *had committed no negligence* to give occasion to the hurt.' "[87]

In short, the general principle of no liability for accident excused harm as faultless only if inflicted absent both foresight and negligence. While thus permitting recovery for unforeseeable harm in Trespass (as well as

Case), the some-negligence doctrine maintained the threshold of moral responsibility at foresight-informed choice. The doctrine conditioned liability on the fact that the defendant received a clear and emphatic warning against inflicting plainly foreseeable negligent harms (or intentional wrongs). Had the defendant complied with the standards of reasonable conduct, the causally related unforeseeable harm would have been avoided.

The following diagram, based on the interpretation of Holmes and his contemporaries, graphically portrays the scope of liability represented by the Trespass decisions:

	Negligent conduct	Non-negligent conduct
Foreseeable harm	*Liability* (negligence rule)	*Liability* (foresight-based strict liability)
Unforeseeable harm	*Liability* (some negligence)	No *liability* (caused-based strict liability)

The some-negligence interpretation of excuse in tort represented the prevailing view in Holmes's time. Indicating its origins in *Weaver,* Cooley stated the doctrine as follows: "An accident may be defined as an event happening unexpectedly and without fault: if there is any fault there is liability."[88] Cooley affirmed that this doctrine created no conflict with *Rylands* and foresight-based strict liability in general.[89] According to Warren Seavey, Jeremiah Smith instructed his students at Harvard Law School that the only excuse in tort law was "accident—an event happening unexpectedly and without fault."[90] A *Harvard Law Review* note on "Inevitable Accident" summarized the some-negligence interpretation.[91] The note reconciled the inevitable accident excuse stemming from *Weaver* with strict liability in *Rylands,* on the grounds that the defense barred only absolute responsibility—the rule that "he who acts voluntarily acts at his peril . . . though the injury be the outcome neither of wilful wrongdoing nor of negligence"—and therefore excused only "a man [who] uses due care [from] . . . responsib[ility] for results which could not have been foreseen."[92]

For support of his some-negligence interpretation of *Weaver* and its English progeny,[93] Holmes relied on the leading American decisions in cases of accidental trespasses. The specific issue in these cases was the question posited in Lecture III concerning precedent for absolute responsibility: whether "if no such excuse is shown [of irresistible force], and the defendant has voluntarily acted, he must answer for the consequences, however little intended and however unforeseen."[94] To Holmes, all that the American courts considered and decided was the relatively narrow, if theoretically testing, claim that the defendant "acts at his peril always, and wholly irrespective of the state of his consciousness upon the matter."[95] The courts rejected arguments that form should govern substance, making "a man's responsibility for the consequences of his acts var[y] as the remedy happens to fall on one side or the other of the penumbra which separates trespass from the action on the case."[96] Instead, they essentially adopted the some-negligence standard of "utterly without fault" prescribed by *Weaver*, requiring the absence of both foresight and negligence for the excuse of inevitable accident, act of God, or simply "accident" (as Holmes preferred), and therefore allowing recovery for unforeseeable harm when there was some fault. Foresight-based strict liability was thus never at issue in these cases. But, to the extent American courts took notice of that rule, they, like their academic contemporaries, recognized its propriety and importance.[97]

Holmes focused on Morris v. Platt to sum up the some-negligence meaning of the American Trespass cases.[98] Like the *Thorns* hypothetical, *Morris* involved injury to a bystander when the defendant fired his gun in self-defense. Echoing *Weaver*'s example of unforeseeable inevitable accident, the court analogized the claim before it to one where "the assailant suddenly and unexpectedly stepped aside, and the ball passing over the spot hit the plaintiff, who till then was invisible and his presence unknown to the defendant."[99] For liability in such a case of unforeseeable harm, the court held that a plaintiff must show that the activity itself was unreasonable ("not lawful")—for example, if no justification for self-defense existed—or that "the act though strictly lawful and necessary was done with wantonness [or] negligence"—if, for instance, excessive force was used.[100]

In generalizing about the some-negligence doctrine in the writ system, Holmes rather loosely paraphrased *Morris* to propose that the "foundation of liability in trespass as well as case was . . . negligence."[101] Taken out of context, this statement could be read as claiming that negligence was a prerequisite for recovery on all claims of Trespass as well as Case. Yet it is clear that Holmes (like the court in *Morris*) was concerned solely with cases involving unforeseeable harm—with rebutting the supposed rule of absolute responsibility and with establishing a some-negligence basis of recovery for unforeseeable harm. The precise declaration in *Morris* to which Holmes referred stated that: "The *foundation* of . . . liability in every case of accident, where it is the result of human agency uninfluenced by the operations of nature, and the act is lawful, is really *negligence.*"[102] Consistent with Holmes's usage, the court explicitly defined "accident" as harm inflicted "undesignedly and unexpectedly."[103]

To read Holmes as concluding that negligence was the universal basis of liability for Trespass would mean he was denying the venerable rules of strict liability for damage to property, a claim which would seem quite implausible to contemporaries and hence appear at odds with his professed empiricism,[104] and which would also contradict his affirmation of those rules immediately before and after the paraphrase of *Morris*.[105] In fact, a few pages later, Holmes relied on dicta in *Morris* as the platform for discussing the policies favoring the use of strict liability for such manifestly risky activities as "the danger to the public of the growing habit of carrying deadly weapons."[106] At that point, Holmes also restated the holding in *Morris* to capture its some-negligence meaning, which did not exclude foresight-based strict liability: "negligence is the foundation of liability for accidental trespasses."[107]

For further support of the some-negligence doctrine and its rejection of absolute responsibility, Holmes relied on Brown v. Kendall, where the plaintiff was "accidentally" injured when the defendant raised a stick to strike and separate two fighting dogs, one of which was his.[108] Holmes apparently set up the *Thorns* hypothetical in part to report its demise in this actual stick case.[109] While pointing out the absence of the necessity for self-defense in *Brown,* which made the case even stronger for his foresight theory than the *Thorns* hypothetical, Holmes emphasized that they were otherwise virtually identical by reducing the "gist of the [*Thorns* hypothetical] action" to the "contact between the staff and his neighbor's head," which "was not intended, and could not have been foreseen."[110] Indeed, Holmes prefaced the entire argument in Lecture III against the causation theory of responsibility in Trespass with a reference to Judge Lemuel Shaw's "politic" decision in *Brown* repudiating the rule of absolute responsibility.[111] Holmes's statement of the question of responsibility in terms of whether an individual "acts at his peril always," regardless of "his consciousness upon the matter," reflected the question Shaw framed for decision: "how far, and under what qualifications, the party by whose unconscious act the damage was done is responsible for it."[112] Shaw refused to allow the direct causation requirement of Trespass to dictate the governing substantive standard of liability, and ruled that without "some negligence" on the defendant's part, an unforeseeable harm must be regarded as "pure accident."[113]

Holmes also relied on Doe's leading opinion in Brown v. Collins—involving a *Gibbons*-type runaway horse that knocked down a post on the plaintiff's property—to show that the American Trespass cases rejected cause-based—not foresight-based—strict liability, and adopted a some-negligence interpretation. Although frequently referred to and quoted today, Doe's opinion is universally misconstrued as adopting a general negligence rule and rejecting *Rylands* along with all forms of strict liability. To be sure, contemporaries regarded Doe, not Holmes, as the arch-enemy of *Rylands* (in fact, as I will show in Chapter 6, the general consensus was that Holmes was among its chief and most effective supporters). But Doe opposed *Rylands* only because he viewed it as authorizing cause-based strict liability. The key question raised by the doctrine of absolute responsibility is whether Trespass extended liability to a defendant who cannot "foresee [his act] will produce any injury to his neighbor, if he thereby unwittingly injure his neighbor."[114] Doe decided that such responsibility existed only if there was fault in the *Weaver* sense of some negligence. Despite the current attention given to his opinion, commentators have ignored his statement of the some-negligence doctrine: namely, that the defendant is "not liable" without "fault" where "the damage was not caused by his voluntary and intended act; or by an act of which he knew, or ought to have known, the damage would be a necessary, probable, or natural consequence; or by an act which he knew, or ought to have known, to be unlawful."[115]

In the text surrounding this statement of the some-negligence doctrine, Doe underscored his focus on unforeseeable harm, and made it clear that his ruling fully accommodated foresight-based strict liability. Invoking *Weaver* and Shaw's opinion in Brown v. Kendall, Doe emphasized that by finding the defendant "without fault" he meant that the harm sued upon was unforeseeable and unavoidable because the injurer took reasonable precautions against all foreseeable risks. Thus the harm was the equivalent of an unforeseeable act of God, and the defendant was as "innocent as if the pole of his wagon had been hurled on the plaintiff's land by a whirlwind, or he himself, by a stronger man, had been thrown through the plaintiff's window."[116] Moreover, and contrary to current assumptions,

Doe affirmed the widespread application of foresight-based strict liability, including "many cases" (also noted by Holmes in the torts lectures) of "taking, converting . . . or destroying property."[117]

In closing his discussion of the American accidental Trespass cases, Holmes referred to a quotation from Harvey v. Dunlop, with which he had briefly introduced the some-negligence interpretation earlier in Lecture III.[118] Directly following his statements of the general principle of no liability for accident, and of the unforeseeable-harm definition of accident, he inserted the some-negligence qualification by quoting *Harvey:*

> "No case or principle can be found, or if found can be maintained, subjecting an individual to liability for an act done without fault on his part . . . All the cases concede that an injury arising from inevitable accident, or, which in law or reason is the same thing, from an act that ordinary human care and foresight are unable to guard against, is but the misfortune of the sufferer, and lays no foundation for legal responsibility."[119]

Holmes's some-negligence interpretation of *Harvey* was consistent not only with that court's reliance on *Weaver,* but also with the facts of the case, which involved a six-year-old defendant who, in play and concededly without any blame, threw a rock that injured the plaintiff's child. As such, *Harvey* apparently fell into one of the special categories of cases of defendants who exhibit a "manifest incapacity" to appreciate and avoid harm, such as infants of "very tender years" or persons afflicted by pronounced insanity, that negated the "moral basis of liability."[120] But, aside from raising an exception to the law's general presumption of ordinary psychological capacities, Holmes considered *Harvey* to resemble *Morris, Kendall,* and the other accidental Trespass cases in excusing a defendant who commits not the "smallest negligence," "unless . . . he might and ought to have foreseen the danger."[121]

Holmes's contemporaries generally recognized and shared his some-negligence interpretation of the English and American cases of accidental Trespass.[122] That understanding has virtually disappeared today.[123] This misperception seems to have occurred largely because current commentators wrongly attribute current "negligence" meanings to the terms "inevitable accident" and "accident" in nineteenth-century texts.[124] They simply treat these terms as redundant of negligence in reading the standard some-negligence formulations—no liability for accident (or inevitable accident) without negligence (or fault)—that appear in those texts.[125]

Indeed, the anachronistic transposition of the negligence meaning to "inevitable accident" and "accident" is so automatic that the practice has arisen, beginning with Gilmore, of quoting the phrase "loss from accident must lie where it falls" closed by ellipses without further explanation.[126] Few commentators go as far as White, who linked the ellipses to the first sentence of the *Harvey* quotation denying "liability for an act done without fault."[127] Apparently, these commentators find the modern negligence meaning so obvious that they never notice its direct conflict with the unforeseeable harm definition of accident in the sentence their ellipses erase. Nor do they heed the sentence directly following the quotation from *Harvey*, where Holmes squared its statement of the inevitable accident defense with his own definition of "accident," affirming that both related solely to claims seeking redress for unforeseeable harm by the rule of absolute responsibility. Without the defense of inevitable accident (and by inference, his notion of "accident"), it would be "sufficient" for liability that a completely innocent "act . . . however remote . . . set in motion or opened the door for a series of physical sequences ending in damage"— equating the examples of "riding the horse" in *Gibbons*-type cases, and "coming to a place where one is seized with a fit and strikes the plaintiff in an unconscious spasm."[128] Moreover, current commentators overlook Holmes's focus on unforeseeable harm and foresight-informed choice that concludes this crucial paragraph, which makes evident not only that the preceding discussion was concerned solely with the role of negligence in cases of accidental Trespass, but that his some-negligence interpretation was consistent with the general foresight theory of responsibility and its support for strict liability:

> Nay, why need the defendant have acted at all, and why is it not enough that his existence has been at the expense of the plaintiff? The requirement of an act is the requirement that the defendant should have made a choice. But the only possible purpose of introducing this moral element is to make the power of avoiding the evil complained of a condition of liability. There is no such power where the evil cannot be foreseen.[129]

In the brief compass of these few sentences, Holmes also stated the essence of his argument against the moral coherence of the causation theory: whatever residual authority existed for absolute responsibility was dry precedent.[130]

Absolute Responsibility as Morally Dry Precedent

At the very opening of the torts lectures Holmes dampened expectations that the case law would prove entirely consistent with his foresight theory. Inconsistency was an inevitable by-product of growth.[131] Moreover, the influence of the contemporary followers of cause-based strict liability could not be totally discounted.[132] It was difficult to believe that so many prominent legal authorities could find attractions in so draconian a rule. But there was no mistaking the support in high places for absolute responsibility, as indicated by Cranworth's opinion for the House of Lords in *Rylands*. Holmes thus acknowledged (or at least conceded for the sake of argument) the possible existence of authority for cause-based strict liability.

By recognizing the possibility of authority for cause-based strict liability, however, Holmes set the stage for the second, decisive phase of his argument against the causation theory. Whatever the empirical evidence, any authority claimed for cause-based strict liability was but "dry precedent." First, no intelligible conception of moral responsibility could be satisfied by mere causation. Second, given the conception of moral responsibility actually embedded in the basic operational requirements for tort liability, it would be arbitrary, that is, both functionally irrational and unjust, for the law to pursue the ends of compensation and deterrence by holding accountable individuals who could not reasonably foresee and therefore choose to avoid the harm in question.

Source of the Moral Element of Choice

To remain consistent with the new jurisprudence, Holmes could not simply posit an *a priori* moral criterion for assessing the functional rationality and justice of cause-based strict liability. The moral conception of responsibility had to be extracted from the law in operation. A norm of such fundamental character would likely be represented by the most basic necessary and broadly required conditions for liability. In addition to "temporal damage," causation was indisputably a necessary element under virtually all liability rules.[133] Holmes surely would occasion no protest from cause theorists in focusing on the defendant's causal act as signifying "the principles on which the peril of his conduct is thrown upon the actor."[134] Moreover, as noted earlier, he granted cause theorists their two qualifications for causal responsibility: that the defendant's act should be both "willed" and a but-for "factor in the result complained of." But this acknowledgment only fortified his objections to the causation theory. For if cause theorists would not accept "spasmodic muscular contractions as a ground of liability," let alone that the defendant's mere "existence" has adversely affected the plaintiff, they must agree with him that the causal act implied a conception of moral responsibility hinging on the defendant's "choice" to either avoid or inflict harm. The causal act requirement thus signified, but alone was insufficient to satisfy, that "moral element."

Functional Irrationality

In a section of Lecture III headed "argument from policy," Holmes examined whether any claim of expedience could rationally be made on behalf of the functional utility of cause-based strict liability.[135] Specifically, he considered whether it was sensible to think that liability without foresight (or some-negligence)—and consequently without the power of choice to avoid harm—bore any reasonable relationship to the tort functions of compensation and deterrence. He found the notion wholly implausible. Imposing liability for unforeseeable harm was not rationally related to either function. But Holmes did not conclude that strict liability in all forms was arbitrary. On the contrary, *Rylands* and the other major strict liability rules played an essential part in performing the missions of compensation and deterrence, especially when it came to dealing with the estimable "generalized" risks of industrial and other business activities. But, Holmes stressed, this was because these rules fully comported with the foresight requirement.

The compensation side of Holmes's attack on the functional rationality of cause-based strict liability was centered mainly on its incapacity to provide social insurance for unforeseeable risks. If the state, despite its perpetual and captive pool of taxpayers, apparently considered it unwise to establish "a mutual insurance company against accidents," he argued, then surely it was incomprehensible that tort could sensibly accomplish the task.[136] First-party accident insurance supplied by commercial carriers "can . . . better and more cheaply," as well as more consistently, deliver social insurance coverage of foreseeable (not to mention unforeseeable) risks, than can government bureaucracy or even higher-cost strict tort liability.[137]

Before we proceed to elaborate Holmes's reasoning, one current misconception of his argument requires correction. Inattention to context by current commentators, particularly to his unforeseeable-harm definition of accident, has resulted in the erroneous perception that Holmes denied not only cause-based strict liability but also the social insurance function entirely—that for him, as Jules Coleman asserts, "compensation could not be a goal of tort law."[138] This prevalent misconception is largely responsible for the view that Holmes opposed all forms of strict liability because he rejected its principal purpose. In fact, Holmes recognized the full spectrum of redressive as well as preventive functions and, in further demonstration of his specific opposition to cause-based strict liability, emphasized the social insurance role of *Rylands* and other foresight-based strict liability rules in industrial cases.[139] Holmes reiterated the general redressive function of tort liability throughout the lectures, most significantly as a framework for applying his foresight theory in Lecture IV to strict liability and the other two main branches: "the general purpose of the law of torts is to secure a man indemnity against certain forms of harm to person, reputation, or estate, at the hands of his neighbors, not because they are wrong, but because they are harms."[140] In subsequent restatements of his foresight theory, Holmes reaffirmed that compensation was one of the principal functions of tort liability, declaring, for example, in "Privilege, Malice and Intent," that "[a]ctions of tort are brought for temporal damage. The law recognizes temporal damage as an evil which its object is to prevent or to redress."[141]

Characteristically terse, Holmes's critique of the rationality of using cause-based strict liability for social insurance purposes presciently suggests the modern terms of the debate. With respect to the majority of ordinary cases arising from commonplace domestic, recreational, and other nonpecuniary activities, it would be plainly arbitrary to use cause-based strict liability against individual defendants as a vehicle for social insurance against unforeseeable harms.[142] Clearly, the unpredictable losses from accidents were beyond the financial means of individual defendants to absorb or spread. Most individual defendants in these cases would lack sufficient assets to satisfy the judgments, while the frightening prospect of losing everything they had would force them to forgo their preferred, socially beneficial activities. Indeed, Holmes thought that using cause-based strict liability to achieve social insurance would be equally illusory in cases of unforeseeable harm involving business defendants whose markets were too small to spread losses competitively, let alone to any degree of deconcentration resembling a system of insurance.[143]

While these arguments suggested that social insurance would not be well served by using even foresight-based strict liability in cases of ordinary activities and small business defendants, Holmes made clear that such a rule could effectively provide social insurance in suits against business defendants with relatively large markets in which to spread losses.[144] But relatively large markets do not solve the problem of providing social insurance for unpredictable risks. Business risks must be predictable if they are to be evaluated and incorporated in product and service prices to consumers at anything approaching actuarially fair premium rates. Thus Holmes doubted that even the giant industrial firms could bear the losses imposed by cause-based strict liability without running the risk of economic ruin, to the detriment of not only the owners but also employees, consumers, and society generally.

Holmes was not overlooking liability insurance in judging the practicality of cause-based strict liability. Liability insurers have great difficulty in rationally setting premiums and spreading losses for unpredictable risks.[145] But in fact, although first-party insurance was commonly available in Holmes's time to provide effective coverage for such risks,[146] liability insurance was not generally available until the early twentieth century, long after publication of the torts lectures as well as his subsequent commentaries on the subject.[147]

Holmes also saw no rational relationship between the threat of liability for unforeseeable harms and the tort system's deterrence function. Instilling "fear of punishment for causing [such] harm cannot work as a motive" because, as he reasoned, "[i]f a consequence cannot be foreseen, it cannot be avoided."[148] This did not mean, however, that behavior would be unaffected by threats of cause-based strict liability. On the contrary, Holmes saw the potential for overdeterrence of "individual activity . . . tend[ing] to the public good."[149] After noting that the law considered it unjust to impose liability where the defendant lacked the power of foresight to avoid harm, Holmes warned that there is also "obviously no policy in throwing the hazard of what is at once desirable and inevitable upon the actor."[150] Indeed, the threat of cause-based strict liability would terrorize individuals into irrationally curtailing essential activities of daily life.[151]

Holmes contended that the foresight theory eluded the deterrence pitfalls of cause-based strict liability. Conditioning liability on foresight assures defendants a reasonable opportunity to predict risks in order to prevent as well as to compensate the resulting harms. Fairness demanded no less protection of the choice to avoid harm for noncommercial and small-market business defendants who lack loss-spreading opportunities.

On the other hand, foresight clearly facilitates rational deterrence policy for industrial and other relatively large-market businesses who can spread their losses. Indeed, the foresight condition is indispensable. "[S]o far as the threats and punishments of the law are intended to deter men from bringing about various harmful results, they must be confined to cases where circumstances making the conduct dangerous were known."[152] In fact, as Holmes concluded in discussing *Rylands,* foresight-based strict liability was the rule of choice to regulate the activity and safety of industrial firms.[153]

Offense to the Sense of Justice

Cause theorists never denied that the moral condition of choice was a prerequisite for liability, but rather maintained that cause-based strict liability satisfied this requirement by attributing responsibility to the active agent of harm. As Holmes characterized their argument, cause-based strict liability redistributes losses from the "plaintiff [who] has done nothing" to "the defendant [who], on the other hand, has chosen to act."[154] This was seen as justice dictated by the causal paradigm. "As between the two, the party whose voluntary conduct has caused the damage should suffer, rather than one who has had no share in producing it."[155]

Holmes agreed with cause theorists, of course, on the starting point of their argument, but demurred from their conclusion. The causal act requirement—essentially, that the defendant's act was a but-for factor in bringing about the plaintiff's harm—was necessary to further the moral condition of choice. One cannot avoid a harmful consequence that will occur regardless of what one consciously chooses to do. But it did not follow that liability based on mere causation was "defensible as theoretically sound."[156] Causation alone was never sufficient to assure the defendant's opportunity of choice to avoid harm. Therefore, Holmes asserted, beyond its irrationality as a means of compensation and deterrence, the arbitrariness of cause-based strict liability was open to "the still graver [objection] of offending the sense of justice."[157]

Remarkably, proponents of the view that Holmes was a negligence dogmatist rely on his invocation of the "sense of justice" as proof that he "joined in the general rejection of strict liability."[158] Horwitz quotes the entire sentence from Lecture III without recognizing its obvious focus on mere causation and the implicit foresight qualification: " '*undertaking to redistribute losses simply on the ground that they resulted from the defen-*

dant's act' . . . was open to a *'still graver'* objection, that *'of offending the sense of justice.'* "[159] In the portion of the paragraph preceding the quotation, Holmes developed his policy objections to the use of cause-based strict liability as a "mutual insurance company against accidents," which Horwitz also quotes, but without mentioning Holmes's unforeseeable-harm definition of accident.[160] Holmes's objection to cause-based strict liability as unjust referred back to the paragraph (on the preceding page) beginning with the statement of the general principle against liability for accident, and concluding with the statement that the "moral element" of responsibility was foresight-informed choice to avoid harm. Indeed, Horwitz need have looked no further for what Holmes meant by foresight than the sentence immediately following the one he quoted. In it Holmes summarized his arguments from justice and functional rationality, declaring that the imposition of liability for unforeseeable harm was the moral equivalent of making individuals responsible for the unexpectable and uncontrollable vicissitudes of nature and life: "Unless my act is of a nature to threaten others, unless under the circumstances a prudent man would have foreseen the possibility of harm, it is no more justifiable to make me indemnify my neighbor against the consequences, than to make me do the same thing if I had fallen upon him in a fit, or to compel me to insure him against lightning."[161]

To show that his foresight theory rather than the causation theory explained the idea of justice implicit in the causal act requirement, Holmes again turned to the reality of multiple causation. The claim by cause theorists that the justice of choice and self-determination could be achieved wholly within the causal paradigm rested on two central assumptions: first, the equivalence of choice to act with choice to inflict the act's harmful consequences; and second, the notion that cause-based strict liability operated to correct the distributional positions of "passive" plaintiffs and "active" defendants. The pervasive fact of multiple causation rendered both assumptions fallacious.

Under the causation theory, the defendant's choice to commit a particular act makes it just to impose liability "for everything which would not have happened but for his choice at some past time."[162] But while an act "imports intention in a certain sense"—a conscious exercise of will to bring about "a muscular contraction"—this "choice" to act by itself plainly does not satisfy the moral norm of choice to avoid any and all of the act's harmful consequences.[163]

The defendant's act and the harm it causes the plaintiff are factually distinct events. "An act is always a voluntary muscular contraction, and nothing else."[164] It is separated from its harmful results by "[t]he chain of physical sequences which [the act] sets in motion or directs to the plaintiff's harm . . . and very generally a long train of such sequences intervenes."[165] Whether a particular act results in harm or not depends entirely upon contingent conditions of the "environment" of "surrounding circumstances," and whether they include intervening factors conducive of harm.[166] Because there is no essential and unique causal relationship between a particular act and its harmful consequences, the choice to act by itself does not necessarily imply a choice to cause the harmful consequences. "For instance," Holmes argued, "to crook the forefinger with a certain force is the same act whether the trigger of a pistol is next to it or not. It is only the surrounding circumstances of a pistol loaded and cocked, and of a human being in such relation to it as to be manifestly likely to be hit, that make the act a wrong."[167]

Given that "the intent necessarily accompanying the act ends there," no moral significance attaches to the mere fact that the defendant's act was willed and thereby caused harm.[168] "[W]hy need the defendant have acted at all," if not to make the responsibility for harm depend on the power of choosing to avoid it?[169] But "there is no such power where the evil cannot be foreseen."[170] It followed that since the "chance to guard against the result which has come to pass" is the premise of responsibility, then the notion of moral responsibility underpinning tort liability measured justice by the "opportunity of choice with reference to the consequence complained of."[171]

Holmes also disputed cause theorists regarding the claimed morality of favoring "passive" plaintiffs injured by "active" defendants. Cause theorists maintained that application of the rule of absolute responsibility in such cases restored and protected the plaintiff's preaccident distributional position, and thus served justice by equalizing the right of each party to live in freedom without interference by the other. By granting the plaintiff an "absolute right . . . [to be] free from detriment at the hands of his neighbors," cause-based strict liability allowed the active defendant to reap the benefits of risky activity, while insuring that the passive plaintiff would lose nothing thereby.[172]

In response, Holmes reiterated his denial of the reality of the active/passive distinction. "A man . . . must act somehow"; however quiescent the plaintiff's circumstances may appear at the moment of injury, that phase in the continuum of time can always be traced back to remote actions.[173] The reality of multiple causation belied the one-sided theoretical paradigm of an active defendant who infringes on the security of a passive plaintiff, and with it the supposed equitable balance of freedom. In the real world crowded with abutting neighbors engaged in conflicting activities, a rule of absolute responsibility that vouchsafes to one party "unrestricted enjoyment of all his possibilities" perforce "would interfere with the other equally important enjoyments on the part of his neighbors."[174] Under such circumstances, compelling defendants to bear the risk of unforeseeable harm, which they cannot spread through liability insurance or, in most cases, through the market, necessarily will inhibit them from exercising their full freedom. In contrast, plaintiffs insured by cause-based strict liability against such harm will be strongly encouraged to pursue their ends to the limits, and perhaps even further.

To avoid the multiple-cause dilemma, some current commentators argue that the causal act requirement should be given a more colloquial and less scientific meaning. Hart and Honoré are the leading advocates of this position, arguing that the law essentially incorporates "the plain man's causal notions" as to when causing harm imports responsibility.[175] Similarly, Epstein attempts to reduce the amorphous notions of everyday causal responsibility to four paradigmatic situations—A hit or frightened B, or created a dangerous condition that results in B's being hit or frightened—"which best capture the ordinary use of causal language."[176] Holmes rejected such arguments as unprincipled and contrary to the law in operation (as demonstrated by his *Thorns* hypothetical).[177] The causation theory of responsibility provides no moral ground for distinguishing between causal acts. Appeals to normal conventions, custom, directness, and the like necessarily entail consideration of facts and conceptions beyond mere causation.

Of course, this was not to say that the law disdained common and intuitive judgments; as a matter of policy discretion, courts often consulted juries to learn the community sentiment regarding the appropriate norm of behavior or scope of liability for a given class of cases. Rather, Holmes's objection to the common understanding and usage definitions of causal responsibility was that on examination, the exemplifying cases or paradigmatic situations always turned out to require or imply more than the causal act for responsibility—at a minimum, facts satisfying the condition of foresight-informed choice. This is a chief lesson of his analysis of the *Thorns* hypothetical. It is also a main point of his analysis of the classic English Trespass decisions, which showed that despite the causal rhetoric, in operation the law resolved the multiple-cause dilemma by going beyond the causal paradigm to foresight or more.[178]

Holmes concluded that in a world of multiple causation the sense of justice embraced by the law through the causal act requirement could only be served by conditioning liability on foresight. He recognized that the foresight condition placed the burden of unforeseeable loss on the plaintiff, but since the loss was initially imposed by a private act done "without the aid of the law," allowing the loss to lie where it falls does not implicate the political legitimacy of state action.[179] In contrast, tort liability represents state power in its rawest form, when it compels the defendant to pay for the plaintiff's private loss. Ultimately, Holmes sought a political theory explaining the moral legitimacy courts claim for the coercive authority of tort liability. As he stated at the outset of the torts lectures:

> [W]hen A assaults or slanders his neighbor, or converts his neighbor's property, he does a harm which he has never consented to bear, and if the law makes him pay for it, the reason for doing so must be found in some general view of the conduct which every one may fairly expect and demand from every other, whether that other has agreed to it or not.[180]

At the opening of the "Theory of Torts" section of Lecture IV, Holmes announced that the "moral standard" of foresight—that the defendant had reasonable warning of danger before acting—was the "true explanation" of the general principle of responsibility.[181] By "giv[ing] a man a fair chance to avoid doing the harm before he is held responsible for it," Holmes found that the foresight condition "reconcile[s] the policy of letting accidents lie where they fall, and the reasonable freedom of others with the protection of the individual from injury."[182]

4

General Theory of Torts
Part One

Holmes laid out the common ground of tort liability in Lecture IV, specifically in its crucial second half—virtually ignored by scholars for the last fifty years—titled "The Theory of Torts."[1] The general prerequisite for liability was reasonably foreseeable harm; this, "reduced to its lowest term," translated into the defendant's "knowledge of circumstances" accompanying the conduct in question, which "would have led a prudent man to perceive danger."[2] On this empirical basis, Holmes formulated a general theory unifying the several branches of tort liability rules. The theory posited that the principle of moral responsibility marking "the point at which a man begins to act at his own peril" was the individual's power of foresight-informed choice to avoid inflicting harm on the plaintiff.[3] Tort law embodied the following conception of moral responsibility: that it is "impolitic and unjust to make a man answerable for harm, unless he might have chosen otherwise," that is, "the choice must be made with a chance of contemplating the consequence complained of."[4]

Holmes divided his general theory of torts into two parts. The first part, to which the torts lectures were primarily devoted, consisted of his foresight theory of moral responsibility, explaining that courts excused only "accidental" harm—"accident" being a term-of-art in the lectures meaning "a [harmful] consequence which could not have been foreseen."[5] The second part, which he developed more fully in "Privilege, Malice and Intent," explained that courts exercise policy discretion in adopting justifications to allow "escapes" in a given class of cases from otherwise morally authorized responsibility for foreseeable harm.[6]

A key aim of this chapter is to show that Holmes's foresight theory of moral responsibility in tort law accommodated foresight-based strict liability. Specifically, my contention is that, contrary to the negligence-dogma thesis, the foresight condition posited by the theory encompassed any and all risks regardless of the quality of the defendant's conduct and, in particular, was not confined by any *a priori* or other conceptual limitation to the foreseeable harms of negligent conduct.[7] Much of the current confusion about the applicability of Holmes's foresight theory to strict liability results from a failure to understand the nature of his two-part general theory of torts. Therefore, in this chapter I begin by explaining his bifurcated theory and then proceed to discuss the purely empirical nature of the foresight condition, its classificatory function in providing a unifying arrangement of the three main branches of tort liability, and its rationalization of all of the major doctrines of strict liability, including *Rylands*.

The Bifurcated Theory

Holmes's two-part general theory corresponded to the classic distinction in general philosophic discourse differentiating moral responsibility (and excuse) from public policy justification. The first part was essentially a theory of political power and described the conception of moral responsibility that courts implicitly invoked to legitimate the use of liability in constraining individual freedom. Holmes determined that the threshold of moral responsibility in tort law separated *prima facie* responsibility for foreseeable harms from absolute excuse for unforeseeable "accident." In the second part of the theory, relating to justification, Holmes explained that courts exercised discretion to allow "escapes [from such *prima facie* responsibility] upon special grounds" of policy for a given class of cases.[8]

The most striking illustration of the theoretical bifurcation of responsibility and justification was presented in connection with the strict liability rule established by *Rylands*. As Holmes made clear in "The Theory of Torts" (Lect. IV), *Rylands* fully comported with the "principle which exonerates [the defendant] from accident" by imposing responsibility only for "conduct from which [a prudent and intelligent man] would have foreseen that harm was liable to follow."[9] But while courts may enforce the warrant of moral responsibility to the fullest empirical extent of foresight, they may fashion a policy justification for applying a less stringent rule such as negligence or even for denying liability altogether in any given class of cases. Because "[d]anger of harm to others is not the only thing to be considered," Holmes noted, "[t]he strictness of this principle [*Rylands*] will vary in different jurisdictions, as the balance varies between the advantages to the public and the dangers to individuals from the conduct in question."[10]

Holmes did not expressly specify the two parts of his general theory until "Privilege, Malice, and Intent" in 1894. At the outset of the article, he summed up the first part:

> When it is shown that the defendant's act has had temporal damage to the plaintiff for its consequence, the next question is whether that consequence was one which the defendant might have foreseen. If common experience has shown that some such consequence was likely to follow the act under the circumstances known to the actor, he is taken to have acted with notice, and is held liable.[11]

The main subject of the article, however, was the second part of the theory dealing with judicial policy discretion to legislate justifications in the form of affirmative defenses, absolute and conditional privileges, qualified duties, and other limitations on *prima facie* responsibility for inflicting foreseeable harm.

> To sum up, when a responsible defendant seeks to escape from liability for an act which he had noticed was likely to cause temporal damage to another, and which has caused such damage in fact, he must show a justification. . . . [I]n all such cases the ground of decision is policy; and the advantages to the community, on the one side and the other, are the only matters really entitled to be weighed.[12]

The most important justifications were privileges granted on a social cost-benefit calculus, such as the exemptions from liability for nonmalicious defamation in employment and credit recommendations to encourage frank appraisals, or for the infliction of economic harms by business competition to gain the social benefits from a free market.[13] Decisions refusing to favor labor boycotts provided a highly provocative illustration of the political element. But the crucial question of privilege concerned the choice between foresight-based strict liability and negligence: whether compliance with the external standard of due care established by the negligence rule should justify infliction of reasonably foreseeable harm.[14] In all such cases of privilege, Holmes stated, "[t]he ground of decision really comes down to a proposition of policy of rather a delicate nature concerning the merit of the particular benefit to themselves intended by the defendants, and suggests a doubt whether judges with different economic sympathies might not decide such a case differently when brought face to face with the issue."[15]

Thus Holmes's theory of responsibility encompassed foresight-based strict liability, but did not necessitate its application in any given class of cases, let alone universally. The first part of the general theory was perfectly consistent with a theory of judicial policy discretion that recognized the power of courts to regulate the scope of liability for the inexcusable infliction of foreseeable harm by applying the negligence rule or any other standard on the spectrum between foresight-based strict liability and no liability.[16] As Holmes stated, "[t]he external standard [of reasonable foresight] applied for the purpose of seeing whether the defendant had notice of the probable consequences of his act has little or nothing to do with the question of privilege. The defendant is assumed to have had notice of the probable consequences of his act, otherwise the question of privilege does not arise."[17]

The balance of this chapter considers the first part of Holmes's theory, on the nature of the foresight condition and its application to strict liability. The next chapter examines the second part of the theory, with particular reference to his policy analysis on the use of negligence and strict liability.

The Foresight Theory of Responsibility

The "starting-point" of responsibility under Holmes's foresight theory was determined solely by the empirical test of risk cognition—whether the defendant had or should have "perceive[d] danger."[18] Holmes recognized that perception of danger depended on two interrelated, factual variables. The first concerned states of mind—essentially, whether the defendant or a reasonable person representing the particular defendant class possessed sufficient experience and knowledge to appreciate the risk involved. The second variable related to states of time: when, in the course of conduct that resulted in harm to the plaintiff, did the defendant actually or reasonably first have notice of and the choice to avoid the risk? As Holmes explained in the second part of his theory, courts could modulate these variables to expand or contract the scope of liability for foreseeable harm according to the needs of public policy. While preferring that courts make policy by deliberate and open weighing of competing social interests, he did not regard the amenability of the foresight variables to covert manipulation as affecting the findings of the first part of his theory that foresight-informed choice was the basis of responsibility in tort. As I demonstrate below, that theory of responsibility embraced a pragmatic conception of the foresight variables, extending potential liability as far as the empirical limits of risk cognition and choice to avoid harm, and thus explaining the judicial claim of moral legitimacy to enforce all liability rules except absolute responsibility for accident.

States of Mind: External and Subjective

Holmes repeatedly stated that the "external standard" of reasonably foreseeable harm sufficed "to throw the risk upon the party pursuing it."[19] Consistent with his rejection of Austin's "criminal" culpability thesis was Holmes's denial that the moral justification of tort liability required subjective consciousness of risk, let alone anything approaching *mens rea*. The scope of responsibility thus broadly encompassed all cases except those involving "no apparent danger" to the reasonable person, which were classified as "mischance" or accident.[20]

What harmful consequences could reasonably be foreseen was an integral function of two purely empirical factors: first, the actual level of risk from the act or activity in question, and second, the reasonable person's capacity to perceive the risk as determined by such variables as experience, education, and acumen. Neither factor suggested limiting foresight to negligence.

In many cases, Holmes explained, courts and juries would determine whether the harm in question was reasonably foreseeable by drawing rational inferences from "the degree of danger attending given conduct under certain known circumstances."[21] No conceptual or *a priori* "degree of manifest danger" nor any preset level of severity or probability was required to support such inferences. "The possibility of a great danger," Holmes stated, "has the same effect as the probability of a less one, and the law throws the risk of the venture on the person who introduces the peril into the community."[22] Nor was the source or quality of the risk germane to satisfying the foresight condition. The issue was perceived danger pure and simple. According to Holmes's theory, the "evil" addressed by tort liability was the generic problem of "temporal damage," and "the manifest tendency of the act to cause temporal damage in general" provides a "sufficient explanation" for tort liability.[23]

Because the foresight condition required defendants to forecast the actual levels of risk from contemplated conduct, inherent in that condition was the need to make overt use of probability analysis, the "principle of averages."[24] Indeed, Holmes welcomed the increasing use by businesses of statistical data to project their risk and loss exposure. Building upon the probabilistic perspective staked out in the lectures, "The Path of the Law" boldly endorsed actuarial, statistical, and economic methods for "estimat[ing]" risks to enable use of strict liability as a means of spurring development of safety precautions and spreading non-negligent losses.[25] In so doing, Holmes deliberately and radically expanded the foresight authorization for strict liability to deter and compensate industrial injury.

Risk cognition depends not only on the actual level of risk, but also on the capacity of the "prudent man to perceive danger."[26] The main determinants of this capacity are psychological receptivity and reaction to risk signals, risk experience, and the training, technology, and intellectual ability to detect, collect, and process risk information. Designed to express cognitive reality, Holmes's external foresight standard reflected the varying risk cognition capacities of different classes of defendants.

Holmes suggested that tort in operation generally categorized these variations according to three basic models of the reasonable person. The first model described the defendant class composed of individuals afflicted by a "distinct defect," such as infancy or "manifestly incapacitating" insanity.[27] Those who exhibited such disabling traits were stereotyped as completely incapable of minimally adequate risk cognition and avoidance and, despite the fact of a willed act in most cases, were thereby excused from legal responsibility for the harms they inflicted.

The second model depicted the "average man," whose capacity to foresee harm was determined by faculties of "ordinary intelligence" and the test of "general experience."[28] Holmes explained that the "average man" was not a natural or preformed entity, but rather a compound of selective features which depicted a subclass of society and were pragmatically amalgamated to achieve the compensation and deterrence functions of tort liability.[29] With respect to activities of pronounced danger, like carrying firearms in public, foresight of the risks was virtually irrefutable.[30] But envisaged mainly as an individual rather than a business entity, the "average man" encountered ordinary risks sporadically, suddenly, and without premeditation, while engaged in conventional domestic, recreational, or small-scale business activities. Embodying only an ordinary and common level of experiential and psychological capacity to appreciate risk, the representative "average man" often would fail to perceive the small and remote risks—in Holmes's terms, "comparatively slight" though "familiar" dangers—associated with conventional activities, such as the possibility of sudden bolting while quietly riding a normally docile horse or lighting an ordinary fire in a fireplace, "having no knowledge that the fireplace was unsafely constructed."[31] Interestingly, Holmes's intuition anticipated recent studies documenting the tendency of individuals to underestimate and ignore the small, remote, and transitory hazards of daily activity, especially those comprehended only statistically rather than through vivid first-hand example.[32] Difficulties experienced by individuals today in foreseeing such risks were greatly exacerbated in Holmes's time, especially during the period in which he composed the lectures, given the limited means of collecting, communicating, evaluating, and maintaining adequate records of risk data.

While Holmes is most often associated exclusively with the reasonable person of common experience, this emphasis is due more to the prosaic and historical orientation of the lectures than to any preference on his part for this standard. In fact, the lectures plainly indicated a third model of the reasonable person, representing the class of "expert" defendants, mainly professionals and business entities, who possessed specialized cognitive powers and experience for predicting risks.[33] Given the relatively technical nature of the risks involved in many of the cases to which Holmes referred in the lectures, a foresight explanation would be credible only if specialized analytical capacity and experience were imputed to the defendants in those cases.[34] Endowed with the relevant type and level of expertise, the third model of the reasonable person was compelled "to exercise the foresight of which he is capable."[35] Holmes's later restatements of the foresight theory formally incorporated the expert model. Establishing a far-reaching warrant for applying strict liability to industrial risks, the subsequent restatements made clear that the reach of strict liability broadened under the external measure of foresight in direct proportion to specialized business or other "more than common" experience possessed by the defendant class.[36] Moreover, he noted that courts could prescribe stringent standards of foresight compelling those who contemplate engaging in particular activities to augment their knowledge of and capacities for appreciating the special risks involved, on pain of strict liability for failing.[37]

Holmes argued forcefully for the external standard of foresight, but he also emphasized two subjective elements of the foresight condition. The first related to the case where a particular defendant subjectively "foresees that harm will result from his conduct."[38] From the standpoint of responsibility for choosing to run a risk and, in particular, for preventing the external standard from creating an arbitrarily low ceiling on responsibility, subjective foresight obviously must take logical and moral precedence over objective, reasonable foresight.

> The reason one resorts to the external standard is to determine the minimum consequences which a man *must* contemplate under given circumstances. If he actually contemplates more the ground for his escape is wanting, *viz.* that as life is action a man cannot be charged for the consequences of his living beyond what in a general way might be contemplated as the result of choosing this course rather than that.[39]

An individual may gain superior foresight by happenstance or idiosyncratic circumstance or, more systematically, by virtue of special training or simply possession of above-average capacity relative to the defendant class involved. In cases where such individuals become subjectively aware of risk that the reasonable person representing the defendant class would not have contemplated, the legitimate scope of liability will expand beyond that authorized by the external standard.[40]

The second subjective aspect of the foresight condition was of even greater theoretical significance to Holmes, because it generally qualified the external character of the foresight condition. This was the prerequisite confining the finding of responsibility "to cases where circumstances making the conduct dangerous were [actually] known" by the defendant, with the question of knowledge being "a question of the actual condition of the defendant's consciousness."[41] As he concluded: "All foresight of the future, all choice with regard to any possible consequence of action, depends on what is known at the moment of choosing."[42] The extent of the reasonable person's foresight was thus extrapolated from and determined by the defendant's subjective perception of the risk-creating circumstances. If the defendant possessed no actual knowledge of such risk-enhancing circumstances, neither knowledge of those circumstances nor knowledge of the ultimate fact of their dangerous character could be attributed to the reasonable person. "The Theory of Torts" (Lecture IV) was devoted mostly to the specification of the minimum "circumstances necessary to be known [subjectively by the defendant] in any given case in order to make a man liable for the consequences of his act."[43]

In setting the bounds of danger perceived by the reasonable person, the subjective element required consideration only of what the defendant actually knew of the raw circumstances surrounding the act in question, not of whether the defendant actually appreciated their risky significance. But the effect of this "limitation[]" on the subjective element was that an individual "must find out at his peril things which a reasonable and prudent man would have inferred from the things actually known."[44] This external result of invoking the subjective requirement for responsibility was designed to prevent defendants from ignoring risky circumstances to avoid responsibility.[45] Moreover, in some cases, such as statutory rape, for example, actual knowledge of certain circumstances, which the reasonable person would regard as benign yet were cause for further investigation, would require the defendant to make such additional inquiry or suffer the consequences.[46]

Requiring the defendant's subjective knowledge of risky circumstances provided an essential cognitive bridge between the external standard of foresight by the reasonable person and the morality of individual choice to avoid harm. "[W]ithout that knowledge," Holmes argued, "[the defendant] cannot be said to have intelligently chosen to subject the community to danger."[47] Yet mere knowledge of the raw facts does not guarantee that every defendant will subjectively understand their risky import and, consequently, that all those who choose to act have actually chosen to run the risk of harm. This is particularly true for those possessing capacities for risk cognition below the mark set by the reasonable person standard for a given defendant class. The problematic nature of equating knowledge of circumstances with understanding their dangers apparently prompted Holmes to moderate his claim that liability was founded on actual informed choice by the individual defendant. Hence at certain points the lectures phrase the foresight theory in terms of constructive choice, that the subjective element of requiring actual knowledge of the risky circumstances at least affords the defendant "an opportunity of choice with reference to the consequence complained of."[48] In later phrasings of the theory, Holmes characterized the moral significance of requiring such subjective knowledge as that of assuring the defendant "reasonable warning" and "notice" of danger.[49] Ultimately, as he observed in regard to the rule against excusing ignorance of the law, "[p]ublic policy sacrifices the individual to the general good."[50]

States of Time: Proximate and Remote

Crosscutting the psychological plane of the foresight premise was a temporal one. As Holmes explained to cause theorists, the moment of causal responsibility based on foresight-informed choice is not fixed *a priori* to any "proximate" point in time relative to the injury alleged. In virtually every case, the plaintiff's injury can be referred to a more remote act and perception of danger, and the only question is whether the harm that ultimately flowed from that act was within the accompanying "picture of a future state of things."[51] The defendant's activity was thus a temporal continuum of contributing causal acts. This continuum begins with the act most remote in time from the injury, typically involving the defendant's decision of whether and where to engage in the particular activity. At the opposite end of the temporal continuum was the defendant's most proximate causal act, usually involving some aspect of performing or managing the activity. The proximate causal act is normally the last point when the defendant might, with foresight, have chosen to avoid the ensuing harmful consequences before a series of intervening "physical or irresponsible agencies" were set in motion that led inevitably to the plaintiff's injury.[52]

Holmes's foresight theory posited *prima facie* responsibility from the most remote to the most proximate act on this causal continuum, encompassing perceptions of danger in any degree of generality consistent with the morality—the sense of justice and functional rationality—of affording the defendant the choice to avoid inflicting the harm in question. As he concluded:

> The cases in which a man is treated as the responsible cause of a given harm, on the one hand, extend beyond those in which his conduct was chosen in actual contemplation of that result, and in which, therefore, he may be said to have chosen to cause that harm; and, on the other hand, they do not extend to all instances where the damages would not have happened but for some remote election on his part.[53]

The only limitation on this expansive conception of foreseeability was the empirical fact that the actual harm sued upon was so freakish that at no point along the continuum of time was it within the "class which a man of reasonable prudence could foresee."[54] In accord with the first part of the general theory, this limitation ensured the consistency of the norms of justice and functional rationality implied by the broad conception of foresight. At the same time, this encompassing conception of foresight autho-rized courts and juries to exercise wide discretion in mitigating liability as well as enlarging its domain to the farthest reaches of statistically gener-alized foresight. Holmes accounted for this discretion—including judicial use of concrete, bureaucratic rules to minimize uncertainty, inconsistency, deceptive practices, and litigation costs—under the second part of his gen-eral theory, which concerned the role of public policy in determining the scope of liability.

As Holmes explained in the lectures, the negligence rule could fulfill the entire panoply of tort functions in a large majority of cases: those involv-ing prosaic horse-and-buggy torts where relatively particular foresight of the causal mechanism of harm usually accompanied the proximate act.[55] "Ordinary cases of liability," he observed, "arise out of a choice which was the proximate cause of the harm upon which the action is founded," and where there was "a reasonable opportunity to avoid" the injury.[56] Given the commonplace nature of the risk, such proximate foresight afforded the defendant ample opportunity to take whatever risk-proportioned care might be required under the circumstances to avoid harm, and compliance with the applicable standard of care nullified all foreseeable risks of this activity.[57]

By contrast, in cases arising from industrial and other business activities it was often impossible at the moment of the proximate act to foresee the harm sued upon, or the flaw or other dangerous mechanism that created the risk of such harm. This was especially true not only of risky circum-stances arising from undiscoverable latent defects, such as the one that undermined the reservoir in *Rylands,* but also of businesses characterized by sudden and unexpected hazards, including sporadic acts of worker negligence as well as non-negligent workplace risks. Unlike some of his contemporaries, Holmes recognized the logic of, and, in many of these cases, the need for, looking "further back" from the proximate point on the temporal continuum to determine the existence of a foresight-informed choice to act.[58] A basis for liability in this context, he main-tained, might be found even at the remotest point, provided that the defendant was or ought to have been conscious of danger. In reference to the rule of strict liability for the foreseeable harms from escaping "fero-cious" animals, for example, he emphasized "the comparative remoteness of the moment of choice in the line of causation from the effect com-plained of."[59]

Whatever moment of choice was being considered as the basis of *prima facie* responsibility, remote or proximate, it was not necessary "to foresee the specific harm."[60] It was merely necessary to apprehend that "some such consequence was likely to follow the act under the circumstances known to the actor," so that the defendant could be "taken to have acted with notice."[61] Generalized foresight thus extended responsibility to the level of the entire enterprise or industry, encompassing estimable harms regardless of whether the particular harm or the causal path by which it occurred could reasonably be foreseen.[62] When it came to industrial activities—for instance, building a reservoir to power a mill—foreseeable danger of some substantial risk to person or property was essentially inherent in the undertaking from the moment of inception. Indeed, Holmes argued that the remote generalized foresight necessary to support strict liability could be presumed conclusively from the mere fact of engaging in certain activities or using certain instrumentalities, if the harm involved could be found characteristic of the activity or its instrumentality. Strict liability for the property damage done by trespassing cattle was the paradigmatic example, and Holmes traced the history of the rule's vibrant growth from its biblical codification to its modern adaptation in *Rylands*.[63] But strict liability based on generalized foresight coincident with a remote act was not confined to such cases. Although the foreseeability of an improbable type of risk could not be presumed or even inferred from engaging in a given type of activity, remote generalized foresight could still be established and used to support a *scienter*-based claim of strict liability if the defendant knew some additional fact of danger "due to the specific tendencies of the individual thing, . . . [albeit] not characteristic of the class to which it belongs."[64]

Whether the choice to engage in a given activity by itself entailed sufficient notice to warrant *prima facie* responsibility for the ensuing harm was entirely an empirical question; "[e]xperience has measured the probabilities and draws the line."[65] Yet Holmes never explained why the courts should think, for example, that trespassing on land was a generally foreseeable risk of choosing to take a walk, while the runaway horse in cases like *Gibbons* was not an expected hazard of saddling-up for a ride. To be sure, he criticized some decisions for understating the cognizable risk of activities like keeping bulls, and approved statutes bringing the law "a little nearer to actual experience."[66] But he was obviously more intent on explaining the trend in decisions than on evaluating and correcting inaccuracies in foreseeability assessments regarding the variety of activities involved in the cases. Noting the "[c]onfused" state of the law that applied strict liability when a defendant trespasses on land, but only negligence when "[h]e . . . run[s on foot] a man down in the street," Holmes commented that "hard as we may find it to arrive at any perfectly satisfactory general theory, it [the law] does distinguish in a pretty sensible way, according to the nature and degree of the different perils incident to a given situation."[67]

Holmes's acceptance of less than perfect foreseeability assessments hardly warrants the current charge that he reconciled conflicting evidence by forced interpretation of the cases or, in Howe's words, "buil[t] decisions from a general theory."[68] These critics fail to appreciate that under Holmes's two-part structure of his general theory of torts, there was no necessary conflict between the foreseeability appraisals in, for example, the land trespass and runaway horse cases. Both types of cases confirmed the predictions drawn from the first part of his theory, that courts would adopt foresight-informed choice as the threshold of moral responsibility in tort. Moreover, even if courts were deliberately understating the foreseeability of runaways, this could be explained by the second part of the theory, positing that judges often exercised policy discretion to narrow the scope of responsibility in a given class of cases through covert manipulation of the liability rules. Holmes himself noted the challenge for his theory from evidence indicating that courts and juries seemed to overstate foresight in industrial cases. In accord with the empiricism of his new jurisprudence, he held his theory "open to reconsideration" in light of this possible evidence of cause-based strict liability.[69] In the end, he retained the foresight theory because, as a matter of empirical fact, the "generalized" risks of industrial activity could be statistically "estimated."[70]

Foreseeable Harm and "Blameworthiness"

The relationship between Holmes's foresight theory and his occasional and ambiguous use of the term "blameworthy" in the torts lectures requires clarification. In Lecture II on criminal law and through roughly the first half of Lecture III, "blameworthy" denoted the general category of inexcusable conduct—the infliction of foreseeable harm for which tort made the actor *prima facie* responsible. Thus Holmes equated the harm that a defendant "might and ought to have foreseen" with the harmful conduct for which "a man of ordinary intelligence and forethought would have been to blame."[71] As he made clear in refuting the causation theory of Trespass, the only excuse from blame and hence from responsibility recognized by tort law is for the infliction of unforeseeable harm without any negligence: "[W]here a natural cause or physical factor intervenes after the act in some way not to be foreseen, and turns what seemed innocent to harm . . . [or] where such a cause or factor intervenes, unknown, at the time . . . a man is excused . . . because he is not to blame."[72] Generalizing this finding as the basis of his theory of responsibility, Holmes concluded: "Ignorance of a fact and inability to foresee a consequence have the same effect on blameworthiness. If a consequence cannot be foreseen, it cannot be avoided [and therefore has no bearing on responsibility for that consequence]."[73]

Midway in Lecture III, however, Holmes abandoned this use of blameworthiness in favor of the term "wrong," suggesting that blameworthy harms represented most but not all wrongful harms. "What the law really forbids, and the only thing it forbids," he declared, "is the act on the wrong side of the line, be that act blameworthy or otherwise."[74] Holmes made clear that the foresight basis of his theory and the inclusion of strict liability were unaffected by this change in terminology. "Wrong" was to be understood in the generic terms of foresight-based responsibility, for, as he stated, "[a]n act cannot be wrong, even when done under circumstances in which it will be hurtful, unless those circumstances are or ought to be known."[75] But he failed to clarify the factor that distinguished blameworthy from simply wrongful harms.

It might be thought that "blameworthy" cases involved infliction of foreseeable harm by negligent conduct. If this were Holmes's meaning, then it would indicate that he viewed foresight-based strict liability as having little theoretical significance, for "in general" the courts hold defendants liable "for what would be blameworthy in the prudent man . . . based on the teachings of experience as to the tendency of the act under the known circumstances."[76] Such a view, however, would conflict with his prominent and elaborate reliance on *Rylands* and the other major strict liability doctrines.

Early in "The Theory of Torts" (Lect. IV) Holmes acknowledged that the meaning and relevance of the blameworthiness characterization "has been left ambiguous" in Lecture III.[77] He explained the meaning of blameworthiness by specifying the nature of the paradigmatic nonblameworthy cases. Those cases comprised the "exceptional" class of "necessity" claims, where the foresight theory authorized strict liability and the courts went the "full length" of imposing it for the infliction of foreseeable but not blameworthy harm. Holmes's distinction between blameworthy and nonblameworthy turned on the social value (or benefit) from the foreseeable harm inflicted. Necessity cases involved individuals acting under circumstances of duress or pronounced need, for whom the infliction of harm on another provides the only practical alternative to suffering far greater loss. Holmes illustrated the point with Gilbert v. Stone, where the defendant robbed the plaintiff to avoid being murdered by third parties. While the court imposed foresight-based strict liability in *Gilbert,* he insisted that rather than signifying blame, the law approved the defendant's choice "to ransom his life as he best may."[78]

Thus Holmes's "assum[ption]" that the conduct a reasonable person would "perceive to be dangerous under the circumstances, would be blameworthy if pursued by him," meant that the usual case involved reasonable foresight of socially undesirable harm.[79] Such cases arise from non-negligent as well as negligent conduct. Generally, foresight-based strict liability applies to cases where the foreseeable harm being redressed is a socially detrimental by-product of reasonable conduct; that is, the infliction of the foreseeable harm yields no good in and of itself and only detracts from the activity's benefits. Prior to acting, the reasonable person mentally projects such harmful consequences, which "would be blameworthy *if* pursued by him." For example, as Holmes read *Rylands,* the reasonable mill owner perceived harmful consequences of a blameworthy nature from building a reservoir, including the risk of collapse and flooding of the adjacent productive mine. The blameworthy attribution is external in the sense that the defendant merely anticipated a risk of such consequences inhering in the type of activity; if the defendant in *Rylands* had known or should have known of the reservoir's "latent defect"[80] but nonetheless filled it with water, then the attribution of blame for the ensuing flood would have been subjective, and in all probability the defendant would have been charged with negligence.[81]

In referring to the nonblameworthy category of strict liability cases as "exceptional," Holmes was speaking quantitatively only. Indeed, drawing an analogy to the "mill acts," he indicated that the necessity cases provided the foundation for expansive use of foresight-based strict liability as a means of delivering just compensation for "judicial takings" to foster economic development and other social welfare objectives.[82] But he also made clear that *Rylands* was among the majority of strict liability cases involving the regrettable overhead residual cost of reasonable activity. Such activity frequently entails risks that simply cannot be eliminated by even the utmost care, and latent defects that cannot be discovered and therefore cannot be cured by reasonable precautions. In closing his discussion of the necessity cases Holmes stated that their distinctive test of mere foresight of danger would not be "considered in what follows," because all of the cases he was about to examine satisfied the tests of both manifest danger and blameworthy harm.[83] What followed was the crucial application of the foresight theory to justify all of the major rules of strict liability in force, the most important being foresight-based strict liability under the *Rylands* doctrine. To correct any misimpression left by the ambiguous reference to blameworthiness in Lecture III, Holmes explicitly classified many of the major strict liability rules—rules founded on "Policy apart from Negligence, [including] *Rylands v. Fletcher*"—under the heading of "Liability for unintended Harm . . . determined by what would be Blameworthy in average Man."[84]

Holmes never explained why the blameworthiness distinction—between undesirable and beneficial harms resulting from reasonable conduct—disappeared after the torts lectures, dissolving into the all-encompassing generic "evil" of "temporal damage."[85] He may have recognized the fallacy in applying the distinction to strict liability cases. In all strict liability cases, not merely necessity and takings cases, the creation of a residual risk is indispensable to increasing social welfare. As he noted in his discussion of *Rylands* in "The Theory of Torts" (Lect. IV): "The law allows some harms to be intentionally inflicted, and *a fortiori* some risks to be intentionally run."[86] In contrast to the harm involved in necessity and takings cases, the harm resulting from the residual risk of reasonable conduct usually does not contribute any benefit; however, its avoidance would in many if not most situations doom the beneficial enterprise, leaving society and frequently the very plaintiffs themselves worse off. If blameworthiness is determined by whether the infliction of harm itself benefits the parties and society, then the taking of a reasonable risk that results in an unproductive harm, as in *Rylands,* should be regarded equally as blameless as the outright infliction of productive harm in *Gilbert* or under the mandate of the mill acts.

Whatever the explanation, by the close of the torts lectures Holmes had virtually abandoned the blameworthiness distinction, asserting that it was "generally unimportant" for purposes of the foresight theory.[87] Reminding the reader that his theory of responsibility was foresight-informed choice, not blameworthiness, he recurred to the term "wrong" in characterizing the concept of moral responsibility which courts invoked to legitimate tort liability. As he stated, "[i]f there is danger that harm to another will follow, the act is generally wrong in the sense of the law."[88] Thus "the known tendency of the act under the known circumstances to do harm may be accepted as the general test of conduct."[89] Liability might therefore extend to redress or prevent all harms, blameworthy or not, as the law "deems it sufficient if the defendant has had reasonable warning of danger before acting."[90]

The Foresight Arrangement

One main purpose of a general theory of the moral conception unifying tort liability was to reveal the dynamic order of the system, thereby facilitating informed prediction of the future course of legal development, and reformation of that order to suit changing social values and needs. This unifying basis for "comprehensive arrangement" had eluded Holmes in "The Theory of Torts" (1873), which had merely reproduced the problem of reconciling the three branches, particularly negligence and strict liability, by relying on related but nonetheless operationally distinct subclasses of primary duties.[91] By the time he delivered the torts lectures, Holmes had determined that foresight-informed choice marked the threshold of moral responsibility for all liability in tort. Thus in "The Theory of Torts" (Lect. IV) he declared that upon this discovery of the foresight theory, "we possess a common ground of classification, and a key to the whole subject."[92] This finding of the "ultimate ground," as he stated later, made it possible to explain the operational universe of tort law not merely as a collection of "several rights and duties," but "on a principle capable of generalization—*viz.* all acts which under the circumstances known to the actor manifestly tend to produce temporal damage are actionable, unless the plaintiff is in a position when for special reasons he must take his chances or on ground of public policy the defendant is permitted knowingly to inflict the damage."[93]

To base the arrangement of torts on the actual political forces shaping the law was consistent with modern scientific theories of classification. The result was the very opposite of a formalist structure of *a priori,* logically exclusive categories. Viewing the law as the product and prophecy of an evolutionary process of gradual adjustment of constantly competing interests, Holmes stressed the interconnectedness and indeterminacy of the tort categories to make clear the inevitable and pervasive role of judicial policy discretion. Plotted out on a spectrum, the three branches of tort liability described a "philosophically continuous series" calibrated by degrees of "manifest probability of harm."[94] In general, the foresight spectrum delineated by Holmes encompassed the full empirical range of risk cognition. At one end, there was infliction of harm with a very high degree of foresight, up to and including torts that show actual intent and malice. At the other end, danger was apparent in some externalized degree. Beyond this threshold point of responsibility lay the realm of "accident."

Accident

As we have seen, Holmes designated the category of accident for cases of non-negligent unforeseeable harm, where liability would be grounded on mere causation. These were cases of "mischance," in other words, where defendants were excused from responsibility because there was "no apparent danger" of the harm sued upon, and, tested by the some-negligence doctrine, there was no negligence with respect to any foreseeable risk.[95] Holmes located rules of absolute responsibility outside the foresight spectrum in the accident category to signify that any precedent for such liability was a dry and valueless relic of evolution, which the law had long ago discarded from its moral domain of responsibility as unjust and impolitic.

Intentional Wrongs

Clustered at the end of the foresight spectrum opposite from accident were cases in which the "manifest probability of harm is very great, and the harm follows."[96] These Holmes characterized as harms "done maliciously or intentionally."[97] As such, this category encompassed both cases of intentional wrongdoing and those governed by rules of strict liability that required actual intent, subjective foresight, or a high chance of injury, but involved neither malice nor unreasonable conduct.[98] Near this pole of the spectrum were strict liability rules for entirely reasonable and praiseworthy "takings" compelled by personal necessity or social welfare.

To refute Austin's personal culpability theory, Holmes promoted his historical thesis: it was that the "law everywhere" tended "to transcend moral and reach external standards" to avoid the anarchy of individualism that would reign if the minimum threshold for responsibility required subjective foresight, let alone malice.[99] Despite their "moral phraseology," he argued, even those rules most often associated with subjective standards—such as fraud, deceit, and defamation—generally required neither malice nor any subjective state-of-mind.[100] In most cases, malice was entirely "superadded," arising by conclusive presumption from proof of mere foresight of harm.[101] The courts made foresight an alternative to malice either by explicit doctrine, or, in effect, by accepting evidence of foresight as sufficient circumstantial proof of malice. In general, Holmes emphasized, "[t]he standard of what is called intent is thus really an external standard of conduct under the known circumstances."[102]

This point was also basic to the new jurisprudence: when courts accept reasonable foresight as proof of malice, then in reality the liability rule is external, not subjective or based on malice, and should be classified accordingly. Just as he opposed converting strict liability rules into negligence by mere presumption, Holmes rejected the presumptive equation of foresight with malice or any notion of personal culpability as "only helping out a false theory by a fiction."[103] Although it may have been probative evidence of malice, the fact of reasonably foreseeable harm—or even subjective foresight—was a very far cry from irrefutable proof that the defendant's state of mind was "wicked."[104] Many motives other than malice induce people to inflict foreseeable harm, even intentionally—including the socially approved reasons of necessity or self-defense. Holmes employed the same analysis to conclude in Lecture II that the unifying basis of responsibility in criminal law was foresight of harm. By the end of the first half of Lecture IV, he could declare success both in refuting Austin's personal culpability theory and in demonstrating that the minimum threshold of responsibility in criminal and tort law was the externalized standard of foresight-informed choice.

Because the requirement of reasonable foresight represented only the minimum sufficient condition for liability and was always satisfied by subjective foresight, intent, and malice, it followed that inability of the reasonable person to foresee the harm in question—however stringent the applicable external standard—would not necessarily shield a given defendant from *prima facie* responsibility. "[W]hen he fails to exercise the foresight of which he is capable [if greater than the external standard requires], or exercises it with evil intent . . . he is answerable for the consequences."[105] Moreover, it would not affect the foresight theory if courts made greater use than Holmes had predicted of malice and other subjective standards to narrow the *prima facie* scope of liability. The first part of his general theory of torts necessarily accommodated policies calling for more stringent state-of-mind conditions, which narrowed the scope of liability to create greater protection for the defendant's freedom of choice and incentives for the resulting personal and social benefits. But the primary role of intent and malice conditions was in regulating privileges to inflict foreseeable harm, as explained by the second part of his theory concerning judicial policy discretion to allow "escapes" from *prima facie* responsibility.[106]

Significantly, these motive or purpose qualifications on privileges could also be established by circumstantial and therefore external proof, and consequently they were not confined by a requirement for such rarely available direct evidence as admissions.[107] In thus emphasizing the external character of the proof, Holmes endorsed potent regulatory enforcement of policies against abuse of privilege. His main point, however, was not concerned with the factual determination of a given defendant's purposes, but rather with showing that by distinguishing between appropriate and inappropriate motives, courts were making legislative judgments about the relative costs and benefits of general classes of social conduct and relationships. In effect, by regulating the purposes for acting, the law could prohibit a particular "use" of privilege based on what substantively was an external policy judgment, and operationally amounted to an external "qualified" privilege.[108] Moreover, by approving certain purposes for acting, courts often created an external privilege where none existed, as exemplified by the labor cases exempting employee strikes and boycotts for collective bargaining purposes from the general prohibition against concerted refusals to contract.[109]

Apparent Danger: Negligence and Strict Liability

According to Holmes's arrangement, the rules governing unintentional infliction of harm under circumstances of "apparent danger" comprised a broad spectrum between the poles of intentional infliction of harm and accident. This middle ground encompassed all applications of negligence and strict liability which required a showing of manifest probability of harm that was "not so great, but still considerable."[110] Although Holmes did not delineate the relationship between the specific negligence and strict liabilty rules in force, he indicated that for purposes of the first part of his theory the distribution would reflect relative requirements of the degree of manifest danger, and of generalized or statistical foresight.

Holmes characterized all unintentional harms on the spectrum as "harm . . . done negligently,"[111] but the context makes clear that he was using the term "negligence" to refer to the general category of liability for unintentionally inflicted foreseeable harm, which included strict liability. In his time, negligence conventionally had this premodern, state-of-mind meaning, in addition to being used as the name of the cause of action for harm from unreasonable conduct—its exclusive use in American legal argument today.[112] For example, given its foresight basis, *Rylands* was typically classified by Holmes's contemporaries under "culpa," or "negligence."[113] This culpa-negligence characterization, according to Thomas Beven, translated into a foresight-based rule of strict liability: "[i]f a man puts upon his land a new combination of materials, which he knows, or ought to know, are of a dangerous nature, then either due care will prevent injury, in which case he is liable, if injury occurs, for not taking that due care, or else no precautions will prevent injury, in which case he is liable for his original act in placing the materials upon the ground."[114] And, Beven declared, "Holmes . . . takes the same view."[115]

Holmes used "negligence" in both senses, often relying on context to indicate which meaning.[116] However, he left no doubt that his use of the term in "Privilege, Malice, and Intent" characterized all unintentional foreseeable harms to include strict liability. He explicitly affirmed that the foresight arrangement encompassed foresight-based strict liability— "[where] liability for an act depends upon its probable consequences without more."[117] No predetermined level of manifest probability of harm was required for these strict liability rules: such liability, Holmes stated, "usually is not affected by the degree of the probability if it is sufficient to give the defendant reasonable warning."[118]

Foresight-Based Strict Liability

In Lecture IV, where Holmes demonstrated that his foresight theory of responsibility unified the three principal branches of tort law, strict liability was the branch he considered first and most extensively. Yet his findings—which are summarized below—have been omitted from present-day accounts of his theory of torts. Holmes applied the foresight theory to rationalize all of the major extant rules of strict liability. These included the venerable doctrines governing defamation, trespass to land, conversion of personal property, and injury from animals, and also the important category of necessity takings. But the defining moment of the exposition occurred when he applied the theory on the basis of generalized foresight to explain *Rylands,* thus providing an intellectual foundation for the modern uses of strict liability to prevent and compensate damage from industrial and other business activities.

Defamation

According to Holmes, the law of defamation made it actionable *per se* to issue a false statement holding another in disrepute. Defamation utilized a strict liability rule because neither the *prima facie* case nor the defense turned on the facts showing the defendant's innocence or reasonableness in attempting to avoid making a false statement. Defamation buttressed Holmes's point that many rules traditionally classified as intentional wrongs were completely unrelated to moral culpability or malice, and imposed nothing more than strict liability determined by an external standard. Moreover, defamation fully demonstrated the generalized level of foresight which accommodated strict liability. Despite the usual lack of proximate knowledge that a particular derogatory statement might prove untrue, "the peril of the conduct here begins farther back."[119] Common experience of the evident risk of maligning another's character creates a remote generalized consciousness of that danger in the reasonable person. As Holmes concluded, the strict rule for defamation "falls in with the general theory, because the manifest tendency of slanderous words is to harm the person of whom they are spoken."[120]

Trespass to Land

Holmes next applied the foresight premise to justify strict liability for land trespass. This was an example of concrete or specific rules of liability, again founded on the highly generalized perception of risk derived from the mere fact of knowingly engaging in a particular activity. Strict liability for land trespass was therefore based solely on the "knowledge thus necessarily implied" from consciousness of walking in public.[121] Such knowledge put a pedestrian on reasonable notice of the danger of unauthorized entry on someone's premises. "He is thus warned, and the burden of his conduct is thrown upon himself."[122]

Conversion of Personal Property

Following the reasoning that brought trespass to land under the theory, Holmes extended the foresight explanation to strict liability for innocent conversion. The mere knowledge that one "is exercising more or less dominion over property, or that he is injuring it" provides the necessary warning of conversion.[123] This gives the law ample basis for holding that the defendant "takes the chance of how the fact [of ownership] may turn out, and if the fact is otherwise than as he supposes, he must answer for his conduct."[124]

Necessity and Takings

If there is a singular test of Holmes's commitment to extend the foresight theory to strict liability, it arises in the necessity-takings cases. Application of the foresight rationale to cases of necessity or judicial takings would undoubtedly represent comprehensive coverage of strict liability, and, consequently, a proponent of the negligence-dogma thesis might well presume that Holmes would exclude them from his theory on some *a priori,* negligence limitation. In these cases, not only have defendants acted reasonably in every respect, but their conduct and the resulting harm is considered socially beneficial and in many instances morally desirable. Nor are the defendants in the ordinary position of making marginal choices from among relatively close alternative courses of action; rather, the pressures of social and individual need generally allow the defendants no practical alternative to engaging in the risky or harmful conduct in question.

Still, Holmes determined that the foresight theory squarely applied to necessity-takings cases. Indeed, immediately after announcing discovery of the foresight theory, he used the necessity cases to demonstrate its "full length."[125] Foresight justified even so harsh a rule of strict liability as the one enforced in *Gilbert,* where the source of compulsion was not nature or society in general, but rather criminally responsible individuals. Under the foresight theory, Holmes explained, the defendant was responsible, and liability could be imposed strictly when courts exercising their policy discretion "deem[] it sufficient if the defendant has had reasonable warning of danger before acting."[126] Even though the defendant in *Gilbert* was acting under murderous threats when he robbed the plaintiff, and it was reasonable and morally justifiable for him "to ransom his life as he best may," nevertheless, given the notions of justice and functional rationality served by foresight-informed choice, it is "enough if the defendant has had a chance to avoid inflicting the harm complained of."[127] The imposition of strict liability in such cases, Holmes concluded, did not "impair[] the force of the argument in the foregoing Lecture, which only requires that people should not be made to pay for accidents which they could not have avoided."[128]

Holmes did not miss or mute the policy significance of the foresight rationale for strict liability in such necessity cases. By drawing a direct parallel between these cases and the mill acts, he underscored the implications of his theory of responsibility for the modern regulatory state. The "tax" levied by strict liability to provide just compensation legitimated both the "taking" and the judicial mode of eminent domain to promote industrial development through the transfer of property from one private party to another.

Risks to Person and Property from Animals

The longest and most consistent tradition of strict liability noted by Holmes involved cases of damage caused by animals. While they are considered of little consequence today, in his time the rules of strict liability for damage to person and property from animals were regarded as highly significant. This was so in part for practical reasons, but also because these rules provided the primary theoretical and precedential pillars of support for modern doctrines of strict liability, particularly *Rylands*.

Cases involving trespass by cattle and other farm livestock were perhaps the most important area governed by strict animal liability. As Holmes emphasized, the rule governing cattle raising demonstrated the social policy of applying strict liability not merely to nonessential activities, like a circus, but to business enterprises that were "clearly beneficial to the community."[129] Holmes evinced no difficulty bringing this strict liability rule within his foresight theory's ambit. Courts applying "good sense" rather than logic enforced strict liability in this area according to a "distinction based on experience and policy between damage which is and that which is not of a kind to be expected."[130] "Cattle generally stray and damage cultivated land when they get upon it," but "only exceptionally hurt human beings."[131] Foresight-based strict liability was thus justified for the activity of keeping cattle in regard to the palpable danger of trespass to property, but in the absence of some negligence in the face of a foreseeable risk, the law refused to impose "responsibility for damage of a kind not to be expected from such animals."[132]

Strict liability also could apply to uncharacteristic risks, which normally were too slight to be apparent from the mere fact of engaging in the activity. All that was required to warrant foresight-based strict liability was simply "another concomitant circumstance known to the party in addition to those of which the knowledge is necessarily or practically proved by his conduct. The cases which naturally suggest themselves again concern animals."[133] Holmes explained that consistent with the foresight theory, courts enforced strict liability for the remote choice to engage in the activity where the owner "knows or has notice that the particular animal kept by him has the abnormal tendency which they [animals of the type] sometimes show."[134]

In addition to the rule of strict liability for cattle trespass, Holmes used the rather exotic cases of ferocious animals which have escaped from zoos and circuses as a metaphorical vehicle for introducing and justifying application of strict liability to extra-hazardous activities. Here, the strict rule applied to the remote choice of keeping any such characteristically dangerous animals. That the "owner is liable simply on proof that he kept" such an animal was consistent with the reasonable foresight hypothesis, since the choice to engage in that type of conduct alone "necessarily imports" knowledge of the inherent risk of escape and consequent danger of personal injury.[135] "Experience has shown," Holmes explained, "that tigers and bears are alert to find means of escape, and that, if they escape, they are very certain to do harm of a serious nature."[136]

Rylands, Extra-Hazardous, and Industrial Risks

To the extent the lectures considered strict liability rules for risks from modern industrial, transportation, and urban conditions, it was largely in connection with the category of extra-hazardous activities. As noted, this category also included strict liability for the nuisances and perils of activities ranging from menageries to risks of building structures to the pastoral hazards of foraging cattle. But as a practical matter, the crucial test of Holmes's theory was undoubtedly the encompassing generalization of extra-hazardous sources based on *Rylands*. This was not only because of the controversial and hostile reception of *Rylands* by American courts, but also because the extra-hazardous classification had clear and present application to the emerging industrial sector. Nevertheless, Holmes found *Rylands* in its broadest implications—including areas where it had been rejected by English and American courts alike—as fully consistent with his theory as the ferocious animal cases.[137] Although sufficient to falsify the negligence-dogma thesis, this evidence of his support for *Rylands* has never been discussed—beyond the occasional but always obfuscatingly superficial reference—by proponents of that thesis in its nearly fifty years of existence.

In *Rylands,* as in the animal cases, it was irrelevant that all reasonable efforts had been made to discover and prevent the risk of flooding. Because experience showed that activities such as building reservoirs were fraught with danger, "[t]he period of choice was further back," and *prima facie* responsibility attached to the characteristic risks upon the mere fact of engaging in the danger-prone activity.[138] Therefore, the defendant in *Rylands* and similar cases "was bound at his peril to know that the object was a continual threat to his neighbors, and that is enough to throw the risk of the business on him."[139] In "The Path of the Law" Holmes deployed the same generalized foresight rationale, based on statistical risk "estimate[s]," to justify the application of strict liability for the hazards of industrial activity generally.[140] His foresight explanation of the strict liability rules applicable to *Rylands* and broadly to extra-hazardous activities was widely known and shared by his contemporaries.

In one of his last opinions for the Supreme Judicial Court of Massachusetts, Holmes concluded: "When knowledge of the damage done or threatened to the public is established, the strict rule of *Rylands v. Fletcher* . . . is not in question. The general principles of tort establish liability unless some special privilege can be made out."[141] The remaining questions of "special privilege," as explained by the second part of Holmes's general theory, concerned matters of public policy in determining whether strict liability would "best accomplish" the functions of compensation and deterrence.[142]

5

General Theory of Torts Part Two

The law in operation often stopped short of fully enforcing the moral warrant of foresight-based responsibility. Courts frequently recognized justifications for inflicting foreseeable harm and allowed "escapes" from responsibility for inexcusable conduct by reducing the scope of liability for a given class of cases from foresight-based strict liability to negligence, or even to no-liability. In its second part, Holmes's theory explained that such justifications—manifested in limited duties, affirmative defenses, qualified privileges, and immunities, as well as in modifications of the necessary elements for liability—represented judicial legislation. This reflects Holmes's functional view of tort liability as an instrument for achieving the public policy objectives of compensation and deterrence.

This chapter will explore Holmes's evaluation of the relative effectiveness of negligence and strict liability as means of redressing and preventing tortious injury.[1] His views on these liability standards appear only sporadically in support of his jurisprudential arguments, and must be inferred from terse statements. Nevertheless, the policy roles Holmes suggested for negligence and strict liability are consistent throughout his writings, and are both insightful and innovative.

As envisioned by Holmes, the functional relationship between strict liability and negligence was complementary, not conflicting. Holmes succinctly summarized this relationship in his first major treatment of the subject, and of *Rylands* in particular:

> The object of the law is to accomplish an external result. When it can best accomplish that result by operating on men's wills, or when it is

secure of what it desires in the absence of wilfulness or negligence, then it may very properly make wilfulness or negligence the gist of the action,—one of the necessary elements of liability. But in other instances it may be thought that this is too narrow a limit; it may be thought that titles should be protected against even innocent conversion; that persons should be indemnified, at all events, for injuries from extra-hazardous sources, in which case negligence is not an element. Public policy must determine where the line is to be drawn.[2]

Contrary to the negligence-dogma and industrial-subsidy claims, the principal role Holmes saw for strict liability was emphatically that of compensating and preventing injuries from industrial and other business activities. His analysis of these liability standards laid a comprehensive intellectual foundation for the ensuing debate over the relative merits of strict liability and negligence throughout this century.

The Negligence Rule

Negligence Failure

To understand why and when the negligence rule would prove functionally sufficient, it is convenient to begin by describing the causes of its failure. Holmes recognized two types of systematic negligence failure that occasioned judicial resort to strict liability. Both primarily involved relatively complex and technologically sophisticated activities typical of industrial and other business enterprise. The first related to process and concerned under-enforcement of the negligence rule. The second involved the substantive inability of negligence to address the residual risk of reasonable conduct—risk which cannot be avoided by compliance with the governing negligence standard, however stringent its demand for care.[3]

Because of the "limit to the nicety of inquiry which is possible in a trial," as Holmes put it, a great deal of unreasonable conduct eludes detection and prosecution under the negligence rule.[4] The chief source of such under-enforcement is the unreasonable conduct element itself. It inhibits plaintiffs from seeking tort remedies by increasing their litigation costs and burdens of proof; by imposing information barriers that prevent the injured from realizing they have grounds for suit; and by creating complicated factual issues coupled with a lack of procedures for discovering relevant evidence. These problems for plaintiffs are compounded by deficiencies of the common law trial process, including delay, uncertainty, inconsistency, fact-finder error, and the difficulty in formulating and applying the standard of care.[5]

Strict liability corrects the negligence failure of under-enforcement by eliminating the need to prove and determine the element of unreasonable conduct.[6] Of course this means imposing liability in some cases of reasonable conduct, so as to catch and deter unreasonable conduct in a number of other cases. Whether this is an expedient trade-off is entirely a matter of judicial policy discretion.

In addition to process-related costs resulting in the rule's under-enforcement, loss from risks that cannot be avoided by reasonable conduct falls by definition beyond the power of the negligence rule to compensate or deter. This functional deficiency was endemic to what Holmes labeled extra-hazardous endeavors, which reasonably, yet systematically, generate substantial amounts of such residual risks. He indicated two classes of extra-hazardous cases where this residual risk called for strict liability— latent defect and marginal cost.

The first, typified by the factual situation of *Rylands,* arises from a "latent defect" in the defendant's operating equipment or facilities, which is undiscoverable with available technology and without unreasonable expense.[7] Because the conventional negligence rule prescribes reasonable precautions to address known or knowable risks, the rule necessarily fails to reach cases where the undiscoverable nature of the hazard thwarts the application of reasonable precautions to avoid injury.

In contrast, strict liability covers the residual risk from undiscoverable latent defects, as Holmes affirmed in his theoretical justification of *Rylands.* For, while the specific mechanism of harm may be unexpected and undetectable in the particular case, and thus beyond the scope of the negligence rule, foresight-based strict liability would nevertheless apply where risk of latent defect is characteristic of the type of activity involved. This generalized foresight basis for strict liability may be derived from the particular defendant's or reasonable person's superior experience, whether with the given enterprise or industry or from public knowledge about undertakings involving comparable scale, hazardous features, complexity, novelty, or other risk-related factors. When it is known that the activity poses a "continual threat to his neighbors," Holmes stated with particular reference to *Rylands,* "it is no excuse that the defendant did not know, and could not have found out, the weak point from which the dangerous object escaped."[8] The foresight theory of responsibility thus curtails strict liability only at the margin of freak cases.[9] But to best accomplish compensation and deterrence goals in a given class of cases, courts must tailor the degree of generality in the foresight condition to the ability of the given defendant class to perceive risk.

In the second class of residual risk cases, the negligence rule fails to achieve compensation and deterrence objectives, not because the mechanism of harm is undiscoverable—it may be obvious—but rather because, on the margin, eliminating the incremental residual risk would cost more than the expected value of the loss that additional care might avoid. The negligence rule requires defendants to take precautions up to but not beyond the point of diminishing returns. In introducing the subject of strict liability in the torts lectures, Holmes referred to the possible use of that rule in cases involving the residual risk of marginal reasonable care, illustrated by claims arising from injury to bystanders from shooting in reasonable self-defense, or to property from reasonably mistaken and even well-intentioned trespass.[10]

In particular, Holmes indicated that the *Rylands* doctrine governed cases of this kind.[11] Indeed, he drew principal support for his explanation of strict liability from the strong and highly controversial endorsement of *Rylands* by Massachusetts in Shipley v. Fifty Associates (1870), which involved a claim that snow falling from the defendant's roof injured a pedestrian walking under it.[12] *Shipley* pointedly ruled the "inevitable accident" defense inapplicable to claims arising from the residual risk of marginal reasonable care. Accepting that the defendant had taken such care, and even that "nothing could prevent or guard against" the risk in question, the court nonetheless denied that such facts constituted an excuse where, as in *Shipley,* the danger was foreseeable, indeed, "well known to be frequent."[13] In holding the defendant strictly liable, *Shipley* established Massachusetts as the leading American jurisdiction to endorse *Rylands.* Later, as Chief Judge of the Massachusetts Supreme Judicial Court, Holmes was urged to overturn *Shipley* on the basis of strong criticism in other jurisdictions.[14] With characteristic terseness, he affirmed *Shipley* and its *Rylands* rule without qualification.[15]

Ordinary Cases

In Holmes's view, negligence generally governed the "great mass" of ordinary cases arising from such conventional, prosaic activities as riding horses, using fireplaces, maintaining common fences, or lifting a stick to part fighting dogs.[16] This estimate was empirical, not normative.

Negligence-dogma proponents nevertheless contend that in highlighting the prevalence of the negligence rule, Holmes was "marginalizing" strict liability.[17] Yet despite the implication of deception in their claim,[18] these commentators never dispute, and, indeed, generally agree with his estimate.[19] Even today, negligence governs the majority of cases, which are mostly automobile claims.[20] Moreover, most of these commentators never take into account the evolution of his ideas: when Holmes recognized the great increase in industrial cases, where negligence typically failed to achieve socially desired levels of compensation and deterrence, he readily revised his estimate and issued a corresponding forecast of vastly increased recourse to strict liability.

Holmes seems to have shared the general contemporary view that with respect to ordinary, horse-and-buggy type torts—torts from the "old days," as he later called them[21]—the negligence rule was not prone to failure. They were unlikely to pose systematic problems of latent defect or substantial residual risk. Indeed, enforced by an external standard, the negligence rule provided the functional equivalent in ordinary cases of foresight-based strict liability in both its administrative efficiency and its capacity to prevent or compensate the harm from all reasonably foreseeable risks. As Pollock observed: "Men at work on a building cannot well drop bricks on the passers-by without more or less carelessness, any more than the building itself will fall into the street unless it is ill-built . . . [Hence] reasonable care is sufficient for safety."[22] This operational appraisal appears to have been confirmed by subsequent experience, and it remains the general view today that "[m]ost ordinary activities can be made entirely safe by the taking of all reasonable precautions."[23]

Holmes reflected this understanding of the negligence rule in his differentiation of extra-hazardous and ordinary activities. Extra-hazardous cases called for strict liability to address the characteristic problems of remote and complex risk-avoidance decisions, latent defects, and pervasive residual risk. Negligence generally sufficed for ordinary cases because they did not pose these problems. Defendants had in these cases, Holmes noted, "a reasonable opportunity to avoid [the infliction of harm] at the time of the acts or omissions which were its proximate cause."[24] Moreover, because a simple, conventional, and all-or-nothing response prevented all foreseeable harms, the standard of due care governing ordinary cases would usually be relatively easy for courts to define and enforce, and for the average defendant to satisfy. These considerations explain Holmes's opinion in Quinn v. Crimmings, finding negligence sufficient—

and, therefore, the "more emphatic" command of strict liability in *Rylands* or of the most stringent negligence standards unnecessary—to prevent and redress foreseeable losses from the collapse of a "common fence."[25]

External Standards and Concrete Rules

Holmes's conception of the negligence rule bears no resemblance to the slack, defendant-biased doctrine portrayed in industrial-subsidy and negligence-dogma literature. His advocacy of external standards and concrete rules of negligence rationalized a comprehensive and aggressive mode of regulation.[26] While external negligence standards were widely recognized and used prior to Holmes,[27] he transformed their modern functional significance with his pathbreaking if cryptic explanation of their strict liability effect. His insight was that, beyond overcoming enforcement and substantive limitations inherent in subjective inquiries, the external negligence standard imposed a degree of strict liability on defendants who lack the capacity to satisfy that standard.[28] As such, application of the external negligence standard would deter these defendants from engaging unnecessarily in the risky activity and would compel them to pay compensation for injuries resulting from a necessary activity.

Proponents of the negligence-dogma thesis admit that Holmes's support for the strict liability effect of the external negligence standard contradicts their thesis.[29] Rather than consider the possibility that they have misread Holmes, these commentators attribute the supposed "paradox" to confusion on his part, for which they give glib and fanciful explanations. According to Horwitz, for example, Holmes's opposition to strict liability was so fervent that he sacrificed external standards by insisting on "personal fault" as the basis of tort liability.[30] Robert Rabin finesses the question with the tautological answer that Holmes "eschew[ed] consistency."[31] Holmes's motives were more sinister to Gilmore, who intimated that the external negligence standard was a cynical device designed to palliate contemporary sentiments while halting the spread of strict liability and covertly paving the way toward the ultimate goal of no industrial liability at all.[32] Of course, the "paradox" disappears upon recognition that Holmes's unifying foresight theory reconciled strict liability on a foresight basis with the external standard of negligence.

To reduce administrative cost and increase the clarity of obligations and certainty of enforcement, Holmes also argued that courts should promulgate concrete external rules that specify the policy mandate for due care in a given class of cases. These concrete rules would translate proof of certain acts into rebuttable or, in some cases, irrefutable presumptions of negligence. In formulating such concrete rules, courts might rely on their own policy judgments, or, lacking "clear views of public policy applicable to the matter," they might seek advice from juries regarding the appropriate norms of reasonable conduct—but always exercising discretion to accept or reject this advice.[33] In particular, courts might find it necessary to work out the policy questions themselves when no satisfactory or dominant standard emerged from jury verdicts, and development of concrete negligence rules would promote the functional effectiveness of tort liability.

Most current commentators make Holmes's advocacy of concrete negligence rules the butt of ridicule—"a false dream of hope," Kaplan remarks.[34] Gordon asks derisively: "How *could* anyone have thought that judgments as obviously socially and politically contingent as those about what is and is not reasonable risk-creating activity could be developed into general nondiscretionary rules of conduct?"[35] These criticisms are misguided. Far from quixotic, Holmes's conception of concrete rules of negligence has been a regular enforcement option which courts have commonly exercised under doctrines like *res ipsa loquitur,* negligence *per se,* and breach of professional, industry-wide, and other market-generated customs.[36] Aside from insuperable problems of fraud and cost in deciding cases on subjective and ad hoc grounds, Holmes recognized that more or less specific and concrete external rules were inevitable, as much because of judges determining the legal sufficiency of a given set of facts, as because of lawyers advising clients on predictions of similar future rulings.[37]

Also indicative of the misconceived and unrealistic basis of the criticism is Gordon's characterization of Holmes's concrete rules as "nondiscretionary." In the first place, rules mandating specific safety precautions might sometimes be necessary to achieve functional objectives. Exacting bureaucratic rules not only would avoid the costs and capriciousness of case-by-case decision-making, but, with the addition of collateral, punitive sanctions, could make certain undesirable conduct prohibitively expensive. For Holmes, indeed, a principal objective for concrete external standards was the social welfare benefits from the "strict liability effect" of overriding situational variables. In the second place, concrete standards usually would not entail prohibitory consequences, and, therefore, would effectively make the choice to engage in the regulated conduct a matter of discretion, "an option at a certain price."[38] Moreover, there is no evidence that Holmes ignored the effects of using concrete rules to govern changing and varied behavior patterns. He was well aware that the costs of using concrete rules might outweigh advantages in areas where skills and technology were "rapidly changing, as, for instance, in some questions of medical treatment."[39] It is difficult to say whether he was mistaken in estimating that such cases were the "exception," given the continuing prevalence of ordinary cases, particularly automobile collisions where concrete rules abound.

Enhanced Negligence Rules

Holmes and his contemporaries recognized that extra-hazardous cases arising from industrial and other business activities were not ordinary, and posed the problem of systematic negligence failure.[40] Far from using the law to subsidize industry, jurists—although perhaps not fully appreciating the magnitude of the problem at the start—consistently advocated procedural and substantive enhancements of the negligence rule to overcome its failings in industrial cases.

Most leading commentators of the day thought that with enhanced potency, the modern negligence rule could replace foresight-based strict liability—as epitomized by *Rylands*—in meeting the challenge of industrial hazards.[41] "Few cases are likely to arise in which a railroad company would escape to-day," according to Thayer, "except where the accident was caused by the unforeseeable intervention of some natural force or human being. Yet those are the very things which excuse him also under *Rylands v. Fletcher.*"[42] Thayer recognized that mandating strict liability to insure against residual risk would not necessarily bestow distributional benefits on the consumer, who "pays those bills in the end, especially in the days of liability insurance."[43] Smith reflected a broad consensus in concluding that "[a]t the present time [*Rylands*] is generally unnecessary . . . in order to do justice to a plaintiff."[44]

Holmes's conception of external standards and concrete rules, particularly under the doctrine of *res ipsa loquitur,* supplied the central mechanism for efforts by his contemporaries to enhance the scope of the negligence rule.[45] They understood and embraced not only Holmes's policy arguments touting the increased administrative efficiency and the certainty of enforcement of external and concrete norms of due care, but also his innovative insight that the resulting strict liability effect provided additional compensation and deterrence benefits. Applying such standards, moreover, would overcome problems of uncertain and selective—often "feeble"—enforcement that plagued strict liability because of the indeterminate "line between the danger which calls for care and the 'extra' hazard."[46] Indeed, it was widely believed that this restructuring alone would leave nothing but a theoretical gap between strict liability and negligence. When implemented through external standards and concrete rules such as those authorized under "the law of nuisance, and the presumption expressed by *res ipsa loquitur*," Pollock concluded, "[negligence] would have sufficed to give a simpler and more uniform rule adequate for all practical purposes."[47]

But Pollock and others proposed even more sweeping enhancements for the negligence rule, including many that remain controversial to this day. For example, they endorsed use of the most stringent standards of care to address industrial risks.[48] Many opposed the rigid, three-degree structure of due care—gross, ordinary, and slight—which could lead courts to choose a standard that was too low to avoid one that was too high.[49] The preferable approach, according to commentators like Pollock, was for courts to treat due care as a continuous variable and set the level of precautions directly in proportion to the heightened risk posed by the type of activity involved.[50] In addition to presumptive negligence rules, reformers favored switching to defendants the burden of proving compliance with the applicable negligence standard.[51] They also urged courts and legislatures to revoke defenses based on presumptions that workers assumed the risks of co-worker ("fellow-servant") and even employer negligence, and to restrict contributory negligence to cases where the plaintiff's natural instincts of self-preservation could not be counted upon and where the plaintiff's unreasonable conduct negated the defendant's negligence as a but-for cause of injury.[52] Among the most far-reaching reforms was Pollock's extension of vicarious liability beyond traditional employment boundaries to encompass "servants, contractors, or others."[53]

Holmes favored the various proposals for enhancing the negligence rule to address industrial risks (although he never joined his contemporaries—nor did they ever claim his support—in promoting these reforms as sufficient to preclude resort to strict liability). Application of the external standards and concrete rules he advocated, especially *res ipsa loquitur*, would dramatically shift the practical weight of evidentiary burdens in favor of plaintiffs. Holmes also endorsed heightening reasonable care requirements on a risk-proportioned basis.[54] He approved converting assumption of the risk into contributory negligence, and limiting the latter to cases where additional legal incentives were required to control plain-tiff risk-taking—especially those cases involving property damage—and where the plaintiff's negligence supplanted the causal contribution from the defendant's negligence.[55] His foresight rationale of proximate cause overcame the "direct causation" test, which courts manipulated to erect the greatest barriers against extending liability to industrial defendants.[56] Moreover, Holmes approved the use of vicarious liability (covering inde-pendent contractors as well as employees) in the industrial context, where the firms could not only predict agent negligence, but also effectively police agent care-taking and adjust prices to spread the added burden of liabil-ity.[57]

By deliberately remodeling the negligence rule to meet the needs of the industrial age, Holmes and his contemporaries proved that the common law evolved through a process of instrumental policy adaptations to changing social conditions and values.[58] Holmes joined with his contem-poraries in admiration for the theoretical and technological feats of mod-ern science in the late nineteenth and early twentieth centuries. They saw science poised to take charge over destiny, and regarded their efforts to enhance the negligence rule as consonant with this spirit. The potential of enhanced negligence rules to control industrial risk lay in their capacity to harness the inexorable and increasing power of science to detect, unravel, and master the hazards of life.

Strict Liability
New Industrial Risks

Although Holmes supported reforming the negligence rule to make it a more potent regulatory instrument, from the beginning he doubted that enhanced negligence rules could adequately deal with the demands of new and increasing industrial risks. The question was empirical; experience determined the efficacy of enhanced negligence rules. Recognizing the dimensions of the problem, he promoted greater use of *Rylands* and other strict liability rules to overcome the failures of negligence in industrial injury cases. Even risk-proportioned or presumptive negligence rules would be costly to enforce, especially compared to the administrative effi-ciencies of concrete rules of strict liability. Moreover, unless enhanced neg-ligence rules were simply strict liability labeled "negligence," they would be defeated by cases of latent defect and would fail to keep pace with rapidly advancing technology. Conversely, while the world waited for technological advances, they could entail substantial residual risks from marginal reasonable care.

Holmes's estimate of the volume of negligence failure in industrial cases and the corresponding need for strict liability increased substantially over time. Through the torts lectures he portrayed an accident world dominated by ordinary cases where conventional—and, certainly, enhanced—negligence rules would prevent or compensate all foreseeable harm. In this picture, industrial risks calling for strict liability represented a relatively small percentage of cases. Outside of *Rylands* and the occasional mention of railroads, industrial activities were not described in his writings, but were classified generically as extra-hazardous sources. His references to other business-related risks were confined to such small-scale and preindustrial hazards as cattle trespass and tigers escaping from a circus or zoo.[59]

Whether Holmes's early estimates misperceived the importance of industrial cases remains an open question. When he was preparing the torts lectures, the rapid increase in industrial injuries (mostly from railroads) had just begun, and such injuries still accounted for a minority of tort claims.[60] Moreover, it is doubtful that the most astute observer—even with the advantages of present day record-keeping, statistical methods, and communications technology—would have immediately recognized the historically unparalleled pace of change and the extent to which rapid industrialization necessitated rethinking of even relatively new ideas.[61]

In the short space of two decades, between 1870 and 1890, burgeoning industrial risks led to a major change of perception and reality regarding the nature of accidents and the corresponding need for strict liability. Traditionally geared for handling ordinary cases arising from sporadic and more or less spontaneous interactions between individuals, centuries-old tort law had to be reinvented virtually overnight to address the needs of industrial society. This required a totally new and highly sophisticated understanding of accidents as the result of mass-produced risks—"[ ]generalized torts," in Holmes's terms—that not only threatened an unprecedented amount of injury, but also generated latent defects and residual risks which systematically defeated the negligence rule and demanded resort to strict liability.

While Holmes possessed a sophisticated if theoretical understanding of the relative effects of tort rules in ordinary and extra-hazardous type cases, he was far from being the most astute observer of contemporary social trends, and he may have been slow to appreciate the nature and extent of the new demands that industrialization was making on the torts system.[62] This was partly due to the historical and philosophic cast of most of his scholarly work. As he reminded readers, "[t]heory is my subject, not practical details."[63] Holmes acknowledged the skew of his concerns, admitting that he knew "nothing about politics and live questions, as of necessity [being] wholly buried in dead ones for some time to come."[64] Indeed, he believed that concentrating on specific applications would have been counterproductive, diverting attention and energy from his theoretical objectives to demonstrate the evolutionary interconnectedness of seemingly diverse liability rules and to generalize and unify them. Moreover, the intensity and hurried pace of his theoretical research and writing program during the 1870s left little time for keeping track of new developments in torts, let alone for studying current events. These pressures were magnified by the demands of preparing *The Common Law* lectures for delivery and publication.[65] Seeing the lectures as his last main chance for intellectual achievement and recognition, Holmes retreated into obsessive seclusion to complete the work—a period he horrifically recalled as "a black gulf of solitude more isolating than that which surrounds the dying man."[66]

Whatever the state of his knowledge of the changing nature of accidents, Holmes's functional, empirical approach was fully capable of expanding the role of strict liability to accommodate new industrial risks. When he recognized the changes brought on by industrialization, he did not hesitate to adjust his estimate of both the source and nature of accidents and the corresponding need for strict liability. By the time he wrote "The Path of the Law," Holmes went further than merely acknowledging the enormous increase in industrial injuries and the failure of negligence to address them. He argued, perhaps even more strongly than the data warranted, that the ordinary cases "of isolated, ungeneralized wrongs, assaults, slanders, and the like" no longer comprised the majority, and concluded that judicial policy must address "the torts with which our courts are kept busy to-day [which] are mainly the incidents of certain well known businesses. They are injuries to person or property by railroads, factories, and the like."[67]

The complexity of these industrial activities and the prevalence of residual risk despite reasonable conduct meant that negligence tests would often fail to deter and to compensate. Hence Holmes advocated greatly expanding strict liability for industrial injuries. These were not academic musings; he was fully prepared to put his theory into action. Indeed, in the

Arizona Employer Liability Cases, Supreme Court Justice Holmes enthu-
siastically endorsed strict liability for industrial workplace injuries as not
simply a constitutional, but also a "just" and "reasonable" solution dictated by modern social policy.[68]

Strict liability, in Holmes's view, provided a comprehensive comple-
ment to negligence, so that the regulatory scope of tort law—according to
his epigram of constitutional license for state police power—"may begin
where an evil begins."[69] The "evil" tort sought to redress and prevent was
"temporal damage." This broad mandate necessarily encompassed risks
and harms beyond the reach of the negligence rule; hence the need for
strict liability. As indicated earlier, the negligence rule fell short, not only
because of practical impediments to effective enforcement, but also
because it was conceptually limited to risks and harms from unreasonable
conduct. Holmes consistently affirmed that strict liability could fill the
compensation and deterrence gaps left by negligence, without limit as to
source, severity, or type (personal or property) of harm.

Compensation

Holmes approved strict liability for the full range of tort compensation
goals. These, in current terminology, included corrective justice, just compensation, and social insurance. Although he never used the phrase "corrective justice," it was clear to him that in redressing injury to a plaintiff's
person or property the law may reflect a precept of individual moral entitlement. As such, the law guaranteed absolute protection against any
infringement of such entitlements by compelling the offender to "restore
the injured party to his former situation, or to another equally good."[70]
Thus Holmes endorsed strict liability, for example, when it was "thought
that titles should be protected against even innocent conversion," and,
more broadly, that losses from extra-hazardous activities "should be
indemnified, at all events."[71] Of course, to Holmes, such precepts were
not a priori natural rights, inductive truths, or their logical corollaries, but
judicial expressions of social, positive moralities—equivalents of the
"can't helps" composing his personal code of moral preferences.

Holmes's compensation rationalizations of strict liability also suggested
notions of just compensation. The idea of just compensation evoked individual rights, but without necessary recourse to postulates of absolute
morality. Just compensation, as he indicated by references to necessity
cases and the mill acts, could be predicated on a variety of grounds of

distributive equity and expedience that were primarily concerned with redressing losses from "takings." The basic principle behind the imposition of strict liability for these purposes was the following: "there is no reason why he [the defendant, representing the class of beneficiaries] should be allowed to intentionally and permanently transfer his misfortunes [costs, in modern terms] to the shoulders of his neighbors."[72] Providing just compensation through strict liability thus operated as a tax on socially productive activity, which created appropriate incentives to maximize gains from that activity. At the same time, strict liability safeguarded the welfare and reasonable expectations of those it harmed, at least by assuring that no individual or group would benefit at the expense of another.

By linking the necessity cases to the mill acts, Holmes projected a modern and expansive use of the just compensation rationale of strict liability to legitimate investing industry with what was, in effect, a common law power of eminent domain to promote social welfare.[73] These statutes focused debate over the political legitimacy of using the state's traditional executive authority of eminent domain to promote economic development by transferring property from one private owner to another. Broad political and intellectual acceptance of the just compensation rationale ultimately resolved this question. Importing this eminent domain policy into tort, Holmes transformed the meaning of liability in cases where inflicting harm was necessary to produce greater benefits. Just as it was applied under the mill acts, the compensation requirement in tort imputes no blame to the defendant, but rather signifies that society "approves and encourages" the taking effected.[74] Holmes thus placed strict liability securely within the consensus symbolized by the mill acts, justifying takings in the name of social necessity.[75]

In addition to its role in achieving corrective justice and just compensation, strict liability was seen by Holmes as an instrument of social insurance against personal injury as well as property damage, especially to cover the residual risks from industrial and other business enterprise.[76] His arguments for strict liability in this role reflect both the utilitarian prescription to abate risk aversion and the distributive justice impulse to deconcentrate the incidence of loss. Adopting this reasoning, Justice Holmes vigorously sustained Arizona tort legislation mandating a broad strict liability rule protecting employees in dangerous workplaces. He derided the dissenters' attempt to portray negligence as the foundation of constitutional as well as common law; it was the basis of neither.[77] Not surprisingly, Holmes raised no objection to the dissenters' charge that his support for strict liability imposed "a kind of taxation."[78] He concluded with a general declaration of social insurance policy often repeated (without attribution) by the leading advocates of strict liability in this century:

> It is reasonable that the public should pay the whole cost of producing what it wants and a part of that cost is the pain and mutilation incident to production. By throwing that loss upon the employer in the first instance we throw it upon the public in the long run and that is just.[79]

Deterrence

Holmes also stressed that tort law had a deterrence function. He indicated that in many types of cases, especially those arising from industrial activities, strict liability would more likely achieve the desired deterrence goals—including the modern preventive objective of minimizing the total costs of injury, precautions, and public administration—than would the negligence rule. Holmes did not share the view of some of his contemporaries that strict liability, even when based on foresight, necessarily over-deterred productive enterprise.[80] Rather, because employers' most cost-efficient strategy is to prevent unreasonable risks and compensate the harm from residual risks, they will invest in safety up to but not beyond the point of diminishing returns in reduced injury costs.

Recognizing the effectiveness of strict liability as a deterrence measure, Holmes concluded in the torts lectures—relying mainly on *Rylands*—that when negligence failed at this task, "the safest way to secure care is to throw the risk upon the person who decides what precautions shall be taken."[81] Decades later, upholding the Arizona tort legislation, Holmes reiterated the deterrence function of strict liability: "There is no more certain way of securing attention to the safety of the men . . . than by holding the employer liable for accidents . . . [T]hey probably will happen a good deal less often when the employer knows that he must answer for them if they do."[82] Though characteristically spare, Holmes's formulations and application of them to various types of activities indicate that he recognized and innovated a variety of deterrence uses for strict liability.

For example, Holmes advanced strict liability as a remedy for under-enforcement of the negligence rule. Such under-enforcement tempts potential defendants, particularly business planners, to skimp on safety investments. The inability of courts to keep their standards of reasonable conduct current with new information and technology further erodes incentives to make necessary investments. Courts are hampered by the costs and complexity of defining safety standards for modern and rapidly changing industrial conditions, as well as by industry's desire to control or conceal information regarding potential safety improvements. Strict liability closes these enforcement gaps. Because it reduces litigation costs, proof difficulties, and other burdens that hamper enforcement of the negligence rule, strict liability bolsters deterrence by appropriately increasing the probability and severity of sanctions against unreasonable conduct. To further enhance the economies and certainty of enforcement, Holmes advocated formulation of concrete rules specifying certain foreseeably dangerous activities that would be subject to strict liability. "Escaping dangerous things"—the doctrine applied to reservoirs of water by *Rylands*—epitomized the type of concrete foresight-based strict liability rule Holmes had in mind.[83] Concomitantly, because it does not require courts to evaluate the quality of the defendants' conduct, strict liability circumvents the negligence pitfall of obsolete safety standards which have been outpaced by technological advances. Indeed, strict liability not only avoids locking in outmoded precautions, but also constantly pressures industry to research, develop, and adopt new and more effective safeguards.

Another deterrence benefit Holmes saw in strict liability is that it creates incentives of reasonable conduct not only in choosing safety precautions, but also in deciding how much risky activity to undertake. In many types of cases enforcing the negligence rule, courts confine themselves to the question of safety precautions—the level of care—and fail to scrutinize, or simply presume, the reasonableness of the level of activity—the frequency and intensity with which defendants engage in risky behavior.[84] Judicial reluctance to tackle this question is understandable, since it entails a complicated evaluation weighing the benefits from various levels of the defendant's activity against the costs from corresponding levels of care and resulting risks. Yet ignoring the complications jeopardizes deterrence. Because defendants have no legal incentive to moderate their behavior, they will choose the level of activity that yields the greatest absolute benefit regardless of the corresponding increase in accident costs, rather than the greatest net benefit after taking account of such costs.[85]

Holmes perceived the failure of negligence, even as implemented through external standards, to address directly and adequately the activity level question.[86] To rectify the problem, he suggested resort to strict liability. Just as it deters under-investment in care, strict liability prevents excessive engagement in risky activity by forcing defendants to pay the marginal injury costs associated with their various choices. Holmes indicated that strict liability could be used to control activity levels of industrial and other innovative technologies in which conventional substitutes with well-established safety records were available. In cases arising from activities that pose a high degree of residual risk, he advocated strict liability regardless of the availability of close substitutes, in order, for example, to curtail "the danger to the public of the growing habit of carrying deadly weapons."[87] Moreover, as Holmes pointed out, applying strict liability to affect activity levels also serves to assure a net social benefit from the defendant's enterprise or from the entire industry. The threat of strict liability spurs industrial expertise to devise the most efficacious balance of benefits and costs and to submit the result to a public referendum in the marketplace. Thus the "success" of a business under strict liability "means that the public . . . care[s] enough for it to . . . pay its expenses and something more."[88]

Policy Limits to Strict Liability

Holmes's approach contained innovative policy arguments for applying strict liability to compensate and deter industrial losses. Because the rule fostered competition by requiring that all firms in the same and related industries pay and price their own way in the market, strict liability was not antithetical to industrial development. Indeed, the just-compensation rationale that Holmes advocated for strict liability provided intellectual and political legitimacy for industrial takings. But there was no hard and fast dogma in Holmes's stance; the choice among liability rules was completely open to social policy analysis. Function and fact rather than conceptualizations and logical extrapolation determined the respective roles of strict liability and negligence.

From this perspective, Holmes viewed strict liability as only one of an array of liability rules by which courts serve the compensation and deterrence functions. Strict liability was available to remedy negligence failure, but the application of that remedy depended on the nature of the class of cases or activities involved.[89] Courts make their selection by a functional assessment of the relative benefits and costs of the various rule options. Foreseeability of harm was a crucial policy factor bearing on this choice, but Holmes also indicated the importance of several other policy considerations which might limit resort to strict liability.

Absence of Liability Insurance

A chief constraint on the use of strict liability was the lack of liability insurance. Liability insurance, unknown until near the very end of the last century, was pivotal in bringing about the expansion of strict liability for business risks in this century.[90] Although he never mentioned liability insurance as such, Holmes seems to have been acutely aware of the effect its absence had on the functional usefulness of strict liability, and the relative advantages of negligence.[91]

The adequacy of strict liability to promote compensation and deterrence is largely determined by the defendant's ability to spread losses. Without liability insurance or other means of rationally distributing the burdens of strict liability, the "immediate working" of a damage judgment would effect "simply a redistribution of an existing loss between two individuals," often impoverishing one to reimburse the other.[92] As a means of social insurance, strict liability was not only expensive and often futile, but also generally unnecessary, since plaintiffs could spread their losses more cheaply and effectively through first-party accident insurance.[93] Moreover, fearing the strict liability burden of concentrated loss, risk-averse defendants without liability insurance would refrain from engaging in productive activity, to their own and society's detriment.

In view of the obvious and crucial importance of liability insurance in the history of strict liability, it is astonishing that its unavailability in the last century has been largely ignored by such leading modern legal historians as Friedman and Horwitz.[94] Certainly, instead of leaping to specious ideological and materialist interpretations such as the negligence-dogma and industrial-subsidy theses, those appraising the (presumed) nineteenth-century resistance to strict liability and preference for lax negligence standards should take account of the social facts, particularly those which, like the lack of liability insurance, delimited the practical choices available to the people at the time.

For Holmes, the question of whether the lack of liability insurance constrained recourse to strict liability depended on the defendant's access to a substantially equivalent means of loss and risk spreading. Lack of liability insurance therefore explains his apparent concerns in the torts lectures about applying strict liability in ordinary cases involving individual defendants engaged in conventional domestic and recreational activities. Because of the noncommercial nature of their activities, these individuals would typically have no practical means of spreading their losses.[95] The threat of enforcing strict liability against such individuals—which typically involved executing judgment against their homes and other family assets and mortgaging their future—created paralyzing fear among potential defendants, while providing little or no social insurance to accident victims.

Strict liability also poses problems for small-scale local business defendants—often individual owners and operators—whose markets are not big or rich enough to absorb the costs of liability in any degree approaching liability insurance.[96] For this reason, Holmes criticized courts for indiscriminate use of vicarious liability and uncritical application of strict liability to common carriers, especially in cases of commercial property damage. Judges were blindly and incorrectly assuming that business defendants as a class are always better able to bear accident losses than plaintiffs (frequently businesses themselves, as in common carrier and cattle trespass cases).

As Holmes observed, however, the unavailability of liability insurance presented no necessary obstacles to applying strict liability against industrial, large-scale, or other businesses whose markets adequately facilitated loss spreading. In such cases the cost of strict liability "sooner or later goes into the price paid by the public,"[97] with virtually the same salutary results as liability insurance. "The public really pays the damages," he concluded, "and the question of liability . . . is really the question how far it is desirable that the public should insure the safety of those whose work it uses."[98]

Economic Development That Benefits Risk-Bearers

Holmes recognized that policy inclination might lead courts to temper the use of strict liability against business defendants, not only to reduce risk aversion resulting from the inability to spread losses, but more broadly to promote productive enterprise. But there was no suggestion even here of curtailing strict liability to "subsidize" industry, in the sense of making some better off at the expense of others. As he indicated, courts could moderate strict liability where an activity yielded a high ratio of public benefits to individual risks, and, by implication, the classes of beneficiaries and residual risk-bearers were largely overlapping.[99] In such cases, cheaper first-party insurance could cover the residual risk, and the net price reduction for the goods in question would increase the welfare of all consumers, especially disadvantaged groups, which gained greater access to the goods and benefited the most from increases in marginal income.

Powerful negligence standards would police levels of care and, depending on the degree of externality in the court-established norm of reasonableness (relative to a given individual's capabilities), would induce socially appropriate adjustments in activity levels. But special reasons would still continue to warrant strict liability, for example, to provide just compensation in "taking" cases, where certain individuals or subgroups bore a disproportionate burden of the residual risk that deprived them of the "average reciprocity of advantage."

A frequent refrain in the industrial-subsidy literature is that in addition to underwriting industry, the "transformation" of tort from strict liability (presumably cause-based) to a lax negligence standard inequitably redistributed the burden of residual risk from business defendants who were equipped to bear it to individuals at risk who were not. While the undefined, uncritical, and empirically unsupported nature of the industrial-subsidy claim has been demonstrated by a number of commentators, none has challenged its redistributive supposition, that replacing strict liability with negligence would prejudice workers, consumers, and third-parties. As Holmes's analysis indicated, however, the distributional consequences would not necessarily favor industry—that is, the class of principal capital investors—at the expense of less advantaged classes. In many cases, the price increases entailed by strict liability threatened the perverse consequence of imposing what would amount to a regressive tax on those classes.[100] Indiscriminate use of strict liability would inflate prices in small and less affluent markets, and exclude low-income consumers from access to certain needed goods and services.[101] Further, plaintiffs had access to first-party insurance that generally was cheaper than "tort insurance," whatever the spreading capabilities of the defendant's market, especially given that tort also required the purchase of insurance against nonpecuniary losses.[102] Of course, the absence of liability insurance exacerbated the regressive character of such tort insurance.

Market Allocation of Risks and Benefits

In many cases arising out of a contractual context, the market may be more proficient than the courts in determining which party—seller or buyer—is in a better position, given information and bargaining costs, to obtain the least expensive insurance coverage.[103] In competitive markets, sellers would offer insurance coverage or warranties against loss when it would be cheaper for consumers than buying first-party policies. This was

Holmes's reasoning in urging discriminating use of strict liability against common carriers for social insurance purposes.[104] From his point of view, a key consideration favoring strict liability would be the existence of a market defect that denied the "equality of position between the parties in which liberty of contract begins," or of corporate size or other factors that jeopardized the public interest.[105]

Joint-Care Objective

Holmes recognized that strict liability might not be desirable when the plaintiff's conduct contributes to the risk of accident. Because strict liability insures plaintiffs against accident loss even if they make no effort to avoid it, they have no legal incentives to behave reasonably. Indeed, strict liability invites the "moral hazard" of plaintiffs engaging in risky behavior to collect tort insurance. In certain cases, therefore, strict liability may be less effective than negligence or other rules that induce reasonable conduct in both parties.[106]

Holmes also suggested two practical limitations on the joint-care rationale for denying strict liability. First, the joint-care objective should prevail only when plaintiffs are sufficiently informed and able to control the risks, as well as sufficiently conscious of the legal consequences of unreasonable conduct to have the appropriate incentives.[107] This limit approximates what in modern parlance is known as "cheapest cost avoider" analysis.[108] Such considerations of relative expertise in predicting and minimizing undue risk are reflected in Holmes's approval of strict employer liability for worker injuries.[109]

Second, given the individual's natural instinct for self-preservation, there is little need in cases of personal injury for legal incentives to induce reasonable conduct, let alone deflect moral hazard from plaintiffs. In the property damage case of *LeRoy Fibre Co.*, which presented a claim for fire damage to crops ignited by sparks from the defendant's locomotive, Justice Holmes advocated a contributory negligence defense to deter plaintiffs from deliberately exploiting the defendant's negligence by increasing the risk of property loss.[110] But he qualified the defense to operate only in cases where the plaintiff's contributory negligence completely negated the defendant's negligent contribution to the risk.

In *The Costs of Accidents,* Guido Calabresi portrays Holmes as a negligence-dogmatist, a portrayal that gives the author a dramatic platform for pointing out the "invalid premises" of the arguments against strict liability.[111] Calabresi finds that the opposition to strict liability, personified by Holmes, chiefly errs by ignoring the problems of cost and under-enforcement that plague the negligence rule, and also the deterrence benefits of allocating residual risk to the "cheaper cost avoider."[112] "[T]he best answer to Holmes," Calabresi concludes, is that there are many areas in torts where strict liability effectively reduces "the sum of the costs of accidents and their avoidance," the most obvious example being "ultrahazardous activities."[113] Like many leading commentators today, Calabresi fails to recognize that Holmes anticipated all of these deterrence rationales for strict liability, and, indeed, identified the paradigmatic cases for its application by his classification of "extra-hazardous sources." The next chapter investigates this virtual disappearance from history of Holmes's intellectual legacy to strict liability in torts.

6

Holmes in History

It is enlightening to trace the history of the way in which Holmes's theory of torts, and especially his views on strict liability, have been perceived. In particular, much can be learned from comparing the understanding among Holmes's contemporaries and immediate successors before 1950 to the current (post-1950) interpretation that characterizes Holmes as a dogmatic proponent of a universal negligence rule. This chapter begins by examining the recorded consensus of Holmes's contemporaries during the roughly sixty-year span of his scholarly and judicial career. Analysis of this record overwhelmingly confirms the view that he supported strict liability, and especially the *Rylands* rule for extra-hazardous or industrial risks. A further gauge of the clarity and strength of that support is provided by a comparison of Holmes's writings with those of his contemporaries, which serves to authenticate the meaning of his terminology and concepts and to sharpen the contrast between his views and those of opponents to *Rylands*. This evidence not only impugns the negligence-dogma interpretation, but more broadly also undermines the industrial-subsidy thesis. The next section explores the origins of the current negligence-dogma orthodoxy and suggests the scholarly shortcomings that have led to its relatively recent and precipitous rise. Extrapolating from this evidence, the chapter concludes with brief remarks on the errant tendencies of current legal scholarship.

The Contemporary Consensus
Wigmore's Mirror

Soon after publishing "Privilege, Malice, and Intent," Holmes received a letter from John Henry Wigmore lavishly praising the article's theoretical achievements.[1] Although Wigmore, a professor of law at Northwestern University, was then beginning his long, diverse, and prolific scholarly career, he had already written extensively in torts, particularly on the history of strict liability culminating in *Rylands*. In the letter, Wigmore advised that his forthcoming article, "The Tripartite Division of Torts," would advance a theory similar to Holmes's.[2]

To confirm that they were indeed in agreement, Wigmore proceeded to describe his "tripartite division of tort-questions."[3] The first part pertained to "Damage (or Injury)," and sought to "define the kinds of harm from which under any circumstances he [the plaintiff] has or has not a claim—mental suffering, discomfort, battery, imprisonment, injuries to property, loss of social relations, loss of privacy, common law copyright and statutory, etc."[4] The second part concerned "Responsibility," and in particular considered what minimum factual conditions must exist for the law to deem it "fair" to hold the defendant "rather than another, or than no one at all, civilly amenable . . . as the source of the [legally cognizable] harmful result."[5] "Justification (or Excuse)," the third part, posed a question of policy: "how far the general convenience of others should be allowed to overbalance the particular harm to the plf [plaintiff]."[6] This question was addressed only after "the law declares [the defendant] to be in fairness responsible for [the harm 'which the law declares actionable']."[7]

Wigmore's "Responsibility" and "Justification" divisions corresponded respectively to the two parts of Holmes's general theory of torts: Part One on the minimum factual conditions for *prima facie* moral responsibility, and Part Two on the policy-making power of courts to justify escapes from some or all *prima facie* responsibility in particular classes of cases.[8] Although he was less concerned with the substantive basis of "Responsibility" than with delineating the proper sequence and scope of the question, he concurred with Holmes's foresight theory and its accommodation of strict liability. As Wigmore concluded, "accident, due care, reasonable consequences, acting at peril all flow more or less from the notion (as you have expressed it, Common Law 144) of 'giving a man a fair chance to avoid the harm before he is held responsible for it.' "[9] And, consistent with the second part of Holmes's theory, Wigmore noted that in the justification phase a defendant may "show that under the circumstances he should be excused or privileged, *though* a legal harm has been done and *though* he is the one to whom it has been fairly brought home."[10]

Holmes's reply was immediate and succinct: "As far as I see we agree in our views substantially."[11]

In subsequent articles elaborating his torts theory, Wigmore indicated his understanding and acceptance of both Holmes's foresight theory of responsibility and its support for strict liability. Relying on Holmes's arguments in the torts lectures developing the indispensable link between choice to avoid harm and foresight, Wigmore declared that the "relative" foresight condition provided a crucial barrier against cause-based strict liability, assuring that "one is not made responsible even for every harm actively caused by him."[12] To illustrate the foresight component of Responsibility—what he called "culpable causation"—Wigmore referred to strict liability for libel, an example Holmes used frequently. In most cases, Wigmore pointed out, liability for libel reduced to a bare question of responsibility: whether reputational damage from a derogatory statement "might fairly and reasonably have been anticipated and feared."[13] Generalizing, he observed that foresight of harm was the "sort of question that arises so commonly for injuries to the person and the property," and, in view of that, "whether the test of acting at peril [under *Rylands*] or of due care under the circumstances [apparently, the doctrine of some-negligence] shall be applied."[14]

Wigmore's writings consistently recognized that Holmes's foresight theory supported strict liability. In an article published shortly before "Privilege, Malice, and Intent," Wigmore credited Blackburn for "mastermind[ing]" in *Rylands* the "co-ordination" of various "unhoused and unshepherded" strict liability rules into the "true category" of escaping dangerous things, saving these rules from being enveloped by the elastic conception of negligence that had captured the imagination of many contemporary commentators.[15] But Wigmore's greatest intellectual accolades were reserved for Holmes. Despite Blackburn's synthesis, *Rylands* might still have been washed away by the rising tide of negligence had it not been that Holmes supplied theoretical coherence to the category of escaping dangerous things. "Supplementing Lord Blackburn's judicial utterance," Wigmore asserted, "the theoretical exposition of Mr. Justice Holmes, in cc. iii. and iv. of 'The Common Law,' had served more than anything else to commend and establish the distinction."[16]

In "A General Analysis of Tort-Relations," Wigmore relied extensively on Holmes to develop a set of concrete rules for implementing the foresight basis of strict liability, such as those applied to "keeping of dogs, cattle, and other animals, the storing of explosives, the use of weapons, and other sorts of conduct."[17] These rules demonstrated the discretionary power of courts to supersede juries and legislate foresight presumptions establishing strict act-at-peril liability, along with the far-reaching scope of foresight-based responsibility. According to Wigmore, courts "may declare once for all that certain harms are always to be regarded under certain circumstances as the normally apprehendible consequences of certain conduct; hence, given the conduct and the consequence, . . . the defendant is responsible without further inquiry."[18]

Recognition of Holmes's Support for Strict Liability

In aligning his ideas with those of Holmes, Wigmore represented the prevailing contemporary consensus. The general understanding of Holmes's theory of torts, as reflected in contemporary records, was not completely accurate nor, in the later years, unanimous. Moreover, compared to the intense interest of current legal scholars, Holmes's contemporaries took far less notice of his views on strict liability, or, for that matter, on negligence. In this respect, Wigmore's elaboration was the exception. Nevertheless, the generally expressed understanding was that Holmes's theory affirmed and approved strict liability.

Melville Bigelow, for example, acknowledged the priority and "controlling influence" of Holmes's three-branch arrangement in "The Theory of Torts" (1873).[19] Expressly following that arrangement, Bigelow's organization of torts placed the branches of "evil motive" and "careless conduct" at the "extremes."[20] In between, Bigelow located "the extensive class of cases" comprising the branch of strict liability.[21] Similarly, other contemporaries attributed the intellectual foundation for modern strict liability to Holmes's historical and policy analysis of external standards,[22] and to his antiformalist jurisprudence.[23] In particular, contemporaries relied on Holmes's arguments demonstrating both the strict liability nature and the utility of specific rules, like those governing land trespass and conversion,[24] defamation,[25] injury done by animals,[26] and common carriers.[27]

For Holmes's contemporaries, *Rylands* and its potential application to industrial risks was the litmus test of support for strict liability. No one saw a brighter hue indicative of such support in Holmes's thinking than did Judge Charles Doe in Brown v. Collins. In fact, Doe's angry reaction was the earliest and most comprehensive acknowledgment of Holmes's endorsement of *Rylands* and its far-reaching implications. Doe opened his attack with a scathing critique of Holmes's treatment of *Rylands* in "The Theory of Torts." Condemning *Rylands* as a misguided application of cause-based strict liability, Doe charged Holmes with promoting that rule by rationalizing the decision on the mere "fact of danger."[28] Doe rebuked Holmes for thinking it "politic to make those who go into extra-hazardous employments take the risk on their own shoulders" despite their "not foreseeing it will produce any injury."[29] What most outraged Doe was Holmes's reductive generalization of *Rylands* to invent an expansive branch of strict liability for regulating industrial risks.[30] Making the "danger" test sufficient for liability would, Doe asserted, expose business enterprise to the arbitrary constraints of unforeseen liability, resulting in pernicious consequences which jury caprice and parochialism would compound. In contrast, Doe regarded strict liability conditioned on foreseeable harm as amply grounded in precedent and policy.

Doe's criticism elicited no direct response from Holmes. One explanation is that Doe misinterpreted Holmes as a supporter of cause-based strict liability, and Holmes may have thought that the error was patent and required no response. To specify the foresight condition would belabor what was clear from the obvious, characteristic dangers posed by the reservoir, cattle, and other examples of extra-hazardous sources which he had presented in "The Theory of Torts" as prototypical subjects for strict liability. He had emphasized, moreover, that the general principle unifying the strict liability branch was the shared and characteristic nature of such activities: "things having an active tendency to do damage."[31] But it is also possibly telling that the foresight qualification to strict liability was first explicitly stated and elaborately explained in the torts lectures. It may be that when Holmes wrote "The Theory of Torts" his views were somewhat ambiguous and unformed, or he initially believed the causation theory's tenet that Trespass was dominated by the rule of absolute responsibility. This allows the conjecture that Holmes's recognition of the foresight condition and its unifying potential was prompted to some extent by Doe's arguments against cause-based strict liability and, significantly, by his striking acceptance of foresight-based strict liability.

The general consensus recognizing Holmes's support for *Rylands* and strict liability in industrial cases continued unabated through publication of the torts lectures and subsequent scholarly treatments of the subject. Pointing to "The Theory of Torts" (Lect. IV), Jeremiah Smith, the staunchest opponent of *Rylands* next to Doe, consistently credited Holmes with giving one of the "best" explanations for why strict liability should apply to extra-hazardous activities.[32] From the other extreme of opinion on the merits of such liability, Morris Cohen lauded Holmes in "The Path of the Law" for anticipating the twentieth-century movement towards using strict liability as a means of social insurance for industrial injuries.[33]

Aside from Wigmore, only a few commentators explicitly noted the foresight qualification to Holmes's support for strict liability in the torts lectures and subsequent writings. Among them was Thomas Beven. On the basis of "The Theory of Torts" (Lect. IV) he reported that Holmes endorsed *Rylands* in so far as it applied to activities which the defendant "knows, or ought to know, are of a dangerous nature."[34] Without this foresight qualification, as Beven observed, strict liability would attach on mere causation to any volitional act "irrespectively of whether the immediate cause of the escape is the act of God or anything else which is incapable of forecast or control."[35] Similarly, referring to the passages in Lecture IV where the foresight theory is applied to justify *Rylands,* Rufus Harris presented a just compensation argument for strict liability in cases involving "extra-hazardous things."[36]

Most commentators, however, left the foresight element of Holmes's views on strict liability more or less to inference. This may have been because they usually mentioned those views only in passing, and, at least with respect to *Rylands* and extra-hazardous cases, because they thought the foresight element obvious.[37] Thus an awareness of Holmes's policy arguments favoring foresight-based strict liability seems implicit in Cohen's focus on industrial risks and emphasis on the ability of defendants to spread (thus predict) the costs of tort-supplied insurance through increases in the price of their products. In contrast to Cohen, Smith, like Wigmore, was one of the few commentators to spell out Holmes's foresight theory of responsibility, and indeed, his two-part general theory of torts.[38] Yet Smith never directly related Holmes's foresight theory to *Rylands,* but rather implied that strict liability applied to distinctively extra-hazardous risks.[39]

A. V. Dicey's review of *The Common Law* provides another example of implying the foresight qualification to Holmes's support for strict liability. Dicey notes Holmes's objective to devise a unifying theory of all tort rules, including both strict liability as applied under *Rylands* and the doctrines governing necessity and defamation claims. Yet in quoting Holmes's conclusion that the general test of responsibility was "the degree of danger attending the act or conduct under the known circumstances," Dicey did not expressly relate this statement of the foresight theory to strict liability.[40] It is clear, however, that Dicey did not attach the same meaning to Holmes's emphasis on the danger test in "The Theory of Torts" (Lect. IV) as Doe had with regard to "The Theory of Torts" (1873). Dicey underscored that Holmes's theory rejected cause-based strict liability, in terms of which "X, having acted in a way which has caused damage to A, is liable to an action, simply because his conduct has been the cause of harm to A."[41]

Similarly, Frederick Pollock credited Holmes with formulating the "extra-hazardous risk" classification of strict liability cases, but never explicitly related this understanding to Holmes's foresight theory and policy analysis.[42] Pollock clearly indicated this relationship, however, in relying on Holmes's upholding the strict liability rules governing cases of ferocious animals in "The Theory of Torts." Without suggesting any disagreement with Holmes, and, in fact, completely in accord with the foresight explanation presented on the cited pages of Lecture IV, Pollock rationalized those cases as based on the "presumed dangerous" character of the animals involved, which he juxtaposed against cases of dogs and other domestic animals requiring proof of *scienter*.[43] While far more dubious than Dicey of Holmes's claim to have discovered the unifying theory of tort law,[44] Pollock too stated the foresight condition with no intimation of a negligence limit, but rather with sufficient breadth to encompass the entire panoply of foresight-based strict liability rules. The theory reflected, according to Pollock, "the general rule . . . that a man is not liable for harmful consequences of acts not unlawful in themselves which he had not a fair chance of foreseeing and preventing," a proposition "reducible to foresight" in the external sense of " 'what a man of reasonable prudence would have foreseen.' "[45]

Pollock's understanding reflected the prevailing view of Holmes's foresight theory, that it imported no negligence limitation and extended to accommodate rules of foresight-based strict liability such as *Rylands*.[46] Indeed, though he would have it otherwise, Pollock recognized that when applied at the generalized foresight level to encompass the characteristic risks of extra-hazardous activities, the strict liability rule was "all but absolute."[47]

This perception of the scope of Holmes's foresight theory is further illustrated in views expressed by Thomas Street. Like Pollock, Street doubted that anyone, including Holmes, had discovered a unifying theory of torts. The rules were far too diverse. However, referring to the summary of the foresight theory of responsibility at the beginning of "Privilege, Malice, and Intent," Street acknowledged that Holmes had delineated the basis of "one of the very broadest of legal principles."[48] In Street's restatement, Holmes's theory posited that "tort is a wrong which consists in the infliction of temporal damage by a responsible person under circumstances of such nature that the person inflicting the damage knows, or in common experience ought to know, that his conduct is likely to result in harm."[49] Although Street did not refer to Holmes's theory in subsequent discussion of what he called "the broadest generalization known to the law of torts," the parallel to ideas and language leaves very little doubt of Street's source.[50] After reviewing *Rylands* and other strict liability doctrines, Street stated the basic "criterion" of responsibility in terms of foresight-based strict liability: "one who creates, maintains, uses, or sends abroad a harmful agent [is responsible] for unintended harms which it does, provided a prudent person, having knowledge of the facts which that person knows or ought to know, could foresee harm to others as a natural result of the creation, maintenance, or use of the agent in question."[51]

Contemporaries also recognized that Holmes's some-negligence interpretation of the classic English and American Trespass cases cohered with his foresight theory, which they understood to accommodate foresight-based strict liability and exclude only liability based on mere causation. Thus, like Dicey, Beven expressly noted that the theory opposed only cause-based strict liability and rationalized *Rylands* on foresight grounds, but he also indicated that Holmes presented Trespass as denying liability for unforeseeable harm—referring to Holmes's definition of "accident"—only if the defendant had taken all reasonable precautions against any foreseeable risk.[52] Significantly, Beven portrayed Holmes's some-negligence analysis and the principal Trespass cases he addressed—Morris v. Platt, Brown v. Kendall, and Harvey v. Dunlop—as concerned with the role of negligence not as a general matter, but solely as applied to claims for unforeseeable harm. Pollock also understood Holmes's analysis in Lecture III of these cases and their English counterparts to focus exclusively on the "proposition that a man must answer for all direct consequences of his voluntary acts at any rate."[53] In adopting the some-negligence interpretation of Trespass, Pollock suggested Holmes's concurrence.[54]

The contemporary reaction to the rejection by Holmes of the plaintiff's *Rylands*-based claim in Quinn v. Crimmings further highlights the contrast between the prevailing consensus then and now.[55] Contemporaries understood *Quinn* to represent merely a particular objection based on policies relating to common everyday risks, rather than a general and dogmatic opposition to strict liability. Thus Smith characterized *Quinn* as excluding from *Rylands* only cases involving "an ordinary building or an ordinary fence."[56] Harold Laski, however, blurred the case into a systematic business risk of "building contractors."[57] But his attempt (albeit off point) to allay Holmes's concerns about overdeterrence, by arguing that contractors could raise prices to cover their strict liability exposure, indicates the general perception of the Justice's functionally discriminating approach to *Rylands*. Nor did *Quinn* alter the contemporary appraisal that the Massachusetts court remained in the vanguard of support for *Rylands* under Holmes's stewardship.[58]

Contrary to what one would expect from the current negligence-dogma account of Holmes's leading role in rejecting *Rylands*, contemporary opponents of that rule never claimed him among their number. If anyone was considered the intellectual leader of the movement against *Rylands*, it was Doe. Even after nearly fifty years, Smith found that Doe's comprehensive criticisms "ha[d] never been satisfactorily answered."[59] In light of this, it is all the more remarkable—not to say misguided—that the only evidence negligence-dogma proponents offer of Holmes's alleged anti-*Rylands* influence on his contemporaries is the erroneous claim that Doe used arguments from "The Theory of Torts" against *Rylands*.[60]

In fact, Holmes's name never appears on any roll-call of *Rylands*' opponents. Smith listed in opposition "some of the best modern text writers," including Salmond, Pollock, Street, and Thayer.[61] Smith also placed major reliance on Bohlen and Bishop, and on decisions from New Hampshire, New Jersey, and New York to show that most leading authorities opposed *Rylands*.[62] Similarly, Pollock, who had perhaps the greatest motivation and opportunity to proclaim Holmes an ally against *Rylands*, never did.[63] Pollock did, however, hail Salmond's and Thayer's criticisms of *Rylands* and their doomsaying predictions about the fate of strict liability.[64] But Pollock never even insinuated that Holmes opposed *Rylands*, and indeed he evinced no surprise at all when the Justice strongly endorsed strict liability for industrial injuries in the Arizona Employers' Liability Cases.[65]

Common Vocabulary and Conceptual Framework

Beyond specific reactions to Holmes's views, the general body of contemporary commentary on torts, whether referring to Holmes or not, confirms his support for strict liability. This commentary reveals a strong correspondence between Holmes's usage and contemporary (often more fully explicated) usage of key terms, concepts, and arguments. This correspondence of language and ideas serves as more than a check on idiosyncratic and anachronistic interpretation. The evidence of consistency with the generally accepted empirical basis of case holdings, rules, and doctrines, as well as conventional terminology and concepts, provide added corroboration of Holmes's support for strict liability and reinforce his claim that the foresight theory of responsibility and its application to *Rylands* were descriptive and explanatory.

Holmes employed a vocabulary and conceptual framework that were common among his contemporaries. As demonstrated earlier, contemporary commentators used "accident," "inevitable accident," and "act of God" not as substitutes for non-negligence, but rather in conformity with Holmes's meaning of unforeseeable harm. Like Holmes, contemporaries attributed dual meanings to both "fault" and "negligence." Depending on the context, those terms represented either the modern negligence cause of action, or the classic requirement for unintentional tort liability of a willed and foresight-informed act—Wigmore's "culpable causation"—encompassing not only the negligence cause of action but also strict liability. The some-negligence interpretation of the English and American Trespass claims for unforeseeable harm was also prevalent in the literature.[66] Moreover, many commentators grounded the notion of moral responsibility on foresight.

Consistent with Holmes's concerns about cause-based strict liability, the chief objection of contemporaries to *Rylands* was that the case established a broad rule of absolute responsibility.[67] They split over whether cause-based strict liability as manifested in *Rylands* was a modern creation or had antecedents in Trespass.[68] But whether they based themselves on lack of precedent, which seemed to bother English commentators most, or on moral and functional considerations, which were more a focus of American critics, Holmes's contemporaries generally opposed cause-based strict liability, especially as implemented in *Rylands* by its open-ended classification of escaping dangerous things. As a result, virtually all commentators—whatever their ultimate view of strict liability—welcomed and urged a foresight rationalization of *Rylands* and strict liability for extra-hazardous activities.[69] In support, they offered (without attribution) the administrative, compensation, and deterrence rationales elaborated by Holmes.

Despite differences of opinion over both the appropriate degree of generalized foresight and the significance of the relative danger and benefits of an activity, Holmes's contemporaries overall formulated rules of foresight-based strict liability that extended broad and expansive coverage for industrial risks. Many commentators stated the foresight ground of strict liability in language strikingly similar to Holmes's. Thus Pollock explained *Rylands* on the ground that "[t]he law takes notice that certain things are a source of extra-ordinary risk, and a man who exposes his neighbour to such risk is held, although his act is not of itself wrongful, to insure his neighbour against any consequent harm not due to some cause beyond human foresight and control."[70] Similarly, in rejecting the exclusive alternatives of cause-based strict liability and negligence, Terry found a "middle ground" for *Rylands*-type cases:

> [T]he true ground is that the person acts at his peril if he has any reason to suppose that there is any appreciable peril, even though the peril be so small that it is perfectly reasonable to disregard it or even though the party takes all imaginable precautions to guard against harm . . . Some things are always noxious, and every one is presumed to know their nature. Others are usually harmless, and then the *scienter* must be proved.[71]

Bohlen too rationalized *Rylands* on foresight grounds, and, while denying a defense based on unforeseeability of the mechanism or particular events leading to injury, he limited the Restatement's authorization for strict liability to the harms that the defendant "should recognize as likely . . . from [the type of risk that] makes the activity ultrahazardous."[72] As Thayer concluded, the scope of *Rylands* extended up to the point of "excuse" for "accident . . . caused by the unforeseeable intervention of some natural force or human being."[73] In light of the current claim that Holmes's analysis of strict liability marginalized *Rylands,* it is noteworthy not only that his contemporaries generally accepted foresight-based strict liability for extra-hazardous activities, but also that, following the torts lectures, *Rylands* itself—either in general or on an activity-by-activity basis—began gaining favor in American courts, with Massachusetts in the forefront.[74]

Affirmation of Rylands

Holmes's commitment to strict liability was manifest in his repeated and prominent promotion of *Rylands* for extra-hazardous risks at the very height of the storm of opposition against the rule—a fact that proponents of the negligence-dogma thesis ignore.[75] Holmes consistently and unhesitatingly affirmed the strict liability nature, precedent, and policy of *Rylands*, despite criticism leveled by such leading authorities as Pollock, Thayer, and Smith, who sought to replace *Rylands* with a general negligence rule.[76]

The effort of Pollock, Thayer, and others to ground torts on the negligence rule lends no support to the current negligence-dogma and industrial-subsidy theses. Holmes's contemporaries envisioned the modern negligence rule, particularly in its external and enhanced modes, as the practical equivalent of foresight-based strict liability. They promoted the negligence rule not to subsidize industry but to avoid subsidizing it: statistics and science made the modern negligence rules unceasing and powerful engines of compensatory and regulatory liability. The negligence rule was preferred by many of Holmes's contemporaries because it performed the role of strict liability in industrial cases while realizing the theoretical objective of unifying torts on a single principle. "Those of us who regret [Rylands] do so," Pollock stated, "not in the name of any general dogma, but because we think it undesirable to multiply distinctions, and believe that [the modern negligence rule including] . . . the law of nuisance, and the presumption expressed by *res ipsa loquitur* would have sufficed to give a simpler and more uniform rule adequate for all practical purposes."[77]

Holmes never concurred in these criticisms of *Rylands,* and indeed refuted the principal arguments aimed at replacing its strict liability mandate with a general rule of negligence.[78] In one line of attack, opponents cast doubt on the scope and viability of *Rylands,* suggesting that it was restricted to cases of adjacent landowners and property damage, and asserting that it had been rejected by "the decided weight of American authority."[79] Holmes, by contrast, never intimated any limitations of place or type of injury. Indeed, he effectively rejected such limitations on *Rylands* with his principal examples of extra-hazardous risks from guns and ferocious animals.[80] In reporting the reaction of American courts to *Rylands,* Holmes stated merely that the rule had been rejected by "[s]ome courts"—probably an understatement at the time—which he balanced against the unqualified and wide-ranging enforcement of the rule in Massachusetts.[81]

Opponents of *Rylands* also disparaged Blackburn's reliance on traditional precedent, particularly the rule of strict liability for cattle trespass in formulating the "escaping dangerous things" classification.[82] That precedent was crucial in his effort "to clothe innovation with the appearance of continuity," making *Rylands* seem neither exceptional nor anomalous.[83] Holmes, to the contrary, never doubted that *Rylands* was a "sound" extension of the traditional strict liability rule governing animals.[84] In fact, his independent research not only authenticated the cattle trespass precedent, but also supplemented Blackburn's analysis by linking *Rylands* to the established rules of strict liability for "ferocious animals."[85] In vouching for *Rylands,* its supporters subsequently emphasized this precedent—though failing to acknowledge Holmes—to refute claims that the rule was an historical anomaly.[86]

The main interpretive strategy followed by *Rylands* critics was to convert the decision to a negligence rule. They argued that the Blackburn and Cairns opinions themselves admitted a negligence interpretation, and that, in any event, the obvious negligence grounds for deciding the case rendered the assertion of strict liability unnecessary if not plain dictum. Significantly, Holmes took no part in this effort to convert *Rylands* into a negligence rule, despite his interest in finding a unifying theory of negligence and strict liability.

The conceptual vulnerability of Blackburn's opinion arose from his attempt to define a realm of strict liability distinct from negligence in cases where the actions of both plaintiff and defendant contribute to the risk. He claimed that the class of such cases governed by the negligence rule, where plaintiffs bear the residual risk, was fundamentally distinguishable from the strict liability class, because the plaintiffs in the former have "taken that risk" by knowingly exposing themselves to the defendants' hazardous activities. Examples of such assumption of the risk included cases where plaintiffs "go on the highway, or have their property adjacent to it ... [or] pass near to warehouses where goods are being raised or lowered."[87] Cairns dealt with the same problem of bilateral causation by relegating strict liability to cases of "non-natural use" of property.[88] Doe attacked both distinctions as porous if not meaningless, and many of his contemporaries agreed. Given Blackburn's examples of plaintiffs assuming the risk of non-negligent activity, Doe argued that this reasoning swept in nearly the "whole human race" and thereby reduced the zone of strict liability to a near vanishing point.[89] Doe dismissed Cairns's natural versus nonnatural distinction as incoherent, if it "meant anything more than the difference between a reasonable use and an unreasonable one."[90] The English courts were quickly coming to the same view.[91] Indeed, three years after Doe's opinion, Blackburn himself, now sitting in the House of Lords, lent support to the negligence-conversion effort by acknowledging that recovery under *Rylands* required proof that the activity in question was "carried on in an unusual, unreasonable, and improper manner."[92]

It is noteworthy that Holmes never invoked or even mentioned either of these rather tenuous and contested bases for distinguishing strict liability from negligence cases. Instead, he generalized *Rylands* on the fact of manifest residual risk, formulating a comprehensive rule of strict liability applicable to any class of cases when it would "best accomplish" the compensation and deterrence functions of tort law. As such, he placed *Rylands* on a broader and more durable foundation than had its English authors.

If strict liability could not be converted into negligence through Blackburn's and Cairns' distinctions, then critics of *Rylands* were prepared to enhance the negligence standard to make it the equivalent of strict liability in all but name. Pointing to the ready availability of such negligence rules as vicarious liability and external, concrete standards of presumptive negligence, such as those applied under the doctrine of *res ipsa loquitur,* critics denied that the courts in *Rylands*-type cases ever needed to reach the strict liability question.[93] Although this was a case of strict liability "parading under the thin disguise of conclusive presumptions of negligence, of negligence *per se,* and negligence as matter of law,"[94] these critics were quite willing to entertain the "dogmatic fiction" of negligence, if that was what it took to establish a unified system of responsibility in tort.[95]

Holmes fully appreciated that vicarious liability and external, concrete standards of presumptive negligence moved tort law far along in the direction of strict liability. But these rules were not operationally equivalent to strict liability. And pursuant to the teachings of his new jurisprudence that "a legal fiction does not change the nature of things . . . [and] cannot be allowed to affect a classification," Holmes consistently rejected the negligence-conversion strategy that deemed *Rylands* a case of "remote inadvertence."[96] By classifying *Rylands* according to its operational requirements and effects, he not only stimulated deliberate consideration of the choices of policy involved in using strict liability, but also established the independent existence of strict liability as a principal branch of tort law.

Sources of the Current Misunderstanding

Prior to 1950

Despite the dearth of references to Holmes's views on strict liability during the decade and a half following his death in 1935, the consensus among his contemporaries on these views continued to hold during this period.[97] This assessment also rests on several appellate opinions that were issued in the 1930s and 1940s.[98] The most noteworthy was Judge Scott's opinion in *Read,* marshaling the foresight theory and its application to strict liability in "The Theory of Torts" (Lect. IV) to justify *Rylands.*[99] The contemporary consensus thus ended just as Doe began it in 1873, with clear judicial affirmation of Holmes's support for strict liability.

Yet given the long period of time and the basic types of scholarly errors that produced current misconceptions of Holmes's views, it would be surprising not to find precursors of the current negligence-dogma thesis prior to 1950. A survey of commentary and cases from 1870 to 1950, however, disclosed very few such departures from the prevailing consensus—in fact only three, Arthur Ballantine, John Salmond, and William Prosser, all in the twentieth century.[100] None of them purported to offer more than conclusory assertions based on unelaborated references to *The Common Law,* in particular to the historical analysis in Lecture III refuting the existence of Trespass precedent for cause-based strict liability. Patently mistaken, the claims by these commentators reveal little familiarity with Holmes's torts lectures.

Of the three, Ballantine came closest to the current negligence-dogma view in asserting that Holmes misread Trespass precedent as denying all forms of strict liability, leading him to conclude erroneously that "losses unintentionally caused . . . in the absence of negligence . . . lie where they fell."[101] Like current proponents of the negligence-dogma thesis, Ballantine selectively quoted from the torts lectures, omitting not only Holmes's unforeseeable harm definition of such "losses from accident," but also his explicit support for *Rylands* in Lecture III as well as in "The Theory of Torts" (Lect. IV). Moreover, in attempting to refute Holmes and prove that Trespass precedent for strict liability "has always persisted," Ballantine relied (unknowingly) on the very same strict liability rules governing trespassing domestic animals and *Rylands*-type dangerous activities that Holmes repeatedly invoked to prove the same point.[102]

While neither Salmond nor Prosser stated directly that Holmes opposed strict liability, they implied this view by characterizing his history of Trespass as establishing a subjective requirement akin to malice for recovery in tort. Salmond, a disciple of Austin, relied on Holmes in arguing that tort demanded the equivalent of criminal "mens rea"; Prosser, an admirer of Salmond, simply cited Holmes as predicating recovery on "a large element of personal blame."[103] Salmond's glaringly erroneous portrayal of Holmes's history of Trespass was corrected by subsequent editors of his treatise, but Prosser's misconception continues to be published.[104]

Since 1950

Sustained advocacy of the current negligence-dogma thesis of Holmes's scholarly torts writings began in 1950, with a passing remark by Fleming James suggesting that Holmes denied the expedience of exacting "compensation from one whose conduct is *not unreasonably dangerous*."[105] James attributed this to Holmes's belief that strict liability would "impose an undue burden on desirable, affirmative activity which would be out of proportion to the benefit conferred on victims."[106] James was also the first to suggest an industrial-subsidy motive for Holmes's opposition to strict liability, speculating that he favored the negligence rule "since it combines a considerable incentive towards safety and a minimum of interference with desirable enterprise."[107]

By the close of the 1950s other commentators were voicing these claims with utter conviction instead of James's more tentative surmise. John Fleming, for example, declared that Holmes relentlessly opposed strict liability and embraced negligence to further "a calculated policy of encouraging the burgeoning industry of the new machine age."[108] In 1961 Leon Green linked Holmes's pronouncement of the principle against liability for loss from accident to the nineteenth-century cause of "liberat-[ing] ... the defendant from liability ... under the cover of 'fault'."[109]

The negligence-dogma thesis next appeared in Mark DeWolfe Howe's *The Proving Years* (1963), which analyzed Holmes's scholarly writings from 1870 through *The Common Law*. In Howe's view, Holmes rejected "two theories ... struggling for dominance": the American theory of "personal fault" and the English theory based on *Rylands*.[110] To Holmes, the external negligence standard represented the best "compromise" in both reflecting "current morality" and promoting the "social advantage" of economic development.[111]

A review of the literature published after *The Proving Years* in the 1960s indicates only a few scattered assertions of the negligence-dogma interpretations.[112] In contrast, the 1970s witnessed an outpouring of such claims by most of the leading commentators on torts and students of legal history.[113] Agreeing that at least through the torts lectures Holmes promoted a universal negligence rule exclusive of strict liability in any form, these commentators differed only over whether his motivation was to subsidize industrial development through a transformation of nineteenth-century tort from cause-based strict liability to negligence,[114] or whether his view expressed merely a pragmatic judgment or stemmed from a commitment to formalist jurisprudence.[115] The negligence-dogma thesis continued to attract adherents during the 1980s and early 1990s. Today, this thesis represents the dominant, and heretofore unchallenged orthodoxy.[116]

This does not mean that the negligence-dogma thesis fully occupies the field. From 1950 to the present, a number of prominent commentators affirmed Holmes's support for strict liability, usually in terms of the foresight-based version. But they never note, let alone directly contest, the negligence-dogma thesis and rarely elaborate Holmes's policy and theoretical arguments for strict liability, or even his treatment of *Rylands* and its role in cases of industrial and other extra-hazardous activities. Thus Christopher Schroeder simply asserts that Holmes promoted "a system of strict liability [in which] an agent need know only that an action might cause harm."[117] In the course of arguing for a utilitarian characterization of Holmes's jurisprudence, H. L. Pohlman reports rather abstractly that "Holmes finally chose as the criterion of liability foresight of harmful consequences," and on this basis "considered his external and general theory of legal liability perfectly compatible with strict liability."[118] Far and away the most penetrating and comprehensive analysis of Holmes's foresight theory and its relationship to strict liability is provided by Patrick Kelley.[119] Portraying Holmes as a nineteenth-century positivist, Kelley concludes that among the foresight theory's "triumphs . . . is that it reconciles the application of the negligence standard . . . with the apparently inconsistent application of a strict liability rule . . . [on] the principle . . . [that] the doing of the act alone establishes that a defendant, with the knowledge derived from the common experience of mankind, would realize its potential for danger."[120]

Many other current commentators also have recognized evidence of Holmes's support for strict liability, yet continue to espouse the negligence-dogma thesis. The transparency of this contradiction in their work perhaps indicates the powerful influence exerted by the prevailing orthodoxy. For example, in his exploration of the strands of pragmatism in Holmes's jurisprudence, Thomas Grey hails the 1872 "Jurisprudence Essay" for "plant-[ing] the germ of the whole modern analysis" of "risk allocation" including the use of strict liability, and "The Path of the Law" for "concisely anticipating the turn toward enterprise liability accident law would take as his risk-allocating conception of civil liability gradually took hold."[121] Yet, in almost the same breath, Grey asserts that in the torts lectures, "Holmes claimed that generally strict liability in tort should be rejected as 'offending the sense of justice.' "[122]

A number of commentators, apparently perceiving a contradiction, attempt to minimize or bury it with a superficial retort. Noting Holmes's supportive arguments in the torts lectures for *Rylands* and various other rules of strict liability, Benjamin Kaplan brushes it off opaquely as "gloss," while Harry Kalven dismisses it as not "serious."[123] Similarly, Robert Rabin trivializes the evidence with the assertion that "Holmes gives only cursory attention to *Rylands*."[124] In his illuminating study of nineteenth-century tort law refuting the industrial-subsidy thesis in general, Gary Schwartz also notes Holmes's support for applying strict liability to the industrial sector of "*Rylands*-like 'extrahazardous' activities."[125] Yet, Schwartz also maintains the negligence-dogma characterization by deflating the contradictory evidence with an unelaborated assertion that Holmes favored only a "limited rule of strict liability."[126]

Rise of the Negligence-Dogma Thesis

Mistaken Expectations

The effort to explain historical events and texts inevitably produces varying interpretations, often starkly at odds with each other. Holmes's writings on torts, which have continuously perplexed readers, are especially likely to lead to marked differences of opinion. The difficulty for readers of this work stems largely from their mistaken expectations that these writings offered conventional treatise-like expositions. Failing to recognize that Holmes's torts writings—even the essays titled "The Theory of Torts"—focused only on those particular aspects that had philosophical significance for his new jurisprudence, readers interested in torts mistakenly presume that the absence of a comprehensive and detailed account of negligence and strict liability, for example, signifies confusion or premodern understanding on his part. The same failing tends to lead readers interested in jurisprudence to pay too little attention to the torts essays.

Also, contrary to what most readers expect, Holmes's writings are not easily accessible. They are characterized by peaks of sparkling insight punctuating long passages of dense, abstruse detail; by crucial ideas expressed in delphic aphorisms; by arguments directed to bygone issues, knowledge of which is taken for granted; by use of terms with multiple meanings; and by simultaneous development of multiple lines of thought with only context to guide the reader. Holmes's writings also show signs of the pressures bearing upon those for whom scholarship is an avocation, as it was for Holmes in the early years of practicing law, and later as a judge. Moreover, most of his important works were prepared as public lectures, and reflect not only the strains of meeting stringent deadlines, but also a tendency to prefer provocative expression over more extended elaboration, heeding his father's advice regarding "spoken addresses": "To hold the attention of an audience is the first requisite of every such composition; and for this a more highly colored rhetoric is admissible than might please the solitary reader."[127]

Elementary Mistakes

Nonetheless, promulgators of the negligence-dogma interpretation are not so simply absolved. Its deficiencies go well beyond matters of misplaced weight and judgment, or errors of research or logic. This thesis (considered by itself or in conjunction with the industrial-subsidy claim) displays scholarly defects of the most elementary kind: assertion of major points without supporting or specified references; begging of central and hotly contested questions of fact; anachronistic and oversimplified treatment of key terms, concepts, and ideas; selective quotation; uncritical reliance on secondary sources; and disregard of important aspects of social context. These basic failings are compounded by an example of scholarly neglect nonpareil—utter disregard of "The Theory of Torts" (Lect. IV). The disappearance from history of this crucial text is reflected in the practice of referring to Lecture IV only by the first half of its title, "Fraud, Malice, and Intent," and omitting the second half: "The Theory of Torts."[128]

Ideological Presuppositions

All productive investigations flow from preconceived hypotheses of what should be found given existing knowledge and beliefs. Failure to keep these initial conjectures in critical check, however, risks predetermining and distorting the results. In my view, just such a failure best explains the negligence-dogma interpretation. Current commentators were primed by certain presuppositions to accept the negligence-dogma thesis, and found easy confirmation in Howe's seemingly thorough and reliable analysis of the raw materials.

Holmes's reputation as an ally of "progressive" causes and jurisprudence had been severely traduced during World War II, and continued to suffer decline to the point that even some admirers and biographers branded him a "reactionary monster."[129] In addition, many commentators who went on to promote the negligence-dogma thesis had been educated in the "progressive" history that "laissez-faire economics and late nineteenth-century legal theories were blood brothers."[130] Undoubtedly, they also were inculcated with the industrial-subsidy thesis—including the claim of a transformation of nineteenth-century tort from cause-based strict liability to negligence—which was well established by the 1930s, tracing back to Pound, Bohlen, and, ironically, even to Holmes, who suggested that judicial resistance to strict liability was prompted by fear of socialism. With these background assumptions, combined with a few well-known snippets from the torts lectures, and mixed with some biographical data on his distrust of centralized government, acceptance of classical economic theory, and flouting of heroic individualism and soldierly courage, these commentators might well have come to regard Holmes as the epitome of a misbegotten if not ruthless era.[131] Indeed, they may have thought it inconceivable that tort law could become so biased towards the negligence rule and industrial interests without Holmes's complicity. Reifying their political-economic conceptions of nineteenth-century legal thought and practice, these commentators ignored or effectively dismissed the counterevidence of Holmes's antiformalism and support for strict liability as insignificant contradictions in his thinking.

Many scholars of the generation nurtured in the 1960s on Marxist class-struggle and conspiracy theories were especially receptive to the negligence-dogma thesis. Authority was under siege everywhere, and attacking Holmes was a way of attacking the institutions and elders of the legal establishment, as well as the reigning ideology of politically neutral legal principles and process. In pointing the study of law towards a future of statistics and economics, Holmes also became anathema for this reason to many of this generation. They considered empirical, cost-benefit analysis a guise for the incoherent theory of neutral principles and process, if not a plot to mire their movement for social justice in insuperable complexity.

Of course, not all current scholars accepted the "progressive" history or believed that the law was or should be regarded mainly as a political instrument for redistributing wealth and power. Yet even these commentators found the negligence-dogma thesis congenial to their views. Scholars who explained the turn to the negligence rule in the last century as efficient and wealth-maximizing, used the thesis to fortify their claim that the law generally adheres to determinative tenets of economic rationalism. Still other scholars found support in the negligence-dogma thesis for portraying Holmes as the *deus ex machina* of judicial instrumentalism and redistribution that undermined the organic stability, individualism, and *a priori* justice inhering in the classic common law system.

Howe's Role

Undoubtedly, the negligence-dogma thesis would have taken a different course but for Mark DeWolfe Howe's *The Proving Years.* The precipitous rise of that thesis in the 1970s is attributable in large part to that book. Howe was not merely the recognized expert on Holmes. As a member of the Harvard faculty, he also was uniquely situated to influence elite academic peers like Gilmore and Friedman, and future scholars such as Horwitz, Posner, Gordon, and White. The power of Howe's influence regarding the negligence-dogma thesis derived from the detailed documentation and analysis provided by *The Proving Years.* Even if the book failed to persuade on matters of interpretation, it would certainly engender confidence that the primary sources had been culled for all their worth. Nothing comparable to Howe's extended examination of the torts lectures would be available until Kelley's careful study in 1984.

The fact that most of the salient deficiencies of the negligence-dogma thesis originated with Howe confirms his influential role in propagating that thesis, as well as the second-hand nature of much of its subsequent iterations. For example, Howe's book anticipated such relatively discrete misreadings as White's claim that Doe relied on arguments in "The Theory of Torts" (1873) to attack *Rylands,* and Friedman's mischaracterization of the article in claiming that Holmes depicted *Rylands* as "indefensible ."[132] More broadly, Howe foreshadowed the erroneous claims by Horwitz that Holmes supported the external negligence standard in furtherance of a formalistic customary law perspective, and by White that the arrangement of tort law established a formalistic *a priori* system.[133] Howe also established the practice of presuming fundamental flaws in Holmes's historical arguments, without actually undertaking an independent analysis of the primary sources.[134] Similarly, he provided a model of anachronistic disregard for important elements in the contemporary context bearing upon Holmes's treatment of strict liability, such as the lack of liability insurance, the politically controversial nature of his endorsement of *Rylands*, and the fundamental distinction between "absolute" cause-based strict liability and strict liability qualified by the foresight condition.[135]

Indeed, Howe mapped the strategy of minimizing the evidence of Holmes's support for *Rylands* and other strict liability cases of industrial and extra-hazardous risks. While he purported to provide an exhaustive account of Holmes's early writings on torts, including "The Theory of Torts" (1873), Howe noted only in passing that Holmes recognized strict liability for extra-hazardous activities "imposed by the legislation of judges."[136] Howe never mentioned the possible conflict between this evidence and his negligence-dogma thesis.[137] Nor did he indicate that in "The Theory of Torts" (1873) Holmes created the strict liability branch on the basis of *Rylands*.[138] Even a brief reference to evidence in the early writings of Holmes's support for strict liability in extra-hazardous cases was dropped from Howe's later summary of the importance of those writings for the torts lectures.[139]

In his extended consideration of the torts lectures, Howe cited only the Lecture III reference to *Rylands*, which he buried in an opaquely worded footnote that obliterated any sense of Holmes's innovative policy arguments.[140] But of all Howe's errors, surely the most damaging was his failure to discuss "The Theory of Torts" (Lecture IV) and its application of the foresight theory to *Rylands*.[141] In fact, that section of Lecture IV disappeared without a trace in *The Proving Years*, which, in referring to that lecture, even omitted the second half of its title: "The Theory of Torts."[142] After describing Lecture III and the first half of Lecture IV on "Fraud, Malice, and Intent," Howe abruptly ended the discussion, asserting that it would not be necessary "closely to follow the course of Holmes's argument through the two lectures."[143]

"To Burst Inflated Explanations"[144]

That the negligence-dogma thesis could have flourished is a sad reflection on the state of current legal scholarship. Of course, I am not suggesting that the types of rudimentary errors of research and interpretation involved and the ideological suppositions that fostered and shielded them are unique to the present day. Scholarship entails an inherent danger that intellectual conceptions will seem more real than the evidentiary details, and that the latter will be shaped to fit the former. Still, there is a tendency today among legal scholars, particularly historians, not only to superimpose their (wishful) constructs of a period's ideological, economic, or other essence upon the actual experience, however incongruent the fit, but also to regard this mode of analysis as less a pitfall than a virtue.[145] Indeed, purely emotive depictions (however fanciful and mundane) are being given equal if not preferred scholarly rank with rational analysis and explanation of empirical evidence.

Legal scholars might do well to take some lessons from legal practitioners on the craft of developing theories from a factual record. To be sure, records have no determinate four corners, and lawyers are not mere chroniclers; interpretation, hypothesis, and conceptualization are essential. But because of their training, the high probability of adversarial scrutiny, and the real-world stakes involved in cases, lawyers tend to speculate and argue with a closer eye on the evidence than do many current legal scholars. Indeed, the rudimentary errors of the negligence-dogma thesis might well have been exposed long ago had it been presented in a brief or opinion. It is noteworthy that, though remarkably few in number, the judges who have considered the point since 1950 are almost unanimous in recognizing Holmes's support for strict liability.[146]

A comparison of Judge Scott's opinion in the *Read* case and its treatment in the 1952 edition of the prominent torts casebook by Harry Schulman and James provides a striking contrast between the scholarly and lawyerly approaches to evidence of Holmes's support for strict liability. The casebook intimates the negligence-dogma interpretation by a selective and unrepresentative excerpt from Lecture III, which gives no indication of Holmes's policy rationalization of *Rylands,* and which refers readers generally to "Holmes, *The Common Law,* Chapters 1, 2, 3."[147] *Read* was included to show the fate of *Rylands* in the British courts. But (apparently by mistake) instead of the ruling of the House of Lords, the casebook presents a lengthy excerpt from Scott's opinion in the Court of Appeal in glaring contradiction of the negligence-dogma thesis.[148] Scott pointed out that "Lectures III and IV" established that the "unifying element in all torts" was "the foresight of the prudent reasonable man."[149] Referring to the analysis in "The Theory of Torts" (Lecture IV) as well as in Lecture III, Scott also explained that Holmes thus justified strict liability in

Rylands and other cases of "extra-hazardous" activity on the ground that "the actor ought to have foreseen the likelihood of the harm resulting."[150] Unfortunately, Shulman and James omitted this portion of Scott's opinion. And that, until now, was the last time that any one discussed Holmes's application of the foresight theory to *Rylands* in "The Theory of Torts" (Lect. IV).

Great figures make history no less by the myths we create about them than by their actual contributions to the content and spirit of our intellectual life. Doubtless, Holmes would have preferred recognition for his theoretical insights on torts and jurisprudence. But, just as he believed that a principal hindrance to freedom of thought in the present was complacent acceptance of past thinking as well as misconceptions and misuses of the past, so we also honor Holmes by practicing his critical use of history. Clarifying the record of his ideas is thus imperative precisely because we are, as he hoped, "moving to the measure of his thought."[151]

Abbreviations

CL	Holmes, *The Common Law* (1881)
CL(H)	*The Common Law* (M. D. Howe, ed., 1963)
CL(I)	*The Common Law* (1881) (Holmes's own interlineated copy, Special Collections, Harvard Law School Library)
CLP	*Collected Legal Papers* (1921)
Commentaries	[Holmes and] J. Kent, *Commentaries on American Law* (12th ed., 4 vols. (1873)
CW	S. M. Novick, *The Collected Works of Justice Holmes,* (3 vols. 1995)
EW	F. Frankfurter, "Early Writings of O. W. Holmes, Jr.," 44 *Harvard Law Review* 717 (1931)
FE	F. R. Kellogg, *The Formative Essays of Justice Holmes* (1984)
HC	"The Holmes-Cohen Correspondence," 9 *Journal of the History of Ideas* 3 (1948)
HP	Holmes Papers, Harvard Law School Library
HPL	M. D. Howe, ed., *Holmes-Pollock Letters: The Correspondence of Mr. Justice Holmes and Sir Frederick Pollock* (2 vols. 1953)
1872 Jurisprudence Essay	Book Notice (1872), reprinted at EW, 788–791
1880 Jurisprudence Essay	Book Notice (1880), reprinted at 10 *Hofstra Law Review* 709–711 (1982)

OS M. D. Howe, ed., *The Occasional Speeches of Justice Oliver Wendell Holmes* (1962)

1873 Theory
of Torts "The Theory of Torts" (1873), reprinted at EW, 773–785

Theory of Torts
(Lect. IV) "The Theory of Torts," in Lecture IV, *The Common Law* (Note: the two essays bearing the same title are far different in content.)

UCLP H. C. Shriver, ed., *Justice Oliver Wendell Holmes: His Book Notices and Uncollected Letters and Papers* (1936)

Principal Works

"Codes, and the Arrangement of the Law" (1870)

"Misunderstandings of the Civil Law" (1871)

"The Arrangement of the Law—Privity" (1872)

1872 Jurisprudence Essay

"The Code of Iowa" (1873)

"The Gas-Stokers' Strike" (1873)

Kent's Commentaries on American Law (12th ed. 1873)

"The Theory of Torts" (1873)

"Primitive Notions in Modern Law I & II" (1876–77)

"Possession" (1878)

"Common Carriers and the Common Law" (1879)

"Trespass and Negligence" (1880)

1880 Jurisprudence Essay

The Common Law (1881)

"Agency I & II" (early 1880s)

"Privilege, Malice, and Intent" (1894)

"The Path of the Law" (1897)

"Law in Science and Science in Law" (1899)

"Natural Law" (1918)

Notes

Introduction

1. *The Common Law* incorporated eleven of the Lowell Institute lectures, the third and fourth of which were about tort law (hereafter respectively "Lecture III" and "Lecture IV," and collectively the "torts lectures"). A twelfth lecture, summarizing the preceding eleven, was omitted from the book. I make use of a verbatim newspaper account of that lecture, which was discovered in the course of my research for this book. See *Boston Daily Advertiser*, p. 1 (January 1, 1881). Little, Brown, the publisher of *The Common Law*, reports that its archives contain no drafts or editorial materials of Holmes's book.

2. Letter from Holmes to Arthur G. Sedgwick (July 12, 1879), HP.

3. CLP, "Path of the Law," 183.

4. CL, 35; 1880 Jurisprudence Essay, 710.

5. CL, 1, 35.

6. 1880 Jurisprudence Essay, 711.

7. CL, 1; CLP, "Path of the Law," 181.

8. As Holmes succinctly stated: "Actions of tort are brought for temporal damage. The law recognizes temporal damage as an evil which its object is to prevent or to redress." CLP, "Privilege, Malice, and Intent," 117.

9. I use the concepts of intentional wrongs, negligence, and strict liability in their conventional meaning today, which, aside from certain terminological differences (notably regarding such key terms as "negligence" and "fault"), comports with the understanding of Holmes and his contemporaries. I deal with these differences by comparing the factual elements that are specified as necessary for recovery by the courts and commentators in each period.

For present purposes, *negligence* means liability for unreasonable conduct that inflicts harm unintentionally. Unreasonable conduct is either an activity which generates greater risks than benefits (often termed "illegal" or "unlawful"), or an activity which the defendant pursues without due care, that is, without taking socially appropriate precautions to prevent or minimize any reasonably foreseeable risk. To the extent that conduct is reasonable and nonnegligent but nonetheless exposes others to risk, such a "residual risk" is exempt from liability under the negligence rule and falls, at least initially, on the plaintiff.

Strict Liability means liability without proof or presumption of negligence. By definition, strict liability exceeds the scope of negligence in granting recovery regardless of whether the harm resulted from unreasonable conduct or from the residual risk of reasonable conduct. An important distinction differentiates the "absolute" form of strict liability, which applies merely on the fact that the defendant's act was a contributing cause of the plaintiff's harm, from the form of strict liability qualified by a foresight condition, which limits liability to those harms that were not only caused by the defendant's act but were within the reasonably foreseeable risk created by that act.

To avoid semantic confusion, the phrase "intentional wrongs" is used in place of the standard term "intentional torts." The category of *intentional wrongs* refers to rules of liability for acts of malice—unreasonable conduct purposefully intended to inflict harm. Intentional wrongs are distinguished from negligence by the element of malice and from strict liability by the element of unreasonable conduct.

10. Current scholarship in torts begins with these classifications. But few commentators today attribute the three-branch classification to Holmes. For a notable exception, see J. G. Fleming, *The Law of Torts*, 14 (1983) (adopting the "classification first suggested by Holmes. . . . (1) an intent to interfere with the plaintiff's interests, (2) negligence, and (3) strict liability or liability without 'fault' ").

11. UCLP, 42 (1870) (doubting that codifying the law could or should "put an end to the function of the judge as law-makers"); CL, 35–36.

12. CL, 35–37.

13. CL, 36.

14. CL, 90, 77.

15. CL, 147.

16. CL, 94–95.

17. CL, 57. On the notion of responsibility and its converse, excuse, in moral philosophy, see H. L. A. Hart, *Punishment and Responsibility*, 13–14 (1968), and in the history of tort law, see G. P. Fletcher, "Fairness and Utility in Tort Theory," 85 *Harvard Law Review* 537, 551–564 (1972).

18. CL, 54–55.

19. CL, 1.

20. Letter from Holmes to Pollock (June 7, 1891), 1 HPL 39.

21. Despite its foresight condition, this rule has generally been recognized as imposing strict liability because it authorizes recovery without proof or presumption of negligent conduct. For examples of commentary recognizing the strict liability nature of this rule in present law, see 3 F. Harper, F. James, and O. Gray, *The*

Law of Torts, 228–229 (1986); G. Calabresi and A. K. Klevorick, "Four Tests for Liability in Torts," 14 *Journal of Legal Studies* 585, 588–591 (1985); S. Shavell, "An Analysis of Causation and the Scope of Liability in the Law of Torts," 9 *Journal of Legal Studies* 463, 482, 490 (1980); in nineteenth-century law, see H. Terry, *Some Leading Principles of Anglo-American Law,* 439 (1884); F. Pollock, "Duties of Insuring Safety: The Rule in Rylands v. Fletcher," 5 *Law Quarterly Review* 52, 55 (1886); and in the law prior to the nineteenth century, see Fletcher, "Fairness and Utility," 552, 541 and n.15.

In contrast to its present usage exclusively to denote the cause of action for unreasonable conduct, "negligence" in Holmes's time also had a premodern meaning as the name given to the entire category of foresight-based "unintentional torts" (as opposed to intentional wrongs). In this latter sense, the "negligence" classification encompassed foresight-based strict liability. Thus, while recognizing the strict liability character of the rule, some of Holmes's contemporaries classified it under the heading of "negligence." Holmes appears to have used "negligence" in both its modern and premodern senses, relying (as he often did when using ambiguous terminology) on context to indicate the meaning he had in mind. 2 Commentaries, *561 n.1 (essay entitled "Negligence" covering major rules of strict liability, defined as liability without allegation of "negligence").

The important point is not terminology but the actual requirements and effects of the rules. Gauged in those terms, the scope of liability based on causation and foresight clearly extends far beyond rules which add the further condition of unreasonable conduct. Regardless of what this broader rule is called, its operational impact in the many significant classes of cases involving substantial foreseeable residual risks, particularly those arising from industrial activities, bears no practical resemblance to the conventional negligence rule.

22. CL, 89.

23. *Restatement (Second) of Torts,* §519, Comment e (based on Madsen v. East Jordan Irrigation Co., 125 P.2d 794 (Utah 1942)). Many commentators believe that this form of strict liability was the dominant rule in tort prior to the nineteenth century. See M. Horwitz, *The Transformation of American Law, 1780–1860,* 85 (1977). Application of cause-based strict liability today, as in Holmes's time, sparks the greatest controversy in torts over the threshold of responsibility. G. L. Priest, "The New Legal Structure of Risk Control," 119 *Daedalus* 207, 218–219 (1990). The most heated debate centers on the use of cause-based strict liability in mass tort cases, particularly those involving toxic chemicals and pharmaceuticals. See Beshada v. Johns-Manville Products Corp., 447 A.2d 539 (N.J. 1982); Feldman v. Lederle Labs, 479 A.2d 374 (N.J. 1984); Anderson v. Owens-Illinois, Inc., 799 F.2d 1 (1st Cir. 1986) (objecting to "absolute liability"); A. Schwartz, "Products Liability, Corporate Structure, and Bankruptcy: Toxic Substances and the Remote Risk Relationship," 14 *Journal of Legal Studies* 689 (1985); S. Shavell, *Economic Analysis of Accident Law,* 128–131 (1987).

24. CL, 94. Any case authority for cause-based strict liability represented, on Holmes's analysis, an evolutionary dead-end "dry precedent." CL, 89.

25. Fletcher v. Rylands L.R. 1 Ex. 265 (1866), aff'd Rylands v. Fletcher L.R. 3 H.L. 330 (1868). (Referred to collectively as "*Rylands*"). Justice Blackburn's opinion in the Court of Exchequer Chamber, as endorsed in the opinions of Lords Cairns and Cranworth for the House of Lords, is considered the most authoritative. Fleming, *The Law of Torts*, 306–07. Commentators read Blackburn's opinion as adopting the reasonable foresight qualification to strict liability, id. at 316–317; E. R. Thayer, "Liability Without Fault," 29 *Harvard Law Review* 801, 805–806 (1916), and they find vindication in subsequent rulings by the English courts applying the foresight limitation on *Rylands*. Nichols v. Marsland 2 Ex. D. 1 (1876); Greenock Corp. v. Caledonian Ry. A.C. 556 (1917). Holmes distinguished precisely between Cranworth's support for absolute responsibility and Blackburn's foresight-based ruling. CL, 88 and n.4, 156–157.

26. Brown v. Collins, 53 N.H. 442 (1873). On Doe's judicial career, see J. P. Reid, *Chief Justice: The Judicial World of Charles Doe* (1967).

27. 2 Commentaries, *561 n.1. For a current generalized foreseeability explanation of the major rules of strict liability, see G. Calabresi and J. T. Hirschoff, "Toward a Test for Strict Liability in Tort," 81 *Yale Law Journal* 1055, 1066 (1972) (noting that the various "forms of liability, whether for animals, ultrahazardous activities, *Fletcher v. Rylands* situations or even workmen's compensation, were limited . . . in terms of whether the injury stemmed from the risk whose presence was the reason for making the activity strictly liable. Had a cow trespassed, or had it instead bitten a neighbor; had a tiger mangled somebody, or had it simply chewed grass; had a bomb exploded, or had it just rolled and crushed somebody's foot?").

28. *Restatement of Torts*, §519 (1938) (declaring that those who engage in "ultrahazardous activities" "should recognize as likely" and therefore be held strictly liable for the type of harm that "makes the activity ultrahazardous"). Under §519, and its successor, *Restatement (Second) of Torts*, §519, the strict liability rule is unaffected by the fact that the characteristic harm of the ultrahazardous activity arises by a wholly unforeseeable course of events. Commentators have usually overestimated the existence of cause-based strict liability in tort history, whether by ignoring the foresight-based version altogether or by failing to consider a generalizedforesight explanation such as Holmes offered. They have also underestimated the presence of foresight-based strict liability by misclassifying many cases where courts ostensibly apply the negligence rule but set the standard of reasonable conduct at a level that is stringent enough to eliminate (or compensate) all reasonably foreseeable harm.

29. M. Cohen, "Justice Holmes and the Nature of Law," 31 *Columbia Law Review* 352, 353 (1931).

30. F. James, Jr., and J. J. Dickinson, "Accident Proneness and Accident Law,"

63 *Harvard Law Review* 769, 779 (1950). For convenient reference I label this view the "negligence-dogma" interpretation.

31. M. D. Howe, *Justice Oliver Wendell Holmes, The Proving Years: 1870–1882* (1963).

32. G. E. White, *Tort Law in America: An Intellectual History,* 19 (1980).

33. L. Friedman, *A History of American Law,* 426 (1973); R. Posner, "A Theory of Negligence," 1 *Journal of Legal Studies* 29, 30 (1972).

34. G. Calabresi, *The Costs of Accidents,* 261 (1970); M. Horwitz, Book Review, 42 *University of Chicago Law Review* 787, 790, 796 (1975). See also R. A. Epstein, *Modern Products Liability Law,* 26 (1980) (he includes Holmes among the "academic writers [who] thought that a uniform theory of negligence should in principle govern all physical injury cases"); R. L. Rabin, "The Historical Development of the Fault Principle: A Reinterpretation," 15 *Georgia Law Review* 925, 929 (1981)(in the torts lectures, strict liability was the *bête noire*); Fletcher, "Utility and Fairness," 564. (Holmes dubbed strict liability "unmoral.")

35. G. T. Schwartz, "Tort Law and the Economy in Nineteenth-Century America: A Reinterpretation," 90 *Yale Law Journal* 1717 (1981). Schwartz traces the subsidy thesis to articles published in the 1950s. But the idea originated much earlier. See R. Pound, *An Introduction to the Philosophy of Law,* 19 (1922; rpt. 1954). Ironically, Holmes himself implied the subsidy thesis in suggesting that fear of socialism prompted judicial opposition to strict liability in industrial cases. CLP, "Path of the Law," 184.

Relief from bearing the residual risk of nonnegligent activity represents the "subsidy" for industry from a negligence hegemony—established by switching from or refusing to adopt strict liability. See G. Calabresi, "Some Thoughts on Risk Distribution and the Law of Torts," 70 *Yale Law Journal* 499, 515–517 (1961). The claimed evidence for and effectiveness of using the negligence rule to subsidize industry have been soundly criticized by a number of scholars. Schwartz, "Tort Law and the Economy"; G. T. Schwartz, "The Character of Early American Tort Law," 36 *UCLA Law Review* 641 (1989); S. F. Williams, Book Review, 25 *UCLA Law Review* 1187 (1978); Rabin, "Historical Development of the Fault Principle"; R. Epstein, "The Social Consequences of Common Law Rules," 95 *Harvard Law Review* 1717 (1982).

36. The most prominent exposition of the orthodox transformation theory is presented in Horwitz, *Transformation of American Law: 1780–1860.* Antecedents of this view are found in J. B. Ames, "Law and Morals," 22 *Harvard Law Review* 97 (1908) and J. H. Wigmore, "Responsibility for Tortious Acts," 7 *Harvard Law Review* 441 (1894). For the minority view that tort liability was always conditioned on negligence, see J. H. Baker, *An Introduction to English Legal History* (1979). See also S. F. C. Milsom, *Historical Foundations of the Common Law* (1969). Other commentators deny that either rule held sway before negligence prevailed in the late nineteenth century. See White, *Tort Law in America.*

37. R. W. Gordon, "Holmes's *Common Law* as Legal and Social Science," 10 *Hofstra Law Review* 719, 720 (1982).

38. M. Horwitz, *The Transformation of American Law: 1870–1960*, 13, 124–125 (1992).

39. G. Gilmore, *The Death of Contract*, 16–17 (1974).

40. The term "progressivism" has been attached to the political movement early in this century advocating a set of substantive reforms in response particularly to business monopolies and union-busting. See M. Keller, *Regulating a New Economy: Public Policy and Economic Change in America, 1900–1933* (1990). For an argument associating progressivism and legal realism, see Horwitz, *The Transformation of American Law, 1870–1960*.

On the compound of ideas collected under the phrase "legal realism," see W. W. Fisher III, M. J. Horwitz, and T. A. Reed, eds., *American Legal Realism* (1993); E. A. Purcell, *The Crisis of Democratic Theory: Scientific Naturalism and the Problem of Value* (1973); R. S. Summers, *Instrumentalism and American Legal Theory* (1982). Holmes's jurisprudential thought is generally acknowledged as the wellspring for legal realism. See Purcell, *Crisis of Democratic Theory*, 361; M. White, *Social Thought in America: The Revolt Against Formalism*, 59–75 (1947); P. P. Wiener, *Evolution and the Founders of Pragmatism*, 4, 35–36 (1949); R. A. Posner, *The Problems of Jurisprudence*, 19–20 (1990); Fisher, Horwitz, and Reed, *American Legal Realism*, 3–6; letter from Roscoe Pound to Holmes (Nov. 11, 1919), Special Collections, Harvard Law School Library (Holmes's "functional conceptions of jurisprudence" founded the modern realist "side of legal science"). An examination of that claim is beyond the scope of this book. Although I recognize that many elements of Holmes's antiformalism and new jurisprudence coincide with the methods and purposes attributed to legal realism, my own purpose is to work within Holmes's definitions and conceptions to clarify and elaborate his thinking in jurisprudence and its relationship to his theory of torts.

I do not intend to enter the fray over whether Holmes's jurisprudence should be categorized under the headings and particular schools of "pragmatism," "positivism," or "utilitarianism." For recent important contributions to this much mooted issue, see H. L. Pohlman, *Justice Oliver Wendell Holmes & Utilitarian Jurisprudence* (1984); T. C. Grey, "Holmes and Legal Pragmatism," 41 *Stanford Law Review* 787 (1989); J. Millar, "Holmes, Peirce, and Legal Pragmatism," 84 *Yale Law Journal* 1123 (1975); C. W. Hantzis, "Legal Innovation Within the Wider Intellectual Tradition: The Pragmatism of Oliver Wendell Holmes, Jr.," 82 *Northwestern University Law Review* 541 (1988); P. Kelley, "A Critical Analysis of Holmes's Theory of Torts," 61 *Washington University Law Quarterly* 681 (1984); and the exchange between M. D. Howe, "The Positivism of Mr. Justice Holmes," 64 *Harvard Law Review* 529 (1951), and H. M. Hart, Jr., "Holmes's Positivism—An Addendum," 64 *Harvard Law Review* 929 (1951). I see little chance of this classification effort succeeding, in large part because the categories are so malleable as to be virtually meaningless. Moreover, my research indicates that the main thrust and originality of Holmes's jurisprudence was not in its coherent development of a particular approach, but rather in its more or less eclectic synthesis of various strands of philosophical thought, especially in regard to the nature and uses of scientific methodology in the investigation of law as a social institution.

41. Gordon, "Holmes's *Common Law*," 719–720.

42. Howe, *The Proving Years*, 180–189 and n.11.

43. Friedman, *History of American Law*, 486.

44. CL, 136, 108.

45. This portion of Lecture IV is substantially different in content from Holmes's 1873 essay of the same title.

46. CL(I), 144.

47. See Hart, *Punishment and Responsibility*.

48. CLP, "Privilege, Malice, and Intent," 117.

1. Formalist Legal Science

1. CLP, "Privilege, Malice, and Intent," 122.

2. For the view that Holmes broke from formalism after publication of the Theory of Torts (1873), see M. D. Howe, *Justice Oliver Wendell Holmes: The Proving Years, 1870–1882*, 81–82, 141 (1963). Some commentators argue that the changeover occurred in three stages or gradually during the 1870s. See F. R. Kellogg, *The Formative Essays of Justice Holmes*, 35 (1984). Others, however, believe that Holmes retained much of his formalist approach through *The Common Law* and, indeed, throughout his life. See G. Gilmore, *The Ages of American Law*, 56 (1977).

3. O. W. Holmes, Book Notice, 5 *American Law Review* 343 (1870); O. W. Holmes, Book Notice, 5 *American Law Review* 536 (1870). See also CLP, "Path of the Law," 195–198.

4. CLP, "Law in Science and Science in Law," 229; CLP, 301. For general discussion of Holmes's early dissatisfaction with the state of jurisprudence, see CL(H), xii–xv.

5. CLP, "Law in Science," 223; CLP, "Path of the Law," 195–197.

6. EW, "The Code of Iowa," 792–793; OS, 170.

7. OS, 49. See also CLP, 166; OS, 99.

8. CLP, "Path of the Law," 195–196.

9. O. W. Holmes, Book Notice, 5 *American Law Review* 340, 341 (1870).

10. CL, 78. To avoid confusion, the initial letters will be capitalized in subsequent references to the writs "Trespass" and "Case" (referred to collectively as the "writ system"). For background on the early English forms of action, and development of the various writs of trespass, including Trespass on the Case, see J. H. Baker, *An Introduction to English Legal History* (1979); on the reception and demise of the writ system in America, see C. O. Gregory, "Trespass to Negligence to Absolute Liability," 37 *Virginia Law Review* 359 (1951).

11. Holmes praised Chief Justice Lemuel Shaw of Massachusetts for shunting aside the procedural writs to reach the substance of tort liability in Brown v. Kendall, 60 Mass. 292 (1850): "[F]ew have lived who were his equals in their understanding of the grounds of public policy to which all laws must ultimately be referred." CL, 106.

12. Id. at 90.

13. CLP, "Path of the Law," 196; CLP, "Law in Science," 223; O. W. Holmes, Book Notice, 5 *American Law Review* 359 (1871) (last paragraph attributed to Holmes, see Howe, *The Proving Years,* 64 n.10); EW, "Codes, and the Arrangement of the Law," 726–727.

14. CLP, "Law in Science," 223.

15. Letter from Holmes to Morris R. Cohen (Aug. 3, 1923), HC, 34. See also CLP, "The Use of Law Schools," 38 (observing that "science, like courage, is never beyond the necessity of proof, but must always be ready to prove itself against all challengers").

16. Holmes rejected absolute truth, holding instead that "truth" was merely a strong, if transitory, state of psychological conviction, externally revealed and measured by an individual's willingness to act upon a belief (induced by empirical evidence) in a cause-and-effect relationship. See 1873 Theory of Torts, 779. "When I say that a thing is true, I mean that I cannot help believing it. I am stating an experience as to which there is no choice." CLP, "Ideals and Doubts," 304–305. This probabilistic and skeptical epistemology underlies Holmes's famous dissenting dictum in Abrams v. U. S., 250 U. S. 616, 630 (1919): "The best test of truth is the power of the thought to get itself accepted in the competition of the market." His conception of truth as a belief strong enough to motivate action (or "*bet* on the behavior of the universe" (2 HPL 252)) dates from a book review he published in 1 *American Law Review* 375 (1867). M. D. Howe, *Justice Oliver Wendell Holmes: The Shaping Years, 1841–1870,* 265–267 (1957). See also Letter from Holmes to Morris R. Cohen (Feb. 5, 1919), HC, 14–15. For a general discussion of the intellectual sources for Holmes's understanding of science, see P. P. Wiener, *Founders of Pragmatism* (1949); Howe, *The Shaping Years,* 52–57, 221.

17. For a general discussion of Gray's life and work, see A. H. Dupree, *Asa Gray* (1959). For additional background on Gray's scientific approach, see A. D. Rodgers, *American Botany 1873–1892* (1944).

18. The artificial approach sought a Platonic taxonomy based on the "systematist's subjective apprehension of the ideal organic form." M. T. Ghiselin, *The Triumph of the Darwinian Method,* 52–53 (1984). On the *a priori* mode of classification generally and as applied to the Linnaean artificial system, see also J. A. Moore, *Science as a Way of Knowing,* 123–127, 148–149 (1993); J. Dewey, *The Influence of Darwin on Philosophy,* 6–7 (1910); Dupree, *Asa Gray,* 28, 34, 52–53.

19. In the ranks of Harvard's science faculty, Gray was the lone "agitator" against transcendentalism, final-cause determinism, and other *a priori* explana-

tions, demanding strict adherence to the empiricist methods of stating hypotheses provisionally for constant testing by experiment and observation. Howe, *The Shaping Years,* 52–57; Dupree, *Asa Gray,* 138, 226. Gray saw Agassiz as the principal representative of the German idealistic philosophy, *Naturphilosophie* ("natural theology"), which dominated biological science before Darwin (Dupree, *Asa Gray,* 232). See also E. Mayr, *One Long Argument,* 52–55, 183 (1991). In it classification of species was considered more real than the actual species because the idea more closely corresponded with God's design. Following an *a priori* design, natural theology deduced fixed and immutable categorizations impervious to empirical contradiction. Nonconforming evidence was ignored or explained by special creation of new species or other saltation theories. Although Spencer adopted a natural selection theory of evolution, Gray considered its *a priori* assumptions of inevitable progress and final cause simply another version of natural theology. For an insightful account of the confrontation between empirical science and natural theology in biology, see Wiener, *Founders of Pragmatism.* There was a pivotal debate on this subject at Harvard between Gray and Agassiz, with Holmes in attendance. Dupree, *Asa Gray,* 246.

20. Darwin was first drawn to Gray because of his criticism of Agassiz's natural theology. Gray became one of Darwin's closest confidants in the years just preceding publication of *On the Origin of Species.* In 1857, Gray was included in the exclusive group to receive Darwin's precis of the theory, which later served as critical documentation of his priority over Alfred Wallace. For a discussion of Darwin's relationship with Gray, see Dupree, *Asa Gray,* 239–246. For an excellent explanation of Darwin's theories of evolution and scientific method, their effect on previously prevailing natural theology in biology, and Gray's importance in championing these ideas, see Mayr, *One Long Argument* and Ghiselin, *Darwinian Method.*

21. Letter from Holmes to Morris R. Cohen (Feb. 5, 1919), HC, 14–15. See Howe, *The Shaping Years,* 17–18, 25–26, 285.

22. On Holmes's reading in science, see Howe, *The Shaping Years,* 210, 213, 257–259; Howe, *The Proving Years,* 149–150.

23. Wiener, *Founders of Pragmatism,* chaps. 1–2, 18–25.

24. On the scientific and philosophical background and teachings of Wright and his influence on Holmes and the other members of the Metaphysical Club, see Wiener, *Founders of Pragmatism;* E. H. Madden, ed., *The Philosophical Writings of Chauncey Wright,* vii (1958); Dupree, *Asa Gray,* 289–292; Howe, *The Shaping Years,* 256–258, 269, 312 n.46; Howe, *The Proving Years,* 4, 151.

25. Science, in Wright's view, accepts the diversity of life processes and therefore examines the world from multiple perspectives. Accordingly, it was unscientific for Spencer to presuppose that natural selection explained the totality of living nature, most especially that it applied to evolving legal and other social institutions. Dupree, *Asa Gray,* 290.

26. CLP, "Law in Science," 210; CLP, "Ideals and Doubts," 303–305.

27. CLP, "Path of the Law," 180.

28. Ibid. So long as scientists abide the test of experience, they may find inspiration in whatever "miracle creed" they choose (A. Einstein, *Ideas and Opinions,* 342 (1954)), whether it is Emerson's transcendentalism or a more conventional religion, as in Gray's case. See C. Wright, *Philosophical Discussions,* 47 (1877, rpt. 1971). Holmes consistently adhered to the "scientific canon[s] of evidence," in formulating his legal theories. M. D. Howe, ed., *Holmes-Laski Letters,* 725. "Every wise man was at bottom a mystic," he said, "but one must get one's mysticism like one's miracles in the right place—right at the beginning or end." Letter from Holmes to Lucy Clifford (Nov. 7, 1924), HP.

29. Letter from Holmes to Pollock (Aug. 30, 1929), 2 HPL 252. See also Holmes's letters to Max C. Otto (Sept. 26, 1929), in 38 *Journal of Philosophy* 391 (1941), and to Morris R. Cohen (Sept. 4, 1923), HC, 34–35. ("That we could not assert necessity of the order of the universe I learned to believe from Chauncey Wright long ago. I suspect C.S. P[eirce] got it from the same source.")

30. On Langdell's legal science, see M. W. Reimann, "Holmes's *Common Law* and German Legal Science," in R. W. Gordon, ed., *The Legacy of Oliver Wendell Holmes, Jr.,* 72–114 (1992); M. H. Hoeflich, "Law & Geometry: Legal Science from Leibniz to Langdell," 30 *American Journal of Legal History* 95, 119–121 (1986); T. C. Grey, "Langdell's Orthodoxy," 45 *University of Pittsburgh Law Review* 1 (1983).

31. CLP, 302; J. Austin, *The Province of Jurisprudence Determined* (1832; rpt. 1954); F. C. Von Savigny, *Of the Vocation of Our Age for Legislation and Jurisprudence* (1831). See generally, 2 J. Bryce, "The Methods of Legal Science," in *Studies in History and Jurisprudence,* 607–637 (1901) and J. Dawson, *The Oracles of the Law* (1968). A lucid, thumbnail sketch of analytic and historical legal science is provided in L. L. Fuller, *Basic Contract Law,* 519–526 (1947). For a more detailed discussion of the formalist character of these schools, see Hoeflich, "Law & Geometry" and Reimann, "German Legal Science."

32. FE, "Common Carriers and the Common Law," 223.

33. Ibid. On American contributions to legal science prior to Langdell, see Hoeflich, "Law & Geometry."

34. See Hoeflich, "Law & Geometry," 95.

35. CLP, "Path of the Law," 180.

36. CLP, "Law in Science," 238.

37. Austin, *Province of Jurisprudence,* 77–78.

38. CLP, "Path of the Law," 180.

39. Ibid; CL, 210. The German historical school divided over whether German custom was founded on Roman law or was mainly an indigenous growth. Holmes sided with the latter faction. On the split between the "Romanist" and "Germanist" factions of the German historical movement, see P. Stein, *Legal Evolution,* 63 (1980) and Dawson, *Oracles of the Law,* 460.

40. Savigny, *Legislation and Jurisprudence,* 45.

41. EW, "The Gas-Stokers' Strike," 796; CLP, "Privilege, Malice, and Intent," 126–127.

42. R. Pound, "Judge Holmes's Contributions to the Science of Law," 34 *Harvard Law Review* 449, 451 (1921).

43. FE, "Common Carriers," 222–223; CLP, "Natural Law," 310; Howe, *The Shaping Years,* 209–215; Howe, *The Proving Years,* 174. Holmes denied the relevance of the syllogistic legal structures constructed from essentialist first principles and derivative rights. Postulates drawn from idealized conceptions of human nature, such as the Kantian notion that "freedom of the will . . . is the essence of man," were unverifiable and subjective; proof was in the mind and conscience of the beholder. CL, 207; CLP, "Natural Law," 310. "No doubt behind these legal rights is the fighting will of the subject to maintain them," Holmes argued, "but that does not seem . . . the same thing as the supposed *a priori* discernment of a duty or the assertion of a preexisting right. A dog will fight for his bone." CLP, "Natural Law," 313–314. Moreover, even if determinate rights were deducible from a vague idea like free will, they could not reconcile cultural differences and accommodate changing social conditions. Social need for expedient policy would demand "a sacrifice of principle to convenience," as indeed, according to Holmes, the "spirit of the Kantian theory required" (CL, 211). But then, he queried, "what is left of a principle which avows itself inconsistent with convenience and the actual course of legislation?" (Ibid.) It must either dissolve or dissemble in the face of conflicting experience. That metaphysics offered normative insights, Holmes never denied; but its self-validating, unverifiable musings were as far from scientific explanations as divine revelation.

44. Holmes admired and appropriated many ideas of method and substance from H. Maine, *Ancient Law: Its Connection with the Early History of Society and Its Relation to Modern Ideas* (1861; rpt. 1963). Nevertheless, he sharply criticized Maine for being overly impressionistic, reading too much Roman law into the English common law, and infusing his legal evolution with final cause or progressivist designs. The "English models" epitomized by Maine (as opposed to Maitland) were generally "inferior" to "German methods," which exhibited an "exactness in details" necessary for the "scientific study" of history. O. W. Holmes, Book Review, 11 *American Law Review* 327–329 (1876). See Kellogg, *Formative Essays,* 11–12; M. Keller, *Affairs of State: Public Life in Late Nineteenth Century America,* 343–344 (1977).

45. CLP, "Law in Science," 225.

46. CL, 1, 37.

47. CLP, "Privilege, Malice, and Intent," 126.

48. CL, 35.

49. CL, 36–37.

50. CL, 1.

51. CL, 211.

52. CL, 35.

53. In Chapter 3 I examine "Trespass and Negligence," which was published as a separate essay in 1880 and subsequently incorporated with some significant changes as Lecture III of *The Common Law.*

54. FE, "Primitive Notions in Modern Law," 130.

55. Austin, *Province of Jurisprudence,* 370, 348, 369.

56. Id. at 30–32, 134, 194, 230–231, 262.

57. Id. at 30–32, 230–31, 254, 262.

58. 1 J. Austin, *Lectures on Jurisprudence or the Philosophy of Positive Law,* 346 (5th ed., 1885). See also Austin, *Province of Jurisprudence,* 369, 370.

59. 1 Austin, *Lectures on Jurisprudence,* 102. Although judges did change rules and doctrines, these seeming deviations, Austin explained, were merely ministerial applications of power delegated by the sovereign.

60. FE, "Possession," 181; CL, 213–215, 219. Kellogg suggests a similar interpretation, see Kellogg, *Formative Essays,* 24–25. Holmes's analytic deconstruction of the concepts of rights and duties to reveal their public policy underpinnings anticipated by several decades the work of Wesley Hohfeld. Hohfeld's article, "Some Fundamental Legal Conceptions as Applied in Judicial Reasoning," 23 *Yale Law Journal* 16 (1913) was hailed by legal realists as a major breakthrough. Holmes's characteristic chagrin at seeing his founding contributions ignored may explain his comment to Pollock that Hohfeld's "pretty good and keen distinctions [were] of the kind that are more needed by a lower grade of lawyer than they are by you and me . . . [A]ll those systematic schematisms rather bore[]." Letter from Holmes to Pollock (Feb. 9, 1921), 2 HPL 64.

61. FE, "The Arrangement of the Law—Privity," 95 (quoting with approval Auguste Comte's views). Important examples of incomplete duties effectively converting rights into mere policy compromises could be found in the myriad "restrictions on the use of property by its owners, (*sic utere tuo,* etc.)." FE, "Codes, and the Arrangement of the Law," 82, 83–85; CLP, "Privilege, Malice, and Intent," 120. "Property," Holmes concluded, is "a creation of law." International News Service v. Associated Press, 248 U.S. 215, 246 (1918) (Holmes, J. concurring).

62. CLP, "Privilege, Malice, and Intent," 124–126. Holmes used the same example to the same effect nearly two decades earlier in "Primitive Notions in Modern Law." FE, 129–30 n.2. Moreover, as he pointed out in "Primitive Notions," courts used external standards to draw the policy line demarcating the extent of the defendant's responsibility (duty) and privilege if any; "actual wish or intent to injure is not taken into consideration, except to rebut privilege" (ibid). Many current commentators erroneously claim that "Privilege, Malice, and Intent" was the first time that Holmes acknowledged the use of subjective malice to qualify privileges, and that this dramatic reversal represented his first realization that courts do not merely apply politically neutral customs but inevitably resolve conflicts in policy. See discussions of this point below and in Chapters 2 and 4.

63. 1873 Theory of Torts, 775.

64. Ibid. Throughout his judicial and scholarly writing Holmes reiterated the inevitable policy-making role of courts as they draw "arbitrary" lines to balance by matters of degree the competing and irreconcilable interests at stake that fall within "penumbra or debatable land." CL, 127–129. For example, note his opinions in Vegelahn v. Guntner, 167 Mass. 92, 106 (1896); Hudson Water Co. v. McCarter, 209 U.S. 349, 355 (1908); Schlesinger v. Wisconsin, 270 U.S. 230, 241 (1926); Springer v. Phillippine Islands, 227 U.S. 189, 209–210. Compare with CLP, "Path of the Law," 181; CLP, "Privilege, Malice, and Intent," 125–127; CLP, "Ideals and Doubts," 306–307; CLP, "Law in Science," 232–233.

65. Holmes's views on the exercise of judicial policy discretion in torts are developed in chapters 4 and 5.

66. CL, 81.

67. Id. at 68.

68. H. L. A. Hart, *Essays on Bentham,* 129 (1982).

69. FE, "Codes, and the Arrangement of the Law," 88.

70. Ibid.

71. FE, "Codes, and the Arrangement of the Law," 78–81; FE, "The Arrangement of the Law—Privity," 95; FE, "Possession," 181.

72. FE, "The Arrangement of the Law—Privity," 96–98.

73. Id. at 95.

74. FE, "Codes, and the Arrangement of the Law," 79–81.

75. CL, 215, 213.

76. EW, "Misunderstandings of the Civil Law," 764. The misguiding lure of general principles was well illustrated for Holmes by the implantation of "fragments of the Roman structure" into the common law of bailments, "in such a place and manner as to entirely miss the ends which they originally answered, while at the same time they are equally ill adapted to any new purpose" (ibid). See also UCLP, 30–31.

77. Lochner v. New York, 198 U.S. 45, 76 (1905) (Holmes, J., dissenting).

78. This was a fair criticism, because Austin considered a theory "mere jargon" unless it corresponded with "particular truths." 1 Austin, *Lectures on Jurisprudence,* 115–116; see also J. S. Mill, "Austin on Jurisprudence," in 4 J. S. Mill, *Dissertations and Discussions,* 210 (1867).

79. FE, "Codes, and the Arrangement of the Law," 80–81.

80. Id. at 80–82.

81. 1872 Jurisprudence Essay, 789.

82. 2 Commentaries, *561 n.1.

83. 1872 Jurisprudence Essay, 789.

84. Ibid.

85. 2 Commentaries, *561 n.1.

86. 1872 Jurisprudence Essay, 789–90.

87. Id. at 790–791; FE, "Trespass and Negligence," 225; CL, 82.

88. FE, "Primitive Notions in Modern Law," 129.

89. 1872 Jurisprudence Essay, 790.

90. Id. at 790–791. Trover emerged in the fifteenth century to augment the existing trespass remedies for conversion (misappropriation of personal property). It gave the plaintiff a "forced sale" option to refuse tender of the wrongfully detained or taken goods and to compel the defendant to pay their full, not merely use, value. W. P. Keeton, et al., *Prosser and Keeton on Torts,* 88–89 (1984).

91. Ibid. By showing that tort damages generally had the effect of a tariff or other overhead cost of doing business, Holmes developed a powerful compensation rationale that paved the way for strict liability in this century. G. L. Priest, "The Invention of Enterprise Liability: A Critical History of the Intellectual Foundations of Modern Tort Law," 14 *Journal of Legal Studies* 461 (1985). In addition, the distinction he drew between tort liability which imposes a mere tax versus that which imposes a prohibitive expense foreshadowed modern discussions differentiating the prohibitive effects of property-type rules from the taxing effects of liability-type rules. Current debate begins with G. Calabresi and A. D. Melamed, "Property Rules, Liability Rules, and Inalienability: One View of the Cathedral," 85 *Harvard Law Review* 1089 (1972).

92. Id. at 791.

93. 1873 Theory of Torts, 773.

94. Id. at 774.

95. FE, "Codes, and the Arrangement of Law," 80. See also UCLP, 52.

96. 1872 Jurisprudence Essay, 791. Apparently, Holmes's extensive reading of cases in preparing a footnote-essay on "negligence" for the 12th edition of *Kent's Commentaries on American Law,* 2 Commentaries *561 n.1, led him to reconsider his estimate of the courts' use of external standards of conduct rather than subjective states of mind. This essay summarized the views presented in "The Theory of Torts," and prefigured much of his thinking on the subject. Holmes regarded the work on the *Commentaries* as a necessary but tedious step in launching his career in legal scholarship. For an account of Holmes's labors on *Kent's Commentaries* see Howe, *The Proving Years,* 10–25.

97. 1872 Jurisprudence Essay, 789; see also FE, "Codes, and the Arrangement of the Law," 80.

98. Compare FE, "Codes, and the Arrangement of the Law," 80; 1872 Jurisprudence Essay, 789–791; CL, 317; with CLP, "Path of the Law," 171–175.

99. 1872 Jurisprudence Essay, 791. See also FE, "Primitive Notions in Modern Law," 130; CL, 144–157; 1873 Theory of Torts, 773–774; 2 Commentaries, *561 n.1.

100. 2 Commentaries, *561 n.1. For background on Rylands v. Fletcher, see Introduction.

101. 1873 Theory of Torts, 774, 785.

102. Id. at 773; FE, "Primitive Notions in Modern Law," 130; CL, 155.

103. 1873 Theory of Torts, 773–774.

104. CL, 155; 1873 Theory of Torts, 773–774; FE, "Primitive Notions in Modern Law," 130.

105. CL, 155.

106. 1873 Theory of Torts, 774.

107. CL, 161; see also CL, 117, 156; 1873 Theory of Torts, 774.

108. 1872 Jurisprudence Essay, 791.

109. Ibid.

110. Ibid. See also CL, 156.

111. Suggestive of the way Gray attacked the artificial system in botany, Holmes criticized reliance on the outmoded arbitrary "categories of the forms of action" for classifying the substantive law of tort. CL, 78. He called for a classification system depicting the "practical shape" of the various rules as indicated by "experience" and "considerations of policy," and generally applauded departure from the "ancient ways" of organizing rules and the growing willingness to apply "business-like common sense" in "adapting law to modern requirements." 1 CW 239 (1871); CL, 1, 312, 78; 1 CW 204 (1869); CLP, "Path of the Law," 192. I respond in Chapter 2 to the characterizations of Holmes and his classificatory aims as formalist.

112. 1873 Theory of Torts, 785.

113. Id. at 784.

114. Ibid.

115. Id. at 774.

116. CL(H), 144.

117. CLP, "Ideals and Doubts," 305–307; CL, 43–45, 48, 162–163; 1873 Theory of Torts, 775.

118. 1873 Theory of Torts, 785.

119. Id. at 783.

120. Ibid.

121. Ibid.

122. Ibid.

123. Id. at 781.

124. CLP, "Path of the Law," 179.

125. FE, "Possession," 181. "I became convinced," Holmes later recalled, "that the machinery of rights and duties was a fifth wheel." Letter from Holmes to John Chipman Gray (Oct. 27, 1914), HP. Reduced to the "rudiments," to call something a right is simply to predict what the courts will do in fact, but that statement, like "talk of the force of gravitation accounting for the conduct of bodies in space ... adds no more than ... what we know without it." Letter from Holmes to Pollock (Jan. 19, 1928), 2 HPL 212; see also CLP, "Natural Law," 313; CLP, "Path of the Law," 170–179.

126. Letter from Holmes to Chief Judge Simon E. Baldwin (Feb. 16, 1897), box 35, folder 6, HP.

127. Savigny, *Legislation and Jurisprudence,* 28–30.

128. Id. at 26–29.

129. Id. at 29.

130. G. F. Puchta, *Pandekten,* 25 (2d ed. 1844); quoted in A. von Mehren and J. Gordley, *The Civil Law System,* 67 (2d ed. 1977). Id. at 81, 85–87, 95. This system was ultimately translated into the German Civil Code of 1900, which founded torts on negligence.

131. EW, "Misunderstandings of the Civil Law," 764.

132. FE, "Primitive Notions in Modern Law," 130–131; FE, "Primitive Notions in Modern Law—II," 147; FE, "Common Carriers," 223 and n.1.

133. 1873 Theory of Torts, 773 n.2; FE, "Primitive Notions in Modern Law," 144. Holmes expanded upon his historical criticism of Austin's personal culpability theory in this 1875 essay. "Primitive Notions in Modern Law" furnished the basis for Lecture I of *The Common Law.*

134. CL, 38, 40.

135. Savigny, *Legislation and Jurisprudence,* 30.

136. 1873 Theory of Torts, 775; 2 Commentaries, *561 n.1.

137. CL, 36–37.

138. EW, "The Gas-Stokers' Strike," 795–796.

139. EW, "Codes, and the Arrangement of the Law," 79–82; 1872 Jurisprudence Essay, 789–790.

140. CL, 36.

141. CLP, "Law in Science," 211. See also CLP, "Agency II," 101. In the margin of his copy of *The Common Law* Holmes noted: "Imagination of men limited—can only think in terms of the language they have been taught. Conservative instinct" (CL(I), 2). This was a comment on the following text: "The substance of the law at any given time pretty nearly corresponds, so far as it goes, with what is then understood to be convenient; but its form and machinery, and the degree to which it is able to work out desired results, depend very much on the past" (CL, 1–2). The point of studying history was precisely to liberate the present from the constraints of the past by demonstrating that changes in the law occur not from predetermining first or final causes, but from deliberate choices of expedience for the "here and now" (OS, 96). Thus, in repeating the advice to avoid thinking of continuity with the past as a duty, Holmes pointed out how quickly and pragmatically even the most established doctrines of law can be changed. For example, once a "legislature is able to imagine abolishing the requirement of a consideration for a simple contract, it is at perfect liberty to abolish it, if it thinks it wise to do so, without the slightest regard to continuity with the past" (CLP, "Law in Science," 211).

142. UCLP, 31.

143. CLP, "Natural Law," 311. Evoking a Darwinian image, Holmes illustrated the historical and cultural relativity of law by comparing the different rules governing capture of whales in Greenland and the Galapagos, taking the fact that "courts adopt different rules on similar facts . . . to shake an *a priori* theory of the matter." CL, 212–213; see also CL, 216–218.

144. UCLP 6, 32–33. Holmes suggested the same imagined connection misled Austin and was infecting recent English commentary. See FE, "Common Carriers," 205 n.2.

145. While initially believing that important areas of English law (such as the law of succession) were derived from knowledge of Roman law and were not the "spontaneous growth of the social needs," Holmes was soon convinced by further study that the reverse was true. Compare FE, "The Arrangement of the Law—Privity," 95; with UCLP, 31; FE, "Primitive Notions in Modern Law," 129–130. But even early on, when he attributed English law to Roman sources, he consistently attacked these contributions as contrary to the social needs and good policy of England at the time of their importation and ever since. UCLP, 320; EW, "Misunderstandings of the Civil Law," 764.

146. CL, 164–165. Bailment involves an agreement by the owner of goods (bailor) to transfer custody of them to another (bailee) for storage or shipment. The reason bailment provides the testing case of the minimum operational requirements for possession is that the law treats bailees as owners of property over which they have custody, even though they "do not own it, or assert the position of an owner for themselves with regard to it" (ibid).

147. UCLP, 34. See also letter from Holmes to A. G. Sedgwick (July 12, 1879), HP.

148. It would completely misconceive English common law to view it in terms of the German equation of law with custom, which subordinated judicial decisions and precedent to the status of mere applications or evidence of the law. Holmes strongly defended the value of precedent in the common law for its utility in conveying time-tested wisdom and, more importantly, for its affirmation of the independent law-making authority of courts. UCLP, 35. For an important contribution to understanding the use of Roman law in German historical science, see J. Q. Whitman, *The Legacy of Roman Law in the German Romantic Era*, 130 (1990).

149. UCLP, 5–7.

150. Theory of Torts, 776–80 (1873); FE, "Codes, and the Arrangement of the Law," 81–82. See also 2 Commentaries, *561 n.1.

151. Theory of Torts, 780 (1873). See also, CL 37, 88–103.

152. EW, "Gas-Stokers' Strike," 795.

153. A slightly revised version of this essay was incorporated as Lecture V of *The Common Law*.

154. FE, "Common Carriers," 202–03. Earlier, Holmes appears to have accepted claims that strict liability for innkeepers originated in the "custom of the realm" (FE, "Codes, and the Arrangement of the Law," 87), but in "Common Carriers" he rejected such claims as post hoc and meritless rationales. FE, 205, 209–212.

155. The criticism by some of Holmes's contemporaries that he greatly overstated the evidence for strict liability in common carrier cases, well taken or not, certainly flies in the face of the negligence-dogma interpretation. See, for example,

E. G. M. Fletcher, *The Carrier's Liability* (1932) and J. H. Beale, "The Carrier's Liability: Its History," 11 *Harvard Law Review* 158 (1897).

156. FE, "Common Carriers," 202.

157. Id. at 209.

158. Ibid.

159. Id. at 209, 222.

160. Id. at 220; FE, "Primitive Notions in Modern Law," 129–130.

161. Coggs v. Bernard (1703), in J. H. Baker and S. F. C. Milsom, *Sources of English Legal History,* 370 (1986); CL, 30.

162. FE, "Common Carriers," 221.

163. Id. at 222.

164. CL, 2–9, 20.

165. 1873 Theory of Torts, 774; CL, 5–9.

166. CL, 156.

167. In contrast to today, as I will show in Chapter 6, Holmes's contemporaries well understood the important support *Rylands* received from his analysis in the "The Theory of Torts" (1873) and subsequently from the foresight theory in *The Common Law,* "The Theory of Torts" (Lect. IV).

168. This amplified the point introduced in his first article, FE, "Codes, and the Arrangement of Law." See also CLP, "Agency I," 49–50.

169. FE, "Common Carriers," 221–222.

170. Id. at 222–223.

171. Id. at 222.

172. Id. at 223.

173. 2 Commentaries, *451 n.1 (footnote essay entitled "Deaf and Dumb"); EW, "Misunderstandings of the Civil Law," 759; FE, "Primitive Notions in Modern Law," 145.

174. FE, "Common Carriers," 222.

175. Southern Pacific Co. v. Jensen, 244 U.S. 205, 222 (1917).

176. FE, "Common Carriers," 222–223. Holmes saw no difference in the nature of the legislative policy made by courts from that made by legislatures. See CL, 112–113; CLP, "Agency I," 67; Black and White Taxicab Co. v. Brown and Yellow Taxicab Co., 276 U.S. 518, 532 (1928) (Holmes, J. dissenting).

177. Id. at 223; FE, "Primitive Notions in Modern Law," 145; CLP, "Agency I," 49.

178. Id. at 222.

179. CL, 36; 1880 Jurisprudence Essay, 711.

180. Letter from Holmes to Pollock (Apr. 10, 1881), 1 HPL 17.

181. In calling Langdell "a Hegelian in disguise" and "the greatest living legal theologian," Holmes probably never considered that his remark might be mistaken for encomium let alone require elaboration. 1880 Jurisprudence Essay, 710.

182. Ibid.

183. Ibid.

184. Ibid.

185. Id. at 710–711.
186. Ibid.
187. Id. at 711.
188. Ibid.
189. Id. at 710–711.
190. Ibid.

2. The New Jurisprudence

1. CL, 1.
2. CLP, "Law in Science and Science in Law," 229.
3. Id. at 239.
4. CL, 36.
5. CLP, "Path of the Law," 182.
6. CLP, "Privilege, Malice and Intent," 120; CL, 35–37.
7. 1880 Jurisprudence Essay, 710.
8. CL, 1.
9. CL, 37.
10. On "population thinking" in Darwin's theory, see E. Mayr, *One Long Argument,* 184 (1991) (the population viewpoint emphasized "the uniqueness of every individual in populations of a sexually reproducing species and therefore the real variability of populations," as opposed to "typological thinking" or essentialism). For an excellent analysis of Holmes's theory of legal evolution and its relationship to the evolutionary paradigm in historiography and jurisprudence, see E. D. Elliott, "Holmes and Evolution: Legal Process as Artificial Intelligence," 13 *Journal of Legal Studies* 113 (1984); H. Hovenkamp, "Evolutionary Models in Jurisprudence," 64 *Texas Law Review* 645 (1985).
11. CLP, "Path of the Law," 181.
12. Ibid.
13. CL, 30.
14. CLP, "Privilege, Malice and Intent," 120–126.
15. Id. at 126.
16. CLP, "Path of the Law," 184.
17. Ibid.
18. Id. at 181.
19. CL, 1.
20. CLP, "The Profession of the Law," 30.
21. CLP, "Path of the Law," 184.
22. Anon., "Holmes's *Common Law*," 15 *American Law Review* 331, 334 (1881).
23. Ibid.
24. Ibid. See also R. Foster, "Holmes on the Common Law," 23 *Albany Law Journal* 380 (1881).
25. The intellectual milieu in the late nineteenth century was conducive to Holm-

es's antiformalism, perhaps more so than he realized. As Charles Peirce recalled the 1870s, "agnosticism was then riding its high horse, and was frowning superbly on all metaphysics." Quoted in P. P. Wiener, *Evolution and the Founders of Pragmatism,* 19 (1949). The rapid acceptance of Darwin's theories of evolution among leading scientists and other intellectuals is documented in T. F. Glick, ed., *The Comparative Reception of Darwinism* (1974); G. Himmelfarb, *Darwin and the Darwinian Revolution* (1959). For a description of the nature and influence of empirical positivism and its leading exponents in the nineteenth century, Auguste Comte and Ernst Mach, see G. Holton, *Science and Anti-Science* (1993) and K. R. Popper, *The Logic of Scientific Discovery* (1968). Holmes's antiformalism paralleled (and undoubtedly reflected) Jeremy Bentham's utilitarianism, Rudolf von Jhering's anticonceptualism; and the proto-pragmatism of James Fitzjames Stephen. See H. L. Pohlman, *Justice Oliver Wendell Holmes & Utilitarian Jurisprudence* (1984); Stein, *Legal Evolution,* 65–69; M. D. Howe, *Justice Oliver Wendell Holmes: The Shaping Years, 1841–1870,* 267–269 (1957).

26. Hay v. The Cohoes Co., 2 N.Y. 159 (1848); Brown v. Collins, 53 N.H. 442 (1873); Losee v. Buchanan, 51 N.Y. 476, 483 (1873); see also Shaw in Farwell v. Boston & Worcester R.R., Corp., 45 Mass. 49, 58–59 (1842); Henderson v. Sullivan, 159 Fed. 46 (6th Cir. 1908); Feinberg v. Wisconsin Granite Co., 224 N.W. 184 (S.D. 1929). This evidence conflicts with the widely held view that by 1900 the dominant style of judicial reasoning had become formalist (in current jargon, "classical legal thought"), marking a dramatic shift from the instrumental style of reasoning based on "public policy" and "justice," which had been "paradigmatic in 1850." See W. W. Fisher III, M. J. Horwitz, and T. A. Reed, eds., *American Legal Realism,* xii (1993). The broader implications of the evidence call into question the current vogue of paradigm-shift (transformation) historiography.

27. CLP, "The Use of Law Schools," 42.

28. FE, "Possession," 181.

29. CLP, "Law in Science," 229. A principal reason that the preference of judges for external standards remained a "hidden ground of policy" was that "their thought still clothe[d] itself in personifying language." CL, 30.

30. CLP, "Path of the Law," 171.

31. CL, 148; CLP, "Path of the Law," 171–175.

32. CLP, "Law in Science and Science in Law," 241.

33. CLP, "Privilege, Malice, and Intent," 126–127; CLP, "Law in Science," 230–232, 240.

34. CLP, "Law in Science," 242. Wright's teachings are unmistakable in Holmes's approach. Thirty years earlier, Wright explained that the "tyranny in . . . reputations [words have is] . . . fatal to freedom of thought . . . [that t]rue science deals with nothing but questions of facts . . . free from moral biases." J. B. Thayer, ed., *Letters of Chauncey Wright,* 113 (1878).

35. UCLP, 121.

36. FE, "Codes, and the Arrangement of the Law," 77; CL, 77.

37. CLP, "Law in Science," 231.

38. OS, 134–135. While acknowledging the relativism of knowledge, Holmes also recognized that anyone with an understanding of science would think it "silly" to deny the powers and benefits of pragmatic knowledge founded on probabilistic predictions and tested by experience. He refused to embrace the psychology or politics of irrationality of the "French skeptics," who "profess[ed] to look with haughty scorn upon a world in ruins." CLP, "Natural Law," 315.

39. CLP, "Law in Science," 224.

40. OS, 133. Ironically, Holmes took care to maintain his distance from reality. During the 1870s, he lived and worked almost entirely within the cloistered Brahmin society of Cambridge and Boston. His bent of mind was decidedly speculative and introspective. Of course, one might say that his Civil War experience was quite enough reality for several lifetimes. Nevertheless, he studiously avoided exposure to the very experience which his own theory posited as the principal force shaping the law. Holmes's disinclination to delve into the facts of social behavior and conditions persisted and even seemed to grow with time, despite the prescription of his new jurisprudence to base theory on experience, and his own judicial obligations to found decisions on case records. Indeed, Holmes professed to "hate facts," bragging he refused to read sociological studies recommended by his Supreme Court colleague Louis Brandeis, or even the daily newspaper. Holmes to Pollock (May 26, 1919), 2 HPL 13–14.

41. CLP, "Law in Science," 229.

42. Id. at 238. In "The Use of Law Schools," CLP, 39, Holmes inveighed against the tendency of lawyers to resort to "cheap and agreeable substitutes for real things."

43. Theory of Torts, 776 (1873). See also FE, "Codes, and the Arrangement of the Law," 80–81; 1872 Jurisprudence Essay, 790–791; CLP, "Path of the Law," 181.

44. CLP, "Economic Elements," 282. See also CL, 211. Oddly, Richard Posner interprets Holmes's injunction to "think things not words" as "naive realism" for believing that "words stand in a one-to-one correspondence to things." R. A. Posner, *The Problems of Jurisprudence*, 241 n. 30 (1990). Holmes was making precisely the opposite point; words, especially legal concepts, often go well beyond reality, claiming more morality for the law than its operational requirements and effects can bear. In attributing to Holmes the view that "what is not a thing, is nothing," Posner appears to join the conventional view which misconstrues Holmes's empiricism as denying the existence or relevance of unobservable phenomena, such as the subjective state of mind. Holmes never denied the existence and significance of states of mind or other intangible factors. Indeed, as I discuss later, the prediction theory of law focused on subjective judicial motives, and the foresight theory of responsibility always accepted subjective knowledge and even actual malice as sufficient bases of liability. For Holmes, empirical evidence could provide the inferential basis for beliefs about the existence of such intangible phe-

nomena—including the "important" views of judges on "justice and reasonable-ness"—just as it does with respect to the existence of tangible phenomena. Moreover, Holmes's very quest for an explanatory theory of torts shows that he was not in the camp of nominal positivism, whose advocates objected to making hypotheses or statements beyond describing the specific observable phenomena.

45. CLP, "Path of the Law," 183; 1872 Jurisprudence Essay 790–91; CL, 146–47; CLP, "Economic Elements," 282. Indeed, Holmes illustrated the need to apply the measure of the law in operation in attacking the treatment of strict liability by formalist legal science. According to Austin's analytics and Pandectist readings of German custom, strict liability either never existed or was always deemed a moral outcast. Holmes argued that the evidence belied these legal science theories on both scores. As shown in Chapter 1, he refuted Austin's strategy of converting strict liability to negligence by presumption, along with the efforts of legal science historians to Romanize strict liability out of the law. Pointing to the actual require-ments and effects of the decisions and rules, Holmes demonstrated the existence and widespread application of strict liability in contemporary as well as prior law. Moreover, he showed that strict liability had strong policy justifications, especially in deterring and compensating infliction of harm by industrial and other extra-hazardous activities.

46. CL, 215.

47. Ibid. Thus, in regard to possession, Holmes explained: "When we say that a man owns a thing, we affirm directly that he has the benefit of the consequences attached to a certain group of facts, and, by implication, that the facts are true of him." Ibid.

48. OS, 156; CLP, "Path of the Law," 170–171. Current commentators assume that Holmes first introduced the "bad man" heuristic in "The Path of the Law" (1897), and take this as indicative that he had finally broken with formalism and replaced it with a commitment to empirical science and the law as an instrument of social policy-making. For recent elaborations of this claim, see G. E. White, *Justice Oliver Wendell Holmes: Law and the Inner Self*, 219–221 (1993). The premise that the perspective of the "bad man" heuristic and its policy orientation represent a late development in Holmes's thinking is erroneous. That perspective was present from his earliest writings, under the less provocative label of "lawyers' law." 1872 Jurisprudence Essay, 789. See also 2 Commentaries, *561 n.1. The "bad man" heuristic in "The Path of the Law" challenges moralistic suppositions about civil liability by showing (1) that it is usually a tax; (2) that in contract, the obligation is merely to perform or pay damages; and (3) that responsibility for defamation was an external rule of foresight-based strict liability. All of these applications appeared in *The Common Law* and earlier writings. See CL, 138–140, 148–149, 158–59, 317; 1872 Jurisprudence Essay, 790–791; FE, "Primitive Notions in Modern Law," 129–130 n.2.

49. CLP, "Path of the Law," 174.

50. Ibid.

51. L. L. Fuller, *The Law in Quest of Itself,* 92–93 (1940); H. M. Hart, "Holmes's Positivism—An Addendum," 929. Hart's essay responded to Mark DeWolfe Howe, "The Positivism of Mr. Justice Holmes," 64 *Harvard Law Review* 529 (1951), which, in turn, defended Holmes against Fuller. For a recent iteration of the Fuller-Hart position, see Posner, *The Problems of Jurisprudence,* 243.

52. H. L. A. Hart, *The Concept of Law,* 181–182 (1961). For comparison of the moral concerns of positivism and natural law, see L. L. Weinreb, *Natural Law and Justice,* 99 (1987).

53. CL, 41; CLP, "Path of the Law," 172. Holmes rejected the Kantian moral rationale for external standards—that such standards implement the notion of each individual possessing "equal rights to life, liberty, and personal security," and to being treated "as an end in himself." CL, 43–44. More appealing were arguments of substantive equality, that the "burden of all should be equal." CL, 48. His pragmatic approach gave priority to the public good, which required external rules "to put an end to robbery and murder." Ibid., see also CL, 108. Holmes avoided the positivist's quandary of insisting on the prerogative to criticize the morality of particular applications of the law, while lacking any moral criterion for absolving disobedience to unjust and therefore unlawful commands. The question of moral legitimacy dissolved in the reality of state power: "all law means I will kill you if necessary to make you conform to my requirements." Letter from Holmes to Harold Laski (Sept. 7, 1916), M. D. Howe, ed., *Holmes-Laski Letters,* 16 (1953); see also CL, 43, 213, 219. This pragmatic view meant that courts must make and hence take responsibility for their own moral judgments. Because judges would be held accountable for the social consequences of their decisions, the only source of judicial legitimacy is the degree to which their decisions rationally promote the public welfare. As a result, judicial policymaking must be scientific "in a more far-reaching sense than that of expressing the *de facto* will of the community for the time." CLP, "Holdsworth's English Law," 288. This entailed gauging the worth of a law not by what we "fancy desirable" but by tallying "the bill that has to be paid in reactions that are relatively obscure." Ibid. (an example previously noted in the lectures was judicial disregard of data showing the net cost of imprisonment, given the relatively meager deterrence benefits). See also CLP, "Learning and Science," 139.

54. CL, 213; CLP, "Path of the Law," 194. Being an instrument of social policy, any "sound body of law" will in the end accommodate even the repellent instinct for revenge against criminals if the only alternative is anarchy or vigilantism. "At the same time this passion is not one we encourage, either as private individuals or as law-makers." CL, 41–42.

55. CL, 1.

56. CLP, "Path of the Law," 170.

57. CL, 1.

58. Theory of Torts, 777 (1873); CL, 213, 219; CLP, "Path of the Law," 170–171.

59. CL, 36–37; CLP, "Path of the Law," 195.

60. Hart, "Holmes's Positivism," 930. For views attributing Holmes's contradictions to his psychological as well as intellectual confusion, see White, *Justice Oliver Wendell Holmes,* 121; M. J. Horwitz, *The Transformation of American Law, 1870–1960,* 143 (1977).

61. CL, 137.

62. CL, 148.

63. CL, 90.

64. CLP, "Path of the Law," 179.

65. CLP, "Law in Science," 222. Control was also exerted by accommodating the desire for vengeance through "interventions of public power to give form and moderation to the self-redress." O. W. Holmes, Book Review, 11 *American Law Review* 327, 330 (1876).

66. CL, 45, 48, 57.

67. CL, 144.

68. CL, 95.

69. White, *Justice Oliver Wendell Holmes,* 115–119; M. H. Hoffheimer, *Justice Holmes and the Natural Law,* 89–90 (1992).

70. CL, 77.

71. CLP, "Path of the Law," 190.

72. FE, "The Arrangement of the Law—Privity," 95 (adopting Auguste Comte's views).

73. FE, "Codes, and the Arrangement of the Law," 77.

74. CLP, "Path of the Law," 197–198.

75. CL, 79.

76. CL, 146; CLP, "Path of the Law," 191.

77. CLP, "Law in Science," 224–225; CL, 89.

78. CLP, "Law in Science," 220.

79. CL, 82, 84.

80. I examine this response in detail in Chapter 3.

81. CL, 95.

82. CL, 36.

83. Lochner v. New York, 198 U.S. 45, 75–76 (Holmes, J., dissenting).

84. This supposed "dualism" is asserted in Hart, "Holmes's Positivism," 929.

85. CLP, "Path of the Law," 171, 179. See also CL, 36–37; OS, 7. Law is also prophecy for judges; they must discern trends to reform law effectively and to apply rules equally to similarly situated parties, taking account of their reasonable expectations.

86. 1880 Jurisprudence Essay, 710.

87. CLP, "Law Schools," 37.

88. FE, "The Arrangement of Law—Privity," 95–96 n.2; CLP, "Path of the Law," 196; see also EW, "The Code of Iowa," 792 (finding that conventional enumerative arrangements "are in truth the most unpractical and destructive of sound legal thinking").

89. CL, 219.

90. CL, 131, 161.

91. CLP, "Ideals and Doubts," 307; EW, "The Gas-Stokers' Strike," 796.

92. White, *Justice Oliver Wendell Holmes,* 41.

93. Ibid.

94. Ibid.

95. Ibid. White claims that while Holmes abandoned his initial effort to devise a duty-based "analytical classification scheme" akin to Austin's, he continued to pursue classifications in the syllogistic ideal. Id. at 113. White is mistaken. Holmes only made the basic assumption of the "law of cause and effect" that is conventional to empirical science. CLP, "Path of the Law," 180. He postulated no *a priori* premise for classifying tort law, whether based on the notion of legal duty or otherwise. White fails to note that Holmes stated he was attaching none of Austin's culpability meaning to the term "duty," but was using the word simply for want of a better term to denote generic legal obligation. FE, "The Arrangement of the Law—Privity," 95 n.2; 1873 Theory of Torts, 781 n.14. White's interpretation misses the chief antiformalist import of Holmes's injunction to judge the scope of asserted rights solely in terms of the policy-calibrated duties courts actually enforce. Holmes was denying the possibility that deductions from general conceptions of free will, property rights, personal security, and other generalizations could ever logically or practically decide particular cases and preempt judicial policy-making. This was precisely the point Holmes made through his duty classifications of the three branches of liability rules in 1873 Theory of Torts.

96. On the nature and development of experimental philosophy, see F. Copleston, *A History of Philosophy* (Book Two, 1985).

97. For recent, concise overviews of the history of modern empirical science, see J. A. Moore, *Science as a Way of Knowing* (1993) and G. Holton, *Science and Anti-Science* (1993).

98. E. H. Madden, ed., *The Philosophical Writings of Chauncey Wright,* vii (1958); C. Wright, *Philosophical Discussions,* 136 (1971).

99. Thayer, *Letters of Chauncey Wright,* 109. See also 2 J. S. Mill, *System of Logic* (1875); D. Hume, *An Enquiry Concerning Human Understanding,* 35, 37, 43 (1748).

100. Wright, *Philosophical Discussions,* 47.

101. Id. at 136.

102. Id. at 185.

103. C. Darwin, *On the Origin of Species,* 420 (1964).

104. FE, "Codes, and the Arrangement of the Law," 80; 1880 Jurisprudence Essay, 711. See also CL, 312 ("The distinctions of the law are grounded on experience not on logic. It therefore does not make the dealings of men dependent on a mathematical accuracy."); CLP, "Law in Science," 238, 240; CLP, "Natural Law," 313–315; Letter from Holmes to Pollock (May 26, 1919), 2 HPL 13. On the split in the seventeenth century between mathematical and empirical science, and its consequences for jurisprudence, see H. J. Berman, "The Origins of Histor-

ical Jurisprudence: Coke, Selden, Hale," 103 *Yale Law Journal* 1651, 1726–1727 (1994); K. R. Popper, *The Logic of Scientific Discovery,* 34 (1968).

105. CLP, "Natural Law," 315.

106. CLP, "Ideals and Doubts," 304–305.

107. Ibid.

108. CLP, "Natural Law," 311; OS, 133. Holmes's appreciation for the relativity of knowledge—that it was a function of social and historical context as well as psychological distortions—has generally been overlooked in current accounts. Horwitz, *The Transformation of American Law, 1870–1960,* 5–6 (attributing "cognitive relativism" to twentieth-century Legal Realism).

109. CLP, "Natural Law," 311; see also OS, 134–135.

110. OS, 168–169.

111. FE, "Codes, and the Arrangement of the Law," 80. See also Patsone v. Pennsylvania, 233 U.S. 138, 144 (1914). Roscoe Pound adopted a "functional" theory of classification that closely resembled Holmes's, using one of his principal examples, the foresight explanation of strict liability for trespassing cattle, to illustrate the power of empirical classification to disclose and explain the policies underlying the rules. R. Pound, "Mechanical Jurisprudence," 8 *Columbia Law Review* 605, 608–609 (1908); R. Pound, "Classification of Law," 37 *Harvard Law Review* 933, 935, 940–944 (1924); R. Pound, "The Call for a Realist Jurisprudence," 44 *Harvard Law Review* 697, 700 (1931).

112. Holmes apparently heeded Wright's stern warning against generalizing the substance of Darwin's theories to subjects other than biology. Thus, while Holmes's theory of legal evolution paralleled Darwin's theory of biological evolution on many major points, such as gradualism, probabilism, and population perspective, there were marked differences between the two theories. Most important, Holmes's jurisprudence did not adopt Darwin's hypothesis of natural selection, by which species developed as a changing environment took its toll on individuals who lacked the characteristics necessary for survival and reproduction. Rather, the process Holmes posited had Lamarckian overtones in the specific sense that judges deliberately adapted the body of law to meet the demands of changing conditions. EW, "Gas-Stokers' Strike," 795.

113. CLP, 245. Tort law evolved from "a single germ [animistic revenge] multiplying and branching into products as different from each other as the flower from the root." CL, 18, 34, 37. This finding provided the key evidence for the critical test of a Darwinian hypothesis of stochastic evolution, the conversion of one species into another, so that the descendants differ greatly from their remote ancestors. Moore, *Science as a Way of Knowing,* 7, 148.

Holmes also pointed out that extensive and important bodies of doctrine, especially in property, and very likely in contract, represent accommodations of biological instincts of self-preservation. O. W. Holmes, Book Notice, 11 *American Law Review* 329, 330 (1876); CL, 44, 213; CLP, "Path of the Law," 200. In noting the limits of historical explanation of the social values and needs motivating judicial legislation, he appears to suggest a genetic disposition in humans to make law that was similar to the instinct Darwin and modern theorists believe exists to acquire language. Cf. S. Pinker, *The Language Instinct,* 20 (1994). All societies, in every epoch, make laws to address certain basic concerns, for example, "[s]ome arrangements and the rudiments of familial institutions seem to be necessary elements in any society," and likewise, "some form of permanent association between the sexes—some residue of property individually owned—some mode of binding oneself to future conduct—to the bottom of all, some protection of the person." Letter from Holmes to Canon Patrick Sheehan (July 17, 1909), D. H. Burton, ed., *Holmes-Sheehan Correspondence,* 27–28 (1977). Like the language instinct, which has no determinative effect on the choice of a society to speak French, Chinese, or English, the biological instinct for law entails no particular system of marriage, property, or contract. The ceaseless "conflicts between tradition and the instinct of justice" have yielded a great diversity of institutions and rules for fostering productive activity and controling antisocial behavior. FE, "Possession," 188; EW, "The Gas-Stokers' Strike," 795–796; CLP, "Privilege, Malice, and Intent," 126–129; CLP, "Path of the Law," 181–183. Existence of such variations contradict claims that law has an *a priori* design or source in innate custom of the people; for example, contrary to social contract theories, communal property arrangements preceded the law of private property, and "witness the Bolsheviki." 2 Commentaries, *319 n. (c); 4 Commentaries, *441 n. 1; Letter from Holmes to Pollock (Jan. 24, 1919), 2 HPL 3.

114. Some current commentators, such as Thomas Grey, recognize that Holmes's classification objectives rejected the syllogistic ideal, but claim nonetheless that his objectives were "conceptualist" and "formalist." T. Grey, "Holmes and Legal Pragmatism," 41 *Stanford Law Review* 787, 822 (1989). In Grey's view, Holmes's idea of making the law knowable meant establishing a structure of highly "abstract," "fix[ed]" categories. While matching these categories to experience, Holmes supposedly determined their contours and contents by some nonexperiential conceptual criterion of "correct[ness]" (undefined by Grey), and formalistically distributed borderline rules and cases among the categories by arbitrary fiat. Ibid.

To the extent he finds conceptualism in Holmes's classification objectives, Grey makes the same mistake as White of simply equating scientific classifications with schemes that imbue concepts with a reality independent of the empirical phenomena. Grey's formalist characterization of Holmes also fails. First, by equating Holmes's "goal of objective predictability" with "formalism," Grey gives that term a meaning completely alien to Holmes's (and the conventional) notion of "deduc[ing] the *corpus* from *a priori* postulates." Id. at 822; CL, 36. The instrumental, bureaucratic rules which Holmes labeled "arbitrary" are today called "formal"; the change in meaning seems to have contributed to Grey's confusion. Second, Grey seriously misconstrues Holmes in stating that Holmes arbitrarily distributed the borderline cases and rules among certain "artificially fix[ed]" categories. Grey, "Holmes and Legal Pragmatism," 822. In fact, the idea of "arbitrary" line-drawing was Holmes's descriptive explanation of one of the chief means that *courts* actually use when confronted with the inevitable clash of policies and interests that arise in most litigated cases. Holmes presented these formal rule-decrees of external, bureaucratic distinctions as phenomena, not ready-made, formalist structures deductively derived from postulates beyond judicial discretion. He explained that the needs of greater social organization prompted courts to adopt such external rules to accomplish collectivist or social welfare policies, as well as to minimize uncertainty, caprice, fraud, and costs of particularization, especially involving subjective states of mind. Grey patches over the holes in his formalist characterization of Holmes by merely asserting that his claimed discovery of judicially created bureaucratic rules is "wholly unconvincing," and therefore that Holmes's real meaning was not scientific explanation but rather normative "social theory." Unlike Holmes, Grey offers no evidence to support his conclusion.

115. Wright, *Philosophical Discussions,* 131–132. On the presumption in modern science of the law of cause and effect, see R. L. Merton, *Social Theory and Social Structure,* 547 (1957).

116. CLP, "Path of the Law," 180. This assumption involved nothing of the final cause or other normative postulates that White and others assert in their formalist interpretations, but simply made Holmes an empirical scientist.

117. CL, 37. See also CL (I), 6.

118. Ibid; CLP, "Path of the Law," 184.

119. CLP, 186–187.

120. CLP, 186.

121. CLP, 198.

122. CLP, "Path of the Law," 186–187. Once theory provides a testable and durable explanation, then, in Wright's less florid words, "practical science comes in to determine what, in view of the facts, our feelings and rules of conduct ought to be; but practical science has no inherent postulates any more than speculative science." Thayer, *Letters of Chauncey Wright,* 113.

123. There were prudential and practical constraints which counseled against unnecessarily radical reformation, including lack of judicial resources and training in political economy, statistics, and other general intellectual disciplines; public expectations generated by settled law; the resistance of basic human instincts and needs to government intervention; the avoidance of anarchic self-help and rebellion. Holmes explained his own reluctance to make wholesale and precipitous renovations of the received traditions derived from a purely pragmatic sense of limits, personal as well as institutional, and not from any "duty" of consistency or notion that such law "represents an eternal principle." CLP, "Law in Science," 239; CL, 36.

124. Southern Pacific Co. v. Jensen, 244 U.S. 205, 221 (1917)(Holmes, J., dissenting).

125. CLP, "Law in Science," 239.

126. Holmes's deference theory was a pragmatic response to experience—the remoteness of the "ideal" of law based on scientifically crafted policy, and the inclination of judges who, if left too much room for discretion, were apt to issue a "wholesale prohibition" of any rule that smacked of socialism. CLP, "Path of the Law," 184. To be sure, Holmes did not intend his theory of constitutional review to endorse the "progressive" agenda. Even though he saw the social advantage of having labor unions serve as a counterweight to the market and political power of organized capital, of the morality of restricting child labor, and of the justice of strict liability for industrial injuries, for the most part, his "Malthusian" skepticism of social transformation prevailed. Social reformers "forget that we no more can get something for nothing by legislation than we can by mechanics." Letter from Holmes to John Henry Wigmore (Aug. 2, 1915), HP; CL, 44; OS, 173; CLP, "Ideals and Doubts," 305. CL, 44; OS, 173.

127. CLP, "Path of the Law," 185–186; see also EW, "The Gas-Stokers' Strike," 795. On the various schools of social Darwinism, see P. Edwards, ed., *Encyclopedia of Philosophy*, 302, 304–305 (1967).

128. Wright, *Philosophical Discussions*, 398–405.

129. Id. at 74.

130. CL, 37.

131. CL, 45.

132. CL, 46.

133. CL, 36–37.

134. CLP, "Law in Science," 225; OS, 156; CLP, "Path of the Law," 224–225; EW, "The Gas-Stokers' Strike."

135. CLP, "Learning and Science," 138.

136. CLP, "Law in Science," 225.

137. Id. at 229.

138. CLP, "Learning and Science," 139.

139. CLP, "Path of the Law," 186.

140. Id. at 195.

141. CLP, "Learning and Science," 139.

142. Horwitz, *The Transformation of American Law, 1870–1960*, 125, 130, 140–141.

143. Id. at 125.

144. Ibid.

145. 1880 Jurisprudence Essay, 710. Indeed, a primary objective of Holmes's attack on historical legal science in "Possession" and "Common Carriers and the Common Law" was to demonstrate that major fields of law, such as bailment, evolved through judicial policy inventions entirely independent of custom.

146. A striking example of Holmes's consistent antiformalism, also contradicting Horwitz's thesis, appears in his last major scholarly work, "Law in Science and Science in Law." Recurring to the form-and-substance paradox, Holmes stressed

the use of history to pierce the facade of customary beliefs and practices, and to reveal the judicial policy choices that actually shaped the law. His own use of critical historicism included, for example, the demonstration of the inequity and irrationality of perpetuating the customary presumption, despite clear experience to the contrary, that the "deaf and dumb" lacked the capacity to contract. CLP, "Law in Science," 225–229. This account recapitulated examples and arguments deployed against historical legal science three decades earlier in EW, "Misunderstandings of the Civil Law," 759, and sketched in 2 Commentaries, *451 n.1.b.

147. Theory of Torts, 775 (1873).

148. EW, "Gas-Stokers' Strike," 796.

149. Id. at 795.

150. Horwitz, *The Transformation of American Law, 1870–1960*, 125 (quoting CL, 36) (Holmes's words underscored).

151. Id. at 125, 130.

152. On its face, the quoted phrase—a descriptive not prescriptive statement—simply says that judges tend to decide cases on the basis of their more or less unexamined political preferences. While the judges might well treat these preferences as self-evident and popularly shared, there is absolutely no suggestion that Holmes endorsed their assumptions, or their lack of candor and deliberateness in making policy. Indeed, in his view, these judges were victims of the paradox of form and substance, who failed (or refused) to confront the doubtful policy choices and contentious interests involved. Holmes made this clear in the sentences surrounding the quoted phrase. He repeated the point in later essays. See CLP, "Path of the Law," 184 ("the result of the often proclaimed judicial aversion to . . . [acknowledging the 'duty of weighing considerations of social advantage'] is simply to leave the very ground and foundation of judgments inarticulate, and often unconscious," as is exemplified by the fear of socialism among "the comfortable classes" that influenced judicial decisions against strict liability).

153. CL, 36.

154. Ibid. See also CL, 23–24, 27–28; CLP, "Agency I and II."

155. CL, 36, 37. Immediately before the phrase Horwitz quotes, Holmes declared that the law "is legislative in its grounds." CL, 35. By this, according to Horwitz, Holmes "meant only that the law is '*at bottom the result of more or less definitely understood views of public policy.*'" Horwitz, *The Transformation of American Law, 1870–1960*, 125 (quoting CL, 35) (Holmes's words underscored). To equate Holmes's statement with the "customary law perspective" is, however, unpersuasive. Again, on its face, the phrase Horwitz quotes hardly suggests an apolitical customary law perspective, but rather confirms Holmes's view that the law is the product of judicial policy-making. It also indicates that not all judges fail to articulate and examine their political preferences. Horwitz's interpretation is even less plausible when his words, "meant only that the law is," are replaced with Holmes's actual language: "Every important principle which is developed by litigation is in fact and. . ." CL, 35. The fact of litigation signifies the irreconcilability

of the interests and values involved. 1873 Theory of Torts, 775; CL, 127–129; CLP, "Law in Science," 239. In the directly preceding sentences, moreover, Holmes explained the paradox of form and substance and stated that despite the "official theory . . . that each new decision follows syllogistically from existing precedents," courts make law in the "deeper sense" based on "considerations of what is expedient"—the factors of substantive experience that provide motives for judicial policy discretion. CL, 35.

To support his interpretation, Horwitz first argues that by the time of "The Path of the Law," when Holmes characterized the choice to use strict liability or negligence as representing "a concealed, half conscious battle on the question of legislative policy," he was referring to the law as politics. Horwitz, *The Transformation of American Law, 1870–1960*, 125. From this premise, Horwitz draws a bald inference that fifteen years earlier, in *The Common Law*, Holmes gave similar expressions and terminology a decidedly customary law meaning. Lacking any textual support for the alleged radical change of mind, Horwitz turns to social context. Horwitz claims that Holmes lost faith in an evolving apolitical custom when he was awakened to the fact of social conflict by the economic depression and labor strife of the 1890s. But this surmise completely neglects the cataclysm and trauma of the Civil War to which Holmes himself frequently referred. H. B. Zobel, "The Three Civil Wars of Oliver Wendell Holmes," 26 *Boston Bar Journal* 13 (1962).

156. EW, "Gas-Stokers' Strike," 795, 796. Like Wright, Holmes was emphatic: no theological or metaphysical final cause rationalizes social and legal evolution. Rather, its hallmark is continuous struggle and competition in a changing, contingent environment, often resulting in one class or interest temporarily dominating another. Progress, therefore, cannot be assumed for either the norms developed by custom or the policies made by courts. Many rules, instead of making improvements, either worsen the situation, like usury laws that make "the burden of borrowers heavier," or simply "favor[] one class at the expense of another." EW, "Gas-Stokers' Strike," 796. Holmes objected to the *a priorist* claim that law, satisfying the utilitarian morality of greatest good for the greatest number, necessarily represented apolitical moral improvement: "Why not the greatest good of the most intelligent and most highly developed?" Ibid. Rather than indicating social progress, some rules pragmatically accommodate "feelings and passions" which have persisted from the "earliest barbarian" despite education and legal sanctions. CL, 2. The chief evidence against evolutionary progressivism was the existence of "dry precedent" and "mere survivals." A presumption that law reflects social progress lacks a basis in fact; indeed, the presumption ought to be reversed: "State interference [including judicial policy-making in tort] is an evil, where it cannot be shown to be a good." CL, 96. See also CLP, "Path of the Law," 185–186.

157. CL, 43; see also CLP, "Ideals and Doubts," 307.

158. CL, 35–36. See also CLP, "Agency I and II."

159. CL, 36.

160. CL, 37.

161. Ibid. For a late iteration of these ideas, see CLP, "Law in Science," 225–229. If customary law had been the key to Holmes's jurisprudence in *The Common Law*, surely he would have stated it explicitly somewhere. But no such statement appears in Lecture I or anywhere in the book, and there is much to the contrary. Indeed, he rejected that perspective at the outset of Lecture I, warning "writer and reader" against imbuing the process of legal development with *a priori* necessity, and advising them to avoid two temptations in particular. The first was that of assuming that the law develops by a "natural" customary process of undeliberative consensus, rather than through being "laboriously fought out or thought out in past times." The second mistake was "asking too much of history" by assuming that the legal or customary resolutions of conflicting interests inevitably produced progress. CL, 2. See also CLP, "Law in Science," 220.

162. CL, 78–79. Thus, even though Holmes thought that the general rejection of cause-based strict liability represented "sound policy," he insisted on "careful analysis" of the issue and was unwilling to accept the verdict of a prevailing "daily practice" where "the true principle is far from being articulately grasped." CL, 89. Moreover, his explanation of the general use of external rather than personal culpability standards in negligence cases gave no hint of the customary law perspective. Instead, he explained the prevailing practice exclusively in terms of deliberate choices of social regulatory policy: first, "the impossibility of nicely measuring a man's powers and limitations," and second, "a more satisfactory explanation is, that, when men live in society, a certain average of conduct, a sacrifice of individual peculiarities going beyond a certain point, is necessary to the general welfare." CL, 108.

In fact, the historical thread connecting *The Common Law* lectures was the increasing use of concrete external standards of strict liability as well as negligence to regulate organized society by the "criterion of social welfare." CLP, "Law in Science," 232–233; CL, 43–48, 56–57; CLP, "Ideals and Doubts," 307. To illustrate his hypothesis of historical correspondence and causal relationship between increasing social organization, use of "arbitrary" external standards to compromise conflicts, and preference for social over individual interests, Holmes turned to torts. He noted that to gain the benefits of a strict liability effect, as well as to minimize cost and uncertainty, courts formulated "arbitrary" distinctions and classifications—for example, determining claims of obstructing "ancient windows" or lights according to a "mathematical rule . . . that a building cannot be complained of unless its height exceeds the distance of its base from the base of the ancient windows." 1873 Theory of Torts, 775–776.

163. CL, 100; Boston Ferrule Co. v. Hills, 159 Mass. 147, 150 (1893) (in all cases "of adjustment between conflicting rights . . . what risk shall be attached to any relation is a pure question of policy").

164. CL, 122–129; 150–151; 1873 Theory of Torts, 780; 2 Commentaries, *561 n.1.

165. CL, 123.

166. Ibid.

167. CLP, "Path of the Law," 182.

168. 1872 Jurisprudence Essay, 791. Indeed, in questioning whether *Rylands* was explained by the evolutionary lineage of tort law in ancient animistic rules of *noxæ deditio* (CL, 154, 156, 158), Holmes suggested that *Rylands* may represent the future ideal of judicial legislation, when courts would be liberated from the constraints of tradition to make policy deliberately and scientifically.

169. CLP, 183–184, 190–191.

170. CL, 62; CLP, "Privilege, Malice, and Intent," 122.

171. CLP, 300–301.

172. CLP, "Law in Science," 223 (quoting Pollock).

3. The Common Ground of Liability

1. CL, 89, 80. This chapter uses Holmes's phrase "absolute responsibility" interchangeably with cause-based strict liability to emphasize that the focus of his quest for the common ground of tort liability was the concept of moral responsibility (and excuse) that courts invoked to legitimate their legislative decisions in tort.

2. CL, 97–98, 94, 149.

3. Apparently, Holmes felt that developing the foresight theory by rebuttal of the causation theory made his explanation all the more persuasive. As he noted earlier, "a conclusion based upon the refutation of its opposite is very different from the same opinion based on ignorance of the arguments by which such an opposite could be maintained." 1880 Jurisprudence Essay, 711.

Holmes reiterated his previously published arguments rejecting Austin's personal culpability theory—in particular, its effort to convert strict liability decisions into facts or presumptions of negligence. Significantly, the torts lectures evince increased reliance on the presence and importance of the major rules of strict liability in contemporary tort law, including *Rylands*. CL, 23–24, 116–117, 154–157.

4. This new interpretation concerns the crucial references to "negligence" in the classic English cases before the nineteenth century that are today taken as the best evidence of the general rule for recovery under the writ system. The current standard interpretations agree that the negligence rule exclusively governed the system if "negligence" meant unreasonable conduct. Denying that "negligence" had this meaning, many commentators argue that the term described the state-of-mind requirement of foresight, encompassing rules of strict liability as well as negligence. Others claim that "negligence" merely connoted the generic fact of "neglect" of a legal duty, suggesting that liability in tort approached the strictness of the cause of action for breach of contract.

The present disagreement only relates to the meaning of "negligence" references in the classic English cases, not its universal import for understanding the writ system. In contrast to the all-or-nothing premise of the current debate, the interpretation proffered by Holmes and his contemporaries allowed both for multiple meanings of "negligence," including unreasonable conduct, and for a diverse system embracing all rules of negligence and strict liability short of absolute responsibility. In essence, the interpretation understood the English cases as concerned solely with the question of recovery for unforeseeable harm, and as conditioning such recovery on the existence of "some," even the "smallest," negligence by the defendant toward some other causally related but foreseeable harm. Losee v. Buchanan, 51 N.Y. 483, 488 (1873); Aston v. Heaven, 170 E.R. 445, 446 (1797) (hereafter, "some-negligence interpretation").

    5. CL(I), 81.

    6. G. Gilmore, *The Death of Contract,* 16 (1974). Gilmore reads this portion of Lecture III as disproving the existence of the rule that, quoting Holmes, "'a man *acts* at his peril,'" and "unveil[ing]" with "breathtaking abruptness [and] . . . without citation of authority" "'[t]he general principle . . . that loss from accident must lie where it falls.'" Ibid. Gilmore's interpretation is fundamentally flawed, but, as will be seen, not atypical of much current treatment of this material. Of course Holmes's statement of the general principle against liability for accident may seem abrupt and lacking in citations if one disregards his arguments and references, as Gilmore does. It should suffice to note that, in addition to discussing the classic English Trespass decisions rejecting absolute responsibility (CL, 85–94, 103–105), Holmes analyzed the American decisions "to the point." CL, 105–107. Most important, Gilmore fails to note that Holmes's theory excluded only cause-based strict liability. Gilmore makes no mention, for example, of the fact that in the paragraph referring to the "*acts* at peril" rule, Holmes objected to this rule only insofar as it was thought to rest on the causation theory that "the whole and sufficient ground [for holding a defendant liable] . . . is supposed to be that he has voluntarily acted, and that damage has ensued." CL, 82. Like many other commentators, Gilmore also ignores Holmes's explicit foresight definition of "loss from accident" (CL, 94) and rationalization of *Rylands* under the foresight theory. CL, 156–157.

    7. While appropriate for a first-year classroom, the unwitting repetition of causation debates from the last century contributes little of scholarly importance. For an example of current causation debates tracking the furrows of analysis cut by Holmes long ago, see R. A. Epstein, "A Theory of Strict Liability," 2 *Journal of Legal Studies* 151 (1973); and the responses from J. Borgo, "Causal Paradigms in Tort Law," 8 *Journal of Legal Studies* 419 (1979); S. R. Perry, "The Impossibility of General Strict Liability," I *Canadian Journal of Law and Jurisprudence* 147 (1988); and J. J. Thomson, *Rights, Restitution & Risk,* 192–224 (1986). An examination of Holmes's multiple-cause analysis also puts in perspective Guido Calabresi's recent claim to have independently discovered an "analysis of causal reciprocity which paralleled that which Coase made so famous in the *The Problem*

of Social Cost." G. Calabresi, Commentary, in F. R. Shapiro, "Most-Cited Articles," 100 *Yale Law Journal* 1482, 1483 (1991).

8. CL, 35–36. Organization of tort law according to procedural writs was, Holmes argued, simply another by-product of the paradox of form and substance. Hence he was not surprised that "rules of conduct" had been "classified under the ['procedural'] forms through and by means of which they [the rules] are developed," but he was adamant that "accidental differences in the way of enforcing" claims could not serve in the new jurisprudence to explain either the substantive requirements and effects of the rules in force, or their motivating policy. EW, 787; CL, 78. No amount of tinkering could save the procedural system of classification in tort. Asserting that "[a]ll actions of trespass are for consequences of acts," Holmes thus quickly dispatched the makeshift distinction "that trespass is for acts alone, and case for consequences of those acts." CL, 91.

9. CL, 90.

10. CL, 93.

11. CL, 90–91.

12. CL, 90.

13. CL, 92.

14. CL, 91.

15. Ibid.

16. Letter from Holmes to Pollock (June 7, 1891), 1 HPL 38; F. Wharton, *A Treatise on the Law of Negligence,* 112 (1878).

17. Holmes's attack on essentialist theories of determinative causation paralleled those published in the early 1870s by Nicholas St. John Green, *Essays and Notes on the Law of Tort and Crime* (1933). In his essay "Proximate and Remote Cause," Green argued that all cases arise from multiple causes, and "[t]he true cause is the whole set of antecedents taken together" (13). Green urged replacing the "abstract theological belief" in determinate causes with the scientific view that proximate causation is "not an absolute but a relative term" (14). This would reveal, he hypothesized in a later essay, that when courts found a defendant's act too remote or indirect a cause, they were actually if covertly making a policy decision that "the plaintiff should not recover" (82).

18. CL, 92. The context clearly indicates that Holmes was not using the term "foresight" in the sense of prudent conduct by the defendant but to connote the mental state of prevision or anticipation of future consequences. "What is foresight of consequences? It is a picture of a future state of things called up by knowledge of the present state of things, the future being viewed as standing to the present in the relation of effect to cause . . . reduc[ed] to lower terms . . . what a man of reasonable prudence would have foreseen." CL, 53–54, 55 (incorporated in Lecture III, CL, 95). This usage of "foresight" was consistent with its primary definition in contemporary dictionaries; see N. Webster, *A Dictionary of the English Language* (1865); J. Simpson and E. Weiner, *The Oxford English Dictio-*

nary (1898), as well in earlier dictionaries, see S. Johnson, *A Dictionary of the English Language* (1796); N. Bailey, *Dictionarium Britannicum* (1730).

19. CL, 90. For a recent argument in this vein, see H. L. A. Hart and T. Honoré, *Causation in the Law,* lxvii (1985).

20. CL, 79.

21. CL, 68–70.

22. See Fletcher v. Rylands, 3 H.& C. 774 (1865) (Bramwell, B); L.R. 1 Ex 265 (1866) (Blackburn, J); Brown v. Collins, 53 N.H. 442 (1873); Ryan v. New York Central R.R. Co., 35 N.Y. 209 (1866); Hay v. The Cohoes Co., 2 N.Y. 159 (1849). Many commentators perceive a correspondence between the rising number of collision cases and increased displacement of strict liability by the negligence standard in the late eighteenth and early nineteenth centuries. See D. Kretzmer, "Transformation of Tort Liability in the Nineteenth Century: The Visible Hand," 4 *Oxford Journal of Legal Studies* 46, 80 (1984); S. F. C. Milsom, *Historical Foundations of the Common Law,* 349–351 (1969); J. H. Baker, *An Introduction to English Legal History,* 345 (1979). Multiple causation posed a philosophical conundrum generally for "first cause" and other *a priorist* claims that a singular, responsible force existed antecedent to all merely empirical events and thus was not itself simply another empirical event. 1 J. S. Mill, *A System of Logic,* 377 (1875). See also Green, *Essays on Tort and Crime,* 9–14.

Advocates of neo-causation theories of responsibility attempt to avoid the multiple-causation critique by arguing that in many cases no causal conflict exists because plaintiffs pose no risk of injury to defendants; for example, the defendant's straying cattle eat the plaintiff's corn, whereas plaintiff's corn does no harm to the defendant's cattle. See Epstein, "Strict Liability," 165. But, as Holmes showed, this argument misses the point that the causal conflict always arises by virtue of the conduct of both parties not only in empirically increasing the risk of plaintiff's injury, but also in claiming mutually exclusive possession of some real or personal property, the legal determination of which grants full freedom of action to one party by curtailing (or at least taxing) the freedom of the other. Reliance on a common law or codified absolute right-of-way to give one party's risk-taking or property interest priority over the other's necessarily appeals to a norm outside the causal paradigm, and ultimately begs the question of the policy choice—which precedes the creation of such a right—as to whose claim of freedom should prevail.

23. The Thorns Case (1466), in J. H. Baker and S. F. C. Milsom, *Sources of English Legal History,* 327 (1986).

24. CL, 90, 97–98; see also 94 (describing "the example of the accidental blow with a stick lifted in self-defense"). Holmes noted that the hypothetical had become one of the "standard illustrations" of the rule of absolute liability repeatedly invoked by judges and lawyers for plaintiffs, including the plaintiff's counsel and Lord Cranworth in *Rylands.* CL, 88 and n.4. For the contemporary view that the *Thorns* hypothetical asserted the rule of cause-based strict liability—liability

without fault for "pure accident," see J. B. Ames, "Law and Morals," 22 *Harvard Law Review* 97, 98 (1908).

25. CL, 94. By assuming the simultaneous occurrence of the raising of the stick and the push by the horse, Holmes ingeniously crafted his hypothetical variant not only to preclude arguments of indirect causation or broken causal chains, but also to underscore the inevitable presence of "intervening" environmental and other causes, however seemingly direct the given causal relationship.

26. CL, 83.

27. CL, 94.

28. Ibid.

29. CL, 131.

30. Gibbons v. Pepper (1695), in Baker and Milsom, *Sources,* 335.

31. CL, 91–92, 94; see also CL, 54, 131–132.

32. CL, 93. This causation reading of *Gibbons* persists. M. S. Arnold, "Towards an Ideology of the Early English Law of Obligations," 5 *Law and History Review* 505, 519 (1987).

33. CL, 92.

34. Ibid. The analysis of *Gibbons* shows that Holmes determined case holdings by the facts and not by what judges said they were holding. He subsequently noted this practice of his and emphasized the "skeptical end" of his "references to the Year Books," possibly in response to Dicey's criticism that *The Common Law* gave too much face value to English opinions. "Agency I" (CLP, 70 n.47); OS, 156; A. V. Dicey, "Holmes's *The Common Law,*" *The Spectator, Literary Supplement* 745 (June 3, 1882), reprinted in 10 *Hofstra Law Review* 712, 714 (1982).

35. CL, 88 n.4. Cranworth's opinion in *Rylands* was regarded by Holmes's contemporaries as the authoritative statement on absolute responsibility. Ames, "Law and Morals," 98; 8 W. Holdsworth, *A History of English Law,* 455 (1923); E. R. Thayer, "Liability Without Fault," 29 *Harvard Law Review* 801, 803 n.7 (1916); J. H. Wigmore, "Responsibility for Tortious Acts: Its History—III," 7 *Harvard Law Review* 441, 443 and n.3 (1894).

36. CL, 156–157.

37. CL, 89.

38. CL, 3, 4, 101–103; CLP, "Agency I," 70 and n.47. Contemporary and current debate continues on the nature of early tort claims. For an alignment of contemporary commentators with and against Holmes, see N. Isaacs, "Fault and Liability," 31 *Harvard Law Review* 954 (1918). It is difficult to understand the charge that Holmes "marginalized" strict liability in the writ system, when, despite assertions of "victory" by proponents of contending "transformation" and continuous negligence theories of Trespass, the ongoing debate shows that the question undoubtedly remains open.

39. CL, 101; CLP, "Agency I," 70, 73. See Milsom, *Historical Foundations of the Common Law,* chap. 11.

40. CL, 23–24, 97, 103; see also CL, 4. For a similar foresight interpretation of

the allegations of direct causation in Trespass, acknowledging Holmes's priority on this point, see P. A. Landon, ed., *Pollock's Law of Torts,* 130 (1951); J. Addison, *Wrongs and Remedies,* 139 (1860).

41. CL, 104–105.

42. CL, 88, 92; Scott v. Shepherd, 2 W. Bl. 892 (1773), reprinted in C. H. S. Fifoot, *History and Sources of the Common Law,* 202 (1949).

43. CL, 92, 104, 95. On the excuse of "automatism" in theories of moral responsibility, see H. L. A. Hart, *Punishment and Responsibility,* 109–112 (1968).

44. CL, 54. Significantly, Holmes did not explain *Scott* on the grounds that the intervening actors were entitled to an excuse for acting reasonably (nonnegligently) from the necessity of self-defense. On his reading of the cases, such an argument might be accepted as justification but not excuse, where circumstances allowed foresight of the harmful consequences of acting in self-defense or in response to some condition of necessity, duress, or compulsion.

45. CL, 93.

46. Ibid. Holmes also explained the spurring reference in *Gibbons* as the court's recognition that the plaintiff's injury could be referred to a remote act, even though the defendant is considered a passive instrument when the horse ran away. Seeing nothing distinctive about spurring, Holmes took the reference as conceding that the passive instrument characterization was fictitious. CL, 92.

Any suggestion by Holmes that hard spurring implied negligence would contradict cases denying liability in negligence on medical and other social justifications for fast riding. For discussion of the contemporary negligence decisions, see H. Terry, *Some Leading Principles of Anglo-American Law,* 175 (1884). The same rule currently holds; see *Restatement (Second) of Torts* §466, Comment on Clauses (a), (c) (1977). Holmes emphasized the need for attention to the circumstances, noting that *Gibbons* might have been decided differently if the facts had been comparable to those in Mitchil v. Alestree (1676) (reprinted in Baker and Milsom, *Sources,* 572), where the owner knew that "the horse had been unruly, and [it] had been taken into a frequented place for the purpose of being broken." CL, 94.

47. CL, 93–94. In another example given by Holmes, "if a man who was a good rider bought a horse with no appearance of vice and mounted it to ride home, there would be no such apparent danger as to make him answerable if the horse became unruly and did damage." CL, 158. According to the some-negligence rule, there would be liability had the defendant ridden the horse on the wrong side of the road, pulled the wrong rein when the horse bolted, or otherwise committed a careless act that contributed to the risk of injury. See also Copeland v. Draper, 157 Mass. 558 (1893) (Holmes, J.).

48. Holmes's view of the sudden bolting by a quietly ridden, docile horse as an event of unforeseeable harm was consistent with the general understanding of *Gibbons* and treatment of runaway cases. R. J. Kaczorowski, "The Common-Law

Background of Nineteenth-Century Tort Law," 51 *Ohio State Law Journal* 1127, 1172–1173 (1990); Aston v. Heaven, 446 (characterizing "horses suddenly taking fright" as "an unforeseen accident or mischance"); Marshall v. Welwood, 38 N.J. 339, 344 (1876). The contemporary commentary on a particular runaway horse case, Holmes v. Mather, L. R. 10 Ex. 261 (1875)("horses being startled by a dog which suddenly rushed out and barked at them") considered the court's denial of liability as a repudiation of cause-based strict liability. See 1 E. A. Jaggard, *Handbook of the Law of Torts*, 65–66 and n.263 (1895); H. Terry, *Some Leading Principles of Anglo-American Law*, 453 (1884)(equating the sudden bolting of a horse without forewarning with an unforeseeable act of God); F. Pollock, *The Law of Torts*, 426 and n.(l) (2d ed. 1890).

49. CL, 95. Holmes was apparently making the usual assumption in such cases of fits and spasms that they occurred suddenly, without prior symptoms or other forewarning. Kaczorowski, "The Common-Law Background of Nineteenth-Century Tort Law," 1172–1173; R. A. Percy, ed., *Charlesworth and Percy on Negligence*, 857 (1983); Hammontree v. Jenner, 20 Cal. App. 3d 528 (1971); cf. CL, 109 (those with impaired sight must anticipate the risks of that handicap).

50. Generally, on the rule of foresight-based *(scienter)* strict liability in animal cases, see 1 H. G. Wood, *The Law of Nuisances*, 1100–1112 (1893); G. L. Williams, *Liability for Animals* (1939); F. Pollock, "The Dog and the Potman: or 'Go It, Bob,'" 25 *Law Quarterly Review*, 317–318 (1909) (relying on Holmes's support for foresight-based strict liability in animal cases and generally in cases of 'extra-hazardous risk'); 1 Wood, *Nuisances*, 1100–1108; Terry, *Some Leading Principles of Anglo-American Law*, 453; F. Buller, *An Introduction to the Law Relative to Trials at Nisi Prius*, 16 (1788); Fletcher v. Rylands, L. R. 1 Ex. 265, 280–282 (1866).

51. CL, 157; see also CL, 23–24, 118–119. For discussion of the application of foresight *(scienter)*-based strict liability in runaway horse cases like *Gibbons*, see Vincent v. Stinehour, 7 Vt. 62 (1835); Hammack v. White, 11 C.B.(N.S.) 588 (1862); F. T. Piggott, *Principles of the Law of Torts*, 212 (1885); G. T. Schwartz, "Tort Law and the Economy in Nineteenth-Century America: A Reinterpretation," 90 *Yale Law Journal* 1717, 1731 (1981); 1 Wood, *Nuisances*, 1109–1112 (1893).

52. CL, 96, 83.

53. CL, 103.

54. CL, 153, 97.

55. CL, 153. Trespass to property cases were thus "very different" from cases where "harm follows accidentally, as a consequence which could not have been foreseen." CL, 97–98.

56. CL, 99–100.

57. CL, 157.

58. *Restatement of Torts*, chaps. 20 and 21 (1938) (respectively providing strict liability for "Possessors and Harborers of Animals," and other "Ultrahazardous

Activities"), and the *Restatement (Second) of Torts*, §§519–520, 822 Comment k, 826 (respectively providing strict liability for "Abnormally Dangerous Activities" and "Nuisance"). Current scholars miss the implications for expansive use of strict liability in Holmes's generalized foresight of the rules governing domestic as well as fierce animals. See Schwartz, "Tort Law and the Economy," 1728–1729.

59. CL, 94.

60. Ibid.

61. Ibid.

62. Ibid. As I show in Chapter 4, Holmes expressly extended this foresight theory to accommodate strict liability, including *Rylands*.

63. G. P. Fletcher, "Fairness and Utility in Tort Theory," 85 *Harvard Law Review* 537, 551–556 (1972). See also E. J. Weinrib, *The Idea of Private Law*, 183 n.22 (1995); M. A. Millner, *Negligence in Modern Law*, 1–2 (1967); 8 Holdsworth, *History of English Law*, 385, 455–457, 468–469, and 9 Holdsworth, *History of English Law*, 608.

64. CL, 83 (giving examples of the defendant being thrown from a horse upon the plaintiff, or of a third party taking the defendant's hand and striking the plaintiff with it).

65. CL, 93. See also C. S. Kenny, *The English Law of Tort*, 606 n.1 (1904) (interpreting the foresight limitation imposed on *Rylands*); F. H. Bohlen, *Studies in the Law of Torts*, 14 (1926); Bratton v. Rudnick, 283 Mass. 556, 561–562 (1933).

66. CL, 148–149. Holmes recognized that in rejecting a justification as well as an excuse for irresistible force in necessity cases, tort law was laying a collectivist policy foundation for the future use of strict liability to compensate and thus politically legitimate judicial "takings" of individual property and personal security for the general social welfare. That he extended his foresight theory to rationalize the strict liability in necessity cases, where the defendant's act is not merely reasonable but socially encouraged, is itself decisive refutation of the negligence-dogma thesis. For further discussion of the necessity cases, see Chapters 4 and 5.

67. CL, 54, 94, 131. See also J. Story, *Commentaries on the Law of Bailments*, 28 (1878) (classifying "sudden death or illness" as an "inevitable accident," which meant "any accident produced by any physical cause, which is irresistible").

68. CL, 57. The submersion of the irresistible force excuse in the excuse of unforeseeability dates back at least to the early seventeenth-century. Keighley's Case, 103 Coke 139a (1603); M. A. Millner, *Negligence in Modern Law*, 1 (1967). Nevertheless, the metaphor of irresistible force retained rhetorical appeal for Holmes; he repeatedly equated unforeseeable harm from volitional acts with harm produced by "an unconscious spasm." CL, 95.

69. Holmes indicated that "accident" had the same meaning as "misfortune," and later "mischance," which he defined as an act under conditions of "no apparent danger." CL, 94; CLP, "Privilege, Malice, and Intent," 117–118. For similar unforeseeable harm definitions of these terms, see Story, *Bailments*, 487–488; cf

M. Hale, *Pleas of the Crown,* 31 (1678) (discussing excuse of "chancemedley"). Unforeseeable chance event was the standard primary definition of the term "accident" in and before the nineteenth century. See Johnson, *Dictionary of the English Language* (1818) ("That which happens unforeseen; causality, chance"); Webster, *Dictionary of the English Language* (1866) ("An event that takes place without one's foresight or expectation; an event which proceeds from an unknown cause, or is an unusual effect of a known cause, and therefore not expected; chance; causality; contingency").

70. T. Cooley, *On the Law of Torts or the Wrongs which arise Independent of Contract,* 568 (1879). Significantly, Cooley was interpreting the "unavoidable accident" defense suggested in Ball v. Nye, 99 Mass. 582 (1868), which was the first case in Massachusetts (and possibly in America) to adopt *Rylands.* See also Terry, *Some Leading Principles,* 439–440 (reading *Ball* as establishing an unforeseeable "act of God" defense to *Rylands*); R. F. V. Heuston and R. S. Chambers, eds., *Salmond and Heuston on the Law of Torts,* 306–307 and n.80 (1981)(*Ball* applies the foreseeability limits expressed in *Rylands*). In Davis v. Rich, 180 Mass. 235 (1902), Holmes affirmed the foresight-based strict liability rule of *Ball.*

71. 1 J. Austin, *Lectures on Jurisprudence or the Philosophy of Positive Law,* 488 (5th ed. 1885). See also R. Campbell, *The Law of Negligence,* 4–5 (1878) (*casus* embraces "act of God," indicating some force which it is beyond human skill or foresight to avert).

72. C. Wright, *Philosophical Discussions,* 131 (1971).

73. Story, *Bailments,* 487–488, 610 (equating "pure accident" with an unforeseeable act of God). For further examples and commentary on the unforeseeable harm meaning of the "accident" excuse, see Parrot v. Wells, Fargo & Co. (The Nitro-glycerine Case), 82 U.S. (15 Wall.) 524, 535, 537–538 (1872); Morris v. Platt, 32 Conn. 75, 79–80, 84–90 (1864); Filliter v. Phippard, 11 Q. B. 347, 357 (1847); C. Whittier, "Mistake in the Law of Torts," 15 *Harvard Law Review* 335, 337 (1902); K. Takayanagi, "Liability without Fault in the Modern Civil and Common Law," 16 *Illinois Law Review* 163, 170 (1921); 11 Holdsworth, *History of English Law,* 608 (regarding fires, "accidentally" means the opposite of "wilfully," but a "better opinion" words it as "'mere chance or incapable of being traced to any cause,' and does not include fire caused by the [defendant's] negligence," quoting *Filliter*). Compare the definition of "accident" as used to determine insurance coverage in Anon., "Accident Insurance," 7 *American Law Review* 585, 587–588 (1873) ("any event which takes place without . . . foresight or expectation"), with Upjohn v. New Hampshire, 438 Mich. 197, 207–208 (1991)("without warning," "unexpected," "by chance"); *Restatement of Torts,* §8 (1938). Regarding the origins of this usage, see M. Arnold, "Accident, Mistake, and Rules of Liability in the Fourteenth-Century Law of Torts," 128 *University of Pennsylvania Law Review* 361 (1979). For current unforeseeable-harm definitions of "accident," see Hart and Honoré, *Causation in the Law,* 151 ("The term [accident] describes the situation in which a consequence that is neither

expected nor desired accrues from the agent's movements"); Hart, *Punishment and Responsibility,* 13–14 (observing that most systems of criminal law will excuse certain cases of homicide as "accidental" on facts showing such "lack of knowledge" as "to render the agent incapable of choice or of carrying out what he has chosen to do").

74. For an example of contemporary commentary giving a non-negligent connotation to inevitable accident, see J. Bishop, *Commentaries on the Non-Contract Law,* 69–70 (1889). Contemporaries were aware of the growing ambiguity of the term (id. at 64); N. S. Green, Book Notice, 4 *American Law Review* 350, 353 (1869); H. Terry, "Proximate Consequences in the Law of Torts," 28 *Harvard Law Review* 10, 24–25 (1914) (expressly rejecting non-negligence meaning, and confining it to very low-probability events traditionally excused under the act of God defense); Brown v. Collins, 53 N.H. 442, 450–451 (1873) (noting but rejecting a broader meaning than unforeseeable harm). On the current non-negligence definition of inevitable accident, see J. G. Fleming, *The Law of Torts,* 285 (1983), and W. P. Keeton, et al., eds., *Prosser and Keeton on Torts,* 162–163 (1984) (both treatises describe the some-negligence rule without recognizing its difference from the general defense of non-negligence).

75. CL, 96. Holmes intimated a foresight definition of the act of God concept and its role as an excuse, noting that when a brick fell from a railroad bridge, a jury must first determine if "the dropping was due, not to a sudden operation of weather, but to a gradual falling out of repair which it was physically possible for the defendant to have prevented"; only then can there be "any question as to the standard of conduct." CL, 125. For the types of "natural accidents" typically treated as acts of God, see Story, *Bailments,* 487 (listing "lightning, earthquakes, and tempests"); see also S. Greenleaf, *A Treatise on the Law of Evidence,* 208–209 (1850; rpt. 1972).

76. Indeed, in Lecture V on bailment, Holmes refers to the "general principle, not peculiar to carriers nor to bailees, that a duty was discharged if an act of God made it impossible of performance," relying on cases of damage resulting from unexpected storms. CL, 201–202 and nn.1, 2. As Holmes subsequently noted, the only question presented for tort liability by an intervention of the "workings of nature . . . is whether it reasonably was to be anticipated or looked out for." CLP, "Privilege, Malice, and Intent," 134.

77. F. Pollock, *The Law of Torts,* 313 (1887); see also Terry, *Some Leading Principles of Anglo-American Law,* 439–441; Story, *Bailments,* 487–488, 592; Greenleaf, *Evidence,* 208–209; Campbell, *Negligence,* 4–5; F. Buller, *Trials at Nisi Prius,* 70 (defining the "excuse" of "act of God" in terms of "sudden" interventions such that "no care of the defendant could foresee or prevent" the resulting harm). Current definitions are in accord; see Keeton, et al., *Prosser and Keeton on Torts,* 314, 564. Although Blackburn in *Rylands* indicated that strict liability was qualified by the defense of unforeseeable act of God (L.R. 1 Ex. 280), whether this was more than dictum remained a matter of doubt for many, including Judge

Charles Doe in Brown v. Collins. Any question that unforeseeable act of God excused liability under *Rylands* was removed by Nichols v. Marsland, L.R. 10 Ex. 255 (1875). Thayer, "Liability Without Fault," 804–805; M. M. Bigelow, *The Law of Torts,* 463 and n.4 (1907); A. Underhill, *A Summary of the Law of Torts,* 21–22 (1932); Fleming, *Torts,* 316–317.

    78. Pollock, *The Law of Torts,* 401 (1887). See also Nichols v. Marsland, 259–260. Act of God remains a foresight qualification on *Rylands* and other strict liability rules. See Bratton v. Rudnick, 562; Greenock Corp. v. Caledonian Ry., A.C. 556, 577 (1917); Oil Pollution Act, 33 U.S.C. §2703(a) (also suggesting the some-negligence doctrine); R. Percy, *Charlesworth on Negligence,* 298.

    79. Story, *Bailments,* 488–489.

    80. CL, 94. For similar inclusive use of "accident," see Morris v. Platt, 85 (defining "accident" as a comprehensive classification covering "an event or occurrence which happens unexpectedly, from the uncontrollable operations of nature alone . . . or an event resulting undesignedly and unexpectedly from human agency alone, or from the joint operation of both"); J. Comyns, *Digest of English Law,* 209 (1822); Story, *Bailments,* 28–29, 36–37, 460 and n.5, 487–488 and n.5; Thayer, "Liability Without Fault," 804–805; E. P. Weeks, *The Doctrine of Absque Injuria,* 269–270 (1879); A. G. Sedgwick, *A Treatise on the Measure of Damages,* 518 (1869); Fletcher, "Fairness and Utility," 552–557; Fleming, *Torts,* 317; Heuston and Chambers, *Salmond on Torts,* 306–307, 310. In effect, Holmes restored the early connection between "accident" and "act of God." Arnold, "Accident, Mistake, and Rules of Liability," 362–363 (tracing the act of God defense back to the ancient plea of "suddenly, by accident"). See also J. Gold, "Inevitable Accident as a Defense in Trespass," 21 *Bell Yard* 5, 5–6 (1938).

    81. Holmes applied the some-negligence doctrine in Hurdiman v. Wholley, 172 Mass. 411, 412 (1899), sustaining liability regardless of *scienter* where the defendant's horse kicked the plaintiff while the animal was illegally on the sidewalk. But see Cox v. Burbridge, 13 C.B., N.S. 431 (1863). Negligence might occur before intervention of the unforeseen factor, for example, in connection with a foreseeable risk arising during preparation to undertake the activity in question, or subsequent to that intervention, in mitigating the newly discovered harm. 1 T. G. Shearman and A. A. Redfield, *A Treatise on the Law of Negligence,* 19–20 (1898).

    The some-negligence rule has many offshoots, including the "cardinal principle" that the commission of any negligence subjects a defendant to liability for the unforeseeable losses suffered in "thin-skull," unexpected use, necessity, and hypersensitive plaintiff cases. J. G. Fleming, "The Passing of Polemis," 39 *Canadian Bar Review* 489, 527 (1961); Ploof v. Putnam, 81 Vt. 471 (1908); Spade v. Lynn & Boston Railroad, 168 Mass. 285, 287–288 (1897). Compare *Restatement (Second) of Torts,* §§519, 524A (limiting strict liability to "harm that reasonably may be expected"); W. Seavey, "Principles of Torts," 56 *Harvard Law Review* 72, 85–86 (1942). Holmes also noted the application of some-negligence rules in bailments. CL, 200–202 (sheriff "excus[ed]" from liability for a prisoner's escape during an "accidental fire" at the prison, since the defendant was not otherwise "in fault"; in another instance, an act of God that destroys bailed property "excused" performance, "provided there was no warranty and no fault on the part of the contractor," citing the classic Mouse's Case, 77 E.R. 1341 (1609)).

The best known modern analog of the some-negligence doctrine is the *Polemis* rule, arising from a decision imposing liability on a defendant, who, while off-loading a ship, negligently knocked over a wooden staging. This caused unforeseeable loss by igniting gasoline vapors and exploding the ship. "[O]nce determined that there is evidence of negligence," the court held, "the person guilty of it is equally liable for its consequences, whether he could have foreseen them or not." In re Polemis and Furness, Withy & Co., 3 K.B. 560, 569 (1921) (quoting Smith v. London S.W. Ry. Co., L.R. 6 L.R.-C.P. 14, 21 (1870)).

Polemis provoked one of the greatest controversies in the history of tort law. Keeton, et al., *Prosser and Keeton on Torts,* 293–297. One court decried the rule's contravention of "justice or morality" for extending responsibility to "all consequences, however unforeseeable and however grave" simply because of some act of negligence "however slight or venial, which results in some trivial foreseeable damage." Overseas Tankship (U.K.) Ltd. v. Morts Dock & Engineering Co., Ltd. (Wagon Mound I), [1961] 1 All E.R. 413. See also Fleming, "The Passing of Polemis," 489, 490–492, 493, 499 (by holding that "the 'threshold tort' . . . carried with it responsibility for all direct consequences of harm, whether foreseeable or not," *Polemis* "committed English law to the most extravagant compass of legal responsibility"); Millner, *Negligence,* 28, 29 and n.1 (portraying *Polemis* as punitive, and simply a "mode of strict liability masquerading as fault").

Despite Frederick Pollock's vehement objection to *Polemis,* Holmes endorsed the decision and took credit for anticipating it in Spade v. Lynn & Boston Railroad Co., 172 Mass. 488, 491 (1899). Letter from Holmes to Pollock (Jan. 23, 1922), 2 HPL 88. Advocating a similar approach in England, Thomas Beven relied upon Holmes's opinion in *Spade,* and Beven's analysis was, in turn, cited for authority in *Polemis.* 1 T. Beven, *Negligence in Law,* 100 (1908); In re Polemis, 574.

82. CL, 116.

83. For contemporary statements of the some-negligence doctrine, see 1 Shearman and Redfield, *Law of Negligence,* 18–20; F. H. Bohlen, "The Basis of Affirmative Obligations in the Law of Tort," 53 *University of Pennsylvania Law Review* 209, 210 (1905); Bratton v. Rudnick, 562; Turner v. Big Lake Oil Co., 96 S.W.2d 221, 227 (1936); and Chapter 6. Current commentators often state the some-negligence rule, but fail to recognize what role it had in overcoming the excuse of unforeseeable harm and how different it is from the conventional negligence rule. See Hart and Honoré, *Causation in the Law,* 234–235 (1959). For justificatory explanations of the some-negligence doctrine see T. Beven, *Principles of the Law of Negligence,* 48–49, 74, 75 and n.1, 83 (1889) (the infliction of unforeseeable harm without any negligence is excused because the defendant lacks the power of "moral choice"); Green, *Essays on Tort and Crime,* 89–90 (quoting

a French commentator); Petition of Kinsman Transit Company, 388 F.2d 708, 723–725 (2d Cir. 1964); J. Feinberg, *Doing and Deserving*, 27–28 (1970).

84. CL, 103–104. Weaver v. Ward (1616), in Baker and Milsom, *Sources*, 331–333 (including a different report of the case they recently discovered).

85. The court in *Weaver* emphasized that the plea of inevitable accident was "in the nature of an excuse, and not of justification." Ibid.

86. CL, 104 (quoting *Weaver*). This suggestion probably inspired Holmes's variation on the *Thorns* hypothetical—where a horse suddenly pushed the plaintiff within range of the stick "just as it was lifted," something that "was not possible, under the circumstances . . . to have anticipated." CL, 94. *Weaver* also suggested that the plea of inevitable accident could be satisfied by an allegation of irresistible force, for example "if a man by force take my hand and strike you." CL, 104. Yet, as Holmes recognized, claims of irresistible force are merely rhetorical devices unless they are taken to imply or require facts showing that the force in question intervened suddenly and without any warning.

87. CL, 104.

88. Cooley, *Law of Torts*, 80 n.2. See also Beven, *Principles of the Law of Negligence*, 48–49, 74, 75 and n.1, 83.

While Cooley used "fault" to mean negligence, many contemporary courts and commentators, including Holmes at various junctures of the torts lectures, also used "fault" in the classic *Weaver* sense to "unify the medley of excuses" based on irresistible force and unforeseeable harm. Fletcher, "Fairness and Utility in Tort Theory," 556. For criticism of this use of "fault," see J. Smith, "Liability for Substantial Physical Damage to Land by Blasting—The Rule of the Future," 33 *Harvard Law Review* 542, 551 (1919).

89. Cooley, *Law of Torts*, 565–573.

90. W. Seavey, "Notes on Torts Lectures by J. Smith," 22 (1904), Special Collections, Harvard Law School Library.

91. Anon., "Inevitable Accident a Defense to Action of Trespass," 5 *Harvard Law Review* 36 (1891).

92. Ibid.

93. Holmes also pointed to "another runaway case," Wakeman v. Robinson, 1 Bing. 213 (1823), which overruled a jury instruction authorizing liability simply on the "immediate act of the defendant," regardless of whether it was "wilful or accidental," and directed a new trial "to consider whether the accident was unavoidable, or occasioned by the fault of the defendant." CL, 105.

94. CL, 83–84.

95. CL, 80.

96. Ibid.

97. The silence of many of these courts regarding foresight-based strict liability follows from the assumption during Holmes's time that most tort claims arose from rather prosaic, horse-and-buggy risks, and that compliance with the negligence standard of reasonable conduct would prevent or compensate all reasonably

foreseeable harms. CL, 103. This assumption continues to hold sway. *Restatement (Second) of Torts,* §520, Comment h. In these cases the scope of the negligence rule (depending on the stringency of its standard of reasonableness) is equivalent (as a tax) to that of foresight-based strict liability. As I discuss later, the failure of current commentators to recognize the possible congruence of these rules in the classic Trespass cases of thorn cuttings, runaway horses, and sticks brandished in self-defense, has led many to overstate the practical meaning of decisions adopting the negligence rule. In effect, the result of applying the negligence rule in many such cases was to limit liability only for unforeseeable harms on the general excuse that set the same limitation on strict liability.

98. Morris v. Platt, 87.

99. Id. at 86. This hypothetical bears a striking similarity to the pleading exemplar offered in *Weaver.*

100. Id. at 87.

101. CL, 106.

102. Morris v. Platt, 87 (emphasis in original). Because (in contrast to foresight-based strict liability) the some-negligence doctrine could apply to unforeseeable harm—usually the principal harm sued upon—commentators classify it as the broadest rule in modern tort law. See W. L. Prosser, "Nuisance without Fault," 20 *Texas Law Review* 399, 406 (1942); A. L. Goodart, "The Third Man or *Novus Actor Interveniens,"* 4 *Current Legal Problems* 177, 182–183 (1951).

103. Id. at 85.

104. My research has revealed no such claim by any contemporary court or commentator. Rather, there was general confirmation of strict liability for land trespass and conversion claims. W. Schofield, Book Review, 1 *Harvard Law Review* 51, 52 (1887); Pollock, *The Law of Torts,* 354 (11th ed. 1920). Indeed, as I demonstrate below, while rejecting *Rylands* in Brown v. Collins, Doe—*Rylands'* chief antagonist—expressly acknowledged these traditional strict liability rules.

Holmes was well aware that the credibility of a descriptive and explanatory theory of responsibility depended on proving his case from the dominant rules, not by appealing to a controversial minority approach, let alone by giving a novel interpretation of those rules. CL, 93 n.2. Of course, it was all to the better if he could demonstrate that his theory also explained a minority or disputed approach, as he did with *Rylands.*

105. CL, 97–98 (discussing strict liability for human trespass to land and conversion of personal property); CL, 116–119 (discussing strict liability for extrahazardous cases, including cattle trespass and the general category of escaping dangerous things governed by *Rylands*).

106. CL, 116.

107. Ibid. 8 Holdsworth, *History of English Law,* 449, 454–457, 468 (equating "pure accidental trespass" with caused-based strict liability under the writ of Trespass). Holmes also stated that in The Nitro-glycerine Case (Parrot v. Wells), 82 U.S. 542 (1872), the Supreme Court "has given the sanction of its approval to

the same doctrine." CL, 106. On the findings that the defendant shippers had no reason to anticipate any possibility of an explosion from opening a routine package, and that there was no negligence regarding any foreseeable risks in handling the package, the Court dismissed the claim as one of "unavoidable accident, for the consequence of which the defendants are not responsible. The consequence of all such accidents must be borne by the sufferer as his misfortune." The Nitroglycerine Case, 538. Holmes's contemporaries regarded the case as involving unforeseeable harm and thus as requiring negligence to establish responsibility. Terry, *Some Leading Principles of the Anglo-American Law of Torts*, 441–442; 1 Jaggard, *Torts*, 65–66 and n.263; Pollock, *The Law of Torts*, 426 and n.(l) (2d ed. 1890); T. A. Street, *The Foundations of Legal Liability*, 84–85 (1906); Palsgraf v. Long Island R.R., 248 N.Y. 339 (1928) (Cardozo, J.).

108. CL, 105–106.

109. The court in *Morris*, 89, suggested this parallel between *Brown* and the hypothetical in *Thorns*.

110. CL, 97.

111. CL, 89; see also CL, 106.

112. Brown v. Kendall, 294; CL, 80. Shaw's analysis also foreshadowed the torts lectures in distinguishing the state of mind that accompanies a willed act from foresight of its consequences; the choice to act by itself does not necessarily imply a choice to inflict the consequences without additional knowledge of circumstances warning of danger.

113. Brown v. Kendall, 297. Illustrative of the contemporary some-negligence interpretation of *Kendall* is Beven's comment that if the dog had not been the defendant's and was beaten for sport, "the complexion of the whole affair would have been different." 1 T. Beven, *Negligence in Law*, 565 (1908); see also Bishop, *Non-Contract Law*, 71 (comparing the case to one where two persons engage in an unlawful fight—"[if] one of them accidentally strikes a third, he must pay the damages"). Beven also argued that the outcome in *Kendall* might have been different if the defendant had acted, though lawfully, for some purpose less compelling than protecting his property. He criticized Holmes for not recognizing gradations of justifications in his some-negligence analysis, with the result that the "quiet citizen must keep out of the way of the exuberantly active one." 1 Beven, *Negligence in the Law*, 565–566. Beven ignored Holmes's multiple-causation critique and confused the questions of responsibility and justification, though he conceded that the torts lectures accurately presented *Kendall* and the other American some-negligence cases as rejecting the causation theory. Ibid; Pollock, *The Law of Torts*, 148 (11th ed. 1920).

For contemporary usage (often based on Shaw's opinion) of "pure accident" as being an excuse for faultless or nonnegligent infliction of unforeseeable harm, and equating recovery for "pure accident" with cause-based strict liability, see Brown v. Collins, 451; H. G. Chapin, *Handbook of the Law of Torts*, 54–55 (1917); Cooley, *Law of Torts*, 80 and n.2; Story, *Bailments*, 610; Street, *Legal Liability*,

80–82; Ames, "Law and Morals," 98; F. Pollock, "Tort," 27 *Encyclopedia Britannica*, 64, 64–65 (1911); Wood, *Nuisances*, 162 (strict liability in nuisance for harms from "apparent defects, or from causes that would reasonably be anticipated, liability . . . but not when the ill results are purely accidental and not in any measure attributable to the negligence of the occupant"). Shaw also defined "inevitable accident" in some-negligence terms, stating that for such an excuse "it must be such an accident as the defendant could not have avoided by the use of the kind and degree of care necessary to the exigency." Brown v. Kendall, 296. In effect, Shaw's formulation of the excuse for inevitable accident paralleled Holmes's foresight resolution of his variation on the *Thorns* hypothetical. While the defendant must take all reasonable precautions necessary to avoid hurting anyone, one cannot guard against a person who suddenly and unexpectedly comes within range of the stick just as it is being raised. See United Elect. Lt. Co. v. DeLiso Construction Co., 315 Mass. 313, 318–319 (1943) (*Kendall* distinguished from case of a "landowner who intentionally sets in motion a force which in the usual course of events will damage the land of another").

114. Brown v. Collins, 445–446.

115. Id. at 450. Doe cited for authority many of the American cases Holmes later relied on, including Morris v. Platt and Brown v. Kendall. Id. at 450–451.

116. Id. at 451.

117. Id. at 450.

118. CL, 106–107, 94–95.

119. CL, 94–95. *Harvey* based the definition of inevitable accident on *Weaver* and the standard formulations of general principle denying responsibility for unforeseeable harm without some negligence. For similar definitions of inevitable accident and the related act of God defense, see Sedgwick, *Damages*, 518; 2 *Commentaries*, *608, 824–25 n.(b); 3 *Commentaries*, *217; Gold, "Inevitable Accident," 5–6; Story, *Bailments*, 598; Campbell, *Negligence*, 4–5; Buller, *Nisi Prius*, 70; The Nitro-glycerine Case; Ball v. Nye; Nugent v. Smith, 1 C.P.D. 423, 436–437 (1876); Greenock Corp. v. Caledonian Ry., 572; Shelley's Case, 1 Co. Rep. 93b, 97b (1581); The Majestic, 166 U.S. 375, 386 (1897); McArthur v. Sears, 21 Wend. 190, 199 (N.Y. 1839).

120. CL, 109–110, 54. For an argument based on *Harvey* and relying on Holmes that the law should excuse infants "whose incapacity to realize the probable consequences of their conduct makes it unjust" to impose liability, see F. H. Bohlen, "Liability in Tort of Infants and Insane Persons," 23 *Michigan Law Review* 9–11 and nn.1, 4 (1924).

121. CL, 106–107, 110. Holmes indicated that his some-negligence interpretation of *Harvey* was confirmed by a later New York case, Losee v. Buchanan. CL, 106 n.3. *Losee* denied liability for damage done by an exploding boiler where the defect was "imperceptible to the defendants or undiscoverable on examination or by the application of known tests." Id. at 492. The court relied on *Harvey* as support for the rule that "[n]o one in such case is made liable without some fault

or negligence on his part, however serious the injury may be which he may accidentally cause," and emphasized that this rule contradicted the cause-based strict liability rule of the *Thorns* hypothetical. Id. at 488–489. Contemporary commentators not only shared Holmes's some-negligence interpretation of *Losee*, but they regarded the case as endorsing a foresight-based strict liability rule for boilers similar to the *scienter* rule for domestic animals, residential fireplaces and other common activities. M. M. Bigelow, *Leading Cases on the Law of Torts*, 499–501 (1878); M. M. Bigelow, *The Law of Torts*, 467 (1907); Beven, *Principles*, 1125; Cooley, *Torts*, 573–574 and n.3. In accordance with Holmes's analysis, such activities were distinguished from cases where *scienter* was established, and from cases of manifestly dangerous activities like blasting or keeping vicious animals. Bishop, *Commentaries on the Non-Contract Law*, 381; Terry, *Some Leading Principles of the Anglo-American Law of Torts*, 441–442; Wharton, *Law of Negligence*, 661–662, 666; Heeg v. Light, 80 N.Y. 579 (1880).

In support of his some-negligence interpretation of accidental Trespass, CL, 107 n.1, Holmes also relied on Vincent v. Stinehour, 7 Vt. 62, 65–66 (1835) (runaway horse case invoking *Gibbons* and *Wakeman* for rule that there is no liability when the defendant is "entirely deprived of the command of his will and actions," as "where a horse takes a sudden fright, and there is no imprudence in the rider, either in managing the horse or in driving an unsafe horse . . . the trespass is wholly involuntary and unavoidable"), and generally referred to several other cases, including Bizzell v. Booker, 16 Ark. 308 (1885) (if defendants were unlawfully camping, they were then liable for the unforeseeable spread of their fire); and Holmes v. Mather (no liability without negligence for harms from a "sudden" runaway).

In the torts lectures, Holmes several times referred to the foresight condition for liability as the standard of social blameworthiness. CL, 110. While this usage of "blame" in the generic sense of attributing responsibility predominated, at one point in Lecture III he suggested a narrower, negligent-harm meaning to "blame." CL 115. In "The Theory of Torts" (Lect. IV), CL, 147–148, Holmes acknowledged and resolved this ambiguity, reconciling the notion of blame with a general foresight theory of responsibility that provided the intellectual footing for expansive application of all of the major rules of strict liability. Further discussion of the meaning he attached to these terms is in Chapter 4, where I elaborate the foresight theory and its application to strict liability.

122. For contemporary statements of the some-negligence interpretations of the principal American and English Trespass cases to which Holmes addressed his analysis, see Campbell, *Law of Negligence*, 4–5; Chapin, *Law of Torts*, 54–55; Underhill, *Law of Torts*, 8–10; Wharton, *Law of Negligence*, 63; T. G. Shearman and A. A. Redfield, *A Treatise on the Law of Negligence*, 6–7 (1880); N. Dane, *A General Abridgment and Digest of American Law*, 484 (relying on Taylor v. Rainbow, 12 Va. 423, 439–40 (1808)); Green, *Essays on Tort and Crime*, 88–90 (some-negligence doctrine in French law); Wigmore, "Responsibility for Tortious

Acts," 442–444, 459–460 (quoting Buller and Comyn); Jaggard, *Law of Torts,* 65–66 and n.263; Anon., "Liability for Blasting," 13 *Harvard Law Review* 600 (1900); Bigelow, *Law of Torts,* 4–5; F. Pollock, *The Law of Torts,* 145, 493 and nn (11th ed., 1920); 1 Comyn, *Digest,* 208–209; Story, *Bailments,* 598; Greenleaf, *Evidence,* 210; Green v. General Petroleum Corp. 205 Cal. 238, 334 (1928); Ploof v. Putnam. The correspondence between Holmes's views and those of his contemporaries is discussed in Chapter 6.

123. Many current scholars, to be sure, recognize that the inevitable accident and act of God defenses in pre-nineteenth-century Trespass cases were not synonymous with non-negligence but required showing unforeseeable harm for excuse. Fletcher, "Fairness and Utility in Tort Theory," 552–555; R. E. V. Heuston and R. A. Buckley, *The Law of Torts,* 372–373 (1987). Yet most of these commentators overgeneralize references conditioning the excuse on the absence of any negligence and use them to apply not only to cases of unforeseeable harm, but broadly to all claims in Trespass. Fleming, *Torts,* 19–20, 316–317. Some state the some-negligence rule without realizing its application to the accidental Trespass cases in and before the last century. D. Kretzmer, "Transformation of Tort Liability in the Nineteenth Century: The Visible Hand," 4 *Oxford Journal of Legal Studies,* 46, 59 (1984); R. Keeton, *Legal Cause in the Law of Torts,* 3–36 (1963); Keeton et al., *Prosser and Keeton on Torts,* 314–315; cf. Feinberg, *Doing and Deserving,* 27–28 and n.4.

In addition to my own work, three other commentators have recently presented the some-negligence interpretation of the pre-nineteenth century, although they conclude that nineteenth-century cases and commentary generally held that negligence controlled Trespass without regard to foreseeability. R. J. Kaczorowski, "The Common-Law Background of Nineteenth-Century Tort Law"; B. A. White, "Risk-Utility Analysis and the Learned Hand Formula: A Hand That Helps or a Hand That Hides?" 32 *Arizona Law Review* 77, 81, 97–99 (1990); S. G. Gilles, "Inevitable Accident in Classical English Tort Law," 43 *Emory Law Journal* 575 (1994). None finds the some-negligence interpretation in Holmes's writings. Among current scholars, only Gary Schwartz has suggested a some-negligence understanding in Holmes's analysis: "Holmes's primary model of conduct that should be nontortious because non-negligent, was conduct the riskiness of which was completely unknowable or unforeseeable by the actor." G. Schwartz, "The Vitality of Negligence and the Ethics of Strict Liability," 15 *Georgia Law Review* 963, 984 n. 107 (1981).

124. Gilles, "Inevitable Accident," 580 and n.23. This error is committed regardless of whether a commentator takes the orthodox position that negligence was a nineteenth-century creation, see M. J. Horwitz, *The Transformation of American Law, 1780–1860,* 90–91 n. 156 (1977); W. L. Prosser, *Handbook of the Law of Torts,* 170, 173 (1941), or holds the minority view that negligence always was a general prerequisite for liability in Trespass as well as Case, J. H. Baker, *An Introduction to English Legal History,* 341–342 (1979); E. F. Roberts,

"Negligence: Blackstone to Shaw to ? An Intellectual Escapade in a Tory Vein," 50 *Cornell Law Quarterly* 191, 192, 204 (1965), or finds that neither rule dominated. G. E. White, *Tort Law in America* (1980). Failure to recognize the some-negligence interpretation seems to have led these commentators to see tort law as either all negligence or all cause-based strict liability, and to miss or minimize the presence or possibility of foresight-based strict liability. Baker, *English Legal History,* 339 (limiting references to a bare mention of the "*scienter* action" of strict liability against owners of dangerous animals); Horwitz, *Transformation of American Law, 1780–1860,* 90 n.151 (dismissing decisions that impose strict liability based on foreseeability as anomalies "groping for the modern distinction between intentional and negligent injuries").

125. Both sides in the debate over whether negligence or cause-based strict liability governed Trespass before the nineteenth century agree on the negligence meaning of the some-negligence references in writings of Holmes and his contemporaries. Those who maintain the negligence view of Trespass ascribe this meaning to some-negligence formulations in cases and commentary prior to the nineteenth century. Advocates of the orthodox "transformation" thesis disagree, arguing that "negligence" references in cases before the nineteenth century generally were not concerned with the cause of action for unreasonable conduct, but were another, if often redundant, way of stating the rule of absolute responsibility. Horwitz, *Transformation of American Law, 1780–1860,* 85–89. On this view, "negligence" meant only "neglect or failure fully to perform a preexisting duty, whether imposed by contract, statute, or common law status," presumably subjecting the defendant to cause-based strict liability. Id. at 87, 93. This "neglect" interpretation of "negligence" was well known to Holmes's contemporaries, who generally dismissed it as vacuous for begging the question of whether in substance the duty required strict liability or merely reasonable conduct. W. Markby, *Elements of Law,* 110 (1871). While Holmes recognized the "neglect" interpretation of "negligence" and stated it broadly as "failure *de facto* to keep safely," he suggested that it related mainly to bailment and other cases arising from contractual relationships (noting that the parties could disavow any strict liability duty by contract). In any event, he concluded that the unreasonable conduct usage of "negligence" was widespread in noncontract cases. CL, 199–201, 205. Subsequent studies substantiate his conclusion. Fifoot, *History and Sources,* 187–195; Kaczorowski, "The Common-Law Background"; Gilles, "Inevitable Accident"; Schwartz, "Tort Law and the Economy." But see Plucknett, *History of the Common Law,* 482, 469 and n.3; White, *Tort Law in America,* 13–16. Moreover, as Holmes found, the strict liability rule implied by the "neglect" concept was limited by the foresight condition, as defendants even in bailment cases could always invoke the excuse of unforeseeable acts of God. CL, 200–201. See also Wigmore, *"Responsibility for Tortious Acts,"* 448.

126. Gilmore, *The Death of Contract,* 16; see also Roberts, "Negligence," 205; M. A. Franklin and R. L. Rabin, *Tort Law and Alternatives,* 69 (1992); C. A.

Auerbach, L. K. Garrison, W. Hurst, and S. Mermin, *The Legal Process,* 239–244 (1961).

127. White, *Tort Law in America,* 18.

128. CL, 95.

129. Ibid.

130. The brevity is explained by the fact that he incorporated a prior, detailed analysis in Lecture II on criminal law, explaining the "[ ]politic and [ ]just" boundary line, which was etched in the law by the cases of civil and criminal liability, and which demarcated excuse and responsibility on the basis of foresight-informed choice. CL, 95 n. 2 (citing CL, 54, 55).

131. Indeed, as Holmes pointed out, the rule of absolute responsibility generally governed claims of property damage against common carriers, although this may not relate directly to the theory of torts as the parties could shift liability for the residual risk by contract. In two essays on "Agency" published in 1891, but written soon after *The Common Law* lectures, he focused on the extension of the rule of vicarious liability into the zone of absolute responsibility by holding non-negligent employers accountable for unforeseeable employee negligence. CLP, "Agency I and II," 49, 81.

132. CL, 88–89 and n.4.

133. CLP, "Privilege, Malice, and Intent," 117. The only limitation, Holmes noted, concerned the class of cases involving "omissions," where the risk arose independently of the defendant's conduct and liability was not imposed "except in consequence of some duty voluntarily undertaken." CL, 82. In view of Holmes's argument against the "passive instrument" notion, it is doubtful that he would classify many cases as "omissions" where the risk in question was not traceable to a more remote act by the defendant.

134. CL, 79.

135. CL, 95–96.

136. CL, 96. Why, indeed, should tort supply insurance for the relatively few who are harmed by human enterprise, while the many must buy first-party insurance against the omnipresent hazards of fate? On the difficulties of insuring unforeseeable risk, see A. Schwartz, "Products Liability, Corporate Structure, and Bankruptcy: Toxic Substances and the Remote Risk Relationship," 14 *Journal of Legal Studies* 689, 729–733 (1985); D. G. Owen, "Products Liability Principles and Justice," 20 *Anglo-American Law Review* 238, 250 and n.54 (1991); Keeton et al., *Prosser and Keeton on Torts,* 44–55.

137. Ibid. There seems little doubt about Holmes's finding even today, notwithstanding improvements in efficiency and consistency made by all systems. 1 American Law Institute, *Reporters' Study: Enterprise Responsibility for Personal Injury,* 28–30 (1991); J. O'Connell, *The Lawsuit Lottery* (1979).

138. J. Coleman, *Risks and Wrongs,* 209 (1992)(referring generally to *The Common Law*). See also W. M. Landes and R. A. Posner, *The Economic Structure of Tort Law,* 4–5 and n.9 (1987).

139. 1872 Jurisprudence Essay, 791; CL, 144–145, 156; CLP, "The Path of the Law," 183. For further discussion, see Chapter 5.

140. CL, 144, 145.

141. CLP, 117.

142. CL, 95.

143. Even if defendants could establish some loss reserve against unpredictable risks—an extremely doubtful prospect—the type of social insurance provided by cause-based strict liability invites undesirable and morally hazardous behavior by tort "insureds," and would negate whatever tenuous benefits the reserves could supply. Absolute coverage, whether provided by tort or conventional insurance, entails well-known dangers of encouraging fraudulent claims, and of fostering indifference towards or preference for risk. On insurance theory and policy concerning such problems as pool size, moral hazard, and adverse selection, see K. S. Abraham, *Distributing Risk* (1986); S. Shavell, *Economic Analysis of Accident Law* (1987).

144. Chapter 5 generally discusses Holmes's views on the types of cases where courts, as a matter of policy discretion, might profitably adopt foresight-based strict liability for social insurance purposes.

145. It is doubtful, moreover, that individuals engaged in nonpecuniary activities could afford liability insurance, even if it were available.

146. Anon., "Accident Insurance," 7 *American Law Review* 585, 586 (1873). G. A. MacLean, *Insurance Up Through the Ages,* 66 (1938); V. A. R. Zelizer, *Morals and Markets* (1983).

147. Although the first appearance of liability insurance in America dates from the mid-1880s, its availability depended on specific statutory authorization, and it was limited to employer liability for employee injuries. Maclean, *Insurance,* 66; G. F. Michelbacher, *Casualty Insurance Principles,* 12–13 (1930). On the public policy concerns inhibiting enforcement of liability insurance contracts, see generally M. McNeely, "Illegality as a Factor in Liability Insurance," 41 *Columbia Law Review* 26 (1941).

148. CL, 55–56.

149. CL, 95; 55–56.

150. Ibid. This concern about cause-based strict liability, which was widespread among Holmes's contemporaries (see Brown v. Collins), fuels present-day resistance to the rule. A. Schwartz, "Remote Risk Relationship," 689; Anderson v. Owens-Illinois, Inc., 799 F.2d 1, 4–5 (1st Cir. 1986). See also L. Kaplow, "The Value of Accuracy in Adjudication: An Economic Analysis," 23 *Journal of Legal Studies* 307, 325 and n.44 (1994).

151. Holmes's concern about overdeterrence was directed to the prospect of risk-averse defendants being compelled to live under a general threat of unexpected liability without even the crude cushion of liability insurance. Cause-based strict liability would induce panicky decisions in choosing among substitute activities. Since, by definition, the various activity options would not reflect their

comparative levels of unforeseeable risks, choices might well be influenced by erroneous assumptions and misleading criteria, with the possible result of increasing risks overall. Moreover, productivity and welfare would suffer as cause-based strict liability pressured individuals to forgo levels and types of activity they would prefer to undertake. Given the difficulty individuals have in spreading losses and establishing adequate reserves, as well as the unavailability of liability insurance for individuals and industry alike, the result of applying cause-based strict liability would be to demoralize and outrage a beleaguered people.

Gilmore misconstrued this overdeterrence analysis as opposing all forms of strict liability, indeed, all liability. Gilmore, *Death of Contract,* 16–17. He erred in ignoring the context of Holmes's policy argument, which leads to the unmistakable conclusion that he was objecting solely to strict liability based on mere causation. As I have noted, this argument followed directly after Holmes's multiple-cause critique of the causation theory and his conclusion that cause-based strict liability failed the criterion of justice implicit in the causal act requirement itself, conditioning moral responsibility on the defendant's foresight-informed power of choice to avoid harm. See also 1 HPL 62–63. Cf. Weinrib, *Private Law,* 152–153 (same point and similar language without attribution).

152. CL, 55. Although Holmes recognized that the burdens of cause-based strict liability could be mitigated by contract in common carrier cases involving commercial transactions, he did not consider using the rule to induce firms to price the chance of unknown risks in their products, to direct research toward discovery of these risks, or to refrain from deceptive or other efforts to thwart discovery.

153. CL, 116–117, 156–157.

154. CL, 84.

155. Ibid.

156. Ibid.

157. CL, 96.

158. Horwitz, *Transformation of American Law, 1870–1960,* 124; see also T. Grey, "Holmes and Legal Pragmatism," 41 *Stanford Law Review* 787, 831 (1989).

159. Ibid. (Holmes's words underscored).

160. CL, 96.

161. Ibid.

162. CL, 55.

163. CL, 54.

164. CL, 91.

165. Ibid.

166. CL, 54.

167. Ibid.

168. Ibid.

169. CL, 95.

170. Ibid. See also CL, 54–55.

171. CL, 94.

172. CL, 84.

173. CL, 95.

174. CL, 144.

175. Hart and Honoré, *Causation in the Law,* 1, 26–28, 91.

176. Epstein, "A Theory of Strict Liability," 165–166, 168 n.48.

177. As I have shown, he also rejected these arguments from the broader jurisprudential perspective that rights cannot be defined by neutral, objective criteria of semantic logic or customary practice—criteria that preclude the necessity of exercising policy choices both in setting the initial distributional entitlements and in applying them to particular cases of conflicting interests.

178. Current proponents of the common usage theories of causation rely more or less explicitly on foreseeability to bridge their causal notions to a coherent idea of moral responsibility. Hart and Honoré, *Causation in the Law,* 151–52, 254, 258–284; Epstein, "A Theory of Strict Liability," 157–171. In fact, these commentators incorporate so many other conditions and qualifications, both in defining the source and nature of ordinary understandings and in avoiding the multiple-causation critique, that they all but concede the view of Holmes and Nicholas St. John Green that causation is largely a stand-in for judicial policy choices. For a more recent statement coinciding with Holmes's thinking on causation, see G. Calabresi, "Concerning Cause and the Law of Torts: An Essay for Harry Kalven, Jr.," 43 *University of Chicago Law Review* 69, 106 (1975), and F. S. Cohen, "Field Theory and Judicial Logic," 59 *Yale Law Journal* 238, 252–253 (1950), which also generally adopts Holmes's new jurisprudence.

179. FE, "Possession," 181. Yet while "rights" were thus pre-legal—"natural powers"—Holmes recognized that the state not only directly regulates or forbids them, but also indirectly affects their exercise by the conditions it imposes on obtaining "protection, restitution, or compensation by the aid of the public force." CL, 77, 144–145, 214. On the related question of liability for "omissions," see CL, 82.

180. CL, 77.

181. CL, 144, 162.

182. Ibid.

4. General Theory of Torts—Part One

1. This is the portion of the torts lectures abbreviated as Theory of Torts (Lect. IV). The 1873 article bearing the same title, but far different in content, is abbreviated as 1873 Theory of Torts.

2. CL, 130, 146–147.

3. CL, 164.

4. CL, 54–55, 95. Many of Holmes's contemporaries embraced the notion that foresight-informed choice to avoid harm was the foundation of moral respon-

sibility in law as well as in ethics generally, not the least of whom was his father. O. W. Holmes, *Mechanism in Thought and Morals,* 79 (1882). See also J. S. Mill, "Auguste Comte and Positivism," in 10 J. M. Robson, ed., *Collected Works of John Stuart Mill,* 261, 266 (1969); E. H. Madden, ed., *The Philosophical Writings of Chauncey Wright,* 43 (1958); N. S. Green, *Essays on Tort and Crime,* 16 (1933); H. T. Terry, "Proximate Consequences in the Law of Torts," 28 *Harvard Law Review* 10, 18 (1914); P. H. Winfield, *The Province of the Law of Tort,* 32–37 (1931); W. A. Seavey, "Principles of Torts," 56 *Harvard Law Review* 72, 84–86 (1942); and on the foresight-based choice element of Kant's theory, see E. Weinrib, *The Idea of Private Law,* 104–105, 109 (1995). For current statements of the foresight theory of responsibility, see H. L. A. Hart, *Punishment and Responsibility,* 90–112 (1968); J. Feinberg, *Doing and Deserving,* 149–150, 222–224 (1970); L. L. Weinreb, *Natural Law and Justice,* 91–93, 201–202, 208 (1987).

   5. CL, 97–98, 94, 149.

   6. CLP, "Privilege, Malice, and Intent," 117.

   7. To be precise, I am claiming that Holmes did not restrict his general theory of responsibility to foreseeable harms that could be avoided by reasonable conduct, or were the causally related consequences of unreasonable conduct. For suggestions that Holmes's theory was limited to this area and did not extend to harms that were foreseeable but were neither the result of negligence nor avoidable by reasonable conduct, see G. E. White, *Justice Oliver Wendell Holmes: Law and the Inner Self,* 526–527 n. 54 (1993); R. W. Gordon, "Holmes's *Common Law* as Legal and Social Science," 10 *Hofstra Law Review* 719, 728 (1982). On the distinction between foresight of unreasonable or negligent harms and foresight of harm irrespective of the quality of the defendant's conduct, see I.S. Bushey & Sons, Inc. v. United States, 398 F.2d 167, 171 (2d Cir. 1968) (Friendly, J.); F. James, Jr., "Strict Liability of Manufacturers," 24 *Tennessee Law Review* 923–925 (1957).

   8. CLP, 117. In effect, Holmes substituted standard philosophical conceptions for what he regarded as morally loaded terms like rights and duties, which he had grudgingly used in the 1873 Theory of Torts. See Letter from Holmes to Frederick Pollock (Mar. 25, 1883), 1 HPL, 20; Letter from John Henry Wigmore to Holmes (Apr. 29, 1894), MS Box 51, Folders 21–31, HP; Letter from Holmes to Wigmore (May 3, 1894), MS Box 51, Folders 21–31, HP. For a discussion of the notions of responsibility (and excuse) and justification, and their relation to the morally legitimate and policy-moderated scope of liability, see Hart, *Punishment and Responsibility,* 13–14 (noting that in contrast to a justification, such as self-defense, which stems from a policy decision that the usual sanctions for inflicting foreseeable harm should not apply in a particular class of cases, excuse is a "requirement of fairness or of justice" that sets minimum threshold conditions for responsibility in any degree). See also Weinreb, *Natural Law and Justice,* 196, 242; on the distinction between excuse and justification in tort law, see G. P. Fletcher, "Fairness and Utility in Tort Theory," 85 *Harvard Law Review* 537,

558–559 (1972); J. H. Wigmore, "The Tripartite Division of Torts," 8 *Harvard Law Review* 208 (1894); F. Buller, *An Introduction to the Law Relative to Trials at Nisi Prius,* 17, 64, 70, 75–78 (1788).

9. CL, 146–147, 156–157.

10. CL, 156.

11. CLP, 117. For other descriptions of the first part of the theory, see Letters from Holmes to Pollock (Mar. 22, 1891; undated) 1 HPL 35–36, 62–63. Part two of the theory was incorporated in Holmes's famous dissent in Vegelahn v. Guntner, 167 Mass. 29, 105–106 (1896) ("in numberless instances the law warrants the intentional infliction of temporal damage . . . [based on] a justification . . . [t]he true grounds of [which] are considerations of policy and of social advantage," not "logic and the general propositions of law which no body disputes"). Holmes reiterated the two-part theory in "The Path of the Law," CLP, 190, and ultimately incorporated it in constitutional doctrine as the basis for the state police power. Aikens v. Wisconsin, 195 U.S. 194, 204–205 (1904).

12. Id. at 130–131.

13. Holmes regarded judicial use of privileges to permit infliction of inexcusable harm as further evidence for the antiformalist attack on legal science he had been waging from the early 1870s, and took the opportunity to reprise his politics-of-law conception of legal reality. Observing that "decisions for or against [a] privilege" involved "a question of policy," Holmes called on judges to decide these matters "with express recognition" and well-tutored understanding of their legislative character and considerations. Id. at 120, 129–130.

14. As explained by Wigmore, who explicitly adopted Holmes's theoretical divisions, the question of whether acting reasonably (non-negligently) should relieve a defendant of *prima facie* responsibility was a question of justification, a pure matter of policy as to "whether one party's convenience should be subjected to another's." Wigmore, *The Tripartite Division of Torts,* 208. See also Burt v. Advertiser Newspaper Co., 154 Mass. 238, 243–245 (1891). That the torts lectures were primarily concerned with working out a theory of responsibility explains why they treated the negligence rule—that is, whether reasonable conduct justifies inflicting foreseeable harm—in rather cursory fashion. Perplexed by the relative obscurity of the negligence rule in the torts lectures, and failing to understand the two parts of Holmes's theory, some scholars have reached the opposite conclusion from the negligence-dogma interpretation, presenting Holmes as an advocate of a premodern conception of negligence that essentially made foresight-based strict liability the universal rule in tort. This argument is considered later in this chapter and in Chapter 6.

15. CLP, 128.

16. CL, 144–145.

17. CLP, "Privilege, Malice, and Intent," 125–126.

18. CL, 147.

19. CL, 130, 147, 149; CLP, "Privilege, Malice, and Intent," 117.

20. CLP, "Privilege, Malice, and Intent," 117–118.

21. CL, 149.

22. CL, 154–155.

23. CLP, "Privilege, Malice and Intent," 117; CLP, "The Path of the Law," 191; CL, 95.

24. CL, 155–156; see also CL, 53. Cf. UCLP, 86; CLP, "The Path of the Law," 187.

25. CLP, "Path of the Law," 183.

26. CL, 147.

27. CL, 109.

28. CL, 56.

29. CL, 56–57. Foresight standards based on the experience of the "average man" were selected by courts in their policy discretion "simply to make a rule which is not too hard for the average member of the community," where a more stringent standard would overdeter beneficial activity or, perversely, induce recourse to more costly illegal circumvention. CL, 57, 26, 33, 42, 100. In designing the reasonable person standard "by legislative considerations of policy" courts should take account of all factors bearing on the capacity of the class of individuals to comply, including the "circumstances and limited powers" of the poor. Butler v. New York, N.H. & H.R.R., 177 Mass. 191, 193 (1900) (Holmes, J.).

Holmes anticipated Seavey's argument that the test of reasonableness is formulated instrumentally according to the needs of policy, and that there is "no standardized man." W. Seavey, "Negligence—Subjective or Objective," 41 *Harvard Law Review* 1, 27 (1927). Horwitz exaggerates Seavey's point, characterizing it as a refutation of the "whole theory of objectivism" because it claimed that "the only plausible meaning of fault implied an impracticably particularistic subjective test." M. J. Horwitz, *The Transformation of American Law, 1870–1960*, 126–127 (1992). Like Holmes, Seavey denied only that reasonableness constituted an essentialist rather than a pragmatic standard. Neither rejected the possibility of empirically objective standards of reasonableness. Given sufficient expenditures and policy reasons, as Holmes suggested, courts could avoid much of the policy choice involved in fashioning particularistic standards by adopting concrete rules incorporating society-wide demographic averages. Similarly, industrial liability could be based on relatively objective "state-of-the-art" standards formulated from industry-wide averages or customs.

30. CL, 116.

31. CL, 93–94, 160.

32. See K. J. Arrow, *Essays in the Theory of Risk-Bearing*, 24 (1974); H. Latin, "Activity Levels, Due Care, and Selective Realism in Economic Analysis of Tort Law," 39 *Rutgers Law Review* 487, 507 (1987); R. A. Posner, *Economic Analysis of Law*, 166 (1986); S. Shavell, "An Analysis of Causation and the Scope of Liability in the Law of Torts," 9 *Journal of Legal Studies* 463, 491 n.48 (1980); S. Breyer, *Breaking the Vicious Circle: Toward Effective Risk Regulation*, 21, 34, 37

(1993) (referring to Holmes's observation that "most people think dramatically, not quantitatively").

33. CL, 57, 161.

34. In his treatment of *Rylands* Holmes assumed that the reasonable mill owner, and hence mill owners generally, would have knowledge of the danger of reservoir collapse. CL, 157. Holmes suggested that railroad operators were bound by the specialized experience of those engaged in the business to recognize when engine sparks would pose an enhanced risk of fire. CL, 92–93. Those who keep cattle were held to the relatively special experience of the reasonable owner who foresees the danger of trespass on neighboring property. CL, 156.

35. CL, 109.

36. CLP, "Path of the Law," 190.

37. CL, 156–157; see also CL, 75. In his review of *The Common Law*, Pollock suggested that Holmes had failed to state that the negligence standard required persons engaged in trades to exercise the skill commensurate with the average or custom in the trade. F. Pollock, "Holmes on the Common Law," *The Saturday Review*, 758, 759 (June 11, 1881). It is apparent, however, that Holmes addressed this point (as Pollock essentially acknowledged) by noting that it would be negligent for individuals to engage in activities demanding precautions beyond their capacities. CL, 109; Pollock, "Holmes on the Common Law," 759. Pollock himself advocated this interpretation of ordinary reasonable care (F. Pollock, *The Law of Torts*, 396 (4th ed. 1895), and the courts generally accept it. Cayzer v. Taylor, 76 Mass. 274, 276–277 (1857); Hill v. Winsor, 118 Mass. 251, 258–259 (1875); Erie R.R. v. Stewart, 40 F.2d 855 (6th Cir. 1930); Turner v. Big Lake Oil Co., 96 S.W.2d 221, 225 (Tex. 1936). Cf. The Germanic, 196 U.S. 589 (1905) (Holmes, J.). Holmes also dealt with the point by explaining the negligence standard with reference to cases involving technologically complex activities, such as operating railroads and public water mains. CL, 92–93, 107. Moreover, he recognized and supported proportioning the level of precautions to the level of risk presented by a given activity and applying concrete, presumptive standards, such as those propounded under the doctrine of *res ipsa loquitur*. CL, 124–128. The law may induce even greater efforts to discover risk by subjecting defendants to liability for consequences which the legislator apprehends, although they are not predictable from common experience. CL, 59, 75; Commonwealth v. Smith, 166 Mass. 370, 375–376 (1896) (Holmes, J.).

38. CL, 146.

39. Letter from Holmes to Pollock, I HPL, 62–63. See also CL, 57, 146–147.

40. In cases where the defendant's cognitive capacity approximated that of the reasonable person, whether modeled upon average or expert intelligence and experience, Holmes surmised that the only difference between the subjective and external standards would be that the former might be easier to prove in many cases. CL, 136, 159.

41. CL, 55–56, 130–131, 155, 160.

42. CL, 55.
43. CL, 147, see also CL, vi.
44. CL, 75.
45. CL, 48, 55, 147; see also Commonwealth v. Pierce, 138 Mass. 165, 179 (1884) (Holmes, J.).
46. CL, 58–59, 75.
47. CL, 155.
48. CL, 94.
49. CLP, "Privilege, Malice, and Intent," 118, 125.
50. CL, 48.
51. CL, 53.
52. CL, 90.
53. CL, 159; see also CL, 160–161.
54. CL, 56.
55. CL, 154–157.
56. CL, 154, 145.
57. For example, in Quinn v. Crimmings, 171 Mass. 255, 258 (1898) Holmes noted that although gravity predictably caused ordinary fences to fall, public policy justified applying negligence rather than strict liability. Compliance with the standard of reasonable care would reduce the risk to a negligible level and, in the absence of liability insurance, strict liability would merely shift the burden of loss. Unlike large-scale businesses involved in extra-hazardous activities, subjecting noncommercial or small business activities to strict liability would unduly inhibit socially beneficial activity. Compare Ainsworth v. Lakin, 180 Mass. 397 (1902); CL 115–116 (strict liability to address the substantial residual risk from carrying guns in public).
58. CL, 157.
59. CL, 154. Generalized foresight was an "underwriters" perspective. N. S. Green, *Essays on Tort and Crime*, 16. This perspective was also vividly expressed by Baron Bramwell's famous hypothetical applying *Rylands* to the case where "a man kept a tiger, and lightning broke his chain, and he got loose and did mischief." Nichols v. Marsland, 10 Ex. 255, 260 (1875). See also Terry, "Proximate Consequences in the Law of Torts," 24 (*Rylands*-type strict liability based on generalized foresight applies to "actively dangerous things").
60. CL, 147.
61. CLP, "Privilege, Malice, and Intent," 117.
62. CL, 154–156.
63. CL, 4–7; 155–158.
64. Commonwealth v. Pierce, 179; CL, 155–158. Here strict liability is founded on specialized knowledge.
65. CL, 158.
66. CL, 157.
67. CL, 153.

68. Lecture notes of M. D. Howe (Mar. 29, 1961), MS Box 53, Folder 19, Howe Papers, Harvard Law School Library; see also M. D. Howe, *Justice Oliver Wendell Holmes, The Proving Years, 1870–1882,* 193–194, 210 (1963). White, *Justice Oliver Wendell Holmes,* 142–144, 152–154; 170–171 (1993). These charges are merely asserted, without independent consideration of the relevant sources. In fact, Holmes's historical analysis comports with studies by his contemporaries and subsequent investigators. For example, see F. Pollock, *The Law of Torts;* N. Isaacs, "Fault and Liability," 31 *Harvard Law Review* 954 (1918); J. H. Wigmore, "Responsibility for Tortious Acts: Its History.—III," 7 *Harvard Law Review* 441 (1894); J. H. Baker, *An Introduction to English Legal History* (1979); S. F. C. Milsom, *Historical Foundations of the Common Law,* 346–350 (1969); C. H. S. Fifoot, *History and Sources of the Common Law,* 185–194 (1949); R. Kaczorowski, "The Common-Law Background of Nineteenth-Century Tort Law," 51 *Ohio State Law Journal* 1127 (1990); R. Posner, "A Theory of Negligence," 1 *Journal of Legal Studies* 29 (1972). I am not endorsing all of the views in these studies, but refer to them simply to indicate the recklessly dismissive treatment of Holmes's historical analysis by many current commentators.

69. CLP, "Path of the Law," 183.

70. Ibid.

71. CL, 110.

72. CL, 93.

73. CL, 54–56. Indeed, the idea of vengeful blame, which generated most of tort law, authorized strict liability against every source of harm, even inanimate objects and animals. CL, 40; see also CL, 3–4, 8–10, 19, 24, 37; CLP, "Law in Science," 216. See Howe, *The Proving Years,* 180–181, 250–251. For a notable example of the use of "blame" by Holmes's contemporaries to connote the generic attribution of responsibility for foreseeable harm which determined application of the principle that loss from accident lies where it falls, see J. Story, *Law of Bailments,* 603 (1878). See also 8 W. Holdsworth, *A History of English Law,* 457–458 (1923); 1 T. Beven, *Negligence in Law,* 568 (1908); F. H. Bohlen, *Cases on the Law of Torts,* 633 (1941); but see J. B. Ames, "Law and Morals," 22 *Harvard Law Review* 97, 99 (1909) (equating "blame" with negligence). For recent usage of "blame" consistent with Holmes's generic ascription of foresight-based responsibility embracing both foresight-based strict liability and negligence, see R. E. Keeton, "Conditional Fault in the Law of Torts," 72 *Harvard Law Review* 401, 419–420, 427–428 (1959); H. L. A. Hart and T. Honoré, *Causation in the Law,* 254 (1985); G. O. Robinson, "Risk, Causation, and Harm," in R. G. Frey and C. W. Morris, eds., *Liability and Responsibility: Essays in Law and Morals,* 331–332 (1991); C. H. Schroeder, "Corrective Justice and Liability for Increasing Risks," 37 *UCLA Law Review* 439, 451–460 (1990).

74. CL, 110.

75. CL, 55.

76. "The Common Law," *Boston Daily Advertiser,* p. 1 (Jan. 1, 1881) (verba-

tim account of Lecture XII, which summarized the preceding lectures in "The Common Law" series). See also CL, 125 (referring to the "general foundation of legal liability in blameworthiness, as determined by the existing average standards of the community"). Holmes referred to "blameworthiness" in the context of explaining the external standard of negligence. But he immediately generalized his point about external standards to encompass all rules governing "unintentional injury," and stated that what a defendant "might and ought to have foreseen" was the test of "blame for acting as he did." CL, 108, 110.

77. CL, 147. Holmes indicated that the ambiguity in the meaning of "blameworthy" arose in connection with his use of "wrong" as the encompassing classification. CL(I), 110, 147.

78. CL, 148. See also CL, 163. By clarifying the ambiguous meaning of blame, Holmes was able to extend the foresight theory of responsibility to all major rules of strict liability, placing most of them in the subclass of rules focusing on the blameworthy infliction of socially detrimental harm. Holmes never explained the source of the ambiguity, but it may have resulted from a time lag in the preparation of the two lectures; Lecture III was written in 1879 as a separate article ("Trespass and Negligence"), more than a year before Lecture IV was drafted and the two were delivered at the Lowell Institute. At the time "Trespass and Negligence" was written, he may not have fully appreciated the foresight theory's application to *Rylands* and other rules of strict liability for extra-hazardous activities. Indeed, in earlier writings he suggested that some traditional rules of strict liability extended to "accident," which, assuming he was then using the term to mean unforeseeable harm, indicated acceptance of absolute responsibility. 1873 Theory of Torts, 774; FE, "Primitive Notions in Modern Law," 130; Holmes's marginal notes on a reprint of 1873 Theory of Torts, Howe Papers, Harvard Law School Library. Also, the presentation of the foresight theory under the subtitle "The True Theory of Liability," and its application to strict liability in "Trespass and Negligence," FE, 245–252, is far less direct than it was after the revisions for delivery and publication as Lecture III of *The Common Law*. Those revisions eliminated the subtitle and grouped both negligence and strict liability together as generally based on the generic conception equating blameworthy responsibility and the infliction of foreseeable harm. A newly written elaboration of the foresight theory of responsibility was incorporated as Theory of Torts (Lect. IV), which deployed the theory to rationalize *Rylands* and the other major strict liability rules.

79. CL, 147–148.

80. Fletcher v. Rylands, L.R. 1 Ex. 265, 278 (1866).

81. CL, 158, 160.

82. CL, 148–149. The early-nineteenth-century mill acts encouraged investment in mills by permitting owners to flood neighboring land so long as they paid compensation—a "tax," according to Holmes—for the "taking." CLP, "Path of the Law," 173–174. The mill acts were forerunners of present-day legislation that promotes projects of economic and social development by authorizing private

parties to "take" and use land owned by others on condition of paying compensation, usually the market value of the appropriated property. The mill acts symbolized what Holmes referred to as the "emphasi[s of] the criterion of social welfare as against the individualistic eighteenth century bills of rights," CLP, "Ideals and Doubts," 307. For discussion of the significance of the mill acts in reshaping legal thought to accept the subordination of notions of individual rights to those of public welfare, see M. J. Horwitz, *The Transformation of American Law: 1780–1860,* 47–53 (1977); F. H. Bohlen, "The Rule in Rylands v. Fletcher," 59 *University of Pennsylvania Law Review* 298, 374–378 (1911).

83. CL, 149.

84. CL, vi. Although foresight-based strict liability applies to the "party taking another man's property" both under the mill acts and by conversion, the harmful consequences of the two forms of takings were distinguishable respectively "in terms of praise" and "in terms of blame." CLP, "Path of the Law," 173–174 (the bad man, however, was indifferent to the social judgment). Holmes's theory of responsibility, specifically the blameworthy category of foresight-based strict liability, substituted the explanation of foresight-informed choice for superficial "primary rights, duties, and consequences or sanctioning rights, or whatever you may call them." Letter from Holmes to Pollock (Mar. 25, 1883), 1 HPL 20. Nevertheless, his contemporaries continued to describe *Rylands* as expressing a sense of social disapprobation and enforcing a general prohibition or entitlement against inflicting foreseeable harm. See F. Pollock, *Essays in Jurisprudence and Ethics,* 120–123 (1882) (*sic utere tuo* maxim); T. Beven, *Law of Negligence,* 914 (1889); R. Campbell, *The Law of Negligence,* 52 (1878); A. Underhill, *Law of Torts,* 209 (1932); J. Salmond, *The Law of Torts,* 191 (1902); Terry, "Proximate Consequences," 24; Justice Blackburn in *Rylands* ("absolute duty," L.R. 1 Ex. at 279). See also J. H. Wigmore, "A General Analysis of Tort-Relations," 8 *Harvard Law Review* 377, 395 (1895) ("right to have certain harmful results not produced").

85. CLP, "Privilege, Malice, and Intent," 117.

86. CL, 156.

87. CL, 162. Yet some degree of ambiguity remained. The last sentence of Lecture IV said that it was "certainly arguable" that responsibility in tort law required "blame" in addition to the foresight condition that afforded "a fair chance to avoid bringing harm to pass." CL, 163 (in context, the remark suggests he had doubts concerning the wisdom of imposing liability in *Gilbert*-type necessity cases). Later, Holmes noted in his copy of *The Common Law* that "at the bottom of liability there is a notion of blameworthiness." CL(I), 107. But none of Holmes's subsequently published or unpublished statements of the theory of torts contains any reference to blameworthy harm (as opposed to risk), or similar conceptions limiting responsibility beyond the foresight condition.

88. CL, 162.

89. Ibid.

90. Ibid.

91. 1873 Theory of Torts, 778–782.

92. CL, 146.

93. Letter from Holmes to Simon E. Baldwin (Feb. 16, 1897), MS Box 37, Folders 23–24, HP.

94. CL, 131; CLP, "Privilege, Malice, and Intent," 117. Judicial formulation of specific or concrete rules—a trend Holmes applauded as well as predicted—increased the difficulty of classifying strict liability and negligence doctrines because, once a rule becomes established, courts rarely advert to its underlying policy. CL, 150–152, 155. Moreover, because the process of sociolegal evolution tended to increase the complexity of institutions and rules, he organized discussion of the several branches of tort to show that they also differed (though by degree) in the "number of concomitant circumstances necessary to throw the peril of conduct . . . on the actor." CL, 152. This additional dimension highlighted a correspondence, on the one hand, between rules of strict liability and external concrete standards and, on the other, between the branches of negligence and intentional wrongs where "circumstances become more numerous and complex, [and] the tendency to cut the knot with the jury becomes greater." Ibid. His treatment of the relative complexity of rules was descriptive, not qualitative. CLP, 301. Indeed, he urged courts to legislate concrete—factually simplified—rules of strict liability and negligence as a practical yet decisive step towards scientific policy-making and liberation from the binds of history. On descriptive complexity in biologic classifications, see J. W. S. Pringle, "On the Parallel Between Learning and Evolution," 3 *Behavior* 90 (1951).

95. CLP, "Privilege, Malice, and Intent," 118.

96. Id. at 117.

97. Ibid.

98. On the purpose of the subjective knowledge element in intentional torts, and the distinction between intent, meaning actual foresight, and malice, denoting a purposeful and unreasonable objective, see CL, 68; CLP, "Agency II," 105; Aikens v. Wisconsin, 203; Letter from Holmes to Pollock (Dec. 28, 1902), 1 HPL 110.

99. CL, 135.

100. CL, 79. See also Green, *Essays on Tort and Crime,* 53. For a recent statement of similar findings, see J. H. Baker, *An Introduction to English Legal History,* 349 (1979).

101. CL, 130, 133–136.

102. CL, 134.

103. Ibid. Holmes ridiculed such attempts to "reconcil[e] the formal theory" with experience: "Whenever it is said that a certain thing is essential to liability, but that it is conclusively presumed from something else, there is always ground for suspicion that the essential element is to be found in that something else, and not in what is said to be presumed from it." Ibid.

104. CL, 132–133. As Holmes noted in cases of deceit, there may be personal

reasons for a defendant's "unwillingness . . . to state the truth" that have absolutely nothing to do with a motive to lead the plaintiff to place detrimental reliance on a false representation. CL, 133. Similarly, actual intent to inflict harm implies that infliction of harm is the "motive of the act," but that intent "is perfectly consistent with the harm being regretted as such, and being wished only as a means to something else." Malice requires "something more." CL, 52.

105. CL, 108–109, 142.

106. While Holmes most fully developed this point in "Privilege, Malice, and Intent," his prior writings consistently affirmed that courts exercised policy discretion to balance competing social interests by varying the elements that controlled the scope of liability, including those dealing with subjective states of mind. This included regulating defendant motives, or more accurately, regulating the purposes of the privilege involved; for example, by prohibiting employers from issuing derogatory recommendations simply to harm employees, or railroads from disclaiming liability to exploit market power over "individual[s] at their mercy." FE, "Primitive Notions in Modern Law," 129–130 n. 2; FE, "Common Carriers and the Common Law," 222; CL, 139. Holmes did not associate judicial policy discretion only with subjective limits on privileges. Indeed, in his view, courts discharged their legislative function primarily by varying the stringency of external standards (including the primary duties and privileges), as, for example, in modulating the "strictness" of liability under *Rylands*. CL, 156.

107. Holmes stated this finding in Lecture IV, CL, 139, and nothing in the more detailed treatment of motive constraints on privileges in "Privilege, Malice, and Intent" suggests any retreat from that view. See also CLP, "Path of the Law," 176–177. Today, the same type of externalized proof determines the limit "malice" places on the constitutional privilege to defame public officials. Cantrell v. Forest City Publishing Co., 419 U.S. 245, 251 (1974).

108. CLP, "Privilege, Malice, and Intent," 126. See also CL, 139; CLP, "The Path of the Law," 190–191.

109. Horwitz claims that "Privilege, Malice, and Intent" represented a "complete about-face" for Holmes on the role of malice, motive, and subjective standards generally, signaling abandonment of support for external rules. Horwitz, *The Transformation of American Law, 1870–1960*, 133. This is an exaggeration. To demonstrate the alleged "about-face," Horwitz quotes from "Privilege, Malice, and Intent" that "[i]t is entirely conceivable that motive . . . should be held to affect all, or nearly all, claims of privilege." Horwitz, *The Transformation of American Law, 1870–1960*, 133. But the ellipses in the quotation replace "in some jurisdictions," a qualification which Holmes stressed. CLP, "Privilege, Malice, and Intent," 130. See also CLP, "Path of the Law," 176–177, 190–191. Horwitz then presents an excerpt from Lecture IV as asserting the opposite position: "Indeed, [Holmes] specifically denied that 'the plaintiff may meet [that is, defeat] a claim of privilege . . . by proving actual malice, that is, actual intent to cause the damage complained of'" (133). Horwitz's framing of the quotation creates a neg-

ative assertion out of a neutral statement. The complete passage reads: "It is said that the plaintiff may meet a claim of privilege thus made out on the part of the defendant, by proving actual malice, that is, actual intent to cause the damage complained of." CL, 139. Horwitz also neglects to mention Holmes's next sentence: "But how is this actual malice made out?" As the discussion following his question makes clear, Holmes was not denying that actual malice could defeat a privilege, but rather was arguing that subjective standards did not imply or usually require direct evidence. As in the case of privileged defamation, the plaintiff could prove malice or bad motive by externalized proof, showing merely "that the defendant knew the statement which he made was false, or that his untrue statements were grossly in excess of what the occasion required." Ibid.

Although Holmes apparently found more judicial use of subjective motives in defining the scope of privileges than he had predicted in the torts lectures, this was a purely empirical adjustment that did not modify his jurisprudential approach or theory of torts. More importantly, the changed estimate related solely to the second part of his theory focusing on judicial policy discretion; it had no bearing on his external foresight theory of responsibility. Indeed, in the torts lectures he noted the possibility that his prediction might not be confirmed, and added that even so, this would not "affect the general views maintained here." CL, 145. Accordingly, Holmes opened "Privilege, Malice, and Intent" by reaffirming the first part of the general theory of responsibility and his view that the foresight "standard applied is external." CLP, 117; CL, 145. In the article and in subsequent writings, Holmes continued to underscore the importance of external standards as means of implementing collectivist judicial policies, and to take credit for illuminating the role and pervasive use of such standards. CLP, "Law in Science," 241. But he emphasized that the external foreseeability standard incorporated both the subjective element of knowledge of the dangerous circumstances and also proof of actual foresight as sufficient (though not necessary) for *prima facie* responsibility. CLP, "Privilege, Malice, and Intent," 117, 123; Letter from Holmes to Pollock (1895), 1 HPL 62–63.

110. CLP, "Privilege, Malice, and Intent," 117–118 ("considerable" meaning appreciable or perceptible). Holmes assumed that negligence required foresight. CL, 92–93. He does not appear to have considered a hindsight rule of negligence, which determines liability simply on the reasonableness of the act that caused harm, without regard to foresight at the time the act was committed. For discussion of this rule, see generally G. Calabresi and A. K. Klevorick, "Four Tests for Liability in Torts," 14 *Journal of Legal Studies* 585 (1985).

111. CLP, "Privilege, Malice, and Intent," 117–118.

112. L. Green, "The Negligence Issue," 37 *Yale Law Journal* 1029 n.1 (1928). See also 1 T. A. Street, *The Foundations of Legal Liability*, 49–68, 73 (1906). For contemporary use of "negligence" to denote the broad category of unintentional tort covering both causes of action for unreasonable conduct and strict liability, see 1 J. Comyns, *Digest of English Law*, 207–208 (1822); 1 Beven, *Negligence in*

Law, 18 (1908); F. Wharton, *Law of Negligence,* 3, 661–663 (1878); W. E. Ball, *Leading Cases on the Law of Torts,* 322 (1884); J. B. Thayer, *Lex Aquilla,* 35 (1929); P. H. Winfield, "The History of Negligence in the Law of Torts," 42 *Law Quarterly* 184, 196–198 (1926). The equation of negligence and foresight-based strict liability was often expressed in terms of a duty of care "to provide against all contingent damage as might reasonably be anticipated." Turner v. Big Lake Oil Co., 222; 1 Beven, *Negligence in Law,* 481 (1908). The unintentional tort connotation of "negligence" may have resulted from the pre-nineteenth century use of "negligence" to mean "neglect" of duty, which Holmes accepted, although he generally limited that interpretation to bailment and other contractual settings. CL, 194, 201. English usage continues to refer to responsibility for unintentionally inflicting reasonably foreseeable harm as "negligence," and to include strict liability within this category. Stone v. Bolton, 1 K.B. 851, 857–858 (1950); Weinrib, *The Idea of Private Law,* 148–152; S. R. Perry, "The Impossibility of General Strict Liability," 1 *Canadian Journal of Law and Jurisprudence* 147, 170–171 (1988). For an example in the torts lectures of such usage of negligence, as distinguished from its meaning to denote the cause of action for unreasonable conduct, see CL, 146 ("Foresight is a possible common denominator of wrongs at the two extremes of malice and negligence"); 147 (reducing negligence to knowledge of circumstances); 163 (courts use concrete external rules "in the domain of wrongs described as intentional, as systematically as in those styled unintentional or negligent").

113. T. Beven, *Negligence in Law,* 481 (3rd ed. 1908); id. at 1137; Pollock, *Jurisprudence and Ethics,* 119–125 (*Rylands* and duties to use reasonable care form a "connected body of doctrine" and "fall under . . . the general head of Negligence or belong to a nearly allied class" dealing with liability for dangerous agencies); cf. B. S. Jackson, ed., *Modern Research in Jewish Law,* 7, 61 (1980). See also F. M. Burdick, *The Law of Torts,* 445 (1905) (classifying the "Doctrine of Rylands v. Fletcher" in the chapter on "Negligence," under the heading "Liability of Landowner or Occupier; and of Others Engaged in Extra Hazardous Undertakings"). On "culpa," see Campbell, *The Law of Negligence,* 4–5, 52–53 ("culpa" included "everything but *casus,*" that is "accident . . . which is beyond human skill or foresight to avert," and therefore "culpa" encompassed *Rylands* at the "extreme degree of responsibility [of] . . . a duty to restrain the thing").

114. Beven, *Negligence in Law,* 481 (quoting Chalmers v. Dixon, 3 R. 461, 464).

115. Id. at 481 n.2 (citing "The Common Law, 157," which was the page in the section of Lecture IV where *Rylands* and other related doctrines of strict liability were substantiated on the common ground of reasonable foresight). Earlier editions of Beven's treatise made no mention of Holmes on this point, and the citation was removed from later editions, prepared by new editors, apparently as part of an effort to anglicize the entire text by eliminating references to all American cases and commentary.

116. Schlemmer v. Buffalo, Rochester, & C. Ry, 205 U.S. 1, 12 (1907) (Holmes, J.). Holmes noted such problems of interpretation. CLP, "The Theory of Legal Interpretation," 203 (observing that "a given word . . . has several meanings," and that "[y]ou have to consider the sentence in which it stands to decide which of those meanings it bears in the particular case").

My research therefore accords with Patrick Kelley's insight that Holmes's notion of "negligence" encompassed foresight-based strict liability. P. J. Kelley, "A Critical Analysis of Holmes's Theory of Torts," 61 *Washington University Law Quarterly* 681, 689, 695, 729 (1984). However, I do not agree with Kelley's broader claim, which essentially argues the antithesis of the negligence-dogma thesis: that Holmes's conception of negligence was synonymous with foresight-based strict liability and never recognized the reasonableness of the defendant's capacity and expenditures for care as limiting liability—the key feature of the modern negligence cause of action. Cf. F. H. Bohlen, "Fifty Years of Torts," 50 *Harvard Law Review* 1225, 1226 (1937) (crediting an article by Henry Terry in 1915 with introducing the definition of negligence in terms of conduct that creates a risk in excess of its social utility).

Terminology aside, Holmes's writings, including the torts lectures, evince a modern conception of the negligence standard that tests the reasonableness of conduct by factors of relative capacity for care, marginal investments in safety, and the overall calculus of social costs and benefits. See CL, 49–50, 116–117, 154–155; and Chapter 5 below, where I elaborate Holmes's understanding of the modern negligence rule. Holmes relied on and was conversant with the leading nineteenth-century cases and commentary, demonstrating facility with these tests and recognition of the role of strict liability in addressing residual risk. See Blyth v. Birmingham Water Works, 156 Eng. Rep. 1047 (1856); Shipley v. Fifty Associates, 106 Mass. 194 (1870); Losee v. Buchanan, 51 N.Y. 483 (1873); Nitroglycerine Case, 82 U.S. 524 (1872); Railroad Company v. Stout, 84 U.S. 657 (1873); Wigmore, *Tripartite Division*, 208 (crediting Holmes); H. G. Wood, *The Law of Nuisances*, 142–149, 747 (1893). Pollock, *Jurisprudence and Ethics*, 124–125 (adopting Holmes's concept of "extra-hazardous" to represent cases where residual risk was expected and strict liability would apply). Indeed, to suggest that the person who first explained the "strict liability effect" of the external negligence standard lacked a modern appreciation for the negligence rule is a virtual contradiction in terms.

117. CLP, "Privilege, Malice, and Intent," 118.

118. Ibid.

119. CL, 139–140, 158.

120. CL, 138.

121. CL, 152–153.

122. CL, 153.

123. CL, 154.

124. Ibid.

125. CL, 148.
126. CL, 162.
127. CL, 148.
128. CL, 149.
129. CL, 155.
130. CL, 23, 156.
131. CL, 156.
132. CL, 23–24.
133. CL, 157.
134. Ibid.
135. CL, 154–155.
136. CL, 154. Holmes also extended the foresight theory of responsibility to cover employer vicarious liability, although he did not consider the doctrine a true rule of strict liability because its application hinged on employee negligence. CLP, "Agency I and II," 51–52 (relying on CL, 54, 55, and the torts lectures), 80, 101; CLP, "Privilege, Malice, and Intent," 132–134; CLP, "Path of the Law," 182–183. The only cases falling outside the theory were sporadic, transitory, totally unexpected: uncontrollable acts of negligence by low-level employees that were expressly forbidden by the employer. Experience teaches that people generally comply with the law. Like owners of otherwise docile runaway horses, employers were *"presumed not to contemplate"* the abnormal; thus employer vicarious liability would be denied in the absence of some reason to know (*scienter*) of an unusual propensity on the part of a particular employee for misfeasant conduct or to pose a substantial residual risk. Letter from Holmes to Pollock (Mar. 22, 1891), 1 HPL 36–37; see also R. Pound, "Classification of Law," 37 *Harvard Law Review* 933, 935 (1924). Holmes considered it unproblematic to apply employer vicarious liability where employee negligence occurs in performing tasks directed by the employer or by a supervisor or other employee with actual or apparent authority to speak for the employer. Indeed, as indicated by his support for foresight-based strict liability in animal cases and for extra-hazardous activities under *Rylands,* he readily approved strict liability against employers for the non-negligent foreseeable harms committed by their agents because, if authorized, their non-negligent conduct was *per force* reasonably expected. By the same analysis, he held that while those who make a defamatory statement are not responsible for its wrongful repetition by a third party, they are responsible for its privileged repetition. Burt v. Advertiser Newspaper Co., 247; May v. Wood, 172 Mass. 11, 15 (Holmes, J. dissenting).
137. Holmes's analogy to the strict liability rule for fierce animals not only supplemented the precedent marshaled by Blackburn, who had relied solely on the cattle trespass doctrine, but also substantially expanded the scope of the rule. On Holmes's analysis, *Rylands* or strict liability for extra-hazardous activities extended to personal injury as well as property damage, and to harm wherever it occurs, whether on the property of the one who owns the dangerous agency or on the property to which it escapes.

138. CL, 157.

139. Ibid. Holmes's reading of *Rylands* as a foresight-based strict liability case was consistent with Justice Blackburn's authoritative opinion, which excluded harms resulting from acts of God, and restricted the scope of the rule to the "natural and anticipated consequences" of a "dangerous" thing, which the defendant "knows to be mischievous if it gets on his neighbor's [property]." L.R. 1 Ex. 265, 279, 280 (1866). See also Nichols v. Marsland, L.R. 10 Ex. 255, 259–260 (1875); Greenock Corp. v. Caledonian Ry., A.C. 556 (1917).

140. CLP, "Path of the Law," 183. See also Arizona Employers' Liability Cases, 250 U.S. 400, 431 (1919) (Holmes, J. concurring) (sustaining constitutionality of workers compensation statute that incorporated strict tort liability for employee "injuries due to [inherent] risks in specified hazardous employments"). Most current commentators accept—without recognizing the source in Holmes—that the generalized foresight conception of strict extra-hazardous liability provides the intellectual foundation of modern strict liability.

141. Davis v. Rich, 237.

142. 1872 Jurisprudence Essay, 791.

5. General Theory of Torts—Part Two

1. Unless otherwise indicated, strict liability refers to the foresight-based version.

2. 1872 Jurisprudence Essay, 791. See also CL, 117, 156; CLP, "The Path of the Law," 182–183.

3. Land trespass represented an important nonindustrial class of cases involving systematic negligence failure of this second type.

4. CL, 117.

5. One reviewer of *The Common Law* suggested that Holmes's promotion of the legislative function of courts might be frustrated by, and might well exacerbate, the "law's delay, its excessive cost, the frequent miscarriages of justice, the uncertain and arbitrary awards of juries." Anon., "Holmes's Common Law," 15 *American Law Review* 331, 333 (1881).

6. CL, 117. Strict liability played a similar role in common carrier cases. FE, "Common Carriers and the Common Law," 221; 2 Commentaries, *603. Cf. Southern. Pac. Co. v. Darnell, 245 U.S. 531, 534 (1918) (Holmes, J.) and Commonwealth v. Perry, 155 Mass. 117, 123, 124 (1891) (Holmes, J. dissenting). Holmes's procedural justification for *Rylands* repudiated Judge Doe's arguments in Brown v. Collins, 73 N.H. 442, 450 (1873), vigorously denying any such reasons for adopting a strict liability rule. Today, however, the procedural rationale for strict liability is invoked routinely. See Siegler v. Kuhlman, 502 P.2d 1181 (Wash. 1972); Escola v. Coca-Cola Co. of Fresno, 150 P.2d 436 (Cal. 1944) (Traynor, J. concurring). Even streamlined by strict liability, however, torts may still prove unnecessarily expensive compared to alternative means of spreading losses, particularly commercial first-party insurance. CL, 96.

7. Fletcher v. Rylands, L.R. 1 Ex. 265, 278 (1866) (Blackburn referred to the "latent defect in the defendant's subsoil").

8. CL, 157.

9. Holmes's analysis anticipated the modern rules of strict enterprise liability, which hold defendants accountable for the characteristic residual risks of their activity, however unforeseeable the means by which harm occurs. This understanding of using generalized and statistical foresight to drive strict liability in regulating industrial activities prefigured the modern rules of strict enterprise liability adopted by the *Restatement of Torts* (1938), chaps. 20 and 21; *Restatement (Second) of Torts,* §§519–520; §822 comment k, §826 (1977). These rules hold defendants strictly liable whenever the harm sued upon results from the activity's perceived "ultrahazardous" or "abnormally dangerous" type of residual risk, even though such harm is brought about in the particular situation by "acts of God," or the intervention of other sudden and unexpected causes.

10. CL, 115–116. Another set of cases where strict liability addresses the problem of residual risk from marginal reasonable care involved situations where the defendant harms the plaintiff out of reasonable necessity. CL, 148.

11. CL, 115–117.

12. Commentaries, *561 n.1 (noting the external nature of strict liability rules applied to hold defendants "liable for damage resulting from extra hazardous sources, without any allegation of negligence, as in Rylands . . . ; Shipley v. Fifty Associates, 106 Mass. 194"); see also CL, 156–157 (relating *Rylands* to various types of risks, including the hazard involved in *Shipley*).

13. Shipley v. Fifty Associates, 196, 199.

14. Cases which had rejected *Shipley* included Garland v. Towne, 55 N.H. 55 (1874), one of the most influential precedents against *Rylands,* and Underwood v. Waldron, 33 Mich. 232 (1876).

15. Fitzpatrick v. Welch, 174 Mass. 486 (1899). See also CL, 156–157.

16. Theory of Torts, 774 (1873); CL, 154–155.

17. M. J. Horwitz, *The Transformation of American Law, 1870–1960,* 13 (1992); see also J. Vetter, "The Evolution of Holmes: Holmes and Evolution," in *Holmes and The Common Law: A Century Later,* 87 (1983); G. E. White, *Tort Law in America: An Intellectual History,* 13 (1980).

18. G. E. White, *Justice Oliver Wendell Holmes: Law and the Inner Self,* 264 (1993) (using charged terms of "undermining" and "subvert[ing]").

19. M. J. Horwitz, *The Transformation of American Law, 1780–1860,* 99 (1977); White, *Tort Law in America,* 16–17; Vetter, "The Evolution of Holmes," 87–88. See also F. James, Jr., "Tort Law in Midstream: Its Challenge to the Judicial Process," 8 *Buffalo Law Review* 315, 316 (1959). Moreover, as Holmes and his contemporaries understood, by adopting a general "duty" of reasonable care, courts and commentators were greatly expanding the scope of tort liability. R. L. Rabin, "The Historical Development of the Fault Principle: A Reinterpretation," 15 *Georgia Law Review* 925 (1981).

20. American Law Institute, Reporters' Study, *Enterprise Responsibility for*

Personal Injury, I, 8 (1991); P. W. Huber, *Liability: The Legal Revolution and Its Consequences,* 9 (1988); Rand Institute for Civil Justice, *Compensation for Accidental Injuries in the United States,* Chap. 5. (1991); S. Shavell, *Economic Analysis of Accident Law,* 31–32 (1987).

21. CLP, "Path of the Law," 183.

22. F. Pollock, *Essays in Jurisprudence and Ethics,* 125 (1882). See also C. J. Peck, "Negligence and Liability Without Fault in Tort Law," 46 *Washington Law Review* 225, 229 (1971) (noting that Trespass presumed negligence in pre-industrial cases because any one directly causing harm "probably had departed from community standards of behavior").

23. *Restatement (Second) of Torts,* §520, comment h; Shavell, *Economic Analysis of Accident Law,* 31–32; R. A. Epstein, "The Social Consequences of Common Law Rules," 95 *Harvard Law Review* 1717, 1725 (1982); J. G. Fleming, *The Law of Torts,* 301 and n.10 (1983). On this empirical assumption, the negligence rule was virtually the functional equivalent of foresight-based strict liability in ordinary cases.

24. CL, 145.

25. Quinn v. Crimmings, 171 Mass. 255, 258–259 (1898).

26. These rules would be even less hospitable to industry to the extent they were formulated, as Holmes advised, from patterns of jury verdicts, which were notoriously skewed in favor of plaintiffs.

27. The Germanic, 196 U.S. 589, 596 (1905). See Blyth v. Birmingham Waterworks, 156 Eng. Rep. 1047, 1049 (1856); Brown v. Kendall, 60 Mass. 292, 296 (1850); F. Buller, *Introduction to the Law Relative to Trials at Nisi Prius,* 25 (5th ed. 1788); F. Pollock, "Mr. Justice Holmes," 44 *Harvard Law Review* 693, 695 (1931) (denying that Holmes invented the external standard).

28. CL, 50, 108.

29. M. J. Horwitz, Book Review, 42 *University of Chicago Law Review* 787, 788, 796 (1975) (describing the "paradox" of Holmes's hostility to strict liability and "equally emphatic championing of objective standards of liability, which are, after all, but another form of absolute liability").

30. Id. at 796. Horwitz offered no evidence for these conclusions. As I have noted, he now claims the opposite, that the torts lectures relentlessly embraced the external negligence standard even while rejecting strict liability. He makes no mention of the paradoxical implications for Holmes's supposed opposition to strict liability.

31. R. L. Rabin, "The Historical Development of the Fault Principle: A Reinterpretation," 15 *Georgia Law Review* 925, 930 (1981). See also R. W. Gordon, "Holmes's *Common Law* as Legal and Social Science," 10 *Hofstra Law Review* 719, 737 n. 123 (1982) (noting without attempting to explain the paradox).

32. G. Gilmore, *The Death of Contract,* 16–17 (1974).

33. CL, 123.

34. B. Kaplan, "Encounters with O. W. Holmes, Jr.," in *Holmes and The Common Law: A Century Later,* 5 (1983).

35. R. W. Gordon, Book Review, 94 *Harvard Law Review* 903, 917 (1981).

36. R. A. Posner, "A Theory of Negligence," 1 *Journal of Legal Studies* 29, 52–73 (1972); S. G. Gilles, "Rule-Based Negligence and the Regulation of Activity Levels," 21 *Journal of Legal Studies* 319, 323 (1992). Greater reliance on concrete rules is forecast by K. Abraham and G. O. Robinson, "Aggregative Valuations of Mass Tort Claims," 53 *Journal of Law and Contemporary Problems* 137, 144 (1990). See also L. Kaplow, "The Value of Accuracy in Adjudication: An Economic Analysis," 23 *Journal of Legal Studies* 307 (1994) (indicating the distributional as well as deterrence and administrative justifications for averaged bureaucratic rules).

Holmes's conspicuous blunder in Baltimore & Ohio R.R. Co. v. Goodman, 275 U.S. 66, 70 (1927), where he promulgated a concrete contributory negligence rule requiring drivers to stop, look, and listen at railroad crossings—Holmes enjoyed car rides but never himself drove a car—makes an amusing target but not much of a case against his method of regulation. (The Court discarded the rule soon after he left the bench, Pokora v. Wabash Ry. Co., 292 U.S. 98 (1934), although questions of federal diversity jurisdiction may have had more to do with the outcome than the merits of the stop, look, and listen rule, which apparently prevails in most states). Critics would have a more difficult time sneering at the idea if instead *Goodman* had involved negligence by the railroad, and Holmes had adopted a concrete rule requiring railroads to place guards or mechanical gates at urban grade crossings. Doubtless these critics would find nothing implausible or formalistic about the prospect of administrative regulations concretizing safety precautions to the same effect as he sought to achieve by judicial legislation. Although criticizing Holmes's advocacy of external standards, Horwitz hails Learned Hand's opinion in The T. J. Hooper, 60 F.2d 737 (2d Cir. 1932) for subjecting an entire industry to a concrete external standard of due care that most members opposed, and thus for assuming "the regulatory function of transforming actual economic practices in the interest of an independent social ideal." R. A. Epstein, *Cases and Materials on Torts,* 175 (5th ed. 1990) (quoting unpublished lecture). In fact, Holmes adopted the same approach as Hand three decades earlier in Texas & Pacific Ry. Co. v. Behymer, 189 U.S. 468, 470 (1903).

37. CL, 111–112; CLP, "Path of the Law," 167–170. Holmes contemplated the notion that concrete rules would specify the public policies judges derived on their own or by accepting the "suggestions" of juries, especially when they reached the same verdict in many similar cases. CL, 122–129; 150–151. Yet law as prophecy meant that "judge-made [rules] are never authentically promulgated as rules, but are left to be inferred from the cases." FE, "Codes, and the Arrangement of the Law," 81. Probabilistic prediction necessarily reduces the significance of any operational distinction between indefinite standards and specific rules.

38. 1872 Jurisprudence Essay, 790.

39. CL, 123.

40. Pollock, *Jurisprudence and Ethics,* 124–125; H. Terry, *Some Leading Principles of Anglo-American Law,* 172 (1884); J. Smith, "Liability for Substantial

Physical Damage to Land by Blasting—The Rule of the Future," 33 *Harvard Law Review* 542, 550–551 and n.35 (1920).

41. E. R. Thayer, "Liability Without Fault," 29 *Harvard Law Review* 801, 806–807, 815 (1916). Cf. 1 T. G. Shearman and A. A. Redfield, *A Treatise on the Law of Negligence*, 57 (1898).

42. Thayer, "Liability Without Fault," 805–806.

43. E. R. Thayer, Notes for Lectures on Torts, file 5–11, Special Collections, Harvard Law School Library.

44. Smith, "Liability for Blasting," 552 and n.43.

45. Thayer, "Liability Without Fault," 807; See also J. P. Bishop, *Non-Contract Law*, 386–387 (1889); cf. Mather v. Rillston, 156 U.S. 391, 399 (1984).

46. Thayer, Torts Lecture Notes, file 5–7; Smith, "Liability for Blasting," 550–551 n.35 (quoting Thayer, "Liability Without Fault," 811).

47. F. Pollock, "A Plea for Historical Interpretation," 39 *Law Quarterly Review* 163, 167 (1923).

48. 1 Shearman and Redfield, *Law of Negligence*, 56–59.

49. Advocates of the three-degree structure responded by stressing the elasticity of the most stringent level defined as "great care," which could be raised "sufficiently high" for industrial cases to command all practical precautions known to a given industry. Ibid., 57.

50. F. Pollock, *The Law of Torts*, 409, 410 (4th ed. 1895). Horwitz asserts that the real object of these commentators was to eliminate the category of "gross" negligence and thus the authority of juries to award exemplary damages. Horwitz, *Transformation of American Law, 1870–1960*, 115. Yet he cites no critic of the three-degree structure who opposed exemplary damages. Those who discussed the subject of exemplary damages affirmed their availability on the traditional ground of wantonness or malice. In fact, according to one of the commentators to whom Horwitz refers, juries would not be required to find any particular degree of negligence or even a subjective intention to cause the harm but rather could predicate exemplary damages merely on the unreasonable "character of the act or omission" as determined from the "particular circumstances of each case." 2 S. D. Thompson, *The Law of Negligence*, 1264–65 (1880). For a similar view see Pollock, *The Law of Torts*, 174–176 (4th ed.). Support for punitive damages waned in the late nineteenth century because its function as a surrogate means of compensating pain and suffering and other nonpecuniary losses was being replaced by express inclusion of nonpecuniary loss components in damage awards. Anon., "Exemplary Damages in the Law of Torts," 70 *Harvard Law Review* 517–520 (1957).

51. J. Smith, "Tort and Absolute Liability—Suggested Changes in Classification," 30 *Harvard Law Review* 409, 413 (1917); Pollock, *The Law of Torts*, 435 (3d ed. 1892).

52. Pollock, *Jurisprudence and Ethics*, 132–135; Pollock, *The Law of Torts*, 395–406 (3d ed.); N. S. Green, Book Notice, 4 *American Law Review* 350, 352 (1869).

53. Pollock, *The Law of Torts,* 435 (3d ed.).

54. Manning v. West End Street Railway Company, 166 Mass. 230, 231 (1896) ("What is due care depends on the nature of the accident and the degree of danger according to common experience under the known circumstances"). Holmes seems to have approved replacing the rigid three-degree structure of negligence. O. W. Holmes, Book Review, 5 *American Law Review* 343 (1870) (agreeing generally with N. S. Green, Book Review, 350, 351 (1869)). Subsequently, he exhibited indifference on the point. Commentaries, *561 n.1; cf., CL, 120. He indicated support for punitive damages in the lectures (CL, 41), in which he outlined the modern deterrence rationales for such sanctions, and generally, by approving the external foresight theory of responsibility for criminal cases. Commonwealth v. Pierce, 138 Mass. 165, 176, 180 (1884) (finding sufficient evidence to convict a physician of manslaughter for gross negligence on the basis of externalized proof of deviation from the medical competence required to treat seriously ill patients).

55. CLP, "Law in Science and Science in Law," 232; LeRoy Fibre Co. v. Chi, Mil. & St. P. Ry., 232 U.S. 340, 353 (1914); Schlemmer v. Buffalo, Rochester, &C. Ry., 205 U.S. 1 (1907). There is some indication that he supported requiring defendants to bear the burden in personal injury cases of proving the plaintiff's contributory negligence. Holmes, Book Review, 343 (1870) (adopting views stated in Green, Book Review, 353 (1869)).

56. A negligence-dogmatist would likely have approved the restrictive proximate cause rule propounded in Ryan v. New York Central Railroad Company, 35 N.Y. 210 (1866), a case which is considered one of the most blatant examples of industrial subsidization by tort law. Yet Holmes never even mentioned *Ryan,* and his foresight analysis refuted the causal theories advanced to rationalize the decision. For rejections of *Ryan* by contemporary commentators, see T. M. Cooley, *Law of Torts,* 77–78 and n.1 (1879); J. Smith, "Legal Cause in Actions of Tort," 25 *Harvard Law Review* 223, 248–249 (1912).

57. Holmes supported vicarious liability by employers for negligence by their independent contractors or employees in cases when the agent's misfeasance could be foreseen or was committed within the scope of employment and under some supervisory control (however low-level and non-negligent). CLP, "Agency I," 51–52, 54, 80; Woodman v. Metropolitan Railroad, 149 Mass. 335, 340 (1889); Ainsworth v. Lakin, 180 Mass. 397 (1902). In opposing only the indiscriminate extension of vicarious liability, he argued for its use in "special cases upon special grounds" of policy and demonstrable benefit. CLP, "Agency II," 101, 115 and n.104 (incorporating the discriminating approach based on deterrence, market failure, and social insurance considerations which he had outlined for common carrier liability). He enforced the exceptions to the fellow-servant defense as broadly as possible short of expressly overruling the doctrine; he urged legislatures to eliminate the defense and sustained the constitutionality of such enactments. Minnesota Iron Company v. Kline, 199 U.S. 593 (1905); Santa Fe Pacific R.R. v.

Holmes, 202 U.S. 438 (1906); Standard Oil Co. v. Brown, 218 U.S. 78 (1910); Brooks v. Central St. Jeanne, 228 U.S. 688, 694 (1913).

Holmes's call for "special" justifications to use vicarious liability was a demand for functional precision in policy-making, and should not be taken to imply that such applications were minor, anomalous, or nonempirical. For example, he invoked vicarious liability in defense of legislation adopting strict liability for dangerous industries. Arizona Employers' Liability Cases, 250 U.S. 400, 432 (1919) (Holmes, J. concurring). Compare CL, 50 (arguing that given the costs of shifting loss, tort liability should not be used without "special reason[s]," but recognizing the existence of such reasons to justify extensive use of negligence and strict liability, CL, 108, 116–17); CLP, "Privilege, Malice, and Intent," 117 (noting the prevalent practice of courts to moderate *prima facie* responsibility for inflicting foreseeable harm upon "special grounds" of policy).

58. Some commentators claimed that this also demonstrated that needed reforms could be left to the judiciary rather than to populist legislation, but Holmes was not among this group.

Horwitz asserts erroneously that Holmes opposed legislative codes because they were likely to overturn the distributional status quo, particularly by mandating strict liability for industrial cases. Horwitz, *The Transformation of American Law, 1870–1960*, 123–124. Quite to the contrary, Holmes's main objection to codes was that they were apt to stultify the law by enacting the status quo. FE, "Codes, and the Arrangement of the Law," 77; EW, "The Code of Iowa," 793–794. He favored the common law process because it could more quickly and flexibly adapt to emerging social needs. Horwitz's surmise also ignores the historical context in which industry was apt to fear juries far more than legislatures; see G. T. Schwartz, "Tort Law and the Economy in Nineteenth-Century America: A Reinterpretation," 90 *Yale Law Journal* 1717, 1742–1746 (1981). As indicated by the Austinian and German codification movements, codifiers were more apt to adopt a universal negligence rule. Moreover, contrary to Horwitz's claim, Holmes consistently recognized the redistributive role of democratically elected legislatures. EW, "The Gas-Stokers' Strike," 795. This is not to deny that he regarded much of the social legislation to be ill considered and likely to worsen conditions for the putative beneficiaries. A notable exception was strict liability legislation. Indeed, he supported legislation in Western states that made railroads strictly liable for running down cattle, and, most dramatically, he backed legislation establishing workers' compensation programs. 1872 Jurisprudence Essay, 791; 1873 Theory of Torts, 774; CLP, "Path of the Law," 182–184. See also Arizona Employers' Liability Cases, 431–434.

59. CL, 99, 155–156.

60. L. M. Friedman, "Civil Wrongs: Personal Injury Law in the Late 19th Century," 1987 *American Bar Foundation Research Journal* 351, 353; E. A. Purcell, *Litigation and Inequality*, 1929 (1992); Posner, "A Theory of Negligence," 29, 63, 85. On the delayed emergence of public perceptions of industrial risk, see C. Siracusa, *A Mechanical People: Perceptions of the Industrial Order in Massachu-*

setts, 1815–1880 (1979); F. W. Munger, "Social Change and Tort Litigation: Industrialization, Accidents, and Trial Courts in Southern West Virginia, 1872–1940," 36 *Buffalo Law Review* 75, 80–81 (1987).

61. L. M. Friedman and J. Ladinsky, "Social Change and the Law of Industrial Accidents," 67 *Columbia Law Review* 50, 72, 74–76 (1967). Although changing conditions continuously exert influence on judicial perceptions, full realization by courts usually awaits a singularly dramatic ruling that breaks new doctrinal ground on a pithy synthesis of the social and legal changes that have taken place, such as was accomplished by Benjamin Cardozo in MacPherson v. Buick, 217 N.Y. 382 (1916), and, more recently, by the California Supreme Court in Sindell v. Abbott Laboratories, 607 P.2d 924 (Cal. 1980). On the delay attending recognition by modern courts and legislatures of the distinctive problems of mass tort cases, see J. B. Weinstein and C. B. Hershenov, "The Effect of Equity on Mass Tort Law," 1991 *University of Illinois Law Review* 269, 288.

62. Despite the empiricist prescriptions of the new jurisprudence, Holmes was averse to observing the facts of social conditions at first-hand, and disinclined to make a systematic collection of data. D. J. Boorstin, "The Elusiveness of Mr. Justice Holmes," 14 *The New England Quarterly* 478, 484–485 (1941); L. B. Boudin, "Justice Holmes and His World," 3 *Lawyers Guild Review* 24, 29 (1943).

63. CLP, "Path of the Law," 200; see also CL, iv.

64. L. Baker, *The Justice from Beacon Hill,* 248 (1991) (quoting Holmes without citation).

65. Ibid., 247–252.

66. OS, 31. See also Letter from Holmes to A. G. Sedgwick (July 12, 1889), HP.

67. CLP, "Path of the Law," 183.

68. Arizona Employers' Liability Cases, 433. This expression of approbation markedly contrasted with the disdain Holmes normally expressed for the economic and social programs that he ruled constitutional because they were not "manifestly absurd." Weaver v. Palmer Bros. Co., 270 U.S. 402, 415 (1926) (Holmes, J. dissenting).

69. Truax v. Corrigan, 257 U.S. 312, 343 (1921) (Holmes, J. dissenting).

70. CL, 41.

71. 1872 Jurisprudence Essay, 791.

72. CL, 148.

73. CL, 42–43; CLP, "Path of the Law," 173–174. Holmes advanced his just compensation principle in Spade v. Lynn & Boston Railroad, 172 Mass. 488, 489–490 (1899), where he suggested a sophisticated calculus to determine the extent of loss from a taking where, as in most cases, the defendant's non-negligent expropriating activity confers benefits on the injured parties that make them better off than they were before—at least, in the expected-value sense. A similar calculus determines modern strict liability for abnormally dangerous activities, *Restatement (Second) Torts,* §520, and explains the constitutional norms of just com-

pensation. F. I. Michelman, "Property, Utility, and Fairness, Comments on the Ethical Foundations of 'Just Compensation' Law," 80 *Harvard Law Review* 1165, 1218 (1967). Indeed, in Pennsylvania Coal Co. v. Mahon, 260 U.S. 393, 415–416 (1923), Holmes interpreted the Fifth Amendment "Takings Clause" with reference to the principle he advanced in *Spade,* "that a man's misfortunes or necessities will [not] justify his shifting the damages to his neighbor's shoulders," and generalized the expected-value test for just compensation as deriving below "average reciprocity of advantage" from the expropriating activity.

74. CL, 148–149.

75. Chancellor Kent foreshadowed these arguments in Gardner v. Village of Newburg, 2 Johns. Ch. 162, 168 (N.Y. 1816). Some of Holmes's contemporaries put the point in terms of primary or secondary duties to compensate or privileges to commit harmful acts conditioned on payment of the resulting losses. W. Markby, *Elements of Law,* 116–117 (1871); F. H. Bohlen, "Incomplete Privilege to Inflict Intentional Invasions of Interests of Property or Personality," 39 *Harvard Law Review* 307 (1926). But political controversy over the mill acts continued into the twentieth century. See Bratton v. Rudnick, 283 Mass. 556, 562–563 (1932) (the court dropped its long-held objections to a view espoused by Holmes: that both the mill acts and strict liability for extra-hazardous activities under *Rylands* were kindred devices for effectuating private takings by levying taxes to pay just compensation). For examples of twentieth-century commentators deploying similar just compensation rationales of *Rylands* and strict liability to give political and moral legitimacy to industrial takings, see R. E. Keeton, "Conditional Fault in the Law of Torts," 72 *Harvard Law Review* 401, 427–429 (1959); R. C. Harris, "Liability Without Fault," 6 *Tulane Law Review* 337, 356–357 and n.75 (1932)(relying in part on Holmes's explanation of *Rylands* in "The Theory of Torts" section of Lecture IV).

76. For a history of the social insurance or loss-spreading rationale as the principal motive behind the general academic acceptance of strict liability in this century, see G. Priest, "The Invention of Enterprise Liability: A Critical History of the Intellectual Foundations of Modern Tort Law," 14 *Journal of Legal Studies* 461 (1985).

77. Letters from Holmes to Pollock, (June 17, 1919), and (Aug. 21, 1919), 2 HPL 15, 22, and from Pollock to Holmes (Aug. 6, 1919), id. at 21.

78. Arizona Employers' Liability Cases, 439 (McKenna, J., dissenting).

79. Id. at 433 (Holmes, J. concurring).

80. Compare Arizona Employers' Liability Cases, 452 (McReynolds, J. dissenting)

81. CL, 117. See also 1872 Jurisprudence Essay, 791, CL, 145; EW, 792–793; 1873 Theory of Torts, 776; CLP, "Privilege, Malice, and Intent," 117. Holmes also suggests a rights-based deterrence function of tort liability in protecting the value of entitlements from depreciation (1) by exposure to risks which create "a general insecurity [that] does not admit of being paid for" and (2) by grave per-

sonal injury because of the "impossibility of estimating the worth of the suffering in money." CL, 40–41; see also CL, 68–69.

82. Arizona Employers' Liability Cases, 432–433.

83. CL, vi, 157–158.

84. Shavell, *Economic Analysis of Accident Law,* 25–26; *Restatement (Second) of Torts,* §291, comment e. See also Gilles, "Rule-Based Negligence and the Regulation of Activity Levels," 339–341 (arguing that courts often examine the reasonableness of activity levels on a class-wide basis, though very rarely as applied to a particular case).

85. See Shavell, *Economic Analysis of Accident Law,* 21; see also R. A. Posner, "Strict Liability: A Comment," 2 *Journal of Legal Studies* 205, 208 (1973).

86. For Holmes, one of the main benefits of the external standard of care under the negligence rule was that its strict liability effect induced "sacrifice" of activity level to "a certain average of conduct." CL, 108.

87. CL, 116.

88. Arizona Employers' Liability Cases, 433. Use of the negligence rule to assess the reasonableness of a defendant's activity and care levels subjects the fate of both industry and the public to the untutored and unaccountable opinions of judges and juries, increases the administrative burden on courts, and raises the stakes of potential error, particularly where new technology is involved. Strict liability solves these problems by transferring reasonableness questions from courts to other more resourceful, informed, administratively efficient, and "democratic" institutions. Sometimes it stimulates a legislative response that restricts the scope of tort liability or provides financial aid to lower-income groups to increase the market for and affordability of the benefits from certain risky activities.

89. In certain cases, such as those addressing harms which business competitors inflict on each other, the best practical solution for negligence failure would be to apply no-liability rules. Given the enormous costs of regulation, courts might go so far in some cases as to absolve defendants from liability for inflicting harm maliciously. CL, 144–145, 156, 161.

90. F. James, Jr., "Accident Liability Reconsidered: The Impact of Liability Insurance," 57 *Yale Law Journal* 549, 549–551 (1948); J. G. Fleming, *The Law of Torts,* 132, 179 (1983) (pointing out that the advent of liability insurance expanded the scope of negligence as well as the use of strict liability); P. S. Atiyah, *Accidents, Compensation and the Law,* chap. 10 (1987).

91. CL, 95–96. Holmes's contemporaries also recognized the difficulties that the absence of liability insurance presented for any expansion of the scope of tort liability. Ryan v. New York Central R.R. Co., 216 (asserting the lack of liability insurance as a reason for restricting negligence liability for railroad fires).

92. CL, 50.

93. In contrast to liability insurance, which predicts the rate of tortious risk from particular firms or industries, first-party insurance forecasts the incidence of certain generic types of harm irrespective of cause. For this reason, and because the

incidence of tort injuries comprises a small to minuscule fraction of annual losses, first-party insurance can, as a practical matter, disregard the rate of foreseeable as well as unforeseeable tort injuries in setting premiums. Keeton, "Conditional Fault in the Law of Torts," 438; Shavell, *Economic Analysis of Accident Law,* 243–244, 263–264 (comparing costs of first-party and liability insurance, and noting that first-party insurance ignores causation where the injured party is unlikely to influence risks).

94. Discussion of the absence of liability insurance and its consequences for expanded use of strict liability in the nineteenth century is nowhere to be found in their major works on the history of American tort law. L. M. Friedman, *A History of American Law* (1985); Horwitz, *The Transformation of American Law, 1870–1960,* 57 (ridiculing *Ryan* without mentioning its concern about the absence of liability insurance).

95. For a contemporary discussion of the inability of noncommercial actors and small businesses to spread losses, see J. Smith, "Sequel to Workmen's Compensation Acts," 241 and n.17.

96. Shavell, *Economic Analysis of Accident Law,* 207–208 (noting risk aversion of firms with small, low-income markets and relatively few assets); K. S. Abraham, *Distributing Risk: Insurance, Legal Theory, and Public Policy,* 48 (1986).

97. CLP, "Path of the Law," 183.

98. Ibid.

99. CL, 117, 156. Judicial preferences for negligence rather than strict liability in two other major types of cases was also explained by Holmes's net-benefit reasoning. The first type usually arises from a contractual relationship where the plaintiff incurs injury from a risky act undertaken by the defendant for the "common interest" of the parties. Spade v. Lynn and Boston Railroad Company, 489 (denying strict liability for mental distress suffered by a passenger when the conductor forcibly but non-negligently removed a rowdy drunk from the streetcar). Common benefit constitutes a standard defense to strict liability under *Rylands.* Carstairs v. Taylor, L.R. 6 Ex. 217 (1871). The second type of case involves common activities, such as riding a horse, using a fireplace (or even a steam boiler in an industrial sector) in Holmes's time, or driving a car today. If the activity involves any residual risk, on average it is borne reciprocally and equally by all participants in the activity. Because strict liability would simply create a mutual insurance system, reliance instead on cheaper, more efficient first-party insurance makes everyone better off. See Bamford v. Turnley, 3 B&S 62, 83 (1862). For similar arguments in the current literature, see *Restatement (Second) of Torts,* §§519–520; R. Keeton, and J. O'Connell, *Basic Protection for the Traffic Victim* (1965); C. Fried, *An Anatomy of Values* (1970).

100. Holmes doubted that the tactical application of rules for redistributional purposes, such as juries awarding excessive damages, would accomplish substantial or enduring gains for lower income groups. Market adjustments generally make the "public pay the damages" or "make the business impossible and thus . . .

injure those whom [we] might wish to help." Southern Pac. Co. v. Darnell, 534; Arizona Employers' Liability Cases, 433–434. Generally on the problem of perverse distributional effects of redistributional largess in the making and application of rules, see EW, "Gas-Stokers' Strike," 796; CLP, "Learning in Science," 139; Plant v. Woods, 176 Mass. 492, 505 (1900) (Holmes, J. dissenting); CLP, 282; CLP, "Ideals and Doubts," 306–307.

101. The assumed distributional advantages of strict liability were also far from apparent in many conflicting use contexts, such as those which frequently arose between existing agrarian and emerging industrial interests. Strict liability tended to favor traditional and established activities over new and socially destabilizing enterprises, thereby entrenching the political status quo, decreasing economic mobility and opportunity, and even maintaining relatively higher levels of risk. This conservatism was mitigated by the encouragement and protection which strict liability gave to the best of the new enterprise; in its turn this venture, if successful, would receive similar protection from other upstarts.

102. CLP, "Path of the Law," 183–184. The perverse distributional effect of strict liability was most apparent, Holmes suggested, in ordinary cases of conflicting uses, such as highways and residential areas, where those who engage (nonnegligently) in the particular activity bear the resulting residual risk in roughly reciprocal degree. Strict liability essentially forces the participants to pay for relatively high-priced tort insurance to cover the losses suffered by others from such risk, rather than allowing them to buy first-party insurance to cover their own losses.

103. The notion that the market adjusts residual risks more effectively than tort appears to underlie and explain Holmes's opinion in Middlesex Company v. McCue, 149 Mass. 103 (1889), in which the court refused to apply strict liability on behalf of the owner of property on the lower portion of a hill, whose millpond was fouled by water runoff from the upper owner's cultivating and manuring of a garden. This constraint on the lower-owner's use resulting from the reasonable and expected use of the upper property would have been reflected in the market price paid by the respective parties when they bought the land. It was a "matter of degree" for the jury to determine whether the particular burden was within the range of uses which the market would have taken into account. Id. at 104–105. To impose strict liability would merely shift the loss or cost of prevention from the lower-plot owner to the upper-plot owner, resulting in an expenditure of judicial resources without reducing, spreading, or more equitably distributing the risk. Although the market could adjust prices to accommodate strict liability against upper-plot owners, in most cases the other owner has better information and control regarding the special use of that property, and therefore can most effectively bargain for a risk-discount in purchasing the property, or build a wall to prevent troublesome runoff. Another application of these ideas by Holmes may be found in Robins Dry Dock Repair Co. v. Flint, 275 U.S. 303, 308–309 (1927). Similarly, the reality of land price adjustments to long standing legal rules and land

uses affected his views on just compensation for takings, nuisances, and other land use conflicts. Rideout v. Knox, 148 Mass. 368, 372–373 (1889); Boston Ferrule Co. v. Hills, 159 Mass. 147 (1893).

104. FE, "Common Carriers and the Common Law," 222. Horwitz is thus mistaken in claiming that Holmes's general preference for contract rather than strict liability in common carrier cases—Holmes never advocated contracting out of negligence—distributionally disadvantaged commercial shippers relative to carriers. Horwitz, *Transformation of American Law, 1870–1960,* 13–14. Horwitz's history is also incorrect in asserting that Holmes was supporting only a recently developed option to disclaim strict liability by contract. While that option had been contemporaneously reaffirmed by the Supreme Court in Railroad Co. v. Lockwood, 84 U.S. 357, 360 (1873), the right of common carriers to disclaim strict liability or, alternatively, to adjust their rates to cover strict liability exposure was already well established in the United States, and in England dated back to well before Coggs v. Bernard. FE, "Common Carriers," 209; EW, "Misunderstanding of the Civil Law," 772. For an excellent account of this history, see R. J. Kaczorowski, "The Common-Law Background of Nineteenth-Century Tort Law," 51 *Ohio State Law Journal* 1127, 1139–1153 (1990).

Horwitz quotes Holmes out of context, and thus creates the impression that he condemned mandatory rules of strict liability for common carriers or innkeepers as "monstrous." Horwitz, *Transformation of American Law, 1870–1960,* 13–14. A similar misimpression is created in White, *Justice Oliver Wendell Holmes,* 170. In fact, Holmes used that term only to characterize an old, outmoded rule that forbade common callings to refuse to contract with any customer who makes a reasonable request for service. FE, "Common Carriers," 221. Strict liability was simply not at issue; indeed, as Holmes pointed out, there was no general authority for common carriers or callings to disclaim liability for negligence. 2 Commentaries, *608 n.1. Apparently, the old rule was aimed at preventing carriers and innkeepers from "holding-out" to extort exorbitant payments from stranded travelers in isolated and rural areas. Indicating approval for this rule in its time, Holmes opposed its general application in modern, urban, and competitive markets. Invoking the same competitive-market grounds, he objected to labor injunctions that barred concerted employee refusals to contract with employers, CLP, "Privilege, Malice, and Intent," 127–128.

105. Coppage v. Kansas, 236 U.S. 1, 27 (1915) (Holmes, J. dissenting); FE, "Common Carriers and the Common Law," 222.

106. On the moral hazard and lack of joint-care effects of strict liability, see Shavell, *Economic Analysis of Accident Law,* 16–17, 195.

107. *Rylands*-type activities were principal examples where, in Holmes's view, "the safest way to secure care is to throw the risk upon the person who decides what precautions shall be taken." CL, 117.

108. For insightful elaboration of the cheapest-cost-avoider approach in Holmes's thought, see S. G. Gilles, "Negligence, Strict Liability, and the Cheapest

Cost-Avoider," 78 *Virginia Law Review* 1291, 1340–1349 (1992); see also P. S. Atiyah, "The Legacy of Holmes Through English Eyes," in *Holmes and The Common Law: A Century Later,* 38 and n.54 (1983). For a general discussion of the cheapest cost-avoider approach, see G. Calabresi and J. T. Hirschoff, "Toward a Test for Strict Liability in Torts," 81 *Yale Law Journal* 1055 (1972).

Holmes suggested the perspective of cheapest cost-avoider in Middlesex Company v. McCue and earlier, in explaining abandonment of strict liability for cattle trespass in "some of the Western states" on the ground that it was impractical to enclose the "vast prairies" and cheaper for the railroads to build the necessary fences. 1872 Jurisprudence Essay, 791; 1873 Theory of Torts, 774. Unlike some of his contemporaries, Holmes insisted that such decisions were not augurs of universal rules but should be understood as examples of the process of local, contextual policy-making by which the law generally evolves. What was appropriate for Western states might not serve community needs in dealing with the crowded and conflicting uses in the East.

109. The negligence-dogma account asserts that Holmes gutted the Massachusetts Employers' Liability Act by inserting common law defenses, such as contributory negligence and assumption of the risk. M. Tushnet, "The Logic of Experience: Oliver Wendell Holmes on the Supreme Judicial Court," 63 *Virginia Law Review* 975, 1031 (1977); Gordon, "Holmes's *Common Law* as Legal and Social Science," 731 n. 87; cf. White, *Tort Law in America,* 41–42. This claim is misleading because it fails to mention that these defenses were mandated or directly implied by the 1887 statute involved. See 1887 Mass. Acts 899, Ch. 270. Contrary to the anachronistic impression left by the negligence-dogma account, the Massachusetts compensation scheme did not resemble the strict liability legislation of today. Under the Act, employees could recover for injuries resulting solely from "the negligence of the employer," and that were not in any degree the result of contributory negligence. Essentially, employees assumed all non-negligent risks of employment, no matter how dangerous the job. Holmes consistently used such assumption-of-the-risk phraseology only in cases denying liability where there was no allegation or proof of employer negligence. Ryalls v. Mechanics' Mills, 150 Mass. 190, 195 (1889). See also Meistrich v. Casino Arena Attractions, Inc., 155 A.2d 90, 93 (N.J. 1959) (noting that such phrases were commonly used in the nineteenth century to characterize cases of non-negligence). Moreover, the Act expressly provided for an assumption-of-the-risk defense where an employee (presumably not contributorily negligent) undertook a negligent risk created by the employer without giving the employer reasonable notice of the defect.

110. LeRoy Fibre Co. v. Chicago, Milwaukee & St. Paul Ry., 353 (Holmes, J. concurring). From its modern inception, the contributory negligence defense was designed to thwart moral hazards by plaintiffs. Butterfield v. Forrester, 103 Eng. Rep. 926, 927 (1809). Cf. FE, "Common Carriers," 218–219.

111. G. Calabresi, *The Costs of Accidents,* 261 (1970).

112. Calabresi mistakenly asserts that Holmes denied any social benefit to loss-

spreading. In fact, Holmes recognized the social insurance advantages of strict liability in industrial injury cases. Beyond the problem of foreseeability, he was reticent to extend strict liability to ordinary cases because there was no liability insurance and because he realized (as Calabresi himself finds quite plausible, id. at 315–316) that first-party insurance spreads losses more cheaply and efficiently than "tort-insurance" supplied by strict liability.

113. Id. at 263 and n.19. Calabresi acknowledges that "efficiency" favors the negligence rule in ordinary cases—Holmes's "ungeneralized torts." Id. at 307 n.7.

6. Holmes in History

1. Letter from John Henry Wigmore to Holmes (Apr. 29, 1894), MS Box 51, Folders 21–31, HP.

2. Actually, Wigmore published two articles in quick succession on the subject: "The Tripartite Division of Torts," 8 *Harvard Law Review* 200 (1894) and "A General Analysis of Tort-Relations," 8 *Harvard Law Review* 377 (1895).

3. Letter from Wigmore to Holmes.

4. Ibid.

5. Ibid.

6. Ibid.

7. Ibid.

8. In contrast to Wigmore, who treated as interchangeable the terms "justification" and "excuse," Holmes used "excuse" in the classic sense to connote the converse of "responsibility." Holmes and Wigmore also differed over a more fundamental point. Instead of treating injury as a distinct part, Holmes distributed the subject under the responsibility and justification parts of his theory. For purposes of responsibility, the question of injury was simply one of generic fact: had the defendant caused "temporal damage" to the plaintiff? The legal cognizability of specific types of harm was a matter of judicial policy discretion under "justification."

9. Letter from Wigmore to Holmes. Wigmore's citation is to the first page of Theory of Torts (Lect. IV), which applied the foresight theory of responsibility to the three principal branches of tort law. As indicated by his contemporaneous writings, Wigmore used "acting at peril" to mean strict liability, and "due care" for negligence. Wigmore, "Tripartite Division," 208; J. H. Wigmore, "Responsibility for Tortious Acts: Its History—III," 7 *Harvard Law Review* 441, 454 (1894). Wigmore employed the cumbersome phrase "Due Care Under the Circumstances" instead of "negligence," apparently to avoid confusion with the possible early use of negligence as expressing the notion of breach or neglect of duty, which encompassed strict liability as well as duties of reasonable care. Ibid., 453–454. See also Wigmore, "Tripartite Division," 206.

10. Letter from Wigmore to Holmes.

11. Letter from Holmes to Wigmore (May 3, 1894), MS Box 51, Folders 21–31,

HP. While Holmes does not identify the Wigmore correspondence to which he is responding, I have reconstructed the exchange not only from the dates and other evidence in the letters, but also from post office records of the average delivery time for mail between Chicago and Boston, and Holmes's practice of answering every personal letter "scrupulously, almost within the hour." E. S. Sergeant, "Oliver Wendell Holmes," *The New Republic* 58, 64 (Nov. 8, 1926).

12. Wigmore, "Tort-Relations," 387–388. Consistent with Holmes's findings, Wigmore noted that in addition to foresight, "responsibility" required only "causation" and "activity" (as opposed to "mere nonfeasance"). Id. at 386, 387.

13. Wigmore, "Tripartite Division," 206–207 (quoting Lynch v. Knight, 9 H.L.C. 577).

14. Id. at 207–208. The some-negligence interpretation relates to Wigmore's assignment of the question to "responsibility." Wigmore distinguished this question of Responsibility from the question of Justification that typically arose from conflicting uses in urban and industrial contexts, where due care was invoked as a general "excuse" to relieve a clearly responsible defendant of liability, "because he is conducting his business in an ordinary and otherwise fair and reasonable manner." Id. at 208.

15. Wigmore, "Responsibility for Tortious Acts," 454–455.

16. Id. at 455 n.2.

17. Wigmore, "Tort-Relations," 388–389.

18. Id. at 388.

19. M. M. Bigelow, *Leading Cases on the Law of Torts,* vii (1875). See also 1 E. A. Jaggard, *Handbook of the Law of Torts,* 107–108 and n.429 (1895). But see W. Schofield, Book Review, 1 *Harvard Law Review* 51, 52 (1887) (crediting Frederick Pollock's 1887 treatise with devising the arrangement, and particularly a broad strict liability branch encompassing *Rylands*).

20. M. M. Bigelow, *Elements of the Law of Torts,* v and n. 1 (1878).

21. Ibid.

22. See N. Isaacs, "Fault and Liability," 31 *Harvard Law Review* 954, 962–967, 977 (1918); A. V. Dicey, "Holmes's *The Common Law,*" 10 *Hofstra Law Review* 712, 714–716 (1982) (reprinted from *The Spectator,* 745–747, June 3, 1882); H. W. Edgerton, "Negligence, Inadvertence, and Indifference; The Relation of Mental States to Negligence," 39 *Harvard Law Review* 849, 867–869 (1926) (indicating the salutary strict liability effect of the external negligence standard on defendant activity levels).

23. H. J. Laski, "The Basis of Vicarious Liability," 26 *Yale Law Journal* 105, 107 and n.15, 130, 135 (1916); R. Pound, "The End of Law as Developed in Legal Rules and Doctrines," 27 *Harvard Law Review* 195, 196 and n.6 (1914) (advocating strict liability on the strength of Holmes's realist, market-failure justification for workers' compensation legislation).

24. C. K. Burdick, *The Law of Torts,* 12 (1926); C. B. Whittier, "Mistake in the Law of Torts," 15 *Harvard Law Review* 335, 343–344, 346–347 (1902); J.

Smith, Notes for Lectures on Torts, "Papers," Part 9, pp. 26–27 (Harvard Law School Library).

25. Dicey, "Holmes's *The Common Law*", 714–715.

26. F. Pollock, "The Dog and the Potman: Or 'Go It, Bob,'" 25 *Law Quarterly Review* 317, 318 (1909); J. Smith, "Tort and Absolute Liability—Suggested Changes in Classification," 30 *Harvard Law Review* 241, 319, 330 (3 pts. 1917); Nash v. Lang, 268 Mass. 407, 413 (1929).

27. E. G. M. Fletcher, *Carrier's Liability*, 5, 33–35 (1932) (challenging Holmes's claim that strict liability continuously governed common carriers); Laski, "Vicarious Liability," 113, 129 and n.149 (arguing for general use of vicarious liability on the basis of Holmes's economic justification for attaching "special liabilities" to carriers).

28. Brown v. Collins, 53 N.H. 442, 445–446 (1873).

29. Id. at 445 (quoting with disapproval first from "The Theory of Torts," and then from an English opinion adopting cause-based strict liability).

30. Ibid.

31. 1873 Theory of Torts, 785. It is significant that Bigelow, who supported strict liability under *Rylands* "when the thing which escapes is obviously dangerous," had no difficulty in adopting Holmes's conception of the strict liability branch. Bigelow, *Elements of Torts,* 258–259.

32. R. Avery, Notes on Torts Lectures by J. Smith, 177–178 (1897), Special Collections, Harvard Law School Library; J. Smith "Absolute Liability," 328. Smith also quoted rationales for strict liability in extra-hazardous cases offered by Pollock and Salmond (id. at 328–329), but, as Smith apparently recognized, they repeated Holmes's arguments based on substantial residual risk, the difficulty of proving negligence, and just compensation for takings. J. Smith, Notes for Lectures on Torts, 70, Special Collections, Harvard Law School Library; W. Seavey, Notes on Smith's Torts Lectures, id. at 72. Significantly, as I discuss later, Smith clearly identified Pollock and Salmond as opponents of *Rylands*, but, like other critics of the rule who frequently listed their academic and judicial allies, never named Holmes among them.

33. M. Cohen, "Justice Holmes and the Nature of Law," 31 *Columbia Law Review* 352, 353 (1931).

34. 1 T. Beven, *Negligence in Law*, 481 and n.2 (1908) (quoting Chalmers v. Dixon, 3 Rettie, 461, 464).

35. Ibid.

36. R. C. Harris, "Liability Without Fault," 6 *Tulane Law Review* 337, 356–358, 368 (1932).

37. Yet, as I show later, many commentators expressly stated the foresight qualification in their own descriptions of the major rules of strict liability in force.

38. Smith, "Absolute Liability," 260; J. Smith, "Crucial Issues in Labor Litigation," 20 *Harvard Law Review* 253, 262–263 (1907).

39. See also Smith, "Absolute Liability," 324 and n.21 (noting Holmes's appli-

cation of foresight-based strict liability in Davis v. Rich, 180 Mass. 235 (1902));
Smith, Tort Lecture Notes, Part 35, p. 22 (citing Theory of Torts (Lect. IV) regarding the presumed knowledge of danger that subjects keepers of ferocious animals
to strict liability). For Smith, the obviously risky business of blasting was the
quintessential extra-hazardous activity. J. Smith, "Liability for Substantial Physical Damage to Land by Blasting—The Rule of the Future," 33 *Harvard Law
Review* 542 (1920).

40. Dicey, "Holmes's *The Common Law*", 714–716.

41. Id. at 715.

42. Pollock, "The Dog and the Potman," 317.

43. Id. at 318. Pollock's reference to Theory of Torts (Lect. IV) signified agreement with Holmes that all of these rules, and, by extension, the strict liability
applied under *Rylands* and broadly to extra-hazardous cases, were conditioned on
foresight, but only foresight. Id. at 321. See also F. Pollock, *Essays in Jurisprudence and Ethics*, 119–124 (1882); F. Pollock, *The Law of Torts*, 400–401
(1887). Pollock opposed these animal rules and *Rylands* in general, but joined
Holmes in rejecting attempts to deny their real nature on suppositions of negligence, or to narrow their scope by unprincipled distinctions.

44. Pollock, *The Law of Torts*, vii (1887) (doubting that a "complete theory"
had been found).

45. F. Pollock, "Holmes on the Common Law," *The Saturday Review* 758, 759
(June 11, 1881), published in revised form, "Mr. Justice Holmes," 44 *Harvard
Law Review* 693 (1930).

46. See also H. Terry, *Some Leading Principles of Anglo-American Law*, 180–
181 (1884) (noting that in the torts lectures Holmes did not limit his foresight
conception to unreasonable risks, and that, "probably because the purpose of his
work did not call for it," he did not elaborate the "degree of likelihood of damage"
required for negligence).

47. Pollock, *Jurisprudence and Ethics*, 119–120. Pollock hoped that the foresight qualification on *Rylands* would be applied narrowly (*The Law of Torts*, 428
(2d ed. 1890)), but the trend was decidedly in the opposite direction, especially
regarding extra-hazardous activities. Greenock Corporation v. Caledonian R. Co.,
A.C. 556 (1917); Bratton v. Rudnick, 283 Mass. 556, 562 (1933); *Restatement of
Torts*, §§519–524 (1938); R. A. Percy, ed., *Charlesworth on Negligence*, 298
(1977).

48. 1 T. A. Street, *The Foundations of Legal Liability*, xxvii (1906). Although
Street referred these principles to the "branch of the law of negligence," he, like
Holmes, defined the negligence branch to encompass all foresight-based rules of
unintentional tort. Id. at xxvii, 73.

49. Id. at xxvii.

50. Id. at 68.

51. Ibid. See also A. J. Harno, "Tort-Relations," 30 *Yale Law Journal* 145,
147, 152 (1920) (noting Holmes's foresight theory of responsibility and arguing

that "the element of foresight should be a determining factor" for strict liability).

52. 1 Beven, *Negligence in Law,* 481, 564–566; T. Beven, *Principles of the Law of Negligence,* 14–15 (1889). See also T. Beven, "The Responsibility at Common Law for the Keeping of Animals," 22 *Harvard Law Review* 465, 483 (1909).

53. Pollock, *The Law of Torts,* 118 (1887). Pollock aligned his some-negligence interpretation of Trespass with his foresight interpretation of *Rylands* as applying to "evidently hazardous" risks, and suggested that to the extent *Rylands* went beyond foreseeable risk, as Cranworth intimated, it rested on a causation theory that the modern some-negligence authorities have explicitly rejected. Id. at 398–399. See also Pollock, *The Law of Torts,* 493 and n.(n) (11th ed. 1920) (specifically cross-referencing discussions of *Rylands* and the some-negligence interpretation of Trespass).

54. Pollock, *The Law of Torts,* 118 (1887). For a similar reading of Holmes's policy arguments—opposed to cause-based strict liability but confining the "inevitable accident" defense to cases of non-negligent "unforeseen accidents"—see 2 S. D. Thompson, *The Law of Negligence,* 1234–1235 (1880) (referring to Holmes's "Trespass and Negligence" article). See also J. Smith, "Sequel to Workmen's Compensation Acts," 27 *Harvard Law Review* 235, 239–240 n.13 (1914) (suggesting Holmes's some-negligence interpretation of liability for "pure accident").

55. Quinn v. Crimmings, 171 Mass. 255 (1898) (as framed by the court, the charge of strict liability arose when the defendant's fence blew over in a violent and unforeseeable storm and killed the plaintiff).

56. Smith, Tort Lecture Notes, Part 41, p. 61. See also Burdick, *The Law of Torts,* 538. This reading of *Quinn* was confirmed in Ainsworth v. Lakin, 180 Mass. 397, 400–401 (1902). Although Holmes was a member of the *Ainsworth* bench, the view that it limited *Rylands* to activities characterized by relatively great danger was generally attributed to Judge Knowlton, the opinion's author. E. R. Thayer, "Liability Without Fault," 29 *Harvard Law Review* 801, 812–813 (1916); Smith, "Absolute Liability," 411 n.6; F. H. Bohlen, "The Rule in Rylands v. Fletcher," 59 *University of Pennsylvania Law Review* 298, 449 n.144 (1911). These commentators appear to have understood Holmes's opinion in Davis v. Rich, issued a month before *Ainsworth,* as disagreeing with Knowlton's position. Smith, "Absolute Liability," 324 and n.21 (referring to *Davis* as specifying foreseeability as the only limit on the danger requisite for *Rylands*).

Wigmore also seemed to approve *Quinn* for refusing to extend *Rylands* to ordinary buildings. J. H. Wigmore, "Justice Holmes and the Law of Torts," 29 *Harvard Law Review* 601, 612 (1916). Wigmore's parenthetical remarks suggest, however, that he thought the main virtue of Holmes's ruling was not related to strict liability; rather, in tailoring the negligence standard to the relatively small risk involved and in excusing the defendant from responsibility for a risk under the exclusive control of the adjoining landowner, Holmes settled an important question arising in cases of joint interest to property.

57. Laski, "Vicarious Liability," 130.

While agreeing that *Quinn* involved an ordinary residential structure and was thus consistent with *Rylands*, Francis Bohlen nonetheless criticized Holmes for adopting a policy of encouraging building construction generally at the expense of neighboring interests. Bohlen, "The Rule in Rylands," 298, 425–426, 440–442. Pointing to the mill acts—which represent the very opposite of the reciprocal or common risks presented by ordinary residential structures—Bohlen asserted that Holmes ignored the just compensation rationale of strict liability, though in the torts lectures Holmes did promote that rationale precisely on the basis of the mill acts. In referring to Holmes's rejection of *Rylands* for "buildings and fences," Bohlen also quoted but disregarded Holmes's express reliance on *Rylands'* unforeseeable harm limitation, which was warranted on the jury findings. Quinn v. Crimmings, 258. Bohlen's criticism was also somewhat disingenuous. He attempted to convert *Rylands* and its American progeny, particularly in Massachusetts, to negligence decisions by claiming that their strict liability holding was unnecessary *dictum.* Bohlen, "The Rule in Rylands v. Fletcher," 299 n.2; 432–436 (applying the negligence conversion interpretation to *Shipley,* and Holmes's reliance on *Rylands* and *Shipley* in *Fitzpatrick*). As Reporter for the *Restatement of Torts,* Bohlen included among the categories exempted from strict liability those activities that did not pose substantial residual risks or that were of "common usage," such as automobiles. *Restatement of Torts,* §§ 519, 520 and Comment a (1938).

58. Burdick, *The Law of Torts,* 538 and n.46; Bohlen, "The Rule in Rylands," 434.

59. J. Smith, "Reasonable Use of One's Own Property as a Justification for Damage to a Neighbor," 17 *Columbia Law Review* 383, 398 n.72 (1917). See also Thayer, "Liability Without Fault," 802 (referring to Doe's arguments); Wigmore, "Responsibility for Tortious Acts," 455 n.3 (favoring *Rylands,* but referring to Doe's "masterly" dissent).

60. G. E. White, *Tort Law in America: An Intellectual History,* 17 (1980).

61. Smith, "Liability for Blasting" 550–551 n.35.

62. Ibid., 683–684 and n.66. See also K. Takayanagi, "Liability Without Fault in the Modern Civil and Common Law," 16 *Illinois Law Review* 163, 163–166, 185–186 and n.85, 285–286 (1921) (suggesting Holmes's foresight theory of responsibility and noting Wigmore's support for *Rylands,* but observing that "most of the best authors" opposed the rule, and naming Thayer, Street, Bohlen, Bishop, Pollock, and Burdick); F. V. Harper, "Liability Without Fault and Proximate Cause," 30 *Michigan Law Review* 1001, 1014 (1932) (opposing *Rylands* and relying on Cooley, Bishop, Smith, and a tentative draft of the Restatement of Torts proposed by Bohlen); R. Pound, *Interpretations of Legal History,* 35–36 and n.1 (1923) (referring to Pollock, Salmond, and Thayer as the leading opponents of strict liability); Letter from Judge R. J. Peaslee of the New Hampshire Supreme Court to E. R. Thayer (July 21, 1913), File 5–10, Special Collections, Harvard Law School Library (placing Thayer alone in Doe's rank of *Rylands'* preeminent critics).

63. Not only did Pollock have the special knowledge acquired from long and close association with Holmes, but his frank and notorious opposition to *Rylands* had placed him out on something of a weak limb in a professional milieu that required deference to precedent.

64. Pollock, *The Law of Torts*, 493–494 nn.(o) and (p) (11th ed. 1920).

65. Arizona Employers' Liability Cases, 250 U.S. 400, 431–434 (1919) (Holmes, J. concurring). See also Letter from Pollock to Holmes (August 6, 1919), 2 HPL 21.

66. The publication history of the Ames casebook on torts dates the time when the distinction of some-negligence from a general negligence rule began to fade. Beginning in 1874, and continuing through the 1889 printing, the first edition included under "Battery" the principal Trespass cases, such as Weaver v. Ward and Harvey v. Dunlop, which presented the question of liability for accident in the classic sense of unforeseen and unpreventable harm. J. B. Ames, *Select Cases on Torts* (1874). In the second edition, issued in 1893 by Smith, these Trespass cases (now including Brown v. Kendall) were organized under the chapter and subheading, "Excusable Trespass (a) Accident or Mistake," and indexed under the heading: "Accident, without negligence, excuses trespass to person . . . excuses trespass to personality . . . whether an excuse for trespass to land . . . through negligence, no excuse for a trespass." 1 J. B. Ames, *A Selection of Cases on the Law of Torts*, 56, 755 (1893). See also id. at 766 (cross-referencing index entry "Negligence" to "accident without. (See Accident.)"); Smith, Tort Lecture Notes, pt. 9, pp. 22–23 (offering in a part of the lectures entitled "Accident or Mistake" a some-negligence interpretation of Brown v. Kendall and other Trespass cases).

The first edition of the Ames casebook contained no general consideration of the negligence cause of action. Although some current commentators have interpreted this omission as evidence of Ames's premodern understanding of negligence and a late development of the modern cause of action (see White, *Tort Law in America*, 18), in fact, as Smith explained in the preface to the 1893 reissue of the book, the first edition represented only a partial collection—indeed, the title page specified it was "Part I." Ames had simply been sidetracked from "extend[ing] the collection over the whole field" by work on other subjects. That extension was completed by Smith in a second volume of the casebook, which included several chapters dealing with negligence, followed by several dealing with strict liability for extra-hazardous and other types of risky activities.

A dramatic rearrangement of the casebook occurred in 1917, under Pound's editorial control. The some-negligence section of "Accident Without Negligence" was eliminated, and *Weaver, Brown,* and other Trespass cases were grouped under a section collecting negligence cases generally, titled "Negligence as a Ground of Liability." R. Pound, ed., J. B. Ames and J. Smith, *A Selection of Cases on the Law of Torts* (1917). A subsequent revision by Beale continued this structure, and also inserted the excerpt from *Brown* a second time, in the chapter "Justification and Excuse" under the subsection "Protection from Consequences of Protected Acts."

2 J. H. Beale, ed., J. B. Ames and J. Smith, *A Selection of Cases on the Law of Torts*, 1319 (1936).

67. Although this crucial distinction is generally recognized in the history of strict liability as well as in its current applications, most commentators overlook its central presence in Holmes's analysis. For example, see G. P. Fletcher, "Fairness and Utility in Tort Theory," 85 *Harvard Law Review* 537, 545–555, 564 (1972) ("The assumption of Holmes's influential analysis is that there are only two doctrinal possibilities: the fault [negligence] standard . . . and strict or absolute liability. The latter is dubbed unmoral; therefore, the only option open to morally sensitive theorists would appear to be liability for fault alone").

68. See generally Isaacs, "Fault and Liability," 954.

69. I have already noted the support of Doe, Bigelow, Smith, Street, and Beven for foresight-based strict liability. Although Laski and Cohen do not invoke the foresight condition directly, it nevertheless seems implicit in their focus on extra-hazardous and industrial activities. Indeed, "the great majority" of extra-hazardous risks were considered "a matter of . . . general notoriety." *Restatement of Torts*, §523, Comment b. For other commentators focusing support for strict liability on extra-hazardous activities, see R. Pound, *An Introduction to the Philosophy of Law*, 90–96 (1954); W. A. Seavey, "Principles of Torts," 56 *Harvard Law Review* 72, 86 (1942); C. A. Bunker, Notes on Lectures on Torts by W. Schofield, 137–139 (1889–90), Special Collections, Harvard Law School Library (noting Schofield's arguments—like Holmes's—that *Rylands* covers cases "where man goes into extra-hazard[ous] busin[ess], though lawful, courts say he must take the responsibility of damage. Class of cases covered not defined & possib[ly] not capab[le] of defin[ition]. . . [Schofield t]hinks true question is as to policy in such cases").

70. F. Pollock, "Duties of Insuring Safety: The Rule in Rylands v. Fletcher," 5 *Law Quarterly Review* 52 (1886); see also id. at 57 (noting that the "act of God" defense to *Rylands* absolved defendants of liability for an "accident . . . such as human foresight could not be reasonably expected to anticipate"); Pollock, *Jurisprudence and Ethics*, 121–122 (referring to cases where responsibility attached to "all events and hazards which may not be fairly considered as beyond human foresight").

71. Terry, *Leading Principles*, 441–42 (referring, like Holmes, to Supreme Court's *Nitroglycerine Case* as a claim of unforeseeable harm).

72. *Restatement of Torts*, §§519, 523 and Comment; Bohlen, "The Rule in Rylands," 423–424, 436–437.

73. Thayer, "Liability Without Fault," 805–806. See also T. M. Cooley, *The Law of Torts*, 568, 571–575 and n.3 (1879); Takayanagi, "Liability Without Fault," 164–165; Harno, "Tort-Relations," 150–152; W. E. Ball, *Leading Cases on the Law of Torts*, 322 (1884); H. G. Wood, *The Law of Nuisances*, 161, 170–171, 490–491, 748–749 (1893); F. T. Piggott, *Principles of the Law of Torts*, 108 (1885); H. Fraser, *The Law of Torts*, 162–163 (1898); J. Salmond, *The Law of Torts*, 189–190 (1902); H. G. Chapin, *Handbook of the Law of Torts*, 513,

521 (1917); 11 W. Holdsworth, *A History of English Law,* 606 and n.3 (1925); J. M. Guest, "The Natural Use of Land," 42 *American Law Register and Review* 98, 104–105 (1894); P. H. Winfield, "The History of Negligence in the Law of Torts," 42 *Law Quarterly Review* 184, 194 (1926).

74. See Pound, *Interpretations of Legal History,* 108–109; Pound, *An Introduction to the Philosophy of Law,* 92–93; R. Pound, "The Economic Interpretation and the Law of Torts," 53 *Harvard Law Review* 365, 384 (1940). Wigmore, "Responsibility for Tortious Acts," 454 n.3; Thayer, "Liability without Fault," 809–810. *Rylands* was applied in many cases of escape of water or other stored liquids, see Defiance Water Co. v. Olinger, 44 N.E. 238 (Ohio 1896); Kankakee Water Co. v. Reeves, 45 Ill. App. 285 (1892); Berry v. Shell Petroleum Co., 140 Kans. 94 (1934). Cases involving the storage and use of explosives for construction purposes—activities recognized as essential to urban and industrial development—led the way in establishing *Rylands* and other strict liability doctrines in most jurisdictions. See Feinberg v. Wisconsin Granite Co., 224 N.W. 184 (S.D. 1929); 4 J. G. Sutherland, *Law of Damages,* 2957–2958 (1904). Indeed, as Holmes noted (CL (I), 156), the New York Court of Appeals adopted strict liability for explosives soon after rejecting *Rylands* for steam boilers in Losee v. Buchanan, 51 N.Y. 483 (1873). See Heeg v. Light, 80 N.Y. 579 (1880).

75. For example, see R. A. Epstein, *Cases and Materials on Torts,* 93 (1990) (minimizing Holmes's treatment of *Rylands* in Lecture III, while disregarding his previous endorsements of strict liability, the innovative nature of his functional arguments, and the foresight theory of *Rylands* in Theory of Torts (Lect. IV)).

76. A further measure of the controversial nature of Holmes's stance is the fact that the torts lectures were published at the height of judicial reaction against *Rylands,* disregarding both Doe's criticism of the extra-hazardous classification and Wharton's denunciation of strict liability based on generalized foresight as a "communist" threat to "capitalism." F. Wharton, *The Law of Negligence,* 828 (1874). Holmes advocated strict industrial liability in "Path of the Law" and the *Arizona Employers' Liability Cases,* despite rampant antiunionism and judicial repudiation of workers compensation laws as "revolutionary" and unconstitutional. Ives v. South Buffalo Ry., 201 N.Y. 271, 309–311 (1911).

77. Pollock, *A Plea for Historical Interpretation,* 163, 167 (1923); see also J. Salmond, *The Law of Torts,* vii (1924) (Speaking of *Rylands:* "No decision in the law of torts has done more to prevent the establishment of a simple, uniform, and intelligible system of civil responsibility"); Smith, "Liability for Blasting," 555 (converting strict liability to negligence will produce "just results, and at the same time, the modern statements of law will tend to legal symmetry"). On the continuing efforts to formulate a unified theory of tort law, see I. Englard, "The System Builders: A Critical Appraisal of Modern American Tort Law," 9 *Journal of Legal Studies* 27 (1980).

78. For a description and refutation (in terms paralleling Holmes's) of these strategies against *Rylands,* see Pound, *Philosophy of Law,* 91–96.

79. Smith, "Liability for Blasting," 684 and n.66. On the restricted scope of *Rylands,* see Pollock, *The Law of Torts,* 398–399 (1887); E. R. Thayer, "Judicial Legislation: Its Legitimate Function in the Development of the Common Law," 5 *Harvard Law Review* 172, 185, 186 n.1 (1892).

80. Holmes's view of the scope of *Rylands* far exceeded that which the English courts subsequently allowed. Read v. J. Lyons & Co., Ltd., 2 A.E.R. 471 (1947) (refusing to apply *Rylands* to cover a worker's injuries from an explosion at a munitions factory); P. S. Atiyah, *Accidents, Compensation and the Law,* 157, 163 (1980).

81. CL, 156–157.

82. Smith, "Absolute Liability," 329–330; F. T. Piggott, *Principles of the Law of Torts,* 111–112 (1885); P. H. Winfield, "The Foundation of Liability in Tort," 27 *Columbia Law Review* 1, 7 (1927). In addition to questioning whether the cattle trespass precedent was sufficiently consistent and strict in nature to support *Rylands,* Smith suggested a specific reason for applying strict liability to cattle trespass. The cattle owner, unlike the owner of water in a reservoir, had an "interest . . . that they [the cattle] should get out and feed on the land of another," and the "[d]efense of 'non-negligence' or defense that owner had used proper care would always be set up" and be difficult to disprove, given the cattle owner's incentive to "make out a defense on false testimony." Avery, Notes on Smith's Lectures, 175–176. Holmes seemed to think that despite the difference in motivation to prevent the escape of water and cattle, both warranted strict liability because they posed the same difficulties of proof relating to negligence. CL, 117.

83. C. H. S. Fifoot, *Judge and Jurist in the Reign of Victoria,* 44 (1959).

84. CL, 156.

85. CL, 156–157.

86. Pound, *Philosophy of Law,* 92.

87. Fletcher v. Rylands, L.R. 1 Ex. 265, 286–287 (1866).

88. Rylands v. Fletcher, L.R. 3 H.L. 330, 339 (1868).

89. Brown v. Collins, 449. See also Avery, Notes of Smith's Lectures, 177.

90. Brown v. Collins, 448.

91. Smith v. Fletcher, L.R. 9 Ex. 64 (1874); Crompton v. Lea, L. R. 19 Eq. 115 (1874); Hurdman v. North Eastern Ry. Co., 3 C.P.D. 168 (1878); Farrer v. Nelson, 15 Q.B.D. 258 (1885).

92. Wilson v. Waddell, 2 App. Cas. 95, 100 (1876) (quoting opinion of the lower court).

93. Smith, "Liability for Blasting," 683–684 (citing in support Bishop, Street, Bohlen, and Pollock); Thayer, "Liability Without Fault," 806–807. Although Holmes's opposition to indiscriminate use of employer vicarious liability drew criticism from some of his later contemporaries, as well as from current commentators, it should be noted that in the 1880s and 1890s vicarious liability was considered a negligence rule and was being used by the foes of *Rylands* to convert the case to negligence. Pollock, *The Law of Torts,* 493–494 n.(o) (11th ed. 1920)

(expressing the hope that Salmond would be found correct in characterizing *Rylands* as rule of vicarious liability that thus precluded recovery where there was "no negligence on the part of any one").

94. N. Isaacs, "Quasi-Delict in Anglo-American Law," 31 *Yale Law Journal* 571, 577 (1922).

95. Pound, *Philosophy of Law*, 91–94 (observing that under these fictions "negligence is established by the liability, not the liability by the negligence"). See also Smith, "Workmen's Compensation Acts," 367 (noting the "indirect methods" of accomplishing strict liability "[b]y a very liberal construction of the *res ipsa loquitur* doctrine; by a broad view as to what constitutes *prima facie* evidence of negligence; and by inverting the burden of proof"); Smith, "Absolute Liability," 414–416.

96. FE, "Codes, and the Arrangement of the Law," 88; 1873 Theory of Torts, 773. See also FE, "Common Carriers and the Common Law," 222; FE, "Primitive Notions in Modern Law," 130; CL, 155. Indeed, Smith juxtaposed Holmes's strict liability interpretation of the animal cases against the "high" (if minority) authority favoring the negligence rule. Smith, "Absolute Liability," 330 and nn. 43–44 (referring to Theory of Torts (Lect. IV)).

97. Fifoot, *Judge and Jurist*, 51–52 (noting Holmes's "quest" to find "a single root of civil liability," and that he reduced *Rylands* "to his single criterion" by resorting to a "policy" of securing safety in cases involving "an added element of danger"); W. G. Friedmann, "Social Insurance and the Principles of Tort Liability," 63 *Harvard Law Review* 241, 262–265 (1949) (finding support in Theory of Torts (Lect. IV) for applying tort to serve the social insurance principle).

98. Johnson v. United States, 333 U.S. 46, 55 (Frankfurter, J. dissenting in part) (quoting Holmes in *Arizona Employers' Liability Cases* for support in castigating states for being "laggards in making law conform to the actualities of industry" by replacing "outmoded" negligence rules with "a rational system of workmen's compensation laws"); Moran v. Pittsburgh-Des Moines Steel Co., 166 F.2d 908, 913 and n.15 (3d Cir. 1948) (affirming Holmes's support for strict liability in reliance on the discussion of *Rylands* in Theory of Torts (Lect. IV)); Acme Fast Freight v. Chicago, M., St. P. & P. R. Co., 166 F.2d 778, 782 and n.9 (2d Cir. 1948) (noting Holmes's showing that strict liability governed common carrier cases); Read v. J. Lyons & Co., 1 A.E.R. 106, 109–10 (1945) (Scott, J.) (discussing Holmes's foresight theory of strict liability); Taylor v. City of Cincinnati, 55 N.E.2d 724, 728 (1944) (relying on rationale for strict liability in Theory of Torts (Lect. IV). See also, Exner v. Sherman Power Const. Co., 54 F.2d 510, 514 (2d Cir. 1931) (relying on Holmes's explanation in Theory of Torts (Lect. IV) to justify strict liability for the risks of stored dynamite). The only case I have found that seems to depart from the prevailing consensus is Jacoby v. Town of Gillette, 174 P.2d 505, 511 (Wyo. 1947), where the court relies on a secondary source for its view that Holmes "criticises and condemns" *Rylands*. In context, however,

both the court (refusing to apply *Rylands* to an "act of God") and its source appear to marshal Holmes's arguments against liability for unforeseeable harm without some-negligence. Indeed, the secondary source, A. C. Freeman, 29 *American Decisions* 149, 150 (1910) (note headed "Injuries Occasioned by Accident") draws the some-negligence interpretation of "inevitable accident" from Holmes's treatment of the American accidental Trespass cases (such as Brown v. Kendall, Harvey v. Dunlop, and The Nitroglycerine Case) that in the absence of negligence, "a man is not liable for the unforeseen injuries occasioned by his lawful act."

99. Scott ultimately concluded that policy warranted restricting foresight-based strict liability under *Rylands* to risks that result in harm on adjacent property.

100. J. W. Salmond, *The Law of Torts,* 9–10 and n.9 (1902); A. A. Ballantine, "A Compensation Plan for Railway Accident Claims," 29 *Harvard Law Review* 705, 711–712 and n.30 (1916); W. L. Prosser, *Handbook of the Law of Torts,* 20 and n.93 (1941). I have previously noted criticisms by Laski objecting to Holmes's views on vicarious liability and also, along with Bohlen, suggesting—erroneously, as I have argued—that *Quinn*'s rejection of *Rylands* represented a policy of subsidizing the construction industry.

101. Ballantine, "Railway Accident Claims," 711 and nn. 2, 3 (crediting Holmes's description of the general rule against liability for accident—apparently, liability based on mere causation—but criticizing the suggestion that negligence was the universal ground for recovery).

102. Id. at 711–712.

103. Salmond, *The Law of Torts,* 9–10 and n.9; Prosser, *Law of Torts,* 20.

104. See R. F. V. Heuston and R. S. Chambers, eds., *Salmond and Heuston on the Law of Torts,* 19–20 (1981); W. P. Keeton et al., eds., *Prosser and Keeton on Torts,* 22 (1984).

105. F. James, Jr. and J. J. Dickinson, "Accident Proneness and Accident Law," 63 *Harvard Law Review* 769, 779 (1950) (citing the portions of Lecture III primarily devoted to showing that cause-based strict liability could not be defended on intelligible grounds of justice and functional rationality).

106. Ibid.

107. Ibid.

108. J. G. Fleming, *The Law of Torts,* 4–5, 9–10, 306 (1957) (offering this characterization without elaborating the texts).

109. L. Green, "The Thrust of Tort Law—Part I: The Influence of Environment," 64 *West Virginia Law Review* 1, 7 (1961).

110. M. D. Howe, *Justice Oliver Wendell Holmes: The Proving Years, 1870–1882,* 188–189 (1963).

111. Id. at 187–189. Howe suggested that an essay by Bigelow had alerted Holmes to the "new curiosity" of *Rylands,* and influenced him to see strict liability as a penalty on "enterprising people who had gone forward to their own gain at the expense of others." Id. at 187 and n.8. In fact, Bigelow acknowledged Holm-

es's creation of the strict liability branch and specifically rationalized *Rylands* on foreseeability and just compensation grounds. Bigelow, *Leading Cases,* 500–501.

112. For examples, see E. F. Roberts, "Negligence: Blackstone to Shaw to ? An Intellectual Escapade in a Tory Vein," 50 *Cornell Law Quarterly* 191, 205 (1965); S. J. Donnelly, "The Fault Principle: A Sketch of Its Development in Tort Law During the Nineteenth Century," 18 *Syracuse Law Review* 728, 730, 732–733 (1966).

113. For references, see Introduction.

114. For claims of transformation, see Green, "The Thrust of Tort law," 7; cf. Donnelly, "The Fault Principle," 748. But see R. A. Posner, "A Theory of Negligence," 1 *Journal of Legal Studies* 29, 30 (1972) (denying the transformation and industrial-subsidy claims generally).

115. Those who do not suggest at least a formalist tinge to Holmes's negligence-dogmatism appear to comprise a distinct minority. For a notable example, see G. Calabresi, *The Costs of Accidents* (1970).

116. After seeing early drafts of this book, several commentators have either expressly suspended final judgment on the question of the negligence-dogma thesis or have softened their prior advocacy. See S. G. Gilles, "Negligence, Strict Liability, and the Cheapest Cost-Avoider," 78 *Virginia Law Review* 1291, 1344 n.168 (1992); G. E. White, *Justice Oliver Wendell Holmes,* 526–527 n.54 (1993). R. Epstein has also modified his negligence-dogma stance, albeit without reference to the draft of this book to which he had access. See Epstein, *Cases and Material on Torts,* 93 (reediting the casebook to include a reference, albeit muted and abridged, to Holmes's explanation of *Rylands* in Lecture III); R. A. Epstein, *Teacher's Manual: Cases and Materials on Torts,* 2–6 (1990) (changing claim in prior editions of the *Manual,* 3–1, that *"Rylands . . .* poses the challenge to Holmes's universal negligence principle" by deleting the reference to Holmes).

A number of commentators appear to have expressed no opinion on the question, despite its pertinence to their work, including C. O. Gregory, "Trespass to Negligence to Absolute Liability," 37 *Virginia Law Review* 359 (1951); R. E. Keeton, "Conditional Fault in the Law of Torts," 72 *Harvard Law Review* 401 (1959); C. J. Peck, "Negligence and Liability Without Fault in Tort Law," 46 *Washington Law Review* 225 (1971).

117. C. H. Schroeder, "Corrective Justice and Liability for Increasing Risks," 37 *UCLA Law Review* 439, 463 (1990). Cf. A. W. B. Simpson, "Legal Liability for Bursting Reservoirs: The Historical Context of Rylands v. Fletcher," 13 *Journal of Legal Studies* 209, 214 n.13 (1984) (noting that "Holmes had some difficulty in fitting [*Rylands*] into his general theory of tort law"); P. S. Atiyah, "The Legacy of Holmes Through English Eyes," in *Holmes and The Common Law: A Century Later,* 38 and n.54 (1983) (noting in passing a correspondence between Holmes's rationale for *Rylands* and Calabresi's cheapest cost-avoider justification). Cf. S. M. Novick, *Honorable Justice,* 157–158, 434–435 (1989) (to Holmes, "what a person . . . could not foresee was accidental and therefore blameless").

118. H. L. Pohlman, *Justice Oliver Wendell Holmes & Utilitarian Jurispru-*

dence, 136–137, 44, 150 (1984) (possibly confusing the "strict liability effect" of the external negligence standard for a rule of strict liability that requires neither proof nor presumption of unreasonable conduct).

119. P. J. Kelley, "A Critical Analysis of Holmes's Theory of Torts," 61 *Washington Law Quarterly* 681 (1984). Kelley is almost alone among current commentators to discuss Theory of Torts (Lect. IV). Yet, oddly, he by-passes Holmes's application of the foresight theory to *Rylands,* and, indeed, virtually neglects Holmes's treatment of that rule as well as of strict liability generally for extra-hazardous activities.

120. Id. at 729. While there is much to admire in Kelley's essay, his ultimate expression of perplexity over the relationship between the foresight theory and Holmes's jurisprudence derives in part from a lack of familiarity with terms and concepts contemporary with Holmes, particularly in Trespass cases. Unfortunately, his analysis also suffers from a failure to understand the bifurcated nature of Holmes's theory of torts, which prevents him from seeing the consistency in Holmes's reliance both on cases which apply strict liability to obviously foreseeable risks and on those which apply negligence to such risks.

121. T. Grey, "Holmes and Legal Pragmatism," 41 *Stanford Law Review* 787, 831–832, 834 (1989).

122. Id. at 831 n.205, 834 n.218. For another example of blindness to an apparent contradiction between evidence and interpretation, see R. W. Gordon, "Holmes's *Common Law* as Legal and Social Science," 10 *Hofstra Law Review* 719, 728, 742, 737 n.123 (1982) (asserting Holmes's opposition to strict liability in the torts lectures, yet reporting (possibly without fully appreciating the implications) evidence of his support for foresight-based strict liability). See also James and Dickinson, "Accident Law," 779–780 and nn.49, 51 (positing the negligence-dogma thesis, while on the next page referring to Holmes's functional rationales for strict liability in the *Arizona Employers' Liability Cases*); W. M. Landes and R. A. Posner, *The Economic Structure of Tort Law,* 4–5 and n.9 (1987) (asserting Holmes's opposition to strict liability on the ground that the state should not provide social insurance, while noting that the argument in the torts lectures was confined to liability for injuries that the defendant "could not have foreseen inflicting"); Fleming, *Torts,* 4–5, 9–10, 306 (advocating negligence-dogma and industrial subsidy views while acknowledging that Holmes opposed cause-based strict liability—what Fleming called "faultless causation"—and wrote at a time when there was no liability insurance).

123. B. Kaplan, "Encounters with O. W. Holmes, Jr.," in *Holmes and The Common Law: A Century Later,* 5 n.21 (1983) (quoting but ignoring the meaning of Holmes's application of the foresight theory to *Rylands* in Theory of Torts (Lect. IV)); H. Kalven, Jr., "Mr. Justice Holmes: Torts," 31 *University of Chicago Law Review* 263, 267 (1964) (asserting without explanation that Holmes "is helpful neither as to *Rylands v. Fletcher* nor as to the basis of liability in defamation").

124. R. L. Rabin, ed., *Perspectives on Tort Law,* 14 (4th ed., 1995). Minimizing the evidence of Holmes's support for strict liability, Rabin refers to the discussion of *Rylands* in Lecture III but omits that portion from the lengthy excerpts of the lecture. Compounding the mischaracterization of Holmes's views, Rabin neither suggests the modern nature of the policy rationales Holmes presented nor indicates application of the foresight theory to *Rylands* in Lecture IV. No reference is made to any other writing by Holmes where he rationalized strict liability for industrial and other extra-hazardous activities. This skewed presentation of Holmes's views on torts in *Perspectives* is all the more troubling because it teaches the negligence-dogma thesis to students who are not likely to consult the primary sources on their own. Students receive a similar selective and minimized view of Holmes's treatment of *Rylands* in Epstein, *Cases and Materials on Torts,* 93 (asserting that Holmes "devoted relatively little attention" to *Rylands,* which "he treated gingerly"). See also R. A. Posner, *The Essential Holmes,* 260 (1990) (excerpting extensive portions of Lecture III but replacing Holmes's discussion of *Rylands* with ellipses, and omitting any excerpt from or reference to Theory of Torts (Lect. IV)).

125. G. T. Schwartz, "Tort Law and the Economy in Nineteenth-Century America: A Reinterpretation," 90 *Yale Law Journal* 1717, 1733 n.134 (1981).

126. Ibid.

127. O. W. Holmes, Sr., *Mechanism in Thought and Morals,* 3 (1871).

128. Kalven, "Mr. Justice Holmes: Torts," 264 n.11.

129. Posner, *The Essential Holmes,* xxviii and n.31 (referring to Sheldon Novick's claim that Holmes espoused "a kind of fascist ideology"). See also G. Gilmore, *The Ages of American Law,* 48–49, 67 (1977) (debunking the "great liberal" image, and asserting that while he tolerated social legislation, "the real Holmes was savage, harsh, and cruel, a bitter and lifelong pessimist who saw . . . nothing but a continuing struggle in which the rich and powerful impose their will on the poor and weak . . . [and who] had no use for the gentle optimism of Karl Marx").

130. Gilmore, *Ages of American Law,* 66.

131. Many of these commentators, like James, favored strict liability. But support for strict liability was not necessary for belief in the industrial-subsidy thesis; one could claim that enhanced negligence rules, shorn of defenses such as assumption of the risk or fellow-servant negligence, represented a vast improvement over conditions in the last century. Moreover, many commentators might view negligence as the best rule for tort, with administrative compensation and safety regulations taking up any slack.

132. Howe, *The Proving Years,* 81, 85 and n.55, 184.

133. Id. at 185, 189, 192, 194–196.

134. Id. at 188–189, 193–194.

135. Id. at 186, 187, 188, 192, 205–206 (uncritically equating "absolute liability" with all forms of strict liability).

136. Id. at 80–81. My quarrel with Howe and other commentators on

Holmes's jurisprudence goes beyond the scant attention they pay on the whole to the evidence showing Holmes's support for strict liability. Torts, for Holmes, was mainly a vehicle for developing his new jurisprudence. Most of the commentators ignore or minimize this purpose even when they emphasize the negligence-dogma thesis, and, indeed, use it to validate a formalist reading of his jurisprudence.

137. In contrast to other issues on which he cross-referenced later writings, Howe completely ignored the conflict between his negligence-dogma interpretation and Holmes's extension of the foresight theory to strict liability in "The Path of the Law" and "Privilege, Malice, and Intent"—which Howe understood as a restatement of the theory developed in the torts lectures.

138. Id. at 81.

139. Id. at 184–186 (discussing without reference to *Rylands* Holmes's recognition of strict liability in his arrangement of tort law in 1873 Theory of Torts).

140. Id. at 188–189 and n.11.

141. It appears that this omission resulted from Howe's erroneous assumption that because of the identical titles, the substance of 1873 Theory of Torts had been incorporated in Theory of Torts (Lect. IV). Id. at 136 and n.7, 177.

142. Id. at 189.

143. Ibid. Howe proceeded to discuss "one link in Holmes's chain of argument"—the definition of an "act"—in terms of foresight-informed choice to avoid the consequences. Id. at 190–192. Howe's discussion of this point was wholly disconnected from Holmes's foresight theory of responsibility in torts. According to Howe, Holmes developed this idea solely to support his "theory that the law's standards are objective." Howe highlighted the point only to show that "a most important aspect of Holmes's intellectual inclination" was an "eagerness to find not simply historical, but logical justifications for the objective theory."

144. CLP, "Law in Science and Science in Law," 224–225 (explaining that the "chief good" of historical criticism as a means of carrying out "the scientific study of law" "is to burst inflated explanations").

145. For a well-documented critique of this misguided trend in history-making, see G. Himmelfarb, *The New History and the Old* (1987).

146. Nickleski v. Aeronaves de Mexico, S.A., 228 N.Y.S.2d 963, 966 (S.Ct. 1962) (citing Holmes's "test of foreseeability as the basis of all tort liability" to explain modern as well as historical applications of strict liability); Romanoff v. City of Mansfield, slip opinion on LEXIS (Ohio Ct. App., July 8, 1981) (relying on Theory of Torts (Lect. IV) to explain the strict liability nature of *Rylands*); cf. United States v. White Fuel Corporation, 498 F.2d 619, 622–623 (1st Cir. 1974) (invoking Holmes's foresight theory to justify strict liability in criminal law). But see Williams v. Employers Liability Assurance Corporation, Ltd., 296 F.2d 569 n.1 (5th Cir. 1961) (quoting, apparently without independent verification, Prosser's negligence-dogma description).

147. H. Shulman and F. James, Jr., *Cases and Materials on the Law of Torts*, 48–50 and n.15 (1952).

148. Id. at 71 and n.23. A footnote to the excerpt from Scott's opinion simply notes that the House of Lords dismissed the appeal. Id. at 77 n.24. The editors seem to have mistakenly thought that the Court of Appeal ruling was allowed to stand without further discussion. The apparent error was subsequently corrected by removal of Scott's opinion, and insertion of a reference to the House of Lords decision. H. Shulman, F. James, Jr., and O. S. Gray, *Cases and Materials on the Law of Torts*, 63–64 n.31 (1976).

149. Read v. J. Lyons & Co., Ltd., 109, 113.

150. Id. at 110, 113. On this basis, Scott rationalized *Rylands* and the Restatement's rule for ultrahazardous activity: "In all of these cases the strictness of the rule of duty may be justified on the ground that the defendant was the person who had it in his power to prevent harm, and, as a prudent, reasonable man, ought to have foreseen the likelihood of harm if he let the harmful things escape from his control."

151. CLP, 32.

Index